THE PARIS OF HENRI IV

THE
PARIS
OF HENRI IV

Architecture and Urbanism

HILARY BALLON

THE ARCHITECTURAL HISTORY FOUNDATION
New York, New York

THE MIT PRESS
Cambridge, Massachusetts, and London, England

Frontispiece: Thomas de Leu, frontispiece of Jacques Perret, *Des Fortifications et artifices d'architecture et perspective* (Paris: 1597). Above the triumphal arch, Henri IV rides the winged Pegasus, who is rearing on a globe, an image of the king's supremacy. Henri holds a sword and balance, signs of his valor and his fairness, and is flanked by two angels with branches of palm and laurel, divine guardians of a reign blessed by peace and justice. "Fear God and Honor the King," the inscriptions admonish, encapsulating the Gallican appeal for religious unity to preserve a strong monarchy. The image also represents the importance of Paris to the king's success; at the base of the triumphal arch is a view of Henri IV's siege of Paris in 1594, the crucial victory that enabled the king to gain control of the capital and to consolidate his power. (B.N. Est. rés. Ed 11d)

Hilary Ballon is Assistant Professor of Art History at Columbia University.

Designed by Bruce Campbell.

Published with the assistance of the Getty Grant Program.

Publication of this book has been aided by a grant from The Millard Meiss Publication Fund of the College Art Association of America.

MM

LIBRARY OF CONGRESS CATALOGING-IN-PUBLICATION DATA
Ballon, Hilary.
    The Paris of Henri IV: architecture and urbanism / Hilary Ballon.
        p.   cm.
    Includes bibliographical references.
    ISBN 0-262-02309-1
        1. Public architecture — France — Paris.   2. City planning — France —
    Paris — History — 17th century.   3. Architecture and state — France.
    4. France — History — Henry IV, 1589–1610.   I. Title.
    NA9050.5.B3   1991
    720′.944′36109031 — dc20
                                                                        90-30984
                                                                            CIP

FOR MY PARENTS

CONTENTS

[vii]

Contents

ACKNOWLEDGMENTS

I am grateful to many people and institutions for their help in making this book a reality. I was fortunate that Henry Millon, David Friedman, and Stanford Anderson carefully read my manuscript at the outset of this project, encouraged my approach, and shared their insights. Above all, I thank them for introducing me to the intellectual challenges of architectural history and the craft of scholarship. Orest Ranum and Wim Smit made this a better book by suggesting ways to broaden the historical framework. My approach to maps owes much to the writings of J. B. Harley, who also offered invaluable comments on Chapter Six. At Columbia, I have benefited enormously from a sustained conversation about the seventeeth century with my colleague Joseph Connors; his work on Baroque Rome has served for me as a model of architectural scholarship.

Research for this book was undertaken in Paris at the Archives Nationales, the Archives de l'Assistance Publique, and the Bibliothèque Nationale. Among the librarians and curators who welcomed me, I would especially like to thank Catherine Grodecki, Nicole Felkay, and Anne-Marie Joly at the Archives Nationales. The opportunity to work in Paris was made possible by grants from the Center for Advanced Study in the Visual Arts, Washington D.C.; the Social Science Research Council; the History, Theory and Criticism Program in the School of Architecture at M.I.T.; and the Council on Research and Faculty Development in the Humanities and Social Sciences at Columbia University. A Mellon Fellowship at the Society of Fellows, Columbia University, enabled me to expand my critical horizons during a year of postdoctoral research.

Many colleagues and friends answered queries, posed important questions, and spurred me on with their interest. Special thanks go to Jean-Pierre Babelon, Mirka Beneš, Barry Bergdoll, Richard Brilliant, Richard Cleary, Elizabeth Easton, Béatrice d'Erceville, Emmanuel Jacquin, Mark Jarzombek, Claude Mignot, Francesco Passanti, Myra Nan Rosenfeld, Stephen Rustow, Nicolas Saint Fare Garnot, and Katherine Fischer Taylor. I am also indebted to Julia Rogoff, who worked tirelessly on the drawings, and to my husband, Orin Kramer, who was a superb editor. Victoria Newhouse, Karen Banks, and Jo Ellen Ackerman of the Architectural History Foundation provided exceptional attention and care throughout the publication process.

[ix]

Acknowledgments

The galleys for this book arrived the week that my daughter Sophia was born. I hope that Orin and I can convey to her the pleasure of learning, as my parents did for me. I dedicate this book to Harriet and Charles Ballon, my beloved parents, who taught me the most precious lessons.

INTRODUCTION

The circumstances surrounding Henri IV's ascension to the throne in 1589 were hardly auspicious. Henri IV was a Protestant in a Catholic country torn by religious civil war. His blood relationship to the monarchy, the basis for his claim to the crown, was highly attenuated. And the city of Paris, controlled by radical Catholics, was in open rebellion against the new king. Those bleak conditions in no way foreshadowed a reign that would, within a relatively brief period, end the Wars of Religion that had racked France through most of the late sixteenth century; lay the groundwork for the modern centralized French state; and establish Paris as a true capital city. That latter achievement — Henri IV's role in the urban development of Paris — which is the focus of this book, entailed planning and construction on a scale that would be unmatched in Paris for more than two centuries thereafter. Henri IV had a vision linking Paris as a capital city to the emergence of a centralized national state. In executing that vision, he played an essential role in a process that established Paris as the most powerful single symbol of France itself.

In 1589 Henri III had been assassinated, leaving behind no sons to lay claim to the throne. Since the Salic Law — the venerable standard governing succession in the French hereditary monarchy — restricted the crown to the male line, the death of Henri III brought an end to the Valois dynasty. To identify the new king, it was necessary to go back to the progenitor of the French monarchy, Saint Louis (1226–70), and to trace the descendants of his youngest son, Robert de Clermont.[1] That convoluted process eventually led to Henri de Bourbon, King of Navarre. But two factors undermined the legitimacy of his claim to the throne. The hereditary monarchy accustomed Frenchmen to expect a close blood relationship between the newly crowned king and his predecessor, yet Henri IV was twenty-two degrees removed from Henri III. Furthermore, the fact that Henri de Bourbon was a Protestant precluded any possibility that his authority might achieve broad acceptance. The sacrosanct coronation ceremony compelled the king of France to pledge his allegiance to the Catholic Church and receive consecration as the Most Christian King, *Rex Christianissimus.* In the view of many French subjects, a Protestant could not fulfill the time-honored vows and duties of the French king. In the view of militant Catholics, the circumstances warranted the abandonment of the hereditary monarchy and the election of a new king.

Fig. 1. Philippe II Danfrie, Henri IV as Hercules, obverse, 1602. Legend: ALCIDES HIC NOVVS ORBI. (B.N. Médailles SR Inv. 310)

With the ascension of Henri IV, the issue of monarchical succession moved to the forefront in the ongoing civil conflict. Moderate Catholics joined with Protestants in defending the monarchy and appealing for religious unity. The rebellious Catholic League, its Spanish Hapsburg allies, and noble magnates protecting powerful interests, opposed the Protestant king. Henri IV waged the fight to consolidate his power on military and political fronts. The legend of his military valor sprang from the victories at Arques (1589) and Ivry (1590). With sizable cash payments, he purchased the loyalty of town governors and noble potentates. Ultimately, however, it was his conversion to Catholicism that appeased the popular opposition. The legendary mass that Paris was worth took place on 25 July 1593.

From 1589 until 1594, Paris had been the stronghold of Catholic rebels who refused to recognize the new king. Henri IV had besieged the city in 1589 and again in 1590 with no success, but after the king's conversion, Paris peacefully surrendered. Exhausted by five years of warfare, by blockade and by looting, the city opened its gates to Henri IV on 22 March 1594. Although there were battles still to be fought, the capture of Paris assured the king's victory.

Within the first five years of his reign, Henri IV effectively ended the Wars of Religion that had divided France for nearly thirty years. He restored peace in his country by defeating the insurrectionary Catholic League, expelling Spanish troops, and winning freedom for the Protestants, feats for which Henri IV was acclaimed the Gallic Hercules (Fig. 1).[2] But for all the labors he had successfully performed, still greater challenges lay ahead in healing the wounded state. The image of an omnipotent Gallic king masked Henri IV's political vulnerability, a vulnerability rooted in powerful institutional forces and the king's personal circumstances.[3] Throughout the sixteenth century, despite the nominal authority of the crown, France essentially functioned as a highly decentralized confederacy of semiautonomous local provinces. For example, local authorities exercised significant control over the collection of taxes and raising of troops. Francois I (1515–47) and Henri II (1547–59) had some success in extending the authority of the king, but the incipient trend toward greater centralization suffered a severe setback during the civil wars, as monarchical control disintegrated in the hands of weaker rulers, Charles IX (1560–74) and Henri III (1574–89). When Henri IV (1589–1610) ascended the throne, he found his power substantially limited by this decentralized system. That weakness was only aggravated by his personal circumstances: a Protestant past that continued to provoke residual distrust, and the unusually distant blood relationship to Henri III. Facing a monumental task of economic recovery in a land depleted by thirty years of war, Henri IV could call upon neither the institutional power of a strong monarchical state nor the credibility that would have attached to an undisputed claim to the throne. However, there was a widespread desire for order after the crises of revolt and regicide. Henri IV capitalized on that popular sentiment by asserting strong monarchical control and thus beginning the fitful process of crafting the absolutist state.

The Bourbon king pursued a multifaceted program to centralize the power of the crown. There is a risk of overstating the extent to which his program succeeded, and it must be clear from the outset that neither Henri IV nor his successors on the throne achieved the creation of a fully centralized and absolutist state. The notion of unrestricted royal power was alien to French political theory of the sixteenth and seventeenth century. Theorists claimed that fundamental laws of the French realm limited the power of the king; because France lacked a constitution comparable to the Magna Carta, jurists disagreed on the dictates and limitations imposed by the unwritten laws. Nevertheless they agreed that ultimate authority resided in fundamental laws rather than the king.⁴ Furthermore, throughout the seventeenth century, administrative obstacles restricted the perfect implementation of royal policies. Roger Mettam has gone further than most historians in denying that there was any real increase in royal power during the seventeenth century; it was only because of "their greater skill in balancing and manipulating power groups," he has written, "and not through any extension of their own absolute authority that Henri IV and Louis XIV created the reputation which some later historians have described as strong monarchy." Nevertheless, Mettam conceded that the formation of a centralized absolute monarchy was "the direction in which the royal ministers were hoping to proceed."⁵

In referring to Henri IV's centralization of France, I am only describing the aims of his policies: the assertion of greater royal control and the limitation of local and regional authorities. In one domain after another — taxation, defense, political administration — reforms were instituted to facilitate greater intervention by the state. To diminish the political power and bonds of feudal clientage which noble magnates had so recently turned against the crown, the king brought the cities under royal control and promoted an alternative system of patronage attached to officeholding. Towns lost their independence: municipal councils were overrun by royalists, municipal charters rewritten as instruments of royal power. From these urban bases of royal control, the king undercut the influence of seignorial lords whose local power was tied to feudal landholding. Princes of the blood and nobles of the sword were excluded from important positions in Henri IV's administration. Instead, government posts were entrusted to nobles of the robe, empowered not by seignorial privilege but by the king, men often only two generations removed from their bourgeois roots and ennobled by virtue of their administrative rank.[6]

The centralizing policies were assiduously implemented by the king's chief minister Maximilien de Béthune (1559–1641), the Duke of Sully. Sully's administrative talents, exacting fiscal supervision, and prodigious energy equipped him well for his multiple duties as Superintendent of Finances (1598), Superintendent of Fortifications (1599), Captain of the Artillery (1599), *Grand Voyer* of France (1599), and Superintendent of Buildings (1602).[7] Sully's most valuable accomplishment was his success in bringing tax collection under royal control and keeping the coffers sufficiently stocked to finance the expansionist policies of the crown. In his capacity as Superintendent of Fortifications, Sully pursued a costly program of national defense, building citadels along the boundaries of France. In his capacity as *Grand Voyer,* a new office created by Henri IV, Sully pursued a program of economic integration by building canals and bridges and by regulating the roads and rivers (*voirie*) of France.[8] As we shall see, these were programs that had significant implications for Paris. Through urban administration and through royal office, through fiscal reform and through construction, Henri IV and Sully moved the French state toward greater centralization and unity.

It is in the context of this multitiered effort to centralize the power of the crown that Henri IV's building program in Paris must be situated. There were ways in which specific royal policies — for example, mercantilist measures to promote manufacturing — directly impinged on the development of the city, and one concern of this book will be to chart the imprint of those policies on the physical form of Paris. Yet the changes Henri IV wrought in Paris represent far more than the sum of the incremental effects produced by those individual policies. The creation of a unified state brought about a shift in the conception of the capital itself. As the seat of the centralizing monarch, the city was compelled to assume a national role; it came to stand for the entire realm. We now take for granted the centrality of Paris to every aspect of French life, but Paris only acquired that role during the seventeenth century. The emerging conception of Paris as a national capital shaped the physical character of the city. Henri IV understood that constructing a capital city was fundamental to achieving a centralized state. His vision of Paris and its translation into brick and stone, streets and squares — into the very fabric of the city — these are our concerns.

Since the reign of the first Capetian king in 987, Paris had been the capital of France, the residence of the king, and seat of the sovereign courts. But following the battle of Agincourt (1415), the kings withdrew from the city. Without the presence of the court and the prestige and influence that presence implied, Paris ranked little higher than the other *bonnes villes* of France, with no claim to political or cultural dominance among the patchwork of provinces that made up the country. During the sixteenth century, the Valois rulers roamed the countryside, housing their peripatetic court in the Renaissance châteaux of the Loire Valley and the Ile-de-France, never far from forests and hunting grounds. François I had announced his intention to reside in Paris and to make the Louvre his primary residence in 1528, but the occasional instances of lip service to Paris as the proper seat of government went unsupported by concrete action. More indicative of the crown's commitment to the city is that Renaissance Paris lacked a palace worthy of the king. In 1546, when François I commissioned Pierre Lescot to enlarge the Louvre, it was but a medieval *château fort,* a small fortress hardly fit for the expanding Valois court. Henri II began the century-long process of transforming the Louvre into a royal residence, and his efforts signal a growing royal interest in Paris. But the Wars of Religion interrupted this process and chased the court from the city. It was Henri IV who returned the court to Paris after two centuries of itinerancy. He transformed the city from a neglected station on the royal circuit to the locus of the monarchy.

In 1594, the king entered a ravaged city.[9] After five years of neglect and siege warfare, the physical fabric was greatly in need of repair. The gates and fortifications were battered. The Hôtel Dieu, the general hospital on the Ile de la Cité, was near collapse. Numerous buildings in the city had been destroyed by rampaging soldiers, while the faubourgs had suffered greatly at the hands of attacking and retreating armies. The problem of a crippled infrastructure was exacerbated by the demands of a rapidly burgeoning population. The poor came from the countryside seeking employment and alms, and royal officeholders arrived to staff the new administration. The population swelled to roughly 350,000 at the turn of the century.[10] The king responded with demonstrations of Christian charity, exonerating the rebels and endowing a hospice for wounded soldiers, but the physical repair of Paris was not an immediate priority. Henri IV's urbanism developed slowly; only after a decade in Paris did he initiate significant public construction.

Fig. 2. Mathieu Merian, map of Paris, 1615. (B.N. Est. Va 419j)
Key: 1. Louvre; 2. Place Royale; 3. Place Dauphine; 4. Pont Neuf and Statue of Henri IV;
5. rue Dauphine; 6. Hôpital St. Louis

Once commenced, however, Henri IV's building program was enormous
in scale. Not until 250 years later, when Baron Haussmann scored the city with
boulevards, was anyone to match the activity of the Bourbon king. Immediately
after entering Paris in 1594, Henri IV pursued the enlargement of the Louvre
(Fig. 2). In 1598, he began work on the Pont Neuf, innocently named with a
claim of perpetual newness that all the more honors its standing as the oldest
bridge in modern Paris. Starting in 1605, the seventeenth year of a reign by then
secure, the king initiated several projects in quick succession, all of which
survive today: the Place Royale (1605), now called the Place des Vosges; the
Place Dauphine (1607); the royal equestrian monument on the Pont Neuf, now
replaced by a nineteenth-century statue; the rue Dauphine (1607) extending the
axis of the Pont Neuf across the Left Bank; and the Hôpital St. Louis (1607),
which holds the dubious honor of being the oldest functioning hospital in Paris.
The two final projects, the Place de France (1609) and the Collège de France
(1610), were abandoned after the king's assassination in 1610.

But the scope of Henri IV's activity was not confined to major buildings
and monuments. Quais, ports, and gates were rebuilt with royal funds. In
addition to several projects undertaken in conjunction with the monumental
buildings, the crown remodeled the eastern entrance to the city from the Seine.

On the Left Bank, only the Porte de la Tournelle was rebuilt, but on the Right Bank, the commercial center of the city, numerous improvements were made.[11] An *allée* 250 *toises* long (495m) was laid out on what had been the sloping shore of the river, so that the Seine was no longer bordered by the bastioned walls of the Arsenal but by a landscaped promenade intended for royal games of pall-mall (Fig. 3).[12] The port St. Paul was enlarged, and the adjoining bank, the quai St. Paul, was extended to the Place de Grève.[13] As *Grand Voyer* of France and *Voyer* of Paris, Sully had largely uncontested control over roads, alignments, and building regulations in the capital. He exercised that power during a period when the crown brought within its jurisdiction areas previously administered by the city. For example, the crown paved and cleaned the streets, previously a responsibility of the municipality. The *Grand Voyer* also enacted a building code that prohibited construction in wood, directed owners of empty lots to rebuild along the street edge, and required builders to comply with the alignments established by the *Grand Voyer*.[14] Since the thirteenth century, property owners had been compelled to maintain their buildings in good condition, but Henri IV's measures went further by controlling the street edge. It was in the context of these regulatory changes that the monumental projects were undertaken, not as isolated ornamental objects but as components of a comprehensive program to renovate and redesign the urban fabric.

The surge of urban development under Henri IV, which was largely confined to the last five years of his reign (1605–10), is a deservedly famous example of the power of the absolute monarch to reshape the physical form of the city. But rarely in urban construction is authority unlimited — even the divinely sanctioned dictates of a monarch cannot alone change a city's physical form. Implementation of the royal plans required the participation of many other constituencies and interests: the municipal government, royal officers, merchants, artisans, and building craftsmen. Their visions and interests were not necessarily those of the king. In the course of constructing the king's projects, social conflicts and compromises were played out, the expectations and ambitions of the crown altered, the formal ideas of the architects modified. Though condensed to only five years, Henri IV's urbanism was an evolving enterprise. What was built was the residue of an interactive process, not the reproduction of an unyielding royal

Fig. 3. Vassallieu dit Nicolay, map of Paris, detail of the Arsenal and pall-mall field, 1609. (B.N. Est. rés. Hennin XV 1352)

ideal. From that perspective, the development of Paris in the early seventeenth century is a prism through which we can witness the interaction of the major political, economic, and social forces that shaped Parisian life and culture.

Nevertheless, it was decidedly Henri IV's building program. His passionate enthusiasm and pride about the buildings is amply documented in his letters, such as the one sent to the French ambassador at the papal court, the Cardinal de Joyeuse, in May 1607:

> This is to give you news of my buildings and of my gardens and to assure you that I haven't lost any time since your departure. In Paris you will find my long gallery which goes to the Tuileries completed, the small [gallery] gilded, and paintings placed in the Tuileries; a pond and many beautiful fountains, my plantings and my garden very beautiful; the Place Royale which is near the Porte St. Antoine and the workshops, three of the four parts finished and the fourth will be completed next year; at the end of the Pont Neuf, a beautiful street which goes to the Porte de Buci built, and the houses on both sides, if not finished at least they will be before the end of next year; plus two to three thousand workshops which work here and there for the embellishment of the city, so much that it is unbelievable how much you find changed.[15]

This letter was of course written to publicize the building program at the papal court, but the same unrelenting zeal is demonstrated in countless other letters in which the king asks about his masons, prods his ministers to hasten construction and instructs Sully to procure building funds. Henri IV was the driving force; he established the overarching vision, he propelled the building program at each step of the process, and he set its priorities. He was neither knowledgeable in architectural theory nor experienced in design, but the king probably gave clear instructions about the programmatic aspects of the projects, leaving aesthetic matters to the royal architects.

Who was this man, the populist king of legend, who commanded so many embellishments in the capital? Robert Dallington described Henri IV in 1602 (Fig. 4):

> This King . . . is about 48 yeeres of age, his stature small, his haire almost all white, or rather grisled, his colour fresh and youthfull, his nature stirring and full of life, like a French man. One of his owne people describeth him thus . . . He is of such an extremely lively and active disposition, that to whatsoever he applyes himselfe, to that hee entirely employs all his powers, seldom doing above one thing at once. To joyne a tedious deliberation with an earnest and pressing affayre, he cannot endure: Hee executes and deliberates both together. But in Councels that require tract of time, to say the truth, hee hath neede of

Fig. 4. Thomas de Leu after François Quesnel, portrait of Henri IV, c. 1594–99.
(B.N. Est. Ne 15)

helpe. He hath an admirable sharpnesse of wit. In affayres of Justice, of his Revenues, forrayne Negotiations, Dispatches, and government of the State, hee credites others, and meddles little himselfe. . . . Hee is naturally very affable and familiar, and more (we strangers thinke) then fits the Maiesty of a great King of France.[16]

Architecture was not among the matters that Henri IV delegated; along with war and women, he said, it was his favorite occupation.

To implement the building program, the king relied on Sully, whose ministerial posts gave him jurisdiction over all aspects of building activity in the capital. Sully reviewed the designs, issued alignments, authorized specifications (*devis*), and allocated funds. The duke was also an active architectural patron; he remodeled his residence in the Arsenal where he lived from 1599 to 1610, rebuilt the châteaux of Rosny, Sully-sur-Loire, and Villebon, and founded the new town of Henrichemont (1606).[17] Because of his public responsibilities and private enthusiasms, some scholars have been tempted to see Sully as the strategic intelligence and even the driving force behind the building program. But this view finds no support in the primary sources, with the exception of Sully's unreliable and self-aggrandizing memoirs.[18] Certainly his administrative skills made it possible to execute an ambitious building program in the space of only five years, but the policies were set by the king whom Sully served.

The king's plans for Paris encountered no resistance from the municipal government. Long accustomed to the presence of the crown, the Hôtel de Ville accepted its subordination in the management of Paris. On occasion, municipal leaders contested royal intervention in fiscal matters; when the crown refused to make interest payments to holders of long-term government bonds (*rentes*) issued by the Hôtel de Ville, the city protested strenuously. "It is useless for us to endeavour to amass money for the King if in so doing we lose him the affection of his subjects," municipal leader François Miron complained in 1605.[19] But Miron and the other presiding officers of the Hôtel de Ville were the king's men, chosen by the crown and then nominally elected to their posts. Thus, ultimately, the city's submission to royal policies was assured.

Nevertheless, the crown wanted to preserve the fiction of an independent corporate identity for the municipal government, which was historically identified with the interests of the Parisian merchants. The city council had developed from a medieval merchant organization, as the title of its leader, Provost of the Merchants (*Prévôt des marchands*), indicates; the institutions and ceremonies of civic life were signs of the vitality of the Parisian merchant community which Henri IV wanted to encourage. To project the image of a vigorous Parisian mercantile tradition, the crown instructed the city council in 1605 to

Fig. 5. Hôtel de Ville, Paris, 1533–1609. Engraving by Mathieu Merian after Claude Chastillon, c. 1610–15. (B.N. Est. rés. Ve 9)

complete construction of the Hôtel de Ville, begun in 1533 during the reign of François I and left incomplete in 1550.[20] The building was finished in 1609, with an equestrian statue of Henri IV by Pierre Biard placed above the main entrance signifying the city's allegiance to the king (Fig. 5). During François Miron's tenure as *Prévôt* (1604–6), the municipality played a particularly active role in supporting Henri IV's building program by reconstructing gates, repairing fountains, and completing numerous minor works. While Henri IV waged a campaign to control the cities throughout his realm, the rebuilding of Paris offered dazzling evidence of the benefits of royal power.

The royal building program was harnessed to the burgeoning real estate market in Paris. The Place Royale and Place Dauphine were built not by the crown but by private investors, by nobles of the robe, by merchants and artisans. Their development of the squares signaled the growing value of urban property, a trend that accelerated during the first half of the seventeenth century, when rents tripled in value.[21] The housing shortage caused by the postwar migration to Paris may have been an initial catalyst during the first years of Henri IV's reign, but it was the return of the crown to the capital that provided long-term impetus to the real estate market. Officers of the court required appropriate housing in the city, and the lavish hôtels that sprang up throughout the seventeenth century in the quartier Richelieu, the Marais, the Ile-St.-Louis, and the faubourg St.-Germain-des-Prés were built by royal officeholders, tax farmers, and bankers attached to the court. Henri IV's urbanism took advantage of the inflationary effects on real estate values that followed the court's return to the capital. His residence in the city and his building program initiated the trajectory of urban development that transformed Paris into a monumental capital.

This book is about a crucial episode in the transformation of a medieval city into a modern capital. It is about the relation between city planning under the direction of an absolute monarch and the emergence of the centralized state in seventeenth-century France. Historians agree on the importance of that relationship, but the nature of the relationship has not yet been satisfactorily explained. It has generally been assumed that the ideology of monarchy, centered on the deified king, directly translated into programs of city planning devoted to self-glorification. At least with respect to Henri IV, that view misconstrues the interrelated social and architectural concerns that animated Henri IV's urbanism. Furthermore, the traditional view fails to capture the power of architecture or account for the complex transactions between art and society; to describe works of architecture as passive reflections of a social reality in which they play no active role is to ignore the power of urban form to shape and structure experience. Henri IV appreciated that power. He understood that the rebuilding of Paris played an essential role in the creation and representation of the centralized state. His buildings were far more than decorative backdrops; they played a major role in defining the history of the city. The monuments and the squares functioned not as static, reflective objects but as social creations making their own meaning.

Earlier generations of scholars combed the royal archives without discovering how Henri IV's urban projects came to life. In the case of the Place Royale, for example, documents concerning the distribution of royal land were found, but nothing was learned about the actual construction and settlement of the square. On these critical matters, the king's archives were silent because the crown was not involved in any of the construction. The two squares were built by private patrons, with each lot owner commissioning his own building crew and hiring notaries to record the transactions. It was in the notarial archives that the undiscovered building contracts for the royal squares lay buried, and it is on these rich resources, deposited in the *Minutier central* in Paris, that this study is based. The history of the projects was pieced together from a large number of documents: contracts with brickmakers, stonecutters, and woodsellers; building contracts with masons, carpenters, metalworkers, and glaziers; land sales, leases, and loans; and in the end, inventories after death. I have tried to spare the reader a tedious familiarity with those individual pieces by confining the archival apparatus to appendices. Even so, the reader is asked to observe the buildings at an unglamorous proximity. But by witnessing them as they rise, as products of human aspirations and conflicts, and not as iconic images of urban splendor, we come closer to seeing how architectural form, social forces, and political vision together produced the Paris of Henri IV.

CHAPTER ONE

THE LOUVRE

enri IV's first building project was the enlargement of the royal palace, the Louvre. It was an expensive undertaking, initiated within months of the king's entry into Paris at a time when the royal coffers were depleted. Yet the project's political value was far from negligible. Construction was intended to stimulate the local building economy, putting masons and carpenters, quarriers and woodsellers, bargees and laborers back to work after the impoverishment of war. The project was hard evidence of Henri IV's intention to live in Paris, promising the city a new era of royal beneficence. It also symbolized monarchical continuity, with the Bourbon king following his Valois predecessors in making the Louvre the royal residence.

On 26 September 1594, Henri IV announced his intention to complete the Louvre and Tuileries, "following the designs and plans which were previously established." [1] Whether motivated by a reluctance to modify the existing design or a perceived need for quick action, Henri IV decided to pursue the Valois plan for transforming the medieval fortress into a modern palace. It was a decision he would eventually reverse.

THE VALOIS PROJECT

Philippe Auguste built the Louvre in the 1190s to defend the western approach to the city, choosing an extramural site on the Right Bank along the river. [2] The Louvre was a typical fortress, with a crenellated curtain wall punctuated by towers surrounding a courtyard with a dungeon in the center. The fortress was brought within the city in the mid-fourteenth century when the urban expansion of the Right Bank led Charles V to build an enlarged circuit of walls. From their western extremity at the Tour du Bois, the fortifications extended along the Seine to the old walls, enclosing the river front of the Louvre (Fig. 6). The Louvre no longer had any strategic value, and Charles V adapted it as a royal residence, building residential wings around the courtyard between 1360 and 1380. Excavated in 1984–86, much of the structure built by Philippe Auguste and Charles V is now visible in the archaeological crypt of the Louvre.

For the next 150 years, no significant changes were made to the Louvre, and when Francois I decided to transfer the court from the Loire valley to the

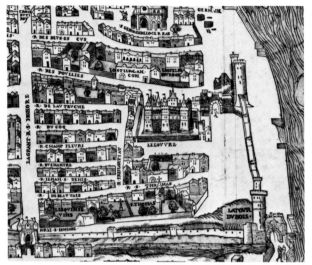

Fig. 6. Olivier Truschet and Germain Hoyau, map of Paris (Basel plan), detail of the Louvre, before 1559. (Bibliothek der Universität Basel AA 124) The Louvre appears as it was in 1528, prior to any sixteenth-century construction.

Ile-de-France, the dilapidated fortress was unfit for the Renaissance king. In 1528, François I announced that he would live in Paris and its environs, and rebuild the Louvre.[3] Although the king never in fact lived in the city — he came about once a year — this edict established the Louvre as the formal seat of the crown. François I demolished the dungeon (1528); built the Porte Neuve (c. 1537), the new gate beside the Tour du Bois; and turned the sloping bank along the river wall into a paved quai (c. 1536). Antiurban by inclination, François I was far more interested in building his châteaux of Fontainebleau, Madrid, La Muette, and Challuau, and he deferred the work of modernizing the Louvre proper until 1546. Serlio produced a design in the early 1540s, probably the city palace for "gran re Francesco" in his manuscript on domestic architecture (Fig. 7).[4] The king preferred Pierre Lescot's design, which is now lost. Presumably it was more modest than Serlio's grandiose sequence of courtyards, because in 1546 Lescot began to rebuild the west wing of the Louvre to the same dimensions as the fortress it replaced.

The decision to enlarge the Louvre radically was made by Henri II. In 1549, he ordered Lescot to demolish part of what had just been built in order to accommodate the expansion; in 1551, he approved Lescot's revised plan, which quadrupled the area of the fortress. Four new wings, each double the length of those standing, were to be built around a square courtyard, the Cour Carrée.[5] By the time of his death in 1578, Lescot had completed only a quarter of the Cour Carrée: half of the west range, which was decorated by Jean Goujon; the connecting half of the south range; and a square pavilion at the corner which housed the king's apartment.

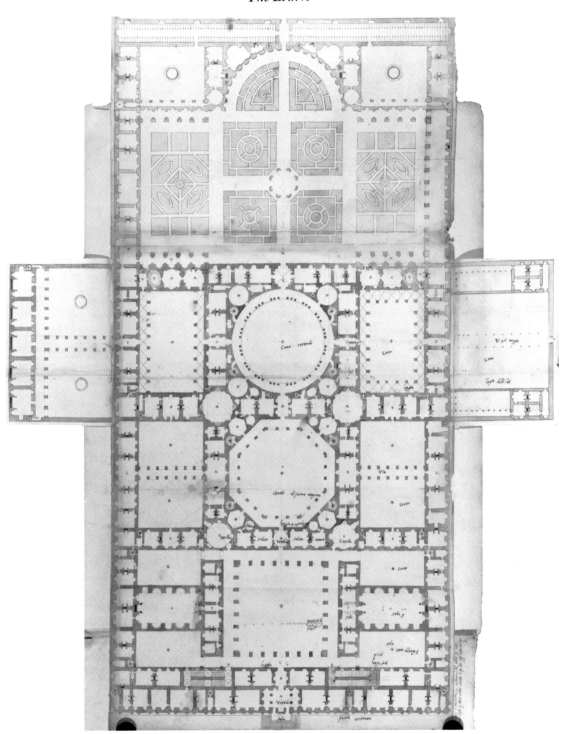

Fig. 7. Sebastiano Serlio, plan of a city palace for François I, Book VI, fol. 71, c. 1541–46. (Avery Architectural and Fine Arts Library, Columbia University, New York)

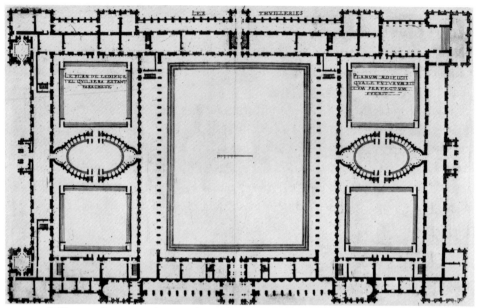

Fig. 8. Philibert Delorme, Tuileries palace, plan, c. 1565. Engraving by Jacques Androuet Ducerceau, *Les plus excellents bastiments de France,* 1576–79. (B.N. Est. Ed 2a) Ducerceau substantially altered Delorme's design, which probably did not include the lateral courtyards.

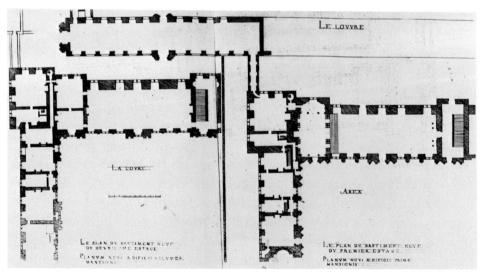

Fig. 9. Louvre, ground plan of the Petite Galerie at top and the connecting Renaissance wings of the Cour Carrée at right, first floor plan at left. Engraving by Jacques Androuet Ducerceau, *Les plus excellents bastiments de France,* 1576–79. (Avery Architectural and Fine Arts Library, Columbia University, New York)

The crown's presence at the Louvre conferred an aristocratic character on the neighborhood. It was here, outside the walls on a site bordering the Seine, that the Queen Mother Catherine de' Medici began building the Tuileries palace in 1564. The only record we have of Philibert Delorme's design of the Tuileries are the engravings by Jacques Androuet Ducerceau, but they include changes made by the engraver (Fig. 8). Anthony Blunt convincingly argued that Ducerceau, influenced by Serlio's Louvre design, added the lateral courtyards, and that Delorme's plan, like those for his other châteaux, comprised only one courtyard.[6] Before his death in 1570, Delorme built the central pavilion of the west range and two adjoining galleries as well as freestanding stables to the north. Whatever the uncertainties about Delorme's plan, there is no question that he conceived the Tuileries as an independent building. He was subsequently overruled by the crown.

Charles IX decided to link the Tuileries to the Louvre, and a plan gradually emerged to traverse the distance with three new buildings. First was the Petite Galerie, a one-story gallery running from the southwest corner of the Cour Carrée to the Seine; begun in about 1566, it was finished by the time Ducerceau published his engraved plan in 1576 (Fig. 9). The gallery was built by Pierre II Chambiges, whom we will encounter again working for Henri IV. In this instance, he was following the designs of an unknown architect, perhaps Lescot, the supervising architect of the Louvre, or Delorme, whose banded columns reappeared here.[7] Second, a gallery was planned along the river wall to connect the Petite Galerie to the Tuileries. Bates Lowry suggested the gallery was inspired by a contemporary Medici project in Florence, the gallery begun by Vasari in 1565 to link the Uffizi and Pitti palaces.[8] It is likely that Charles IX planned a similar, modest structure, although his unexecuted project is not known. Third, Jean Bullant redesigned the Tuileries palace as a single range which extended to the Seine, abandoning Delorme's plan for a courtyard palace. Bullant was able to add only one pavilion to the south end of the Tuileries, which was built between 1570 and 1572. Thereafter, the Valois rulers undertook no further construction on the Tuileries, leaving the palace short of the river.[9]

It was Henri III's intention to continue the projects of Henri II and Charles IX. On orders of the king, Lescot's drawings of the Louvre were transferred upon his death to the new royal architect, Baptiste Androuet Ducerceau, but the civil war prevented the crown from pursuing the Valois design.[10] Henri III built only one minor structure, yet it may have saved his life. He opened a paved walkway inside the river wall which led from the Louvre to the ramparts. It was by this path that the king escaped the city when on the Day of Barricades, 12 May 1588, antiroyalist rebels captured Paris.

Upon entering Paris in 1594, Henri IV found the royal palace in a shabby state of incompletion. The Cour Carrée was bordered by two medieval wings and two Renaissance wings, which were connected to an undecorated gallery abutting the river wall. The unfinished Tuileries lay in ruin beyond the wall of Charles V, and the area between the palaces, pierced by moat and ramparts, contained a sizable neighborhood with two parish churches.

HENRI IV's FIRST PLAN FOR THE LOUVRE: 1594–95

Henri IV adhered to the inherited Valois projects in his first scheme for the Louvre, dating from 1594–95. It is depicted in an anonymous and undated plan, known by its catalogue number as Destailleur 147 (Fig. 10). Although the date of the drawing was once disputed, it has been confirmed by numerous building contracts from 1594 and 1595 that detail the first phase of construction.[11] The Louvre and Tuileries are rendered at different scales in the drawing, and Lowry, in a masterful analysis, concluded that Destailleur 147 is a composite of two Valois plans.[12] We know that Lescot's drawings, which survived at least until 1624, were passed on to the successive architects of the Louvre, presumably accompanied by the Tuileries designs. Henri IV's draftsman simply traced two older plans, one for the enlarged Cour Carrée and the other for the Tuileries, without transposing them into a common scale. He even copied the initials of Henri II and Catherine de' Medici in the parterres of the Tuileries gardens. The tracing procedure explains two other features of Destailleur 147. First, the real dimensions of the two galleries connecting the palaces cannot be read from the 1594–95 plan; the galleries were not drawn to scale in order to mask the inconsistent scales of the palaces. Second, the drawing misrepresents the orientation of the Tuileries and moat; they were not aligned with the Louvre, as shown, but were diagonally oriented to the older palace. By repositioning the base plan of the Tuileries, the draftsman easily aligned the palaces, and his rendering deceptively endowed Henri IV's project with the appeal of geometric regularity. The drawing suppressed the crucial formal issue raised by linking the two palaces: how to resolve their misalignment.

Yet given this design, the misalignment of the Louvre and Tuileries would have been imperceptible because the palaces were separated by intervening courtyards. It is possible that the three courtyards between the Louvre and the moat were copied from the Valois base plan, as is the case for the narrow courtyards between the Cour Carrée and the Seine. These lateral spaces may have been planned under Charles IX in conjunction with the Petite Galerie; however, only the chapel at the east end is documented.[13] Ultimately, the

Fig. 10. Anonymous, plan of Henri IV's first project for the Louvre and Tuileries palaces, 1594–95. (B.N. Est rés. Ve 53i, Destailleur 147)

courtyards derived from Serlio's palace design for François I, where many smaller units were added to one another to form a vast structure (see Fig. 7). This Renaissance segmentation of space also characterized Henri IV's scheme. In order to link the Louvre and Tuileries palaces, the distance was traversed by a series of additive units.

Within this conservative, Valois framework, Henri IV's architects made two important innovations: they reconceived the Grande Galerie and the fortifications of Charles V. Whereas the Valois had envisioned the gallery as little more than a covered passageway, Henri IV's architects designed a monumental structure which served several aulic functions; and whereas the Valois gallery bordered the river wall, dependent on the defensive system, Henri IV's gallery replaced the wall and faced the Seine. The fortifications dividing the two palaces were also demolished; only the two gatehouses — the Porte Neuve and the Porte St. Honoré — survived, continuing to regulate entry to the city. In 1989, excavations uncovered this segment of Charles V's ramparts, documenting their physical form for the first time. Proceeding from east to west, the city was defended by a massive sloping embankment of earth, about 20 meters wide and 6 – 7 meters high, which was buttressed by a stone wall. Beyond it was a wet moat, 30 meters wide, contained on the far side by another masonry wall, the counterscarp; and beyond the moat were advanced earthworks, made up of at least two more ditches with a rise of land in between.[14] This territory was relandscaped in Henri IV's plan of 1594 – 95 (see Fig. 10). On the Tuileries side of the moat, the advanced earthworks were transformed into a garden, the Jardin Neuf. On the Louvre side, the sloping embankment was leveled to make a two-tiered platform or esplanade, a pleasant spot for a stroll overlooking the moat and garden.[15]

The ramparts were gone, but they left their mark on the Grande Galerie. At the point where they intersected the Grande Galerie, a large pavilion was planned. It divided the gallery into two unequal segments, each with a different facade design. On the quai, the pavilion adjoined the Porte Neuve; and on the city side, the pavilion provided access to the esplanade. The esplanade was enclosed at the other end by a freestanding pavilion, aligned with the stables of the Tuileries and apparently conceived as a guardhouse. According to the 1594 – 95 plan, any pedestrian passing through the Porte St. Honoré could reach the lower, eastern platform by stairs at each end, while the upper level was only accessible from the Grande Galerie. There was no means of moving between the two platforms.

Henri IV's first project was ambitious in scale but not in conception. The Louvre and Tuileries had originally been separated by the ramparts; now that

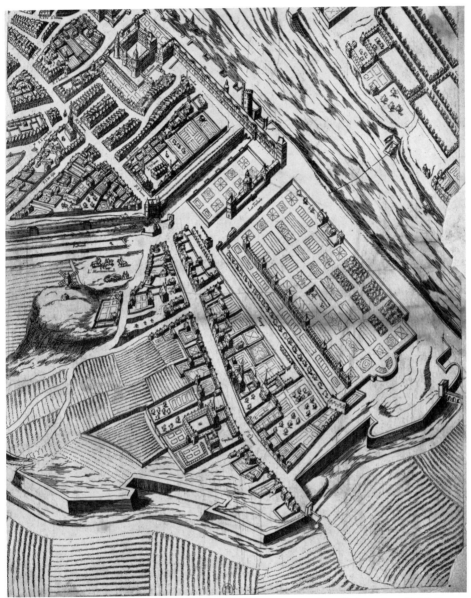

Fig. 11. François Quesnel, map of Paris, detail of the Louvre and Tuileries, 1609. (B.N. Est. rés. AA 3)

barrier was removed, but the palaces were still treated as separate units. Henri IV's architects brought them together in an additive ensemble that was no more than an accumulation of courtyards and connecting wings. From these many parts, the royal design failed to forge one unified palace with an over-reaching architectural order.

Fig. 12. Vassallieu dit Nicolay, map of Paris, detail of the Louvre and Tuileries, 1609. (B.N. Est. rés. Hennin XV 1352)

Fig. 13. Anonymous, Tuileries palace, west facade, c. 1650. (B.N. Est. rés. Ve 53h) This watercolor depicts the palace as it was enlarged by Henri IV, prior to Louis XIV's modifications. From left to right, one sees Delorme's two symmetric wings flanking the staircase pavilion which was probably domed by Henri IV; the Bullant pavilion; and the Petite Galerie des Tuileries and Pavillon de Flore which were both built by Henri IV.

Construction was launched in 1594 and 1595. Two months after entering Paris, Henry IV began repairing the Tuileries. The famous suspended staircase in the axial pavilion, unfinished by Delorme, was completed by mason Martin Boullet. The Quesnel and Nicolay maps, both from 1609, also indicate that the pavilion was domed at this time, although no contracts for this work have been found (Figs. 11, 12).[16] The dome is more accurately depicted in Figure 13, an anonymous drawing of the Tuileries, viewed from the west, which was made before Louis XIV altered Henri IV's additions to the palace. Also under Henri IV, Delorme's southern gallery, to the right of the dome in Figure 13, was largely rebuilt, and the adjoining pavilion by Bullant was partially restored.[17] In the Cour Carrée, Henri IV completed the sculptural decoration of Lescot's south wing.[18] At the same time, the roof terrace of the Petite Galerie was replaced by a second story, seen in Marot's reversed engraving of the east facade (Fig. 14). The masonry contract has not been found, but work was under way in January 1595, and the roof was begun in October 1596.[19]

We learn from Sauval that the upper story of the Petite Galerie was built by masons Florent Fournier and Jean Coin, but they were certainly not responsible for the design, a subject we will turn to shortly. The building was chiefly remarkable for its revetment of multicolored marbles and rich ornamentation. The facade, Sauval wrote, "is so encumbered by bas-reliefs, round bosses, very delicate ornaments, and inlaid marbles in white, black, jasper and colors of all sorts, that it is difficult to describe the inharmonious combination of such motley elements."[20] The Petite Galerie would have been even more richly

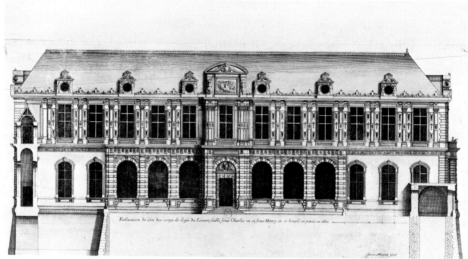

Fig. 14. Petite Galerie, east elevation. Engraving by Jean Marot, "Grand Marot," late 1660s. (B.N. Est Va 217a) The engraving is reversed. As a result, the two-story passageway leading to the king's apartment incorrectly appears at left (in section), while the balcony overlooking the river and the orangery (in section) along the quai incorrectly appear at right.

Fig. 15. Reinier Nooms dit Zeeman, the Louvre viewed from the Left Bank, 1656. (B.N. Est. rés. Ve53g) This watercolor drawing, a preparatory study for a painting in the Musée Carnavalet, shows the river facade of the Petite Galerie and the adjoining five bays of the Grande Galerie as built by Henri IV, prior to their alteration in 1661.

decorated than we see it in Marot's elevation had Henri IV's architect followed his first design. It is described in a contract passed in 1601 with sculptor Jean Mansart (uncle of architect François Mansart) to carve images of Abundance, Peace, and Henri IV, "His Imperial Majesty," for three large pediments on the west facade. The scheme was changed in 1602 to a single pediment above the entrance bay similar in shape to Lescot's pediments in the Cour Carrée. The sculptural program was also revised to focus on Henri IV's military feats; Mansart sculpted a rectangular relief of the king with his armies, framed by figures of Fame and Victory and crowned by a rounded pediment with angels supporting the royal arms.[21] The decoration of the east facade is undocumented, but Marot's engraving shows a figure of Fame above the entrance. Finally, the Petite Galerie presented a one-bay facade to the river. This elevation was distinguished by a second-floor balcony from which the king could enjoy what Sauval considered "one of the most beautiful views in the world" (Fig. 15).[22]

Construction of the Grande Galerie, the centerpiece of Henri IV's project, began in January 1595. The masonry contract called for the demolition of Charles V's river wall and the construction of the gallery on its foundations. A pavilion was to be built at the ramparts, and beyond that point there was a change in the elevation of the extramural segment of the gallery. The contract also included the end pavilion, later called the Pavillon de Flore, and the perpendicular wing of the Tuileries, the Petite Galerie des Tuileries. The contract for the Grande Galerie was awarded to six masons, all *juré du Roi,* the highest rank of their profession: Florent Fournier, Pierre Guillain, Robert Marquelet, Guillaume Marchant, François Petit, and Pierre II Chambiges.[23] Guillain and Marquelet had already been hired to repair the Tuileries. Marchant and Petit built the Pont Neuf, and Petit would go on to play a key role in the Place Dauphine. Chambiges, member of a distinguished family of mason-architects, later supervised the completion of the Hôtel de Ville, which his father had begun for François I.

After three intensive years of construction between 1595 and 1598, the crown fell delinquent in its payments, slowing construction considerably for the next five years. Work had begun at the east end, and about fifteen bays (41 *toises*) were partially built in 1601 when the crown agreed to pay the masons 51,000 *livres* during the calendar year for carrying the walls up to the roof.[24] Finding it difficult to finance the project, the crown accused the masons of inflating costs, a charge which they fiercely denied. Ultimately, the parties agreed to annul the 1595 contract.[25] When construction was resumed by a new team of masons in 1603, Henri IV's architects had reconceived the design of the Louvre.

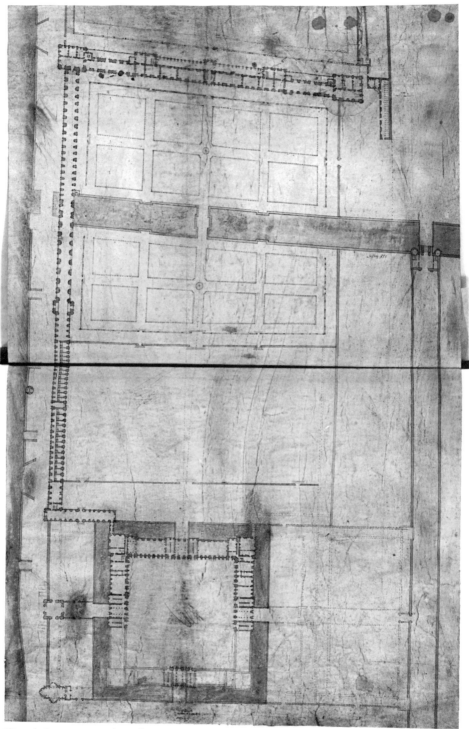

Fig. 16. Anonymous, plan of Henri IV's second project for the Louvre and Tuileries palaces, 1603. (B.N. Est. rés. Ve 53i, Destailleur 148)

Henri IV's Second Design for the Louvre: 1603

In February 1603, a revised masonry contract for the Grande Galerie was awarded to Jean Coin (who had built the Petite Galerie), Isidoire Guyot, and Guillaume Jacquet — three less prominent masons who accepted the low rates imposed by the crown.[26] The gallery was $31\frac{1}{2}$ *toises* short of the Porte Neuve, and the new contract only concerned the remaining section within the walls. The changes specified in the 1603 contract were dictated by a new design, depicted in a second anonymous drawing known as Destailleur 148 (Fig. 16).

The conception of the palace had profoundly changed. Henri IV's architect decided to remove all the buildings between the Louvre and Tuileries so that the palaces faced one another across a vast courtyard. The intervening courtyards and esplanade of the first scheme were eliminated, as of course were all the medieval and Renaissance buildings that actually occupied the site; and the moat was integrated into the enlarged garden. The architect underscored his interest in the visual relation of the two palaces by marking the sight line between the two axial pavilions with a broken line. It is with this visual axis that the main garden path is aligned.

The Grande Galerie was also modified to satisfy the new architectural priorities. In Henri IV's original design, the intersection of the ramparts with the Grande Galerie was marked by a large pavilion. Now that all trace of the ramparts was removed, including the Porte Neuve on the quai, other considerations controlled the design of the pavilion. It was reduced in size and shifted to the east, not placed in middle of the gallery as one would at first suppose, but aligned with the midpoint between the two palaces. The gallery pavilion was thus conceived as a visual marker, bisecting the view between the palaces. There are three points of reference in the courtyard, each with a crowning element: the central pavilion of the Tuileries which was topped by a dome, probably by Henri IV; the gallery pavilion, topped by a cupola and lantern, after which it was called the Pavillon de la Lanterne (see Figs. 11, 12); and the central pavilion in the west range of the Cour Carrée, which was certainly intended to have a prominent crowning element. Henri IV did not execute this third pavilion — he made no additions to the Cour Carrée — and his plans do not clarify the roof design. The two-bay entrance to the pavilion in the 1594–95 plan has been widened to three bays in the 1603 plan, and it is possible that a dome was projected for this enlarged pavilion (see Figs. 10, 16). However it was covered, the 1603 design envisioned three tall pavilions which addressed one another across the vast space of the courtyard.

While the location of the gallery pavilion is explained by the view from the courtyard, its new design was otherwise determined by the view from the Seine.

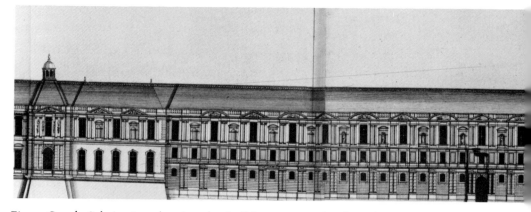

Fig. 17. Grande Galerie, river elevation, detail of the eastern section from the Pavillon de la Lanterne, at left, to the Petite Galerie. Engraving by Jean Marot, "Grand Marot," late 1660s. (Avery Architectural and Fine Arts Library, Columbia University, New York)

The eastern section of the gallery now had a symmetric facade. The river facade of the Pavillon de la Lanterne mirrored that of the Petite Galerie, with a banded ground-floor arch, balcony, and curved pediment broken by a bull's-eye window (see Figs. 15, 17). "The projection and balcony," the 1603 masonry contract specified, ". . . will be made symmetric to the projection of the Petite Galerie."[27] Beside each of the single-bay projections was a five-bay unit with a

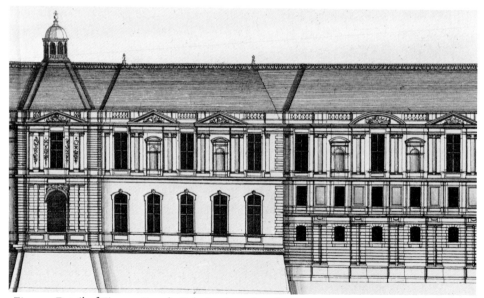

Fig. 17a. Detail of Fig. 17. Grande Galerie, river elevation, eastern section.

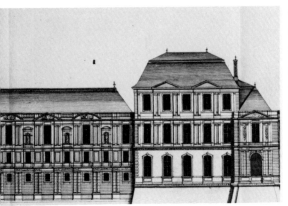

two-story elevation. After a fire in 1661 destroyed the upper floor of the Petite Galerie, Louis Le Vau extended the damaged building to the west and re-worked the facade of the adjoining five bays, adding a third story as Marot's engraving illustrates (Fig. 17).[28] Most views of the Grande Galerie postdate Le Vau's modifications and consequently do not reflect the symmetry of Henri IV's composition. The pendant five-bay units anchored the two-and-one-half-story elevation of the long central section: rusticated ground floor, mezzanine, and first floor with pedimented bays alternating with niches (Fig. 17a). Paired pilasters were carried over from the Petite Galerie, but the vertical axis of the superimposed orders was interrupted by the cornices and the tablets of the mezzanine. The composition gives greater visual weight to the horizontal division of the facade and dissolves the wall into an ornamental surface. Beside this cramped and overcharged elevation, the five-bay units with their austere ground story offered a welcome restraint. The ground floor and mezzanine corresponded to apartments that the

Veue du Louure et de la grande Galerie du cofté des Offices .

Ifrael ex·

Fig. 18. View of the Louvre and Grande Galerie from the north. Engraving by Israel Silvestre, c. 1650–55. (B.N. Est Va 217e)

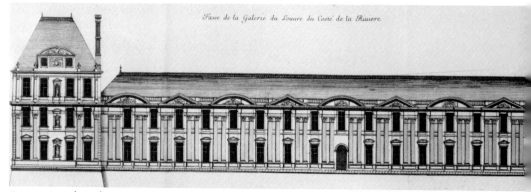

Fig. 19. Grande Galerie, river elevation, detail of the western section from the Pavillon de Flore, at left, up to the Pavillon de la Lanterne. Engraving by Jean Marot, "Grand Marot," late 1660s. (Avery Architectural and Fine Arts Library, Columbia University, New York)

Fig. 20. Grande Galerie, north facade. Philibert Girault de Pangey, daguerreotype, 1841. (B.N. Est. rés. Eg7 557)

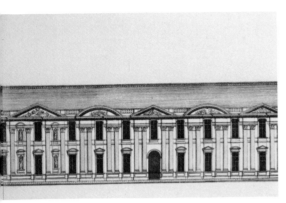

crown built for artists. The only difference in the northern elevation of the gallery was a ground-floor arcade that fronted the artists' workshops (Fig. 18). As Destailleur 148 shows, only one passageway was originally planned through this section of the gallery — the Guichet St. Thomas in the center bay (see Fig. 16). By the 1660s, additional passages were opened in the second apartment (Guichet St. Nicolas) and the Pavillon de la Lanterne (Guichet St. Nicaise), seen in Marot's engraving (see Fig. 17).

The 1603 contract specified that the elevation of the Grande Galerie was to change at the Pavillon de la Lanterne, not at the ramparts as originally planned.[29] On the western section, a colossal order of coupled pilasters framed two floors of windows (Figs. 19, 20). The original design called for an Ionic order, but this was changed in 1603 to a composite order with dolphins in celebration of the dauphin's birth in 1601. The last dauphin to reach the throne was François II (1559–61), and the dolphin order, also used in Henri IV's additions to the Cour Ovale at Fontainebleau, signaled a new era of dynastic continuity (Fig. 21).[30] The alternation of triangular and curved pediments continued across the entire gallery, but the larger pediments and wider bay of the western elevation combined with the colossal order to create a monumentality lacking in the other part (Fig. 21a). This monumentality was achieved despite Mannerist devices that undermined the classical expression of weight and support: the upper range of windows pierced the entablature, reducing it to a series of blocks above the pilasters; the fragmentary entablature did not appear to sup-

Fig. 21 Château de Fontainebleau, Porte Dauphine, detail of the dolphin order. (B.N. Est. Va 77, t. 7)

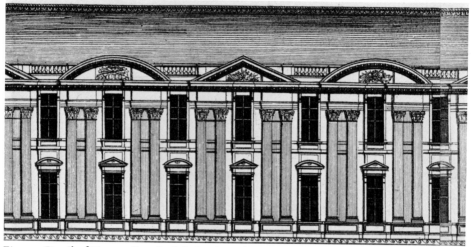

Fig. 21a. Detail of Fig. 19. Grande Galerie, river elevation, western section.

port the roof; the pediments sprang from the recessed window jambs rather than the entablature; and the cornice and pediments projected beyond the pilasters, which appeared weaker than the load they carried. Sauval condemned these "irregularities" which did not suit his classicizing taste, yet this elevation was certainly more successful than its eastern counterpart.[31] The pediment reliefs seen in Marot's engraving were added by Louis XIV in the early 1660s, and we do not know whether the decoration was projected in Henri IV's design.

The ramparts left one imprint on the Grande Galerie: the bay over the moat was enlarged by a file of niches between the pilasters (see Fig. 19). This bay divided the western part of the gallery into two unequal parts. On the 1603 plan, a passageway in each part was aligned with garden paths (see Fig. 16). Only the

Fig. 22. View of the Seine looking east, before 1661. Anonymous engraving published by Nicolas Berey. (B.N. Est. Va 224b) The Grande Galerie is obstructed by the Porte Neuve and Tour du Bois which were not demolished until 1670.

Fig. 23. Pavillon de Flore, river facade. Edouard Baldus, July 1861. (A.N. 64 AJ 500; Service Photographique des Archives Nationales)

garden on the Tuileries side of the moat, the Jardin Neuf, was realized, and the corresponding opening was built according to the 1603 design.[32] On the Louvre side of the moat, where the garden was not built, the river view determined the placement of the *guichet;* as Marot's engraving illustrates, the bay in the middle of that section was pierced. The demolition of the Porte Neuve, Tour du Bois, and ramparts was projected in 1603, but they were not destroyed until 1670. With the exception of the *guichets,* the Grande Galerie was composed in deference to an unobstructed view from the river (Fig. 22).

The Pavillon de Flore visually anchored both the Grande Galerie and the Tuileries with a towering three-story elevation and dormers. The cornice of the Grande Galerie wrapped around the pavilion, and the elevation below echoed that of the gallery but with single pilasters (Fig. 23; see Fig. 19). On the west side of the Tuileries, the Petite Galerie des Tuileries receded between the Pavillon de Flore and the Bullant pavilion (see Fig. 13). On the 1594/95 drawing, it was planned with a gallery, giving it the same width as the Delorme wings (see Fig. 10). The gallery was omitted from the 1603 design, and the staircases were

[35]

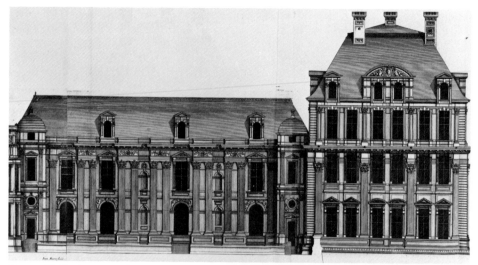

Fig. 24. Tuileries, west elevation, detail of the Petite Galerie des Tuileries and Pavillon de Flore. Engraving by Jean Marot, "Grand Marot," late 1660s. (Avery Architectural and Fine Arts Library, Columbia University, New York)

expressed as separate volumes, housed in small projections at each end (see Fig. 16). The coupled order was repeated on the central block in an asymmetric scheme which apparently resulted from retaining the bay used on the east facade of the Delorme wings. In 1664–66, when Le Vau completed the Tuileries, he widened the Petite Galerie des Tuileries on the west side so that the palace had a uniform width, and his new facade corrected the asymmetry of the original design (Fig. 24).

No contract other than the one passed in 1595 has been found for the extramural segment of the gallery and the connecting wing of the Tuileries, but construction was well advanced by 1608.[33] The cornerstone of the Pavillon de Flore was laid in 1607, and the Englishman Thomas Coryate reported that two hundred masons were working on the west end of the gallery during his visit to Paris in May 1608.[34] The roof of the Petite Galerie des Tuileries was begun a year later, and the buildings were completed by the time of Henri IV's death.[35]

As Destailleur 148 demonstrates, the geometry of the Louvre did not govern the Tuileries, which was planned as an independent building and oriented with the walls of Charles V, on a diagonal course to the Seine (see Fig. 16). The conflicting geometries are more clearly demonstrated on a plan made by Antoine Desgodetz in 1694 (Fig. 25). When it was decided in 1603 to unify the two palaces around an open courtyard, the oblique relationship of the palaces had to be taken into account. The draftsman of Destailleur 148 studied this

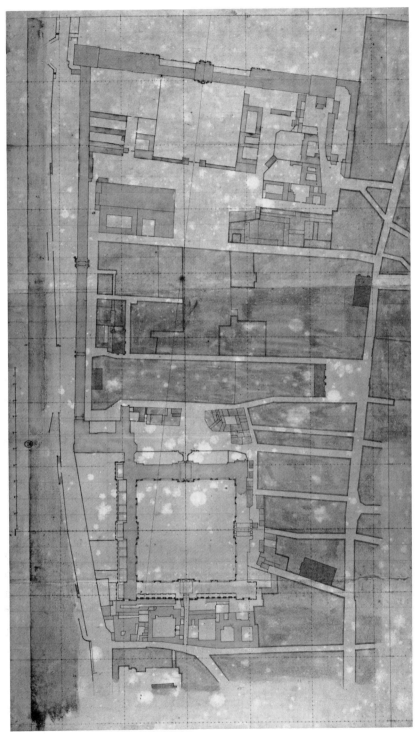

Fig. 25. Antoine Desgodetz, plan of the Louvre and Tuileries, c. 1694. (B.N. Est. Va 440a)

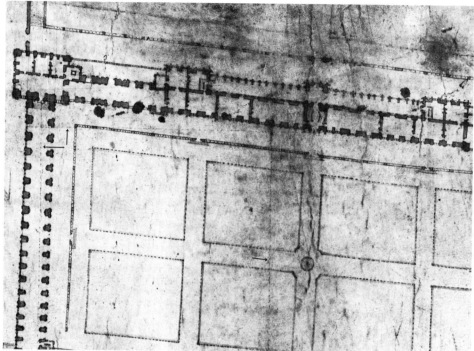

Fig. 26. Detail of Fig. 16 (Destailleur 148). The draftsman projected the geometry of the Louvre on the Pavillon de Flore and Tuileries in three dashed lines.

problem by projecting the geometry of the Louvre onto the Tuileries with three orthogonal lines (Fig. 26; see Fig. 16): a line parallel with the east-west axis of the Louvre is drawn from the center of the Louvre's west range to the Tuileries, sharply diverging from the sight line; a perpendicular line is drawn through the Tuileries and Grande Galerie; and a line perpendicular to it (and parallel to the first line) is drawn through the gallery. As the third line demonstrates, the Grande Galerie also deviated from the Louvre grid because its course was determined by the wall of Charles V (see Fig. 16). Because the gallery was not perpendicular to the Tuileries, the north facade of the gallery was slightly shorter than the river facade. Had the architect been willing to compose the two facades independently, their unequal lengths would not have created a problem; however, he wanted to align the windows, maintaining a normative bay on both facades. The architect reckoned with this problem by contracting one bay on the north side of the gallery — the bay west of the moat — and masked the irregularity by a small projecting stair pavilion, shown both on the 1603 plan and Quesnel's map (see Figs. 16, 11).

The conflicting geometries also impinged on the design of the Pavillon de Flore, which formed an irregular trapezoid in plan (see Figs. 25, 26). Here the architect did not value the alignment of facades; the axial view from the gallery through the pavilion was blocked by a pier as was the view from the Tuileries to the river. The most important consideration was that the entrance to the Grande Galerie be placed in the center of the room. The two exposed facades of the pavilion responded to local conditions: the river facade was aligned with the Petite Galerie, and the west facade, overlooking the garden, was aligned with the Tuileries. This supple approach to design, with its acceptance of irregular geometries and attention to local site conditions, we will again see at the Place Dauphine. Finally, the misalignment of the palaces affected the unexecuted garden east of the moat; bounded on one side by the moat and on the other by a wall parallel to the Louvre, the garden was forced to taper.

THE DESIGNERS

The design of Henri IV's Louvre has traditionally been attributed to the royal architects Jacques II Androuet Ducerceau (c. 1550–1614) and Louis Métezeau (1559–1615). As Henri IV's chief architects, they were probably responsible for designing the Place Royale and Place Dauphine as well. Despite the crucial roles they surely played, we know very little about their specific contributions. There is no documentary basis for the attributions, since none of the contracts for the Louvre or royal squares identifies the architect in charge. Furthermore, there are difficulties in basing the attributions on stylistic grounds; the personal styles of Ducerceau and Métezeau cannot be defined because their oeuvre as a whole is almost entirely undocumented. In the past thirty years, archival research has altered our view of French architecture during the reigns of Henri III and Henri IV, as long-accepted attributions and assumptions about chronology have been invalidated. Given this broader reconsideration of the period and the centrality of Ducerceau and Métezeau in Henri IV's urbanism, it is important to clarify precisely what is and is not known about their work.

Ducerceau had served as royal architect since the reign of Henri III, and he opposed Métezeau's appointment in 1594, claiming that the title could be granted to only one architect. The crown dismissed Ducerceau's complaint in 1599, asserting the king's prerogative to name as many royal architects as he pleased.[36] It is difficult to imagine that the two men amicably collaborated in 1594–95 when their dispute began, and the project was undoubtedly divided between them, as the stylistic differences of the elevations suggest. The Petite Galerie des Tuileries and western section of the Grande Galerie are traditionally

Fig. 27. Jacques Androuet Ducerceau, château de Charleval, elevation of the lower court. Engraving by Jacques Androuet Ducerceau, *Les plus excellents bastiments de France*, 1576–79. (B.N. Est. Ed 2a)

attributed to Ducerceau, the Petite Galerie and eastern section of the Grande Galerie to Métezeau.

The first author to discuss Ducerceau's work at the Louvre was Sauval, writing in the 1660s, from whom we learn that Ducerceau designed the Tuileries wing.[37] Certainly, the same man was responsible for the adjoining section of the Grande Galerie. Yet, while there is no reason to reject Sauval's attribution, neither is there a shred of hard evidence — stylistic or documentary — to sustain it.[38] The attribution has gained acceptance because similarities are noted between the Grande Galerie and the designs of Jacques Androuet Ducerceau the

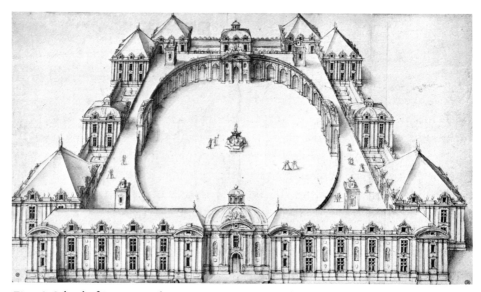

Fig. 28. School of Jacques Androuet Ducerceau, project for a palace. (Ecole nationale supérieure des Beaux-Arts, Paris, dessin 093)

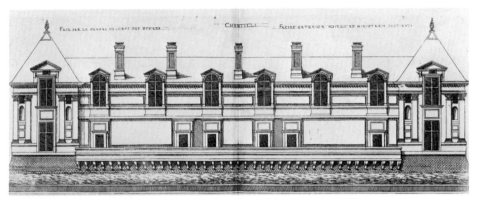

Fig. 29. Jean Bullant, Chantilly, exterior elevation of the Cour des Offices, c. 1557–60. Engraving by Jacques Androuet Ducerceau, *Les plus excellents bastiments de France,* 1576–79. (B.N. Imp. rés. V390)

Elder, and it is assumed that Jacques II designed in the manner of his father. The only documented fact about Jacques II's training is that he worked on his father's chantiers at Verneuil and Charleval (Fig. 27). Some motifs in these châteaux recur in the Grande Galerie, namely the colossal order and the entablature pierced by tall windows. Yet the Grande Galerie elevation rejected the ornamental treatment of the wall surface that characterized the châteaux designs. Are there other designs by the senior Ducerceau, then, which more closely resemble the Grande Galerie? In 1972, Rosalys Coope published a drawing of a palace project in the Ecole des Beaux-Arts, Paris, which she attributed to Jacques the Elder and identified as a prototype of the Grande Galerie (Fig. 28).[39] The strong colossal order of this project, the pedimented end bays with paired pilasters and the windows breaking the entablature, do indeed recall the Grande Galerie.

But the Ecole des Beaux-Arts drawing does not clarify the authorship of the Grande Galerie. In the first place, the drawing is not an autograph work of Ducerceau the Elder: it lacks his refined line; the figures are not characteristically elongated; and the perspective is awkward, particularly the domes of the axial pavilions and the little towers projecting from the roof terrace. The drawing can safely be credited to the circle of Ducerceau senior, but no more precise attribution can be made at this early stage in Ducerceau studies. Jacques Androuet Ducerceau's name is now attached to the dozens of drawings produced by his workshop and his followers, and the first attempts are only now under way to discriminate the hands of studio artists and those of Ducerceau's sons.[40] But even if Coope's attribution were correct, given our ignorance about Jacques II, it is untenable to equate his style with his father's. Indeed, it is clear that the architect of the Louvre was not exclusively shaped by the Ducerceau

Fig. 30. Jean Bullant, Tuileries pavilion, west elevation, c. 1570–72. Engraving by Jean Marot, "Grand Marot," late 1660s. (Avery Architectural and Fine Arts Library, Columbia University, New York)

heritage. Rejecting the decorative approach of Charleval, he turned to the more architectonic designs of Jean Bullant, such as Chantilly and the Tuileries pavilion, and gave his Mannerist vocabulary the pronounced weight of Bullant's forms (Figs. 29, 30). These qualifications by no means rule out Jacques II; they do, however, undermine the ungrounded assumption that the son's work mirrored that of his father. Until his hand is identified and some designs uncovered, the contribution of Jacques II Androuet Ducerceau to Henri IV's Louvre cannot be assessed.

It is only marginally easier to sketch a stylistic profile of Métezeau. His work as an interior designer at the royal palaces is firmly documented; contracts refer to his designs for the king's apartment; the queen's chapel, in the medieval tower abutting Lescot's south range of the Cour Carrée; the upper floor of the Petite Galerie; and the Salle des Antiques, on the ground floor of the Grande Galerie.[41] In his guide to Paris published in 1684, Germain Brice attributed the eastern section of the Grande Galerie to Métezeau.[42] The contracts cited above localize Métezeau's presence in the eastern part of the palace, and the use of marble revetment on the exterior of the Petite Galerie suggests similarities to Métezeau's design of the Salle des Antiques, described below.

Fig. 31. Louis Métezeau, Hôtel d'Angoulême, court facade, c. 1584. (D. Thomson, *Renaissance Paris,* 1984)

Yet this evidence for Métezeau's authorship is circumstantial at best; the stylistic confirmation provided by other buildings is needed. As a result of an archival discovery in 1984, we now know of one, and only one, documented work by Métezeau: the court elevation of the Hôtel d'Angoulême (c. 1584) in Paris (Fig. 31).[43] This building was previously attributed to Baptiste Androuet Ducerceau, Jacques II's older brother, because the colossal order, broken pediment, and attic cornice broken by dormer windows were associated with the Ducerceau heritage. Yet at the Hôtel d'Angoulême, these motifs were not employed in the manner of Jacques the Elder. Rather, they demonstrate an interest in Bullant, as Coope noted; compare, for instance, his dormer windows at Chantilly with those at Métezeau's hôtel (see Fig. 29).[44] There are also echoes of Bullant in the eastern section of the Grande Galerie; the superimposed order and horizontal composition, the niches and tablets refer to Bullant's Tuileries pavilion (see Fig. 30). Though both the hôtel and the gallery demonstrate an interest in Bullant, it remains difficult to define a style for Métezeau based on the Hôtel d'Angoulême, his one documented work, which fully justifies the Louvre attribution.

Ultimately, two factors recommend the established attributions to Ducer-

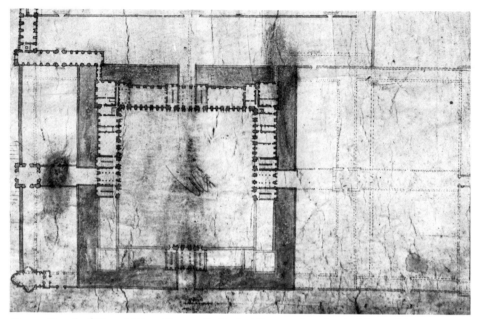

Fig. 32. Detail of Fig. 16 (Destailleur 148). Dashed lines project the doubling of the Petite Galerie, a symmetric gallery and courtyards north of the Louvre, and a gallery facing the Grande Galerie.

ceau and Métezeau: the authority of the seventeenth-century sources and the simple fact that there are no more likely candidates than the two royal architects. We can cautiously accept these attributions, but a far more perplexing issue of authorship remains unexplored. The most significant feature of the 1603 design was the integration of the two palaces around one vast courtyard. We know far too little about the architects to understand their approach to planning on a larger scale, and for this reason the authorship of the Henri IV's Louvre fundamentally remains an open question. We now turn to the conception of the Louvre on an urban scale.

THE *Grand Dessein*

Henri IV intended to make other additions to the royal palace which he did not live to realize. Two projects are shown in bold lines on the 1603 plan (see Fig. 16). The Tuileries is completed by the addition of northern wings symmetric to Ducerceau's buildings, and the Cour Carrée is enlarged by four axial pavilions and two wings at the northwest corner (Fig. 32).[45] Other elements drawn in broken lines suggest more tentative thoughts for a later phase of construction.

The river wing east of the Petite Galerie was carried over from the 1595 drawing and probably was originally planned by Charles IX.[46] The 1603 plan explores widening of the Petite Galerie and the symmetric wing on the north side of the Louvre with courtyards extending to the rue St. Honoré.[47] The draftsman has not resolved the design of these courtyards, and two solutions overlap. One calls for two small rectangular courtyards mirroring those on the south side of the Cour Carrée; in the other, the dimensions of the courtyards are determined by the wall on the north side of the gardens, opposite the Grande Galerie. The most intriguing element is the dotted line parallel to this wall, which outlines a wing equal in width to the Grande Galerie, extending from the projected pendant of the Petite Galerie to the garden.

As the Grande Galerie neared completion in 1608, reports circulated that the king was planning a new gallery, joining the north ends of the two palaces

PUBLICATION·FAITE·A·PARIS LE·25·MARS 1612· DES·MARIAGES·ARRESTEZ ENTRE·
LOUIS·XIII· ROY·DE·FRANCE, ET·ANNE D'AUTRICHE INFANTE DESPAGNE, ET ENTRE
PHILIPPE ROY DESPAGNE, ET ELIZABETH DE BOURBON SOEUR DU ROY·

Fig. 33. Anonymous, Announcement on 25 March 1612 of the engagements of Louis XIII to the Spanish Infanta and of Philip IV to the king's sister, 1612. (B.N. Est. Qb1) The engraving projects the completion of Henri IV's *grand dessein*.

and thus enclosing the courtyard. The project is depicted in a print from 1612, with the completed Tuileries seen in the background (Fig. 33). It was described in some detail by Jean de Saulx-Tavannes in memoirs written between 1601 and 1619:

> If King Henri IV had lived, loving building as he did, he would have made a remarkable one: completing the [west] wing of the Louvre of which the grand staircase [of Henri II] only marks the midpoint; at the end of it, building a gallery symmetric to the one adjoining his apartment [i.e., the Petite Galerie] directed toward St. Honoré; and from there, building a similar gallery to the one facing the river which would terminate between the pavilion of the Tuileries which is not finished and the stables; . . . and destroying all the housing between the two galleries, the Louvre and the Tuileries, so there would be a grand, admirable courtyard.[48]

When an English traveler, Peter Heylyn, arrived in Paris in 1625, he heard similar rumors.

> [The Grande Galerie] . . . was said to have been erected purposely to joyn the Louvre unto the House and Garden of the Tuilleries, an unlikely matter that such a stupendious building should be designed only for a cleanly conveyance into a Summer House; others are of an opinion that [Henri IV] . . . had a resolution to have made the house quadrangular, every side being correspondent to this [the Grande Galerie] which should have been the common gallery to the rest. Which design had it taken effect, this Palace would at once have been the wonder of the world, and the envy of it. For my part, I dare be of this last minde as well because the second side is in part begun as also considering how infinitely this king was inclined to building. . . . Besides the generall love he had to building, he had also an ambition to go beyond example, which also induceth me further to believe his intent of making that large and admirable quadrangle above spoken of to have been serious and reall.[49]

This enormous courtyard—bordered by the enlarged Cour Carrée and the Tuileries, the Grande Galerie and a parallel gallery to the north—was the boldest feature of Henri IV's *grand dessein* for the Louvre. While Destailleur 148 and the contemporary reports do not prove that construction was about to begin in 1610, these sources establish that Henri IV's architects had evolved a plan for a northern gallery enclosing a vast courtyard between the two palaces.

A new spatial concern permeated the *grand dessein* and marked the emergence of planning on an urban scale in Henri IV's Paris. The area between the two palaces, no longer subdivided by the Renaissance courtyards envisioned in the sixteenth century, was larger than any open space ever before seen or even planned in Paris. The Grande Galerie was 232 *toises* (459m) long and the projected courtyard approximately 142 *toises* (280m) wide, yielding an area more than six times greater than the Place Royale (72 *toises* square) which, when it was built, was the largest planned space in the city. The way in which the buildings were seen from a distance became an important aspect of their design. The vistas unfurled in the courtyard were measured by the central pavilions, with the placement and profile of the gallery pavilion determined by the views from the court and the river. While the king enjoyed spectacular vistas of the Seine from his gallery, the building also offered itself to the city as a landmark to be admired in the urban landscape. Its south facade was composed for the sweeping panorama, its great span parsed by three pavilions. Although the *grand dessein* was not realized during Henri IV's reign, its urban scale and its responsiveness to the roaming panoramic view were further developed in his public building projects.

THE PROGRAM AND DECORATION OF THE PALACE: THE ARTISTS' APARTMENTS

Henri IV's Louvre was not only the residence of the king; it was also planned as a forum for diplomatic and cultural activity in the capital. According to Saulx-Tavannes, the king intended to lodge foreign ambassadors in the planned northern gallery.[50] The most important part of the program, one that was linked to the broader social and economic policies of Henri IV's reign, was the provision of apartments and workshops for artists in the eastern section of the Grande Galerie. Artists had previously been lodged in the royal residence at the Burgundian and Valois courts, but only to serve the ruler's household. Henri IV, on the other hand, did not restrict the artists to his private use. Rather than simply compensating artists involved in court decoration, he aimed to raise the level of artisanal activity throughout France "to create a nursery of workers," the royal edict stated, "from which, after an apprenticeship to such fine masters, many will emerge who will spread throughout the realm and will know how to serve the public well."[51]

The crown wanted to remedy a shortage of skilled artisans, which it blamed on guild masters who blocked apprentices from obtaining their *maîtrise* and from establishing independent practices. Henri IV exempted the Grande Galerie residents from guild regulations; each could hire two apprentices plus his children, and they would automatically receive the *maîtrise* after five years of service. This measure undermined the authority of the guild, which enlisted the Parlement's support in fighting the king. The Parlement delayed registering

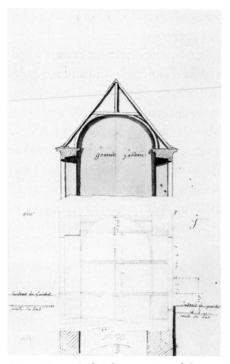

Fig. 34. François d'Orbay, section of the Grande Galerie, c. 1670s. (B.N. Est. Va 217a) Beneath the royal gallery on the first floor, drawn in ink, is an artist's apartment on three levels: cellar, ground floor, and mezzanine.

the edict for a year and a half — the king originally submitted it on 30 June 1607 — but eventually yielded to the crown, approving Henri IV's patent letters on 22 December 1608.[52] The formation of a sizable community of artists under royal protection and exempt from guild regulations was a significant step toward the creation in 1648 of the Royal Academy of Painting, founded by artists to break the guild's monopolistic control. But whereas the Academy differentiated itself from the guild by insisting on the artist's intellectual development, Henri IV's policy had a different goal: it was dedicated to the promotion of artisanship.

There were twenty-six apartments in the Grande Galerie, each with a ground-floor shop facing the city. A staircase in each led below to a cellar and above to living rooms at the mezzanine level (Fig. 34). Carpentry and other finishing work were initiated in mid-1608, and the rooms were ready for their residents at the end of the year, although some artists moved into the palace at an earlier date.[53] Among the men given apartments were the most illustrious artists of Henri IV's reign: royal painter Jacob Bunel, Florentine sculptor Pietro Francavilla, royal engineer and mathematician Jacques Alleaume, and royal architect Louis Métezeau, all of whom we will encounter again in Henri IV's other building projects. But there was an even larger contingent of artisans expert in luxury crafts, whose names are little known today: clockmakers Abraham de Lagarde and Antoine Ferrier, jewelers Pierre Courtois and Nicolas Roussel, swordmaker Pierre Vernier and globemaker Marin Bourgeois, cabinetmaker Laurens Setarbe, gilder Jean Petit, and Estienne Raulin, who made mathematical instruments. Guillaume Dupré, sculptor and controller of the Mint, was given an apartment, and the Mint was also installed in the Grande Galerie, in three bays west of the Pavillon de la Lanterne.[54] Three tapestry weavers were allotted apartments and the five bays east of the Pavillon de la Lanterne to set up a workshop.⁵⁵ One of the *tapissiers,* Pierre Dupont, recounted in his memoirs that Henri IV promised him "in the presence of many gentlemen to establish the manufacture of [Turkish rugs] all over France, as he had done with Flemish tapestry, gold from Milan, cloths of gold and silk, and other enterprises, in order, as he said, to prevent the export of gold and money from the country . . . and to put to work an infinite number of idlers and vagabonds." ⁵⁶ Dupont echoed words reiterated by Henri IV in countless edicts, and it was this same goal that led Henri IV to create the Place Royale, where the cloths of silk and gold mentioned by Dupont were produced. No plans were advanced during Henri IV's reign for the west end of the gallery's ground floor. Under Louis XIII, the Imprimerie Royale, the royal press, was installed in the bays adjoining the Mint, and the remaining stretch was used by the Petite Ecurie, the royal stables.⁵⁷

THE SALLE DES ANTIQUES

Henri IV did not fit the cultural profile of a Renaissance prince. He had no interest in humanist erudition, in antiquity, in collecting artworks or curiosities.⁵⁸ Nonetheless, one room in the palace — the Salle des Antiques — was given over to a display of classical splendor and princely magnificence. As the name implies, antique sculptures were exhibited in this room on the ground floor of the Grande Galerie, between the artists' apartments and the Petite Galerie. While we do not know what works were on view, they presumably included the preeminent pieces from the collection formed by François I. According to Félibien, Henri IV had intended to acquire additional statues from Italy.⁵⁹ Between 1604 and 1608, the room was decorated with multicolored marbles, columns, and reliefs designed by Métezeau.⁶⁰ Its precious surfaces suggested "a reliquary or highly decorated German cabinet" to Sauval, but Métezeau certainly drew his inspiration from antiquity, from the richly colored, sumptuous spaces of imperial palaces.⁶¹ While the lower zone of the room was devoted to the timeless beauty of classical art, the ceiling represented the passage of time and cycle of nature. Jacob Bunel was hired in December 1609 to paint the vault with scenes of the four seasons and signs of the zodiac, and above the windows, the four winds and four elements.⁶²

Antoine Schnapper has suggested that the program of the Salle des Antiques was devised by the antiquarian Pierre-Antoine Rascas de Bagarris (1562–1620), who served as Keeper of the King's Medals and Antiquities. A lawyer and medal collector from Aix-en-Provence, Bagarris was in Paris from 1599 to 1613 and in contact with the king by 1602, when he submitted a proposal for forming a royal cabinet of medals and antiquities.[63] This petition failed, but perhaps Bagarris persuaded the crown to devote this room to antique statuary. It also remains possible that Louis Métezeau conceived the program of the Salle des Antiques, since his decorative designs indicate that he possessed some knowledge of classical culture.

The Salle des Antiques led to a corridor behind the artists' workshops, a sequence that implicitly paired the splendors and virtues of antiquity with the inventions of Henri IV's reign. A vestibule and stair at the east end of the room led to the Petite Galerie. The ground floor remained undecorated as it had been since the reign of Charles IX, but on the upper floor, Henri IV's legendary salvation of France was more dramatically represented than elsewhere in the palace.

THE PETITE AND GRANDE GALERIES

While the ground floor was the domain of art and craft, the upper floor of the palace, from the king's apartment to the Tuileries, was planned as a grand ceremonial sequence. It began in the Petite Galerie with an homage to Henri IV's triumphs. The room was destroyed by fire in 1661, but it can be reconstructed from descriptions. The vault, whose decoration was begun by Toussaint Dubreuil (1561–1602) in 1601 and continued after his death by Jacob Bunel, was painted with scenes from the Old Testament and from Ovid.[64] Sauval tells us that in separate compartments of the vault, Perseus slew the Medusa and rescued Andromeda, references to Henri IV's defeat of the League and his rescue of France. Although both scenes were commonly used in royalist propaganda to celebrate the king's triumphs, to avoid any misunderstanding, Perseus and the other mythological heroes were given the face of Henri IV.[65]

After the vault was finished in late 1606, Bunel began work on the walls of the gallery. They were completed after his death in 1614 by his wife, Marguerite Bahuche. Sully initially considered a map cycle for the walls, a topic to which we shall return in Chapter Six, and vetted his idea with the cartographer André Laval. In an essay written in 1601, Laval rejected both maps and mythology; such representations were appropriate subjects for rulers without a distinguished past, "but for our king who can produce the most venerable and authentic genealogical tree of kings, his ancestors, it would be a great crime to borrow elsewhere what he has so abundantly himself." [66] Since Henri IV's claim to the throne was much disputed, Laval's genealogical program offered the political advantage of affiliating the Bourbon ruler with his predecessors. His suggestion was accepted, and in May 1607 Bunel was commissioned to paint twenty-eight

Fig. 35. Jacob Bunel, Henri IV, preparatory drawing for the Petite Galerie, 1607. (Musée du Louvre, Paris, Cabinet des Dessins, Inv. 33594; Réunion des Musées Nationaux)

full-length portraits of French kings and queens beginning with Saint Louis and culminating with Henri IV, each ruler accompanied by sixteen smaller portraits of important figures of the reign (Fig. 35).

Between 1601 when Laval proposed the portrait cycle and 1607 when the contract with Bunel was drawn up, a new concern emerged. The contract required Bunel to model his work after original portraits, to portray "everything lifelike, in the dress and clothing of the time of each reign and according to the originals which Bunel will be provided with and which he will locate by his own diligence and efforts." [67] The emphasis on historical accuracy was not intended to enhance the political symbolism; rather, it reflects the intellectual priorities of an antiquarian who evidently influenced the program of the Petite Galerie. Since Paulo Giovio (1483–1552) first created a museum of authentic portraits in his villa at Como, Renaissance princes and humanist scholars had formed similar collections. The most famous collection of portraits in early-seventeenth-century France was that of Fabri de Peiresc (1580–1637), who made it readily available to artists.[68] In 1607 he was consulted by a local painter commissioned to depict the kings of France in the Parlement of Aix. In the 1620s, he advised Jacques de Bié, who was preparing a publication on French royal portraits; Peiresc urged him to portray the clothing accurately and to separate the authentic effigies from the fictive portraits, to which the antiquarian attached no value.[69] These were precisely the terms of Bunel's commission in 1607, and it is possible that Peiresc was consulted on the program of the Petite Galerie, perhaps through his friend at court and neighbor in Aix-en-Provence, Bagarris. Whether or not Peiresc played a role in the planning stages, it is more than likely that he provided Bunel with information to fulfill the commission. According to Sauval, Bunel traveled throughout France in order to locate the most accurate images of his royal subjects, and one such trip may have taken him to Peiresc's home.[70] The two men were in contact by 1608 when Peiresc's brother Valavez visited the painter on the occasion of a trip to Paris, and a letter from Peiresc to Bunel in 1614 indicates that they were already well acquainted.[71]

The Grande Galerie, from the Petite Galerie to the Pavillon de Flore, formed one continuous passage 442 meters long.[72] It was a vast and difficult space to decorate, and by the time of Henri IV's death, only one small piece was completed. At each end of the gallery was a triumphal arch built of marble with antique statues set in side niches. In July 1609, statues of Bacchus and Titus on display in the Salle des Antiques were moved to the niches at the east end, and the four marble columns of the western arch were erected.[73] We do not know how Henri IV's artists intended to develop the imperial imagery of the Grande Galerie. Though undecorated by Henri IV, his triumphal arches provided a key to Poussin when he devised his imperial program for the gallery in 1640.

THE TUILERIES PALACE AND GARDENS

We have no information about the decoration of the Pavillon de Flore and the adjoining wing of the Tuileries; construction was not completed until 1609, and the interior work was probably not begun during the king's reign. After repairing the Delorme and Bullant wings, Henri IV furnished the interiors, but neither the building contracts nor contemporary sources describe the rooms in sufficient detail to reconstruct the program.[74] We know only that Bunel painted the main reception room in Delorme's southern gallery beginning in 1604,[75] and that Etienne Dupérac designed a tribune for an unspecified location, perhaps as a pendant to Goujon's tribune in the west range of the Cour Carrée.[76]

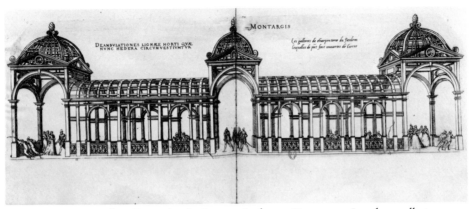

Fig. 36. Montargis, arbor. Engraving by Jacques Androuet Ducerceau, *Les plus excellents bastiments de France,* 1576–79. (B.N. Imp. rés. V390)

In the gardens as in the palace, Henri IV proceeded at first with caution. In 1594, he restored Catherine de' Medici's garden west of the palace and hired the same gardener that the queen had employed in 1572, Pierre Le Nostre, grandfather of André Le Nostre, to replant the parterres.[77] A pond was opened in one compartment, fed by the pump the king built on the Pont Neuf, and a long arbor with seven pedimented pavilions was constructed on the north side of the garden, aligned with the transverse paths, just as it is depicted in Quesnel's map (see Fig. 11).[78] The building contract described a structure that virtually reproduced the arbor at Montargis, which was engraved by Ducerceau (Fig. 36). In order to promote the cultivation of silkworms, a royal undertaking to which we shall turn in the next chapter, the king had an allée of mulberry trees planted on a terrace north of the arbor, and at the end of the allée, Dupérac built an orangery for the silkworms.[79] An exclusive site of court pageantry during Catherine de' Medici's reign, the Tuileries gardens were modified during Henri IV's reign to demonstrate the possibilities of productive agriculture in the space of the princely pleasure.

Between the palace and the moat, Henri IV created the Jardin Neuf. The counterscarp of Charles V's ramparts was rebuilt in 1601 to serve as the retaining wall of the garden.[80] The area was divided into eight parterres with a fountain designed by Dupérac in the center, which can be seen on the 1603 Destailleur plan and on Merian's map of 1615 (see Figs. 16, 2).[81] Dupérac may have also designed the lacework parterres, but after the fierce winter of 1608 destroyed the plantings, they were redesigned by Claude Mollet.[82]

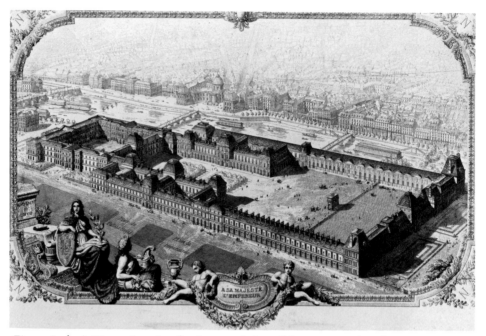

Fig. 37. Ludovic Visconti, project for the completion of the Louvre and Tuileries, 1853. Engraving by Rodolphe Pfnor. (A.N. 64 AJ 287, no. 33; Service Photographique des Archives Nationales)

Fig. 38. Grande Galerie, Pavillon des Lesdiguières (Pavillon de la Lanterne), river facade. Edouard Baldus, 1864. (B.N. Est. Eo 8, t. 3) Lefuel altered the five bays adjoining the pavilion to match Le Vau's design at the east end of the gallery.

Fig. 39. Destruction of the Grande Galerie. Edouard Baldus, August 1861. (A.N. 64 AJ 500; Service Photographique des Archives Nationales)

Epilogue

The *grand dessein* was realized by Henri IV's successors over the next 250 years. Under Louis XIV, the Tuileries and Cour Carrée were completed, and the ramparts of Charles V were destroyed. There were no expansions for more than a century until Napoleon resumed construction of the palaces. His architects, Percier and Fontaine, began the west half of the northern gallery in 1810; they formed a courtyard on the site of Henri IV's Jardin Neuf; and they placed the Arc du Carrousel in the center of that space, aligned with the axis of the Tuileries. The remaining segment of the northern gallery was completed by Napoleon III's architects, Ludovic Visconti and Hector Lefuel, between 1852 and 1857, shortly after massive demolitions between 1849 and 1851 cleared the area between the palaces. For the first time, the misalignment of the Tuileries and Louvre could actually be seen. In order to make the irregularity less glaring, Visconti and Lefuel narrowed the courtyard at the east end by extending new wings from the ends of the Cour Carrée (1852–57; Fig. 37).

No sooner was the *grand dessein* completed than Lefuel began to destroy Henri IV's Grande Galerie.[83] Métezeau's section had been faithfully restored by Félix Duban between 1848 and 1852, but in 1862 Lefuel changed the five bays

Fig. 40. Hector Lefuel, project for the reconstruction of the Pavillon de Flore and the western section of the Grande Galerie, river elevation. (A.N. 64 AJ 583, no. 6; Service Photographique des Archives Nationales)

east of the Pavillon de la Lanterne; he copied Le Vau's four-story elevation at the end of the gallery, reproducing the original principle of symmetry but according to a different scheme (Fig. 38).[84] Between 1861 and 1866, Lefuel directed the demolition and reconstruction of the Pavillon de Flore and the western section of the Grande Galerie (Fig. 39). Percier and Fontaine had copied Ducerceau's elevation when they built the northern gallery, but Lefuel rejected this solution. "The enormous pilasters," he wrote, "were an unhappy invention which had a disastrous influence on French architecture and which all men of taste ever since have criticized."[85] Instead, Lefuel copied Métezeau's elevation, omitting the mezzanine to accommodate the higher grade at the west end of the site (Fig. 40). Finally, in 1869 Lefuel replaced the lantern pavilion with a three-bay *guichet,* the Pavillons La Tremoille and Lesdiguières.

The *grand dessein* survived only briefly. After the devastating fire of 1871, the Tuileries palace was demolished in 1882–83, leaving only the end pavilions which Lefuel had recently rebuilt. Henri IV's decision to link the Louvre and Tuileries raised a problem with which every successive architect of the Louvre has grappled: the misalignment of the palaces. Even after the destruction of the Tuileries palace, the issue persisted because the axis of the palace was still expressed in the Arc du Carrousel, in the Tuileries gardens, and in the Champs-Elysées. I. M. Pei acknowledged that historic design problem in his designs for President Mitterrand's Louvre: while the pyramids are organized by the geometry of the Louvre, the modern cast of Bernini's equestrian statue is placed on the axis of the Tuileries.

Henri IV's *grand dessein* had two legacies. In the long term, it influenced builders of the Louvre for three centuries; in the short term, it introduced formal and urbanistic values that were to evolve in Henri IV's later building projects. The 1603 design for the royal palace was the crucible in which the forms of Henri IV's urbanism were forged.

CHAPTER TWO

THE PLACE ROYALE

I n July 1605, Henri IV announced the creation of the Place Royale, the first planned square in Paris. Now called the Place des Vosges, it appears today much as it did in 1612, just after its completion, when the square was depicted for the first time in a view by Claude Chastillon (Figs. 41, 42). The Place Royale, so the standard account goes, was planned from the start as a residential square for the nobility, enclosed by four uniform ranges of houses, just as we see it in Chastillon's engraving. We know from documents Mallevoüe published in 1911 that Henri IV gave the land at the square to royal officeholders who were required to build the surrounding pavilions, and we know from the work of Lambeau (1902–36) and Dumolin (1925–26) that prominent noblemen lived at the square during the seventeenth century.[1] Yet its function as an aristocratic residential quarter has not been reconciled with other evidence presented by Lambeau linking the origins of the Place Royale to a silk-manufacturing enterprise.

In an edict of 1604, the king granted subsidies for construction of silk workshops on the site of the future square; a year later, when plans for the Place Royale were unveiled, Henri IV explained that it was intended to support the production of silk, supply lodgings for artisans, and provide shops for trade. The early historians of the square paid no heed to the king's stated intentions. They assumed that the square was planned for the aristocrats to whom the land was originally given and that the workshops were destined for destruction from the moment of the square's inception. In the most recent study, Jean-Pierre Babelon indicated that the workshops were not destroyed; they functioned until at least 1612 at some unknown location. But Babelon also adopted the conventional view that the silk enterprise played no role in the design of the square, and he offered no explanation for the king's declaration.[2]

How are we to reconcile the seemingly contradictory evidence surrounding the Place Royale? If the square was planned for aristocrats as scholars have previously maintained, why did Henri IV publicly announce an altogether different commercial program? If, on the other hand, the square was planned as the king stated in 1605 to accommodate silk manufacturing, artisans, and shops, how did it become an aristocratic quarter? These questions have gone unanswered because our knowledge about the early history of the square has been

DESSEIN DES POMPES ET MAGNIFICENCES DV CAROVSEL FAICT EN LA PLACE ROYALLE A PARIS LE V. VI.VII DAPVRIL 1612

Fig. 41. Place Royale, 1612. Engraving after Claude Chastillon. (B.N. Est. rés. Hennin XIX 1677) This view of the square from the east depicts the festivities in honor of the engagements of Louis XIII and his sister.

limited to the names of the original recipients of land. Nothing has been known about the development of the square following the land donations: who actually built, owned, and lived in the houses. Nor has anything been known about the royally subsidized silk enterprise, or even whether such an enterprise was in fact built on the north side of the square. This chapter is based on newly uncovered documents in the notarial archives, construction contracts for the silkworks and business agreements concerning their operation, land sales, building contracts, and leases for the pavilions. From these documents, a new view of the Place Royale emerges.

The royal edict was not wrong. The Place Royale was conceived not as an aristocratic residential square, but as a commercial square, the centerpiece of a royal campaign to stimulate French manufacturing. When the creation of the square was announced in 1605, it was the crown's intention to preserve the workshops on the north side of the site and to build three connecting ranges of brick-and-stone pavilions on the other sides of the square. The pavilions that

Fig. 42. Place des Vosges (Royale), aerial photograph. (Arthus-Bertrand, Paris)

Chastillon portrayed and that circumscribe the square today were originally intended for commercial and residential use by artisans and merchants, with ground-floor shops opening onto the arcaded gallery. The Place Royale was planned to promote the manufacturing venture, not to supplant it; it was planned for artisans, not aristocrats. But two years later, in 1607, the form and the function of the Place Royale were changed. The workshops were razed, and in their place, a freestanding range of pavilions was built (to the right in Chastillon's view). Manufacturing and commerce were banished from the square, and without any alteration in the facade design, the pavilions were transformed into residences for the nobility.

THE ROYAL CAMPAIGN FOR FRENCH SILK

The revival of domestic manufacturing was central to Henri IV's effort to resurrect the war-battered economy of France. The emphasis on domestic production was shaped by Barthélemy Laffemas (1545–1611), a Protestant trader who had served the Bourbon ruler since both were youths. In an incessant flow of pamphlets published between 1596 and 1609, Laffemas argued that the wealth of France was being sapped by the export of gold and silver for the purchase of foreign goods. To stem the flight of capital, he proposed an increased commitment to domestic manufacturing.[3] Laffemas's mercantilist program won the king's enthusiastic support; in 1601, the king created a Commission on Commerce to promote domestic manufacturing under the direction of Laffemas, who was appointed Controller-general of Commerce. As a result of Laffemas's relentless activities, ateliers proliferated in Henri IV's Paris, where foreign craftsmen and their French apprentices produced crystal, tapestries, leather, and cloths of every kind.[4]

Among the many new manufacturing ventures, the production of silk received the highest priority. Despite the uncertainty about whether silkworms and mulberry trees would find the French climate hospitable, compelling economic reasons favored the emphasis on silk production. More than any other luxury item, Italy's fine silks lured French wealth beyond its borders; only a domestic alternative would suffice to stem the outflow of desperately needed capital. Moreover, the growth of domestic silk production could be expected to have ripple effects across the French economy. Fine silk was spun with thread of gold and silver; consequently, promoting the manufacture of finished silk indirectly stimulated trade in precious metals and the merchant banking activity on which a manufacturing economy relied. Henri IV's aggressive campaign during the first years of the seventeenth century to transform France into a silk-producing country was simply a tactical component of a broader strategy: the growth of French commerce and manufacturing and the establishment of Paris as a center for finance and merchant banking. "The introduction of silks . . . ," he declared in 1603, "is the most suitable remedy to avoid the export of currency and moreover is desirable for public embellishment [*la décoration publique*], adornment, and the employment of the population."[5] It was the intersection of the silk program with *la décoration publique* that led to the creation of the Place Royale.

The campaign for domestic silk was waged in the country and the city, with a flood of promotional literature and with large royal subsidies. The preeminent advocate of sericulture was Olivier de Serres (1539–1619), the Protestant agronomist who culled his experience from decades of agricultural experimentation in *Le Théâtre d'agriculture* (1600), a volume in such demand that by 1610 it had gone through four editions, and which throughout the century remained the standard guide to agricultural matters. The manual was dedicated to Henri IV, who had excerpts read aloud to him at mealtime. Probably at the king's request, the chapters on sericulture were published in 1599 as a separate pamphlet, one of many such pamphlets proselytizing sericulture, stressing its profitability and its practicality for owners of estates of all sizes.[6] In his effort to build what was in France at best a fledgling industry, de Serres suggested ways to landscape country estates with mulberry trees and imaginatively advised city dwellers how to build incubation rooms for silkworms which could be used off-season as living space. De Serres targeted one group in particular: dedicating the pamphlet to the municipal leaders of Paris, he spoke for the king in urging them to promote silk production in the capital.

A program to spread sericulture across the country was launched by the crown in 1603. The Commission on Commerce employed two merchants with a staff of experienced workers to disseminate 600,000 mulberry trees, hundreds of pounds of silkworms and mulberry seeds, and 16,000 printed manuals on silkmaking in the regions of Paris, Orléans, Tours, and Lyon.[7] The merchants calculated that 800 pounds (*livres*) of silk were produced during the first year of the experiment, although they encountered various difficulties, notably the high mortality of silkworms and the disinterest of small farmers.[8] Despite these setbacks, the crown pursued its campaign, introducing sericulture in Poitou in 1604 and in Normandy in 1608, where the effort was directed by royal gardener Claude Mollet, who wrote two manuals on the cultivation of mulberry trees and silkworms and produced his own raw silk in Paris.[9] The king "hath caused most of the gentlemen and possessioners of his realm to plant mulberry trees in their grounds for the nourishing of silk-worms," the English ambassador Sir George Carew wrote in 1609, "and told me he hoped to make his realm the staple for all the silk that should be worn in all these northern parts of Europe."[10]

The king set an example for his subjects by cultivating mulberry trees and silkworms in Paris and at the royal châteaux of Fontainebleau and Madrid.[11] In 1601, 15,000 to 20,000 mulberry trees selected by de Serres were planted in the garden of the Tuileries (see Fig. 11). Two years later, royal architect Etienne Dupérac designed a nursery for the incubation of silkworms on the north side of the garden. That project particularly interested the king, who instructed Sully in a letter on 29 March 1603 to bring construction to a speedy conclusion:

> My friend, I ask of you to expedite the frame and roof of my orangery in the Tuileries so that I can make use of it this year to raise the silk-worm eggs that I brought from Valencia in Spain which must be hatched as soon as the mulberry tress have thrown off what can feed them [the worms]. You know how much I favor this, which is why I ask you once again to attend to it and expedite [the construction]. . . .[12]

A staff of Italian experts was brought to Paris to manage the nursery, and Laffemas boasted that the raw silk produced in the Tuileries was "lighter, finer and more lustrous" than foreign silks; ". . . even the workers . . . truthfully attest that 15 ounces [*onces*] of the [silkworm] eggs from the Tuileries produce as much cloth as 18 ounces [*onces*] from Italy." [13] Hardly an impartial appraisal, but whatever its quality, the silk cultivated in the Tuileries demonstrated Henri IV's commitment to French sericulture.

Weaning France from foreign markets would require more than the production of raw silk; the country also had to learn the craft of spinning finished cloth. Several small silk workshops were opened in the capital in 1601 and 1602. [14] But Henri IV wanted to launch a major manufacturing venture on a scale sufficiently grand to attract Italian artisans to Paris, institutionalize the privileged craft in France, and establish the city as a center of manufacturing. In May 1603, Pierre Sainctot, a prominent Parisian cloth merchant, was summoned to Fontainebleau to discuss such a venture with the king's deputies. Three months later, in August 1603, the crown announced the establishment of a royally sponsored business to manufacture silk, gold, and silver cloth "in the Milanese manner," under the direction of six private investors. [15] From the start, this project was cast in a symbolic role by the crown, the model for other workshops and the first step toward solving France's economic problems.

The success of the business seemed assured by its six directors, who were among the most accomplished merchants and financiers in Paris. The experience of Pierre Sainctot, Jean-André Lumague, Nicolas Camus, Claude Parfaict, and Guillaume Parfaict, all veterans in the silk trade, was joined with the fortune of Jean Moisset. Moisset (c. 1570–1620) was an exemplar of the bourgeois ascent to wealth and nobility through tax farming, royal banking, and venal office. From a modest beginning as an apprentice tailor at the court of Henri III, he rose to a high position in Henri IV's fiscal administration, holding lucrative tax farms and executing unpopular royal measures which earned him public contempt but personal riches. When the crown named Moisset receiver and payer of government bonds (*receveur et payeur des rentes*), the municipality fiercely objected to the appointment, denouncing his integrity (which it seems was widely suspect). But the underlying source of friction was the crown's attempt to gain greater fiscal control over the city by consolidating six separate commissions into one. In this episode as throughout his career, Moisset was closely allied with the interests of the crown. Moisset put up one quarter of the capital for the silk business (45,000 *livres*), probably at the crown's request, while the five other managing partners each contributed 27,000 *livres* for a total investment of 180,000 *livres*. [16]

Moisset was the only entrepreneur drawn from the nobility of the robe and closely associated with the monarch; his partners were prominent members of the Parisian merchant community and, in several cases, of the ruling municipal elite, the *noblesse de cloche*. Pierre Sainctot (15?–1640) began his career as a silk dyer and trader. An expert in making gold thread, he ran a business in precious silk cloths before becoming involved in the royally backed operation. A leader of the merchant community, Sainctot was named to one of the two seats on the Commission on Commerce reserved for merchants, and he negotiated terms for the royally backed silkworks with the crown. Sainctot visited the court on a few other occasions, one of which was to present alternative designs for the Hôpital St. Louis, but it was far less familiar terrain to him than the Hôtel de Ville. Elected *quartinier* in 1601, *échevin* in 1604, and *conseiller* in 1606, Sainctot ascended the ranks of municipal government and later represented the Third Estate at the meeting of the Estates General in 1614.[17] Claude Parfaict (1586–1623) followed a path similar to Sainctot's, though less demarcated by official honors. Son of a draper on the rue St. Antoine, he continued the family business on the same busy street and was elected *quartinier* in 1610.[18]

Nicolas Camus (1567–1648), a native Parisian like Parfaict and Sainctot, became active in the domestic production of silk after the import ban was imposed in 1599. Camus moved from commerce into banking and in that domain amassed an unmatched fortune, becoming one of the dominant bankers during Louis XIII's reign.[19] Jean-André Lumague (1564–1637) enjoyed a similar ascent. He came to Paris in 1598 from Lyon, where he had established a successful trading company in silk and currency in the early 1580s with Paul Mascranny. The firm of Mascranny and Lumague, based in Paris and Lyon with correspondents across Europe, flourished during the reigns of Henri IV and Louis XIII, and was well connected to the Italian community in Paris and to international channels of trade.[20] Lumague's participation in the Parisian silkworks illustrates the early-seventeenth-century expansion of the Lyonnais merchant community — with its strong links to Italy — into Paris where new financial opportunities were afforded by the court. Drawing upon Lyonnais capital and even some Lyonnais craftsmen, the royal silk business was an attempt by the crown to invigorate the economy of Paris with Lyon's historic commercial vitality.[21]

The sixth investor, Odard Colbert (1560–1640), was a relative of Nicolas Camus's and a close associate of Lumague in the Lyonnais silk trade.[22] In 1604, Colbert withdrew from the project and was replaced by Guillaume Parfaict (1558–1625). Unlike his brother Claude, Guillaume Parfaict left the world of trade and municipal government (where he had served as *échevin*) to enter the royal fiscal administration, holding the office of Controller-general of the king's household.[23]

The five merchants were all experienced in the production and sale of silk, a business that involved them in the trade of luxury goods and precious metals, in currency exchange, and in banking, activities that the Place Royale was to accommodate. In the decades after Henri IV's death, these men acquired greater wealth and power; they lent money to the crown, bought royal offices which were passed on to their sons, and abandoned the business of manufacturing. The royal silkworks, tied to the world of international finance and to the crown, served them in their passage from trade to royal banking and office-holding. In this respect, the fate of the silkworks and of the Place Royale underscores a problem that vexed *ancien régime* France: the preference of the monied classes to invest in land and office over manufacturing.

Yet, the subsequent departure from manufacturing activity of the silk-works investors in no way reflected a lack of commitment by Henri IV. The king demonstrated that commitment to the business in several ways. The investors were granted titles of nobility, on the condition that they maintain the business for a twelve-year period ending in 1615.[24] Special privileges were extended to the silk artisans; because French workers lacked the expertise to produce the precious cloths, foreign artisans were lured to France with offers of naturalized status as well as exemptions from taxes and guild regulations. Finally, the crown allocated 180,000 *livres* for the business: 30,000 *livres* as a gift, and 150,000 *livres* as a loan to be repaid within twelve years. While these were standard privileges, they were offered here in more generous measure than usual.[25] Moreover, one year later, the king presented the silk entrepreneurs with an unprecedented gift — the gift of land in Paris.

THE SILKWORKS AND THE SITE

Sainctot was invited to court again in November 1603, and the fruits of this meeting were publicized in a decree of January 1604. Henri IV gave the silk entrepreneurs a large tract of land on which they were to build workshops and housing for their craftsmen.[26] The gift amounted to 6,000 square *toises* (23,522 square meters) on the Right Bank of Paris, inside the city wall near the Bastille, which included the land on which the north range of the Place Royale was built four years later (Fig. 43). In an edict on 4 March 1604 instructing Sully to measure the site, the king reiterated the importance of the silkworks.

> Having a particular desire to establish arts and manufacturing in our
> good city of Paris especially those of silk, gold and silver thread in the

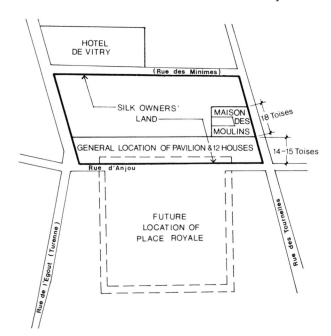

Fig. 43. Reconstruction of the silkworks in 1604. (Drawing by Julia Rogoff based on A.N. Q1*/1099/10C)

Milanese manner, we have brought workers from foreign countries to set up the mills, looms, and other things necessary for the workshops [*manufactures*] as well as to begin working here and teaching those of our subjects who want to learn [the craft]. . . . But in that we did not find in our city any building spacious, clean, or commodious enough to mount the large number of looms and mills which will be needed or to lodge and shelter the workers who will work there, we have considered it appropriate to have one built expressly for this purpose on the site previously called the parc des Tournelles which belongs to us, and after having measured the site, we have promised and accorded it as a gift to the Sirs de Moisset and Sainctot, Lumague, Camus and Parfaict, owners of the said establishment, up to the quantity of 100 *toises* long by 60 wide to have built and constructed the proper and necessary houses for the said workshops and workmen following the design which we have shown them . . .[27]

Other manufacturing ventures had been provided with facilities in which to work. The Italian crêpe atelier was set up in the château de Mantes. Another silkmaker was installed in a building on the rue de la Tissanderie, and for the particularly favored Flemish tapestry works, later called the Gobelins, the crown rented and remodeled two houses in the faubourg St. Marcel. But no other enterprise was given land in the heart of Paris, a gift which signaled unmistakably the importance of the silkworks in the royal economic program.

Fig. 44. Olivier Truschet and Germain Hoyau, map of Paris (Basel plan), detail of the Hôtel des Tournelles, before 1559. (Bibliothek der Universität Basel AA 124)

The design mentioned in the edict cited above was not a specific scheme for the workshops, but most likely a plan indicating the streets and numbered lots of an abandoned Valois project to develop the parc des Tournelles. The park was the former site of the Hôtel des Tournelles, the medieval royal residence where Henri II was killed in a jousting accident in 1559 (Fig. 44). Five years after his death, the crown decided to destroy the hôtel and sell the property in order to finance Catherine de' Medici's construction of the Tuileries. The projected development entailed a grid of streets bordered by uniform housing lots on which construction by the owners was required to comply with a royal facade design. The scheme was never completed, presumably for lack of buyers; only a few parcels were sold at the western edge of the site, near the rue de l'Egout (today the rue de Turenne), and if a facade design was ever established, any record of it has been lost.[28] With the failure of the Valois project, the site was used for a horse market and public dump until Henri IV reclaimed the land for urban development.

Abiding by the Valois street plan, the crown structured the donations to the silk entrepreneurs as well as other gifts of neighboring parcels by the projected grid.[29] Royal carpenter Jean Fontaine measured the site in March 1604, and after having "seen the old plan of streets and lots designated for construction, in order to maintain the streets in their full and straight lines" he demarcated one large tract of land, 5,300 squares *toises* in area, on which the silkworks were built. The balance of 700 *toises* promised to Sainctot and his partners was provided in a separate parcel to the east (lots 38, 39, and 50 of the Valois plan), but evidently they did not press their claim to this parcel, and it is never again mentioned in the documents.[30]

Construction of the silkworks began soon after the king confirmed the donation in April 1604 and was largely completed by the end of the year. The owners anticipated that "for the large number and diversity of workers that they will need to employ in the enterprise, it will be necessary to build up to twenty houses."[31] They began, however, on a more modest scale by building twelve houses, each 3 by 14–15 *toises*, and a pavilion, 4 by 5 *toises*, according to a contract for joinery work passed in September 1604.[32] These buildings spread across the southern edge of the property, from the rue de l'Egout (de Turenne) to the rue des Tournelles; we do not know how they were distributed, but given their dimensions, they could not have formed a solid streetfront across this distance.[33] The silk artisans presumably lived and did finishing work in these buildings, while a larger workshop called the *maison des moulins* was constructed to house the spinning mills. It consisted of a main block on the rue des Tournelles, 18 *toises* long, and two side wings framing a courtyard (see Fig. 43).[34] While the houses and pavilion were simple wooden structures, the *maison des moulins* was a masonry building at least modestly embellished with pediments, keystones, entablatures, and consoles on the dormer windows. Laffemas described it as a "beautiful building . . . more superb" than the orangery in the Tuileries; the king was so proud of the *maison des moulins* that the festivities for the baptism of the dauphin in 1606 were originally planned there, "in the court and place of the building of the Manufactures near the Place Royale of the Tournelles."[35]

The silkworks were in operation by mid-1605. Installed in the houses were master craftsmen, mostly Milanese, and their French apprentices who, it was hoped, would sow a new domestic art with their valuable skills.[36] A Milanese gold worker, Andrea Turato, was hired to administer the business, then dismissed for mismanagement and replaced in 1606 by another Italian, Sigismond Pestalossi, who was lodged in the *maison des moulins*.[37] The owners also opened a shop to sell their cloths, perhaps using the pavilion for this purpose. They spent close to 177,000 *livres* on construction and 30,000 *livres* on inventory in the shop; the total of 207,000 *livres* was roughly equivalent to the cost of building seven brick and stone pavilions with their rear secondary structures at the Place Royale. After deducting the king's subsidy of 30,000 *livres,* the silk partners remained liable for 177,000 *livres*.[38] With Italian craftsmen and brand new buildings, a well-endowed business was launched in 1604, bearing the king's hopes for economic revival.

THE FIRST DESIGN OF THE PLACE ROYALE: 1605

In March 1605, the king advanced another project for the parc des Tournelles. He wrote Sully on 29 March 1605:

> My friend, this is to remind you of what we recently discussed together, the square that I want made in front of the building under construction . . . for the workshops [*manufactures*], so if you have not been there, go have it [the site] marked. By leasing the remainder of the building lots for taxes, there is no doubt they will be taken at once, and please keep me informed.[39]

The king had decided to build a square in front of the silkworks. Two months later, in May 1605, he pressed Sully about the project: "Arnauld [the royal treasurer for Paris] will tell you how often I inquire whether construction of the houses at the site of the horse market has yet begun . . ."[40] The official announcement of the creation of the Place Royale came in July 1605:

> Having resolved for the convenience and ornament of our good city of Paris to make a large square built on four sides which would help establish the silkworks and lodge the workers that we want to attract to our realm in as large a number as possible; and at the same time, the residents of our city, who are very crowded in their houses because of the multitude of people who come here in large numbers from all directions, could stroll [*proumenoir* in the square]; and [it would be used] as well on days of celebration, when there are large assemblies, and on various other occasions when such squares are necessary; We have resolved in our council . . . to commit to this end the site presently called the horse market, previously the parc des Tournelles, and which we wish henceforth to be called the Place Royale . . .[41]

The edict specified three functions for the square. First, the Place Royale was intended to support the silk manufacturing venture and provide housing for the artisans. France suffered from a shortage of craftsmen skilled in the production of precious cloths. The royal silk business, Sainctot told the Commission on Commerce, was hampered by "the lack of spinners and other skilled people who can be found in large enough number to cut and spin the supplies of gold and silver that are already prepared . . ."[42] With its success dependent on the recruitment of foreign artisans, the royal silkworks had to be sufficiently enticing to draw men to Paris from their native lands. The Place Royale was intended to be such an inducement by offering the craftsmen a privileged residential amenity in Paris and a prestigious association with the crown. The English ambassador George Carew noted the king's goal: "He hath erected [in Paris] many of the most rich and substantial manufactures and by great wages drawn thither men skilful and expert in the same, accommodating and fitting them also with mansions and habitations as one who means to tie them fast." [43] It was, in part, to lure Italian craftsmen to the French capital and "to tie them fast" that the Place Royale was planned in 1605.

The square was also intended to provide open ground for a confined population to enjoy a leisurely stroll or promenade. In this objective, we can discern two aspects of an emerging urban consciousness. First, the promenade was conceived as a distinctively urban recreation, a response to the density of the city. It was not that Paris lacked empty land where one could roam about, but strolling required an architecturally defined space. The experience of the promenade existed in relation to the conditions of city life — its concentrated population and its architecture. Second, the Place Royale was planned for the city at large. The function of the square was not defined in terms of a neighborhood or a parish, the traditional units of community organization; it was to serve as a recreational site for all of Paris. This was equally true of its commercial function. The Place Royale was not intended as the marketplace for the parish of St. Paul but as the city-wide magnet for trade in precious goods. The program of the square was defined at the enlarged scale of the whole city; this fact was an important signal that the crown was beginning to think of Paris as a unified entity.

Finally, the Place Royale was conceived as a stage for court ceremonies and public celebrations. The crown had no such public arena in Paris; while municipal ceremonies took place in front of the Hôtel de Ville at the Place de Grève (see Fig. 5), royal festivities were restricted to the exclusive precincts of the court, either the unfinished courtyards of the Louvre or the tight confines of the Arsenal. With the Place Royale, the monarchy acquired a civic forum for its rituals. The appropriation of public space for the periodic staging of royal ceremonies was hardly an unusual practice, but what is distinctive here was the crown's interest in sharing the space with the ignoble pursuits of manufacturing and trade. In effect, the crown was lending its prestige to commerce; that identification of the monarchy with artisanal activity distinguished Henri IV's court and his urbanism from that of the Valois kings who preceded him and the Bourbon kings who were to follow.

The crown could not have dramatized the importance of this agenda more

Fig. 45. Fra Giocondo, Pont Notre-Dame, 1506. Engraving attributed to Jacques Androuet Ducerceau. (B.N. Est. Va 255k)

forcefully than by creating a square. The development schemes (*lotissements*) of the sixteenth century were all structured by a simple grid of streets with no attempt made to carve a public space. Even the regular lot division was used only to systematize the sale of land and did not impinge on subsequent construction. Buyers amassed holdings of varying sizes, making it possible for nobles to acquire large, rectangular plots on which they built hôtels on a regular plan; as a result, the density of construction in the new sixteenth-century neighborhoods just west of the Place Royale was considerably lower than the medieval fabric.[44] But no public space was rescued from this process, and the sixteenth-century projects served primarily to fill the royal coffers. The scheme for the Hôtel des Tournelles would have been the first attempt to regulate the architectural character of a new neighborhood by imposing a uniform facade on the houses, but it was never realized. The only example in Paris of a public space regulated by a building design was the Pont Notre-Dame which, from the time of its reconstruction in 1506, was bordered by uniform houses (Fig. 45).[45] At the Place Royale, not only was a uniform design realized on a larger scale than ever before in the city, but the crown molded the urban fabric to form a unique space in Paris, the city's first planned square.

The Place Royale was situated directly south of the silkworks, in the parc des Tournelles. The royal edict of July 1605 clearly describes the original layout of buildings:

> [We] have had a large square marked off vis-à-vis the building which was recently constructed by the owners of the workshops [*manufactures*], measuring 72 *toises* square . . . [and] have leased the lots . . . around the said square . . . to those who offered to build according to our design; and to this end we have relinquished the lots . . . with the requirement . . . to build on the front of each lot one pavilion with a

facade of dressed stone and brick, opened by arcades and galleries below
with shops to accommodate merchandise, all according to the plan and
elevations which have been drawn, such that the three sides which are to
be built to go round the square in front of the manufacturing establishment [*logis des manufactures*] are all built of the same symmetry for the
decoration of our city . . .[46]

The edict explicitly limited the pavilions to three sides of the square while the
logis des manufactures remained standing on the north side. Nowhere is it implied
that the silkworks were to be destroyed.

To a resident of Henri IV's Paris, the most striking feature of the Place
Royale was, without doubt, its scale and vast, open space, 72 *toises* square (142.6
meters square). Expanded street crossings had been the only open spaces in the
tightly knit fabric of the medieval city, and even the more capacious areas
developed in the sixteenth century did not deviate from a gridded plan. The one
large public space in Paris, the Place de Grève, was surrounded by shops of no
architectural distinction, and the municipal authorities faced a constant struggle
to protect even that space from the encroachments of vendors. Excluding
Henri IV's Louvre, the Place Royale was unique — in its size, its sensitivity to
long-distance views, and its design on what for Paris was a new urban scale. The
spatial qualities first envisioned at the royal palace were now to be available to
the public at the Place Royale.

The crown gave away the land on the three unbuilt sides of the square.
Nine pavilions were planned for each range, with the building charge transferred to the land recipients. The deeds stipulated that the owners were required
to construct "on the front of each lot, a pavilion covered in slate having arcades
and a gallery below with shops opening on the gallery" and a facade of brick and
stone as dictated by the royal design (Fig. 46). To prevent any alteration of the
elevation, the subdivision of pavilions was prohibited. Behind the facade, however, the owners were permitted to build "whatever other buildings and as
many or as few as they desire," and even the depth of the pavilion was left to the
discretion of the owner.[47] The ground-floor arcade was built entirely of stone,
which dignified the commercial function of the square. Above the arcade, a
brick wall rose two stories with window surrounds, quoins, and string courses
picked out in stone, delineating each bay in a repetitive pattern. The brick-and-
stone wall, with its continuous crowning cornice, wrapped around the three
ranges, forming one unified facade with only double files of quoins hinting at
the party walls behind. But in the skyline, steep hipped roofs sharply demarcated each four-bay pavilion (Fig. 47). The formal tension between the planar,
gridded wall and the individual roofs mirrored the social balance between the

Fig. 46. Place des Vosges (Royale), pavilion facade. (Author)

public use of the square and the domestic privacy of the houses.

The pavilions were not embellished by classical motifs. The ornamental effects depended entirely on the richly colored building materials: red brick, cream stone, and black slate. Beginning in the late seventeenth century, the use of brick was devalued in favor of stone as the required material for important buildings. This shift in preference has led many historians to ignore the high regard for brick during the sixteenth century and most of the seventeenth, when it was commonly used in royal and noble buildings: in royal châteaux such as Fontainebleau at the Cour du Cheval Blanc (after 1528), in châteaux of the nobility such as Vallery (c. 1550–59) and Rosny (c. 1595–1610), and in Parisian hôtels such as the Hôtel de Nevers (begun 1582) and the abbatial palace of St.-Germain-des-Prés (1586; Figs. 48, 49).[48] Recent scholarship has also proven that several brick-and-stone châteaux in the Ile-de-France, once dated to the 1620s and 1630s, were actually built during the last quarter of the sixteenth century. These châteaux—Ormesson (c. 1578), Wideville (1580–84), and Grosbois (1597)—were the immediate references for Henri IV's use of brick and stone, both at the Cour des Offices (1606–9) at Fontainebleau and in Paris (Figs. 50, 51).[49] The brick at the Place Royale was not a sign of modest and practical economy, but of lavish and ennobling treatment for shops and artisanal houses.

Fig. 47. Place des Vosges (Royale), view of the north and east ranges, 1905. (B.N. Est. Va 251)

Fig. 48. Château de Fontainebleau, Cour du Cheval Blanc, view of the François I wing, 1911. (B.N. Est. Va 77)

Fig. 49 Hôtel de Nevers, 1580s. Engraving after Claude Chastillon. (B.N. Est. rés. Ve 9)

While the royal edict stated that the Place Royale was intended to provide lodgings for silk artisans, is it possible that the pavilions that have been historically associated with the nobility were actually intended for craftsmen and merchants? The formal affiliations of the design indeed indicate that the pavilions and their facade design derive from traditions of bourgeois housing, that is, the buildings of merchants, craftsmen, and tradesmen. First, the plan of the Place Royale pavilion does not derive from the aristocratic hôtel but from the bourgeois house. By the end of the sixteenth century, it was standard for the hôtel to withdraw from the street, setting the main residential block between court and garden, as at the Hôtel Carnavalet (begun 1545; Fig. 52); even if pavilions occupied the full breadth of the street facade, as in the Hôtel de Donon (c. 1576), they were only used for services (Fig. 53).[50] At the Place Royale, however, the main residential wing bordered the public domain (Figs. 54, 55). The pavilion played this role whether a narrow side wing or a detached, parallel

Fig. 50. Château de Grosbois, court facade, 1597. (Author)

Fig. 51. Château de Fontainebleau, Cour des Offices, 1606–9. (Author)

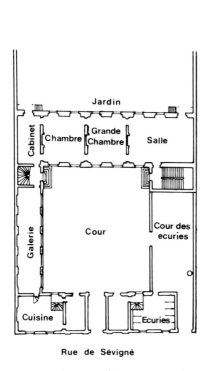

Fig. 52. Hôtel Carnavalet, reconstruction of the original plan, 1545–48. (Drawing by Julia Rogoff after Babelon, *Revue de l'Art,* 1978)

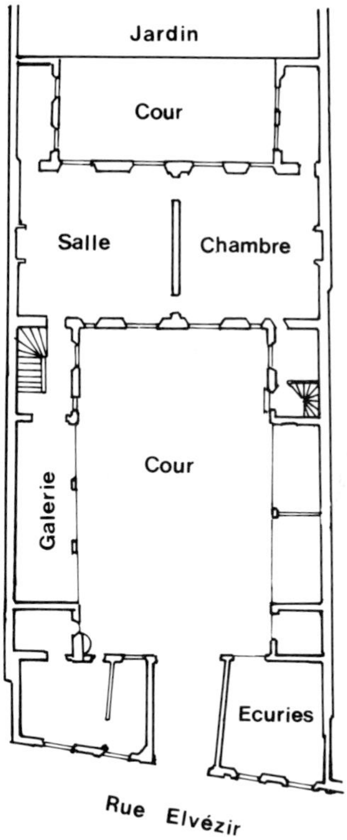

Fig. 53. Hôtel de Donon, reconstruction of the plan, c. 1575. (Drawing by Julia Rogoff after Babelon, *Revue de l'Art,* 1978)

block was built behind it. The placement of the residence at the front of the lot was a feature of the bourgeois house, which typically consisted of a wing on the street and one at the back of the court, often connected by a narrow side wing. Le Muet later codified this arrangement in the plan for the seventh lot in his housing manual, *Manière de bastir pour touttes sortes de personnes* (1623); this lot is only slightly narrower than the Place Royale lots (Fig. 56).

The most elegant example of a sixteenth-century house with this plan is that of Philibert Delorme (Figs. 57, 58). In 1550, the royal architect bought a lot on the rue de la Cerisaie, part of the *lotissement* of the Hôtel St. Pol just west of the Place Royale. His lot was 7 *toises* 5 *pieds* wide and 27 ½ *toises* long, comparable to the dimensions of the Place Royale lots, which were 8 *toises* wide and varied from 22 to 32 *toises* long. Delorme planned a block along the street, one on the far side of the courtyard, and two side loggias—all that the narrow width of the property would allow. The wing at the rear of the court contained the main

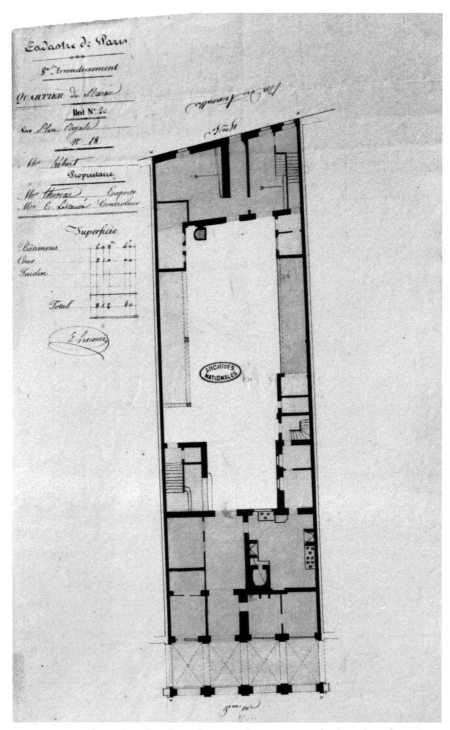

Fig. 54. House of Nicolas Chevalier, Place Royale, east range, third pavilion from the north end, plan, 1846. (A.N. F³¹ 21, no. 178) Lot size: c. 46 *pieds* (15.1 meters) on the square × c. 160 *pieds* (c. 53 meters).

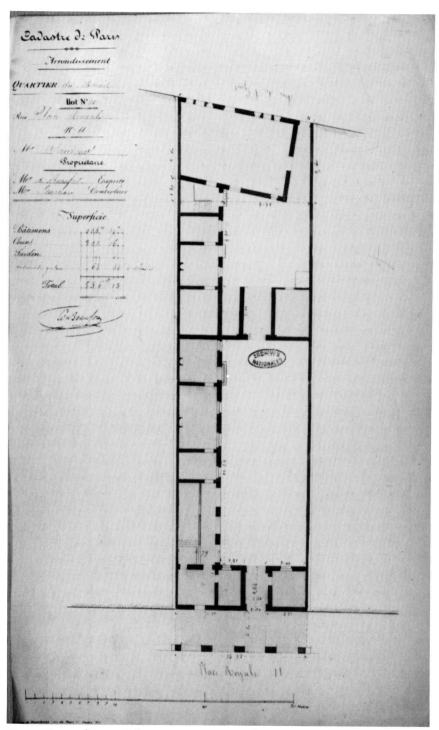

Fig. 55. House of François de Lomenie, Place Royale, west range, third pavilion from the south end, plan, c. 1831. (A.N. F³¹ 21, no. 168) Lot size: c. 43 *pieds* (14.32 meters) on the square × 173 *pieds* (c. 57 meters).

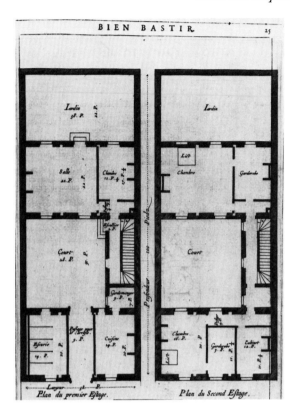

Fig. 56. Pierre Le Muet, house plan for the seventh lot, *Manière de bastir pour touttes sortes de personnes,* 1623. (Avery Architectural and Fine Arts Library, Columbia University, New York) Lot size: 38 × 100 *pieds.*

residential quarters, and the lower priority street wing was never built. Delorme forged a compromise between the bourgeois house and the hôtel, using the dimensions and plan of the former but the functional layout of the latter. He recommended his house as a model for those with lots of modest width who wished to build a respectable residence at reasonable cost, for successful bourgeois such as himself and the merchants for whom the Place Royale was intended. Delorme also replaced pilasters with stone quoins, "to show how the learned and expert architect can devise an elegant building, without great expense."[51] This was precisely the aim of Henri IV's architects, not only in substituting quoins for a classical order, but in adapting Delorme's planning type to the Place Royale. The royal architects made one significant modification, however: whereas Delorme privileged the wing removed from the street,

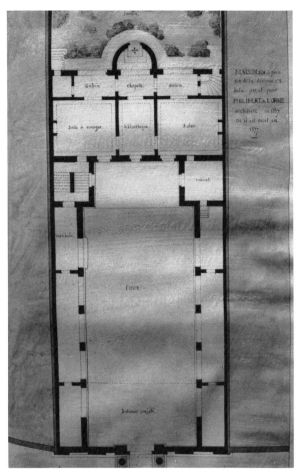

Fig. 57. House of Philibert Delorme, rue de la Cerisaie, Paris, 1554. Plan by A.L.T. Vaudoyer, 1840. (Bibliothèque de l'Institut de France, Paris, N 90A) Lot size: 47 × 165 *pieds.*

Fig. 58. House of Philibert Delorme, rue de la Cerisaie, Paris, court facade, 1554. P. Delorme, *Le Premier Tome de l'Architecture,* 1567, fol. 253v. (Avery Architectural and Fine Arts Library, Columbia University, New York)

Fig. 59. Champ à seille, Metz. Engraving after Claude Chastillon. (B.N. Est. rés. Ve 9)

Fig. 60. Place Notre-Dame, Villefranche-de-Rouergue. (Studio Maravelle, Villefranche-de-Rouergue)

Henri's architects emphasized the front pavilion to take advantage of the wonderful views of the square.

That the pavilions were planned for artisans is clear also from the arcaded gallery, which was a feature of commercial architecture rather than noble housing. Paris provided a local example in the Pont Notre-Dame where the ground-floor shops were arcaded (see Fig. 45). An arcaded gallery typically circumscribed medieval market squares, whether in Arras, Metz, and Pont-à-Mousson in northeastern France where the squares had a marked Flemish influence, or in the *bastides* of southwestern France, such as Montauban or Villefranche-de-Rouergue (Figs. 59, 60). It is from these medieval squares that the Place Royale descended.[52]

The arcaded market square also had its Renaissance variants, but the differences between the Place Royale and the Piazza Ducale in Vigevano (1492–94), for example, clarify the medieval heritage of the French square (Fig. 61). The Piazza Ducale embodied the Renaissance conception of the square as an ancient forum; it was rectangular, enclosed by a colonnade, and dominated by a monumental building (a church), as Vitruvius and Alberti recommended. The Place Royale was not conceived as a forum in the Vitruvian tradition.[53] Yet even at the medieval squares, a monumental building — whether church or town hall — presided over the public space. The Place Royale was unique in that it had no monument to justify the opening of public space.

Fig. 61. Piazza Ducale, Vigevano, 1492–94. (David Friedman)

[83]

The closest model for the facade of the Place Royale pavilions is a design in Serlio's sixth book on domestic architecture, a three-story house with ground-floor shops opening onto an arcaded gallery and a hipped roof (Fig. 62). Serlio identified this design, project I in the Columbia manuscript, as a house for a rich artisan or merchant, "Casa per un ricco artefice o buon mercante e anche per un cittadine," precisely the group for whom the Place Royale was intended. The predominant horizontal lines of Serlio's design were counterbalanced at the Place Royale by stone quoins, satisfying the French fondness for the vertical line (see Fig. 46). Dormer windows were opened in the roof to exploit all available living space, another French custom, and Serlio's five bays were reduced to four, depriving the pavilions of a central axis that would have given greater formal autonomy to each housing unit within the range.

All told, these adjustments inflected Serlio's Italian house with French features. Yet the striking similarity between the two designs raises the possibility that Henri IV's architects actually consulted Serlio's manuscript on domestic architecture, a copy of which was in France, possibly in the library of Salomon de Brosse.[54] On the same folio as project I there was an alternative design "in the French manner," project K, "Casa quasi simile alla passata ma al costume di franza," which Serlio noted was common in Paris, "alla parigina" (Fig. 63).[55] In choosing the Italian model for the Place Royale, Henri IV's architect probably intended to ennoble the square by departing from the vernacular type. It is hard to imagine that the choice had anything to do with attracting Italian artisans, since the handling of the facade is so unmistakably French. The departure of the pavilions from the local tradition of bourgeois housing, their enrichment with brick-and-stone facades, and their presence at a royal space reflected sharp breaks with traditional style. Those stylistic discontinuities may explain why the architectural decorum of the *place* was misread by its noble residents and by latter-day historians who characterized these pavilions as aristocratic residences. The Place Dauphine, Henri IV's second square also planned for artisans and merchants, produced no such misinterpretations; the design similarities between the two squares reinforce the view that the Place Royale was intended for the same social class. The pavilions and the scale of the first square were indeed grander than in the Place Dauphine, but this was to honor the crown's presence at the Place Royale, a presence signified by the King's Pavilion.

The crown retained one lot in the middle of the south range where Henri IV built the Pavillon du Roi (Fig. 64). The king's identification with the square was a valuable asset in enticing foreign artisans to participate in the French enterprise, inspiring lot owners to undertake the architectural charge, and above all encouraging manufacturing in Paris. Construction of the royal pavilion was

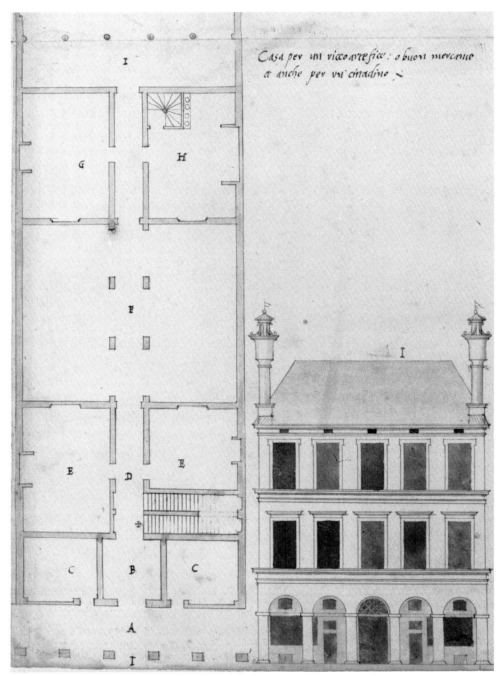

Fig. 62. Sebastiano Serlio, House of a rich artisan or good merchant or citizen, Book VI, fol. 49, Project I, c. 1541–46. (Avery Architectural and Fine Arts Library, Columbia University, New York) Serlio's caption reads "Casa per un ricco artefice o buon mercante et anche per un cittadino."

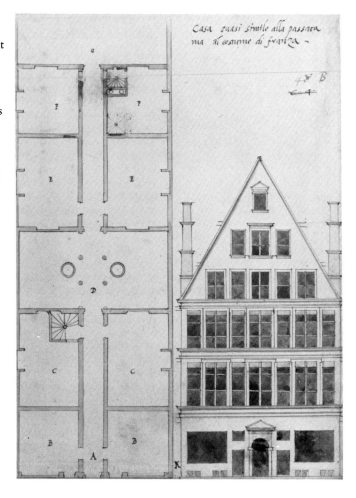

Fig. 63. Sebastiano Serlio, House of a rich artisan or good merchant or citizen in the French manner, Book VI, fol. 49, Project K, c. 1541–46. (Avery Architectural and Fine Arts Library, Columbia University, New York) Serlio's caption reads "Casa quasi simile alla passata ma al costume di franza."

begun immediately, with masonry and carpentry contracts awarded to Jonas Robelin and Gilles Le Redde, respectively, on 1 July 1605. Originally, only one story was planned between arcade and attic, "un estage-carré," which would have produced a modest building no taller than its neighbors. But the design was soon modified and another story added, raising the height of the royal pavilion by nearly 12 *pieds* and giving it greater prominence in the square. Built at a cost of 32,679 *livres,* the King's Pavilion was completed by May 1607 when the first concierge was installed, court painter Charles de Court — another indication by Henri IV that he intended high-ranking artisans to settle at the Place Royale.[56]

The King's Pavilion towered above the ring of houses that enclosed the square. As befit its royal patron, it alone was decorated with ennobling classical motifs, fluted pilasters, and a frieze interlacing the king's cipher with emblems of art and war. It alone was centered on its own axis; five bays of windows scanned the facade, and the middle bay was emphasized by larger openings and more concentrated ornament.[57] And the King's Pavilion alone had no ground-floor shops; the monarch could sponsor commerce, but the dignity of his station prohibited the conduct of trade beneath his symbolic residence. Instead, the royal pavilion served as the primary entrance to the square, with movement through its open arches reinforcing the central axis of the square. The King's Pavilion was conceived as an entrance pavilion, affiliated with those in the enclosed forecourts of sixteenth-century châteaux, as at Fleury-en-Bière or the domed pavilions in Jacques Androuet Ducerceau's designs for Verneuil (c. 1568–76), and later set in an urban context by de Brosse at the Luxembourg Palace (1615).[58] By adapting a building type associated with the nobleman's château, the King's Pavilion retained an appropriate architectural dignity at the bourgeois square.

The principal approach to the Place Royale was from the rue St. Antoine, the Right Bank's primary east-west artery, carrying traffic from the Bastille and the Porte St. Antoine to the Hôtel de Ville and the Louvre (Fig. 65). Turning onto the rue Royale (rue Birague), one saw the King's Pavilion at the end of this short street (Fig. 66). The crown built the rue Birague at the same time as the square, cutting through a partially developed area, but surprisingly it failed to control the design of the houses on this approach road.[59] Nonetheless, juxta-

Fig. 64. Place des Vosges (Royale), King's Pavilion, north facade. (Author)

[87]

Fig. 65. Jacques Gomboust, map of Paris, detail of the Place Royale, 1652. (B.N. Est. Ve 31b)

posed against banal houses on the rue Birague, the Pavillon du Roi appeared all the more splendid, drawing the visitor through its open arches into a space of totally unexpected grandeur.

One entered the square on its central axis and found the space enclosed on three sides by connecting pavilions. On the far side of the square lay the silkworks. This range of buildings extended beyond the sides of the square and was set off by a street, the extension of the rue des Francs Bourgeois, which channeled traffic into the Place Royale from the residential and commercial districts to the west. Circulation into the Place Royale formed T-shaped axes; traffic from the rue St. Antoine delineated the central axis of the square, and traffic from the rue des Francs Bourgeois, the lateral axis (Fig. 67). The pattern of circulation was reinforced by the arrangement of buildings around the square, the King's Pavilion marking the central axis in an otherwise closed ring of buildings and the freestanding workshops reinforcing the lateral axis. This harmony between the square's formal composition and its urban structure distinguished the first design of the Place Royale, although the modest workshops on the north side of the square would have seemed unworthy of the brick-and-stone pavilions.

The designer of the Place Royale is nowhere named in the documents, and his identity is further obscured by the disappearance of all but one of the drawings of the square made during Henri IV's reign. Most likely, one or both of the royal architects, Jacques II Androuet Ducerceau and Louis Métezeau, designed the square.[60] There is also the tantalizing possibility that Salomon de Brosse (1571–1626) participated in designing the Place Royale, a possibility arising out of the attribution to de Brosse of the one contemporary drawing of the square (Fig. 68).[61] Undated and unsigned, it is a study of the upper stories of the King's Pavilion, recording a variant of the final design with a royal escutcheon on the middle dormer and narrow windows framing the central bay. On the verso is a drawing of the *porte cochère* of the Hôtel de Soissons, which de

[88]

Brosse designed sometime between 1605 and 1612, when the Comte de Soissons owned the hôtel. The attribution of this sheet to de Brosse cannot be proven definitively because no signed drawings by the architect survive.[62] Furthermore, it is possible that the sketch of the King's Pavilion represents a revision of the finished building rather than an alternative preliminary design.[63]

In short, the evidence of de Brosse's participation is ambiguous at best, but it would not be unreasonable to suppose that Jacques II Androuet Ducerceau involved de Brosse, his nephew and former student, in designing the Place Royale. De Brosse was already known to the Bourbon court from his work at Verneuil for Henri IV's mistress, Henriette d'Entragues (beginning c. 1600). He was well regarded by Sully who commissioned de Brosse to design the new

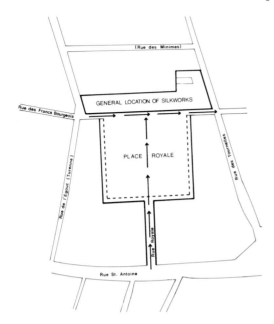

Fig. 67. Place Royale, reconstruction of the first design showing T-shaped axes of circulation, 1605. (Drawing by Julia Rogoff based on A.N. Q1*/1099/10C)

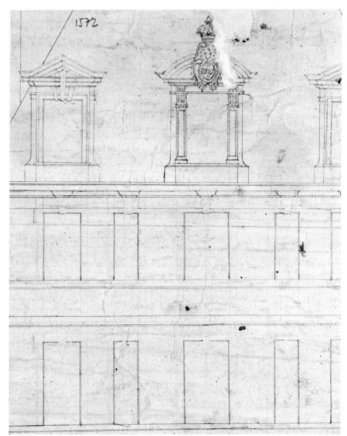

Fig. 68. Attributed to Salomon de Brosse, Place Royale, King's Pavilion, elevation, c. 1605–12. (Stockholm, Nationalmuseum, CC1572v)

town of Henrichemont in 1608. Yet in the end, the fact that none of the numerous building contracts for the Place Royale names its architect suggests that the design was the collective product of the office of the royal architect, and de Brosse may have been significantly involved in that effort.

With three ranges of artisanal housing and an arcade of shops projected across from the workshops, the commercial function of the Place Royale was well understood in 1605. Antoine de Bandole invoked imperial imagery to praise the king's embellishment of Paris: "Caesar and Henry were great architects to embellish their cities with beautiful buildings. One had a magnificent theater built in Rome for public pleasure: and the other, the Place Royale in Paris to have all kinds of artisans work there." [64] But Henri IV soon encountered a problem. The men on whom he relied to build the square did not share his vision of the Place Royale.

THE LAND OWNERS

The alienation of land at the Place Royale was not a lucrative operation for the royal treasury, with the only direct revenue provided by an annual property tax of 3 *livres* per lot. On the other hand, the project provided Paris with a precious amenity at minimal cost to the crown. Unlike the sixteenth-century development schemes, which were undertaken primarily to raise money for the crown, the Bourbon king sacrificed immediate income in order to promote broader policy objectives offering longer-term benefits: the development of French manufacturing and the embellishment of the capital.

In exchange for the gift of land, the recipients were required to build on their lots in compliance with the royal design. About half of the lots were distributed in June 1605 (the east range and most of the south), while the remaining land was assigned two years later, delayed by the crown's efforts to acquire private property on the west side of the square. The king's interest in the Place Royale even extended to these expropriations, and on 27 May 1605, he wrote Sully about the negotiations with one owner who was reluctant to surrender his property:

> Concerning the opposition raised by the sieur de Montmagny after you
> established the foundations for the houses to be built at the horse
> market, my view, which you should convey to him on my behalf, is
> that since it is something that I want for the ornament and embellish-
> ment of my city of Paris, it should not be opposed; at the worst, he will
> be paid for the land taken from his garden, and tell him that being a
> public work he can be compelled to sell it, not at his price, but for what
> is judged fair.[65]

[91]

Needless to say, Montmagny and his neighbors yielded to the king and were compensated at prices far above the market value of their land.[66]

The king gave the lots at the Place Royale to his political allies, mostly high-ranking nobles holding offices in the fiscal administration. The group included Jean de Fourcy, *Intendant des bâtiments;* Nicolas Chevalier, president of the *Chambre des enquêtes,* a parliamentary court; and Etienne de La Fond, *Intendant des meubles* and a key agent in enforcing the crown's economic program. Nicolas d'Angennes and Pierre Jeannin, moderate Catholics who were instrumental in consolidating Henri IV's power in the 1590s, were also rewarded with lots. Six of the recipients were closely associated with Sully and later confirmed their loyalty by building houses in his new town of Henrichemont.[67] Barthélemy Laffemas, the ardent champion of manufacturing, was granted a lot; another recipient was Claude Chastillon, the royal topographer and engineer, whose drawings of the new monuments publicized Henri IV's building program. Some writers have pointed to the land donation as evidence that Chastillon designed the square, but the gift demonstrates nothing beyond the king's appreciation for Chastillon's long-standing support. The only recipient who held no royal post was Charles Marchant. An officer of the city's militia, *Capitaine des archers, arquebusiers, et arbalestres,* Marchant was a pillar of the municipal elite. Moreover, his long-standing support of the king had resulted in his expulsion from League-occupied Paris in 1593.

If the crown intended the pavilions at the Place Royale for artisans and shopkeepers, why then was the land given to noblemen? The king was guided by two considerations. First, he regarded the land donation as a means of rewarding men who had served the crown well; even if the recipients did not want to build, they could sell the land for a quick profit. Second, Henri IV wanted to put the lots in the hands of those who, generally speaking, were most likely to undertake construction. In 1605, there was little reason for optimism that most artisans and merchants would be willing to assume the building charge, particularly in view of the expense imposed by the brick-and-stone facades. By contrast, the financial resources of royal officeholders, coupled with their attachment to the king, enhanced the probability that they would build at the square. As the king's anxiousness to complete the square rose, his priorities in the allocation of lots shifted. In 1605, the king chose to maximize the number of recipients of royal patronage and gave every lot to a different beneficiary. By 1607, Henri IV's overriding aim was to finish construction, and he gave the entire west range to the two men he thought most likely to build the required pavilions. Five lots were given to Pierre Fougeu d'Escures, who had already built one pavilion on the south range; the remaining four lots were given to Charles Marchant, by far the largest developer in Paris (see Appendix D).

It is important to remember that the development of the Place Royale was an experiment. The crown could not predict how the real estate market would respond to an enterprise never before attempted in Paris. It could not gauge to what extent the lots would be considered a boon or a burden: a boon because of the free gift of land, a burden because of the building requirement. On either count, the king had cause to rely on his inner circle, but his expectations were not entirely realized at the Place Royale. The crown learned two important lessons from the development of the square, which it applied to the subsequent development of the Place Dauphine. It learned that the nobility were reluctant to construct rental housing for bourgeois tenants, and that the Parisian real estate market placed a high value on new housing.

There was a substantial turnover of property at the Place Royale. Almost half the lots were immediately put up for sale, and the sellers discovered that their land fetched rather low prices. Property at the Place Royale brought from 4.3 *livres* to 6.8 *livres* per square *toise*, rates that did not compare well with the 75 *livres* commanded at the centrally located Place Dauphine. In 1604, land on the rue des Tournelles, one block removed from the square, commanded 7 *livres*, a higher price than at the Place Royale. In sum, the square not only failed to increase the value of the immediately surrounding property but — perhaps owing to the construction requirement — may even have depressed its value.[68]

Almost half the lots changed hands in 1606 and early 1607, and in the resulting redistribution of property, two different constituencies made claims on the square. The lots were scaled for a large bourgeois house, not for a nobleman's hôtel. Each pavilion was 7 – 8 *toises* wide (13.8 – 15.8 meters), but the lots ranged considerably in length, from 20 to 36 *toises* (40 – 71m), providing areas that were substantially larger than the average lot at the Place Dauphine but comparable in size to Serlio's house for a rich artisan (project I).[69] Consequently, the turnover of land permitted several noblemen to amass larger holdings better suited for the demands of a proper hôtel. They recombined half the lots (thirteen) to form two 2-pavilion parcels and six 1½-pavilion parcels, despite the royal ban against subdividing the pavilions.[70]

The second major constituency consisted of artisans, who were able through turnover to acquire single lots at the square. They were all master masons and carpenters, men whose skills facilitated their compliance with the construction requirement. In two instances, artisans — royal carpenter Louis Marchant and royal mason Jean Fontaine — were given lots after the original owners failed to take any action.[71] But master carpenters Barthélemy Drouin and Antoine Le Redde and master mason Jean Coin all purchased their lots.

Drouin's case illustrates the opportunity afforded by their building skills. Tax farmer François Felissan agreed to sell his lot in the east range to Drouin for 1,200 *livres* (approximately 6.4 *livres* per square *toise*). When the carpenter was unable to raise the money, new terms were negotiated that required an outlay of capital from the seller. Felissan accepted the carpenter's house, which Drouin had recently built in the neighborhood, on the rue Neuve-St.-Paul. In exchange, he gave Drouin the lot at the Place Royale plus 10,500 *livres* to defray construction costs.[72] From Felissan's point of view, it was an economic arrangement; he moved into a new house for about one-half the cost of building a one-pavilion residence at the square (approximately 24,000 *livres*). On the other hand, Drouin's professional skills enabled him to build the house more inexpensively. The emphasis on the court connections of the original land recipients has obscured the major role played by building craftsmen at the Place Royale; nearly 20 percent of the men who built and owned pavilions at the square were accomplished artisans, the group for whom the Place Royale was intended.

Although masked by the uniform facades, aristocrats and artisans began to build rather different kinds of houses at the Place Royale. The crown facilitated the construction process by enlarging the port St. Paul, where building materials for the square were delivered, and by expelling the horse market from the site.[73] As he watched the pavilions rise in 1605, the English agent, Tobie Mathew, had only praise for the project:

> The wonder of a buildinge is that of the old marché aux Chevaux, now call'd the Place Royalle, which is already half built with galleries to walk drye round about, a goodly fountaine in the midst, and a pavillion on one side of the square to lodge the Kinge. . . . This must be destined to the sale of those stuffs of silke and gold which are already made in great abundance by Dutch and Italians who dwell nearby.[74]

However, the redistribution of land produced diverging conceptions of the square. The noblemen who owned large parcels at the Place Royale certainly did not envision it as a precinct for artisans and silk craftsmen, and it became increasingly difficult to harmonize those conflicting visions. In 1607, the conflict was resolved: the silkworks were destroyed, and the commercial program of the square lost its justification.

THE SECOND DESIGN OF THE PLACE ROYALE: 1607

The workshops must have seemed shabby compared to the brick-and-stone pavilions rising opposite them. By April 1607, the king was persuaded that embellishing the north side and making the square symmetrical would much improve the Place Royale. The question was whether to accomplish that goal by attaching a gallery to the front of the workshops, as the king recommended, or by razing the workshops and replacing them with a fourth range of pavilions, as the silk partners evidently wanted. Henri IV raised the matter in a letter to Sully on 27 April 1607:

> I learned from the Controller [-general of buildings Jean de] Donon that there is some problem with the directors of the workshops [*manufactures*], because they wanted to tear down the whole building [*tout le logis*]. This is not my view, and it seems to me that it should be enough if they built a gallery in front with the same facade as the rest.[75]

It is unclear to which building (*logis*) the king is referring in his letter. But his proposal to build a gallery would make little sense unless he wanted to preserve the full complement of houses on the north side of square. Yet if the silkworks were destined for destruction from the time the square was begun in 1605, as is generally believed, how can the king's desire to save the buildings in 1607 be explained? In fact, the presence of the silkworks at the square was not called into question before 1607. The underlying issue that divided the king and the silk entrepreneurs was not the design of the square, which they agreed should be symmetric, but the purpose of the square. Whereas Henri IV remained committed to the original conception of the Place Royale as a manufacturing and commercial center, the silk partners and probably other land owners as well envisioned the Place Royale as a strictly residential square. No other documents concerning this crucial episode have yet been found, and we are left to speculate about the aspirations and motives of the various parties based on their ensuing actions.

Why did the silk partners want to demolish the workshops in which they had just invested a considerable sum of money? They were not simply maneuvering to terminate the business, for they pressed for destruction of the buildings well aware that the terms by which they were granted titles of nobility obliged them to manufacture silk through 1615 — with or without the workshops at the Place Royale — an obligation which they apparently expected the king to enforce. They understood that there was no possibility of dissolving the business, only of relocating it. Nor were the partners seeking greater residential amenities for themselves by building new houses at the square, for not one of them ever lived at the Place Royale. It is possible they were inspired by an aesthetic yearning for symmetry but, as the king pointed out, this could have been satisfied, at least in part, without tearing down the ateliers.

Yet there was apparently a strong economic rationale behind removing the

L.A PLACE ROYALE DE PARIS laquelle fut commancée l'an 1604. par l'ordre de Henry 4. et acheuée quelque temps apres. Son d͞ hangement des particuliers sy sont faits des logemens magnifiques: La statue de Bronze de Louis 13 qui est au mil͞i͞e͞ust de Biar, et le Chev Perelle fecit

Fig. 69. Place Royale, view of the north range. Engraving by Pérelle, mid-seventeenth-century. (B.N. Est. Va 251b) The equestrian monument of Louis XIII was placed in the center of the square in 1639.

manufacturing enterprise from the Place Royale. Whereas the financiers and nobles showed little interest in the silkworks and in French sericulture and manufacturing in general, they found the square appealing as an aristocratic residential quarter. The silk partners presumably discerned the resistance of the noblemen who owned land at the square to develop it as artisanal housing and shops, and they concluded that aristocratic residences would be a more prestigious and potentially more lucrative investment than workshops. As Paul Deyon observed, the broader social context was that the merchant manufacturer in seventeenth-century France was generally eager to abandon his profession:

*...ger des Ouuriers et dy etablir des manufactures, mais par je ne sçay que
de Daniel de Volterre . ils furent posez l'an 1639.
Mariette rüe s.^t Iacque a la Victoire . Auec Priuilege du Roy*

"After 15 or 20 years of manufacturing he would shift his capital to an investment in property or a *seigneurie* or into the purchase of an office or tax-farming contract . . . for manufacturing was not considered a means of social advancement in seventeenth-century France, and even suffered under hostile prejudice."[76] The attitude of the silk partners toward their workshops at the Place Royale illustrates the negative perceptions of manufacturing; it was those biases that defeated Henri IV's strategy of entrusting royal office-holders with the development of a commercial and artisanal square.

There were certainly signs that the noblemen who owned lots at the square did not enthusiastically support the commercial program. They were relatively slow to begin building the pavilions, ignoring the construction deadline the king set for the end of 1606, and their deliberate pace may have resulted from displeasure at having to house artisans and shopkeepers. More than half of the aristocrats who built at the square amassed parcels larger than a single lot, not to provide more ample facilities for artisan tenants but to bestow upon themselves more spacious residences. Personal use of the houses by the nobility did not necessarily preclude the installation of shops on the ground floor. Yet, unlike Rome where such mixed use was a common practice, in Paris it was unusual to combine aristocratic housing with shops; Antoine Le Pautre's Hôtel de Beauvais (1654) was one of the rare seventeenth-century Parisian hôtels to include street-level shops.[77] In at least one known case, a nobleman closed the arched entrances to the shops in his pavilion, adapting the rooms for noncommercial use, as soon as the crown stopped enforcing the commercial program.[78] The resolute separation of shops from noble residences and the resistance to the commercial program of the Place Royale demonstrated the aversion of the gown nobility to investment in manufacturing and trade, an attitude that Robert Dallington observed in 1604. "Trade availeth nothing the French Kings," he wrote, "for they holde it heere a base and sordid kind of profession for a Gentleman, much more for a king, to trade by Marchandize." [79] Finally, there may have been the practical economic difficulty of attracting the high-priced trades to the distant Place Royale, which was far removed from the neighborhood where jewelers, watchmakers, gold traders, and money exchangers traditionally flourished on the bridges of the Seine and within the Parlement on the Ile de la Cité. These were the obstacles that Henri IV unhappily encountered in surrendering his goal of making the royal square a thriving center of commerce and manufacturing. With the enticing vision of a more magnificent Place Royale enclosed by uniform pavilions, the king was persuaded to modify the original scheme.

In April 1607, Henri IV endorsed a second design for the Place Royale. Sainctot and his associates were ordered to demolish the workshops bordering the square and to build a row of nine pavilions in their place, symmetric to the south range. [80] To compensate the entrepreneurs for the loss of their buildings, the king financed construction of the new range. Pérelle, in his engraving of the square, incorrectly depicted eleven pavilions to the north, creating the false impression that the buildings extended beyond the side ranges (Fig. 69). In fact, the symmetric north range was intended to create the image of an enclosed space, suppressing the lateral axis, and this formal concern was made clear in the specifications prepared by Sully for the pavilions "on the site where the building of the *Manufactures* is now located and on the same alignment" (see Appendix C). [81]

> All of the nine pavilions correctly aligned will together have the same length as the nine others which are directly opposite them on the south side, namely the quantity of 72 *toises,* the length and width delimited by the quadrature of the square, and such that the two ends of the nine pavilions to be built must correspond exactly and be made even with the pavilions already built on the east as well as the west sides in order to create a right angle. [82]

While Chastillon's engraving shows that the north range of pavilions was freestanding, Nicolay and Quesnel depicted the Place Royale as a fully enclosed space, capturing the formal ideal to which the square aspired (Figs. 70, 71; see Fig. 41). Sully's specifications also eliminated the reference to shops which had appeared in all prior documents and instead described "an arcaded gallery, public and *commune,* for walking under cover." [83] The ground-floor shops and

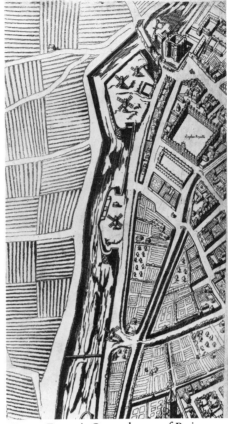

Fig. 70. Vassallieu dit Nicolay, map of Paris, detail of the Place Royale, 1609. (B.N. Est. rés. Hennin XV 1352)

Fig. 71. François Quesnel, map of Paris, detail of the Place Royale, 1609. (B.N. Est. rés. AA 3)

gallery lost their original function as commerce was excluded from the square. In the middle of the north range rose another entrance pavilion, later known as the Queen's Pavilion. It was not owned by the crown and therefore never adorned with the royal ciphers and rich decoration bestowed upon the King's Pavilion. The new entrance pavilion and the road opened beneath it, the rue de Béarn, accentuated the central axis of the square, and the form of the Place Royale was reconceived as a symmetric square, enclosed on all sides.

However more magnificent the symmetric square was, there were discordant elements in the new design. No longer was the axial structure of the Place Royale congruent with patterns of circulation in the city. Now traffic entered the square in ways that undermined its redesigned form and expressed the

Fig. 72. Place des Vosges (Royale), Queen's Pavilion, north facade. (Author)

structure of the first project. The new road to the north, the rue de Béarn, extended the central axis of the square, but the street served no functional role (see Fig. 65). Whereas the southern approach, the rue Birague, funneled traffic into the square from a major artery, the rue St. Antoine, its northern counterpart carried practically no traffic and came to a dead end after two short blocks in the midst of an undeveloped area. To this day, the northern approach to the Place Royale remains unimportant to the city's circulation. It is clear that this was considered a back entrance, hidden from public view, from the north elevation of the Queen's Pavilion, where it was considered unnecessary to make an architectural statement. Indeed, not only was the brick-and-stone facade never built, but instead of the normative five bays of windows, the north elevation had only four bays, which were misaligned with the three arches below (Fig. 72). The axial pavilion on the north side was a formal device to achieve symmetry within the square, but unlike the King's Pavilion, it had no urban significance outside that space.

The two entrances at the north corners of the square were also problematic. Because these openings undermined the formal ideal of an enclosed and symmetric space, additional pavilions were planned by 1630 to mask the intrusive openings.[84] A pavilion was built at the northeast corner (see Fig. 65). But these entrances served a vital axis of circulation, and it proved impractical to obstruct the northwest entrance, which forever remained open. The flow of traffic from the rue des Francs Bourgeois and the asymmetric opening at the northwest corner continued to assert the lateral axis, preventing the square from achieving the perfect symmetry and axiality to which it aspired. It is the continuing importance of this lateral axis of circulation that Pérelle unwittingly captured in his engraving by lengthening the north range of pavilions (see Fig. 69). There was a tension in the new design between the form of the square and its urban context, a tension that was absent from the original project. Nevertheless, with the wooden houses on the north side of the square now replaced by a splendid range of brick-and-stone pavilions, there is little doubt that the second design produced a far more magnificent Place Royale. Indeed the king's consent to abandon the commercial program must have been won by associating it with the vision of this much grander square.

The silk investors retained possession of the entire tract of land that the king had given them in 1604. In agreements dated 2 October 1608 and 8 January 1609, they divvied up their land on the north side of the square and subdivided the pavilions, despite the royal injunction to preserve the four-bay unit.[85] Destruction of the silkworks began in early 1608. Two carpenters were hired in February to disassemble the carpentry in six of the houses, and one week later, the owners signed a masonry contract with Balthazar Monnard to build the new pavilions. The specifications required Monnard to "demolish from top to bottom, for a length of 64 *toises* the buildings where the *manufactures* are at present" (see Appendix A2).[86] The pavilions were finished in 1610, and the owners proceeded with construction of additional wings to the rear.

Despite the destruction of the workshops on the north side of the square, the silkworks continued to operate, and new facilities were built to accommodate them. The partnership of Moisset, Sainctot, Lumague, Camus, and the Parfaicts was dissolved in October 1608, but individually they continued to produce silk, gold, and silver cloth as the original agreement with the king in 1603 bound them to do. Those parts of the silkworks that did not border the Place Royale—the *maison des moulins* and the peripheral buildings extending beyond the north facade of the square—were preserved. Moisset was given the *maison des moulins* and the shop with a stock of merchandise "of long and difficult sale" valued at close to 12,000 *livres*.[87]

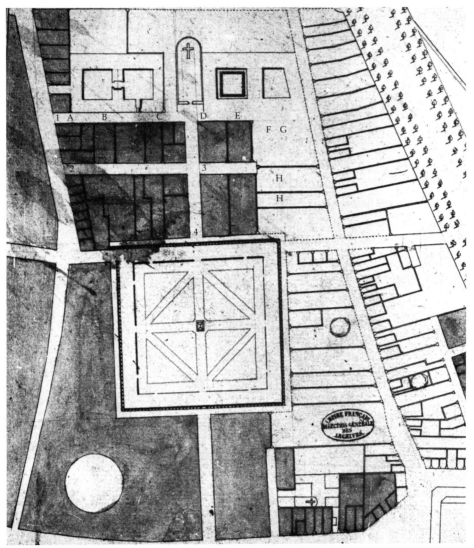

Fig. 73. Place Royale and surrounding area, 1702. (A.N. Q1*/1099/10C; Service Photographique des Archives Nationales) Individual houses (A–H) are identified in Appendix A5. Key: 1. rue des Minimes; 2. rue du Foin; 3. rue Roger Verlomme; 4. rue de Béarn

In March 1609, Moisset hired the director of the silkworks, Pestalossi, to run the shop and mill through 1615, requiring him to bring nine silk artisans to Paris and "in addition to maintain and conduct all business which the *manufactures* can undertake during the said time and in such a way that Moisset receives no complaint from His Majesty." [88] Behind the north range of the square, a new street, the rue du Foin, was opened. Along the street, the entrepreneurs built seven new houses where, by agreement with the crown, they were obliged to lodge silk artisans free of rent until 1615 (Fig. 73).[89] Three houses were already occupied in 1608, and craftsmen moved into the other buildings in 1609, with a house at the corner of the rues des Minimes and des Tournelles reserved for the female gold spinners (see Appendix A5 – 6).[90] Lumague was especially active in maintaining the silk business, hiring a number of Milanese gold beaters and selling substantial quantities of the gold and silver thread produced in his *fabrique*.[91] That the silkworks survived and still generated new construction despite this displacement from the square testifies to the king's continuing enthusiasm for the manufacturing venture. The commercial program was defeated at the Place Royale, but Henri IV remained committed to a capital supported by manufacturing and artisanal activity.

As for the king's vision of establishing France as a great silk-producing country, ultimately it was not realized; continuing strong foreign competition, the French climate, and the resistance of land owners posed insuperable obstacles. But the royal project met at least sufficient success to impress the distinguished economist Antoine de Montchrétien, who concluded in 1615 that France had proven she could "supply herself with the best [silk] in the world without buying at high prices from foreigners."[92]

THE CONSTRUCTION AND SETTLEMENT OF THE SQUARE

When it was decided to destroy the silkworks in the spring of 1607, pavilions were rising around three sides of the square. Only the three lots at the north end of the east range remained empty, and on 10 July 1607, the king threatened to penalize the delinquent owners if they did not begin construction immediately. When neither Barthélemy Laffemas nor the aged Nicolas d'Angennes (1530 – 1611) responded to the threat, the king instructed royal carpenter Louis Marchant and royal mason Jean Fontaine to build the pavilions at the crown's expense, granting them title to the property upon completion.[93] In 1608, the silkworks were razed, and within two years the north range was completed. With the exception of these pavilions (which were all built by master mason Balthazar Monnard), construction at the Place Royale was entirely decentralized, with each lot owner hiring his own workmen and building at his own discretion behind the brick-and-stone facade. Many owners, however, hired the same craftsmen; at least five pavilions were built by the architect whom the king had used for the Pavillon du Roi, Jonas Robelin, and Monnard built eleven pavilions altogether. The masons handled these multiple commissions by acting as general contractors, supplying the building materials and subcontracting each project to a different mason.[94]

When the design of the Place Royale was modified in 1607, the crown did not explicitly reformulate the program of the square. The king did not directly countermand the goals stated in the 1605 edict, and the pavilions continued to express in the silent language of architecture their artisanal and commercial affiliations. But the crown took no steps to prevent the accumulation of subdivided lots or to coerce owners to install shops and artisans in their pavilions. By mid-1607, the king was planning a second square, the Place Dauphine, which was better suited to commerce, if not manufacturing, and he evidently decided against pressing his economic goals upon the reluctant nobles of the Place Royale. Meeting no opposition from the crown, royal officeholders proceeded to develop the Place Royale in accordance with their individual residential needs, yet the contingent of artisan-owners continued to recall the original conception of the square. While uncertainty about the king's intentions persisted during the early years of the Place Royale, both visions of the square were kept alive.

Until now, the clearest picture of the square had come from documents of the late seventeenth century when many owners enlarged and upgraded the houses, giving us an image of the Place Royale as an exclusively aristocratic precinct.[95] But the discovery of many of the original building contracts has revealed the hybrid social and architectural character of Henri IV's Place Royale and its gradual transformation into an aristocratic space after the king's death. These building contracts have certain limitations; they do not describe the floor plans nor the functions of the rooms. Nevertheless, the information they do contain—the owner's name, the size of his lot, and the arrangement of the wings of the house—amounts to an entirely new picture of the Place Royale.

As we have seen, because the lots were scaled for a comfortable bourgeois house rather than a nobleman's hôtel, more than half of the nobles acquired additional land. The case of Pierre Fougeu d'Escures (1554–1621) is particularly instructive about attitudes toward lot size because he built two houses at the Place Royale, a one-pavilion house that complied with the king's original plan and a two-pavilion house built after the square was modified. A trusted royal agent, Fougeu held several important posts in Sully's administration of the *voirie*. He was an active architectural patron in his native city of Orléans, and to please Sully he built a house in Henrichemont.[96] In 1605, Fougeu was given the lot on the east side of the royal pavilion, and he recruited the same building crew used by the king. On 17 March 1606, the mason Jonas Robelin agreed to build a pavilion with four ground-floor shops facing the square and, directly behind them, a second file of rooms facing a courtyard. Stables were built on the far side of the courtyard, which was entered through a *porte cochère* on the rue Birague.

This building fulfilled the crown's intentions for the Place Royale: a house with shops whose modesty was veiled by the brick-and-stone facade, built not for Fougeu's own use but for merchants and bourgeois tenants. It was completed at a cost of 23,711 *livres*, a sum beyond the reach of all but the wealthiest artisans (the smallest houses built at the Place Dauphine cost roughly 6,000 *livres*), but not a crushing burden for a wealthy nobleman.[97]

In March 1607, when construction was well advanced, Fougeu was given five lots on the west side of the square, a generous gift to show the king's appreciation for Fougeu's quick construction of his first house.[98] Fougeu welcomed the opportunity to build a larger house in which he could live. He retained two lots at the south end of the range and, to defray the building costs, he sold the three other lots as well as the completed pavilion. In December 1607, in anticipation of selling the house, Fougeu had the arched entrances to the shops closed, an alteration which he evidently thought made the house more appealing. Three months later, in March 1608, he sold it for 25,500 *livres*, making a 7.5 percent return on his investment.[99] Fougeu never lived in this house, and he surely never intended to do so. With the money that he raised from the various sales, Fougeu built a modified hôtel with two pavilions on the square, at least one side wing, another block on the far side of the courtyard, and a garden extending toward the rue St. Antoine on an additional piece of property that he acquired separately (Fig. 74).[100] This was the only residence at the square that had a larger than pocket-sized garden, although a garden was consid-

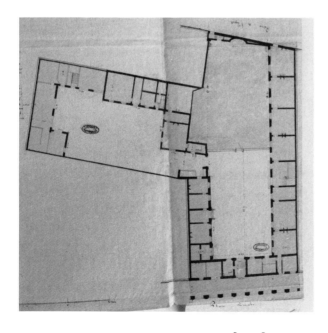

Fig. 74. House of Pierre Fougeu d'Escures (Hôtel de Chaulnes), Place Royale, plan, c. 1831. (A.N. F³¹ 21, no. 167) This residence comprised the two pavilions at the south end of the west range; it did not originally include the garden and service court which were built on land acquired in 1644. Lot size: c. 88 *pieds* (29 meters) on the square.

ered an essential feature of a nobelman's hôtel. That Fougeu was able to include a garden only by annexing additional land to his Place Royale lots is yet another indication that the lots were not intended for aristocratic housing. Fougeu kept the house for his own use throughout his life. In his will dated 18 March 1641, the Place Royale residence was valued at 94,000 *livres,* and it was sold three years later by his daughter for 130,000 *livres* to Honoré d'Albert, Duke of Chaulnes, who enlarged the house and gave it the name by which it is known today, the Hôtel de Chaulnes.[101]

The development of the north side of the square reveals most clearly what

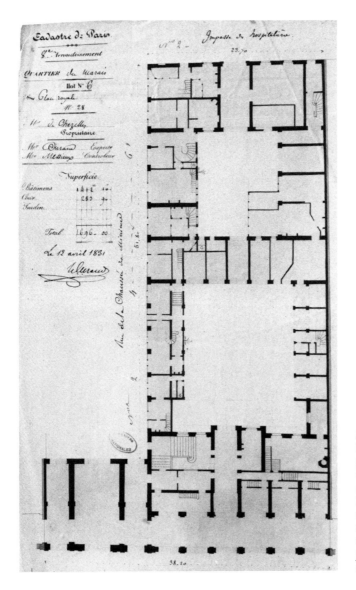

Fig. 75. House of Jean de Moisset, Place Royale, plan, 1831. (A.N. F³¹ 16, no. 269) This residence comprised the Queen's Pavilion and the six adjoining bays to the east on the north side of the square. Lot size: c. 116 *pieds* (38.2 meters) on the square.

the advocates of the design change wanted for the Place Royale. On this side, the partners in the silkworks distributed the nine lots, the Queen's Pavilion included, without respecting the four-bay unit of the pavilion, and the consequences of their irregular subdivision are still clear in the square today where property lines do not coincide with pavilions. On their large plots, some of the most lavish residences at the square were built. Jean Moisset was given the axial pavilion plus another lot and a half—altogether nine bays—and on this parcel he built the largest residence at the Place Royale (Fig. 75). Almost two years after the pavilions were completed, on 2 March 1612, Moisset commissioned the mason Charles du Ry to build a wing along the rue de Béarn, an arcaded screen-wall separating the main court from the service court, and stables bordering the rue du Foin.[102]

Interspersed with the multipavilion residences were more modest dwellings built by the five artisan-owners, consisting of one pavilion and either a short side wing or a block at the rear of the court. Four of these houses were in the east range, where the smallest lots were located; they are featured in the foreground of Chastillon's engraving, perhaps because Chastillon's house was in this row as well (see Fig. 41). For royal carpenter Louis Marchant, who owned the lot at the north end of the range (at the right end in Chastillon's view), mason Balthazar Monnard built a side wing bordering the street (rue du Pas de la Mule); the unusually low rent of 350 *livres* that Marchant charged for the house in 1609 suggests that it was a rather modest dwelling.[103] Carpenter Antoine Le Redde owned the lot at the south end of the range (on the far left in Chastillon's engraving), which he acquired from Jean de Fourcy on terms that are not known. Evidently Le Redde very much wanted to live at the square and sold another house for 4,000 *livres* in order to finance construction of the pavilion and a parallel wing on the rue des Tournelles. Le Redde and his wife lived throughout their lives at the Place Royale; the house did not leave his family until 1681, when it was sold by his children.[104]

However much the twenty-four builders at the Place Royale were motivated by a disinterested desire to support the king and to embellish Paris, the value of the houses amply rewarded their sense of duty. Whereas the empty lots had fetched low prices in 1605 and 1606, property at the square quickly appreciated once the Place Royale was completed. Since very few resold their houses in the first five years, it is clear that speculation was not an important factor; nevertheless, the experience of the first sellers demonstrated that sizable profits were to be had in the Parisian housing market.[105] Isaac Arnauld, *Intendant des finances* and a member of Sully's inner circle, built two parallel *corps de logis* on his lot at the east end of the south range, remembered today as the home of Victor

Hugo. Arnauld acted as his own contractor by supplying his craftsmen with building materials, and in 1608 he made the last payment to his mason Jean Gaucher, who received a total of 11,851 *livres* for his labor. Arnauld lived in the house for four years before selling it in 1612, one week after the royal ceremony in the square depicted by Chastillon, for 48,000 *livres* to Jean de Beaumanoir, marquis de Lavardin. If the total cost of his house were comparable to Fougeu's, approximately 24,000 *livres,* then Arnauld reaped a remarkable 100 percent return on his investment in only four years.[106] Compared with this rate of return, Fougeu had not done very well with his 7.5 percent return, but property was obviously appreciating very quickly over time, no doubt accelerated by the recent royal festivities held in the Place Royale.

It is striking that few of the owners chose to live at the Place Royale: only a third in 1610, and by 1613 the number shrank to about one fifth. François de Lomenie, a royal officer for fiscal matters, quickly had misgivings about living at the square. On a lot that he bought on the west side of the square in 1607, he had Jonas Robelin build a pavilion with a single file of rooms, shops on the ground floor and apartment suites on the upper floors ("salle, chambre, garderobe"). A narrow side wing (2 by 7 *toises*) housed the kitchen, stable, and main stair which was to be "like that in the building of Sir d'Escures, near the King's Pavilion, which was built by the said mason," a phrase typical of these building contracts.[107] After living in this modest house for a year or two at the most, de Lomenie moved out and rented it for 800 *livres* to a Portuguese *gentilhomme.*[108] De Lomenie's neighbor, royal magistrate Jean Péricard, was also eager to live at the square in 1607. He was not the beneficiary of a royal donation and spent 1,200 *livres* to acquire two lots from Fougeu. His two-pavilion hôtel was built quickly, and by July 1608 only the paving was left to be done. But Péricard lived in the house for no more than a year and a half before renting it for 1,200 *livres* to a member of the guard of the king's brother, who then transferred the lease to a merchant for 800 *livres.*[109] As the succession of Péricard's tenants reveals, the social character of the square was still fluid. A proviso which Jean Phélypeaux added to the lease for his Place Royale pavilion in 1608 confirms that there was lingering confusion about the program of the square:

> If His Majesty orders that the shops at the Place Royale be rented to lodge merchants or other artisans, or [if] the other proprietors of houses at the Place Royale rent the shops in their houses, in either case, the owner can rent the four shops which are dependencies of the house at his profit and as if [they were] not included in the present lease, with the requirement that in one of the said shops, he will leave a passageway to go to the Place Royale.[110]

This uncertainty about the function of the square must have been one of the factors that initially diminished the appeal of the Place Royale to the aristocracy. We do not know what kind of residences these men preferred to their Place Royale buildings. We know only that their primary homes were in Paris, a crucial fact. For the royal officeholders who built at the square were tied to the capital, and that attachment inspired their investment in Parisian real estate. There is only one documented case of a Place Royale owner who did not live in Paris; Claude Chastillon lived in his native town of Chaalons and kept the top floor of his Place Royale pavilion for his trips to the capital.[111]

The large majority of owners held the Place Royale houses as rental property, following the example of Captain Charles Marchant (?–1610), the largest investor in the square. The four pavilions that he constructed at the north end of the west range were divided into three rental houses.[112] Until the leases are found, the rental income generated by these houses cannot be estimated, but the scope of his real estate holdings in Paris indicates that he expected lucrative rewards from the rental housing market.[113] Marchant was the largest private builder in Henri IV's Paris. His most celebrated project was the Pont aux Marchands (or Pont Marchant; 1598–1608), a bridge built at his own expense across the north arm of the Seine, which was bordered by fifty-one shops of uniform design (Fig. 76). Including these shops, Marchant collected rent from at least sixty buildings in Paris, fifty-five of which he constructed, though he resided throughout his life in a house on the rue Couture Ste.-Catherine that he did not build. No other individual built, owned, and rented as much residential property in Paris during the first decade of the seventeenth century (see Appendix D).

All of the silk partners rented their Place Royale houses; by the end of their lives, the buildings had become important assets. Pierre Sainctot, for example, in his will in 1639 instructed his heirs to sell the one-and-a-half-pavilion house whose value he estimated at 78,800 *livres,* the most valuable piece of property in his estate.[114] His children were only able to sell the house for 75,000 *livres,* requiring them to renegotiate the division of their father's estate.[115] The parties to that settlement in 1641 illustrate the path of upward mobility in

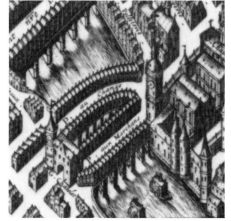

Fig. 76. Vassallieu dit Nicolay, map of Paris, detail of the Pont aux Marchands in the foreground, 1609. (B.N. Est. rés. Hennin XV 1352)

seventeenth-century France, which condemned manufacturing as an inappropriate investment for a nobleman, Henri IV's dreams notwithstanding. The testator was Pierre Sainctot, whose Place Royale house originated in his career as a silk merchant. The male heirs were his sons Estienne, magistrate in the Parlement; Nicolas, treasurer-general to the king; and Jean-Baptiste, master of ceremonies of France, all court officers. The lawyer, by amusing coincidence, was the son of Barthélemy Laffemas who had added a *particule* to his name: Isaac de Laffemas, *maître des requêtes de l'Hôtel du Roi,* a judge with jurisdiction over officers in the king's household.[116]

The social character of the Place Royale was far from homogeneous, with nobles and bourgeois residents commingling as in neighborhoods throughout the city. Masons, merchants, silk artisans, a musician, and a Portuguese *gentilhomme* lived side by side with such distinguished royal officeholders as Michel Tambonneau, president of the *Chambre des comptes* (Phélypeaux's house); Bernardin Pradel, royal treasurer for Montpellier (Claude Parfaict's house); and Prince Henri de Rohan (in Moisset's two-and-a-half-pavilion hôtel). Guillaume Parfaict's tenant in 1613, an officer in the royal guard, was followed in quick succession by a secretary to the Spanish ambassador, the English ambassador, a tax collector, a cavalry officer, and a lieutenant.[117] The turnover was so rapid that despite the long-term leases, Parfaict's building must have been considered temporary housing, although this seems to be a unique case. Rents reflected the premium placed on the square. On his lot and a half, Pierre Sainctot built two houses of equal size back to back, one with a six-bay facade on the square and the other at the rear of the lot facing the rue du Foin. The house on the square was rented for 1,200 *livres* while the back house was half the price; in 1618, the rent of the former was up to 1,400 *livres* while the other stayed at 600 *livres*.[118] Most of the leases gave the landlord the right to use the rooms facing the square whenever royal ceremonies were staged at the Place Royale. But landlords only infrequently had cause to invoke this privilege, for after the death of Henri IV, the Bourbon court preferred the far grander and more expansive grounds of the Louvre to the square that never entirely shed its bourgeois character.

THE PLACE ROYALE CROWNED

In April 1612, with the square enclosed on all sides by brick-and-stone pavilions, the crown staged a lavish ceremony in the Place Royale to celebrate the joint engagements of the king's sister Elizabeth to the future Philip IV, heir to the Hapsburg throne, and of Louis XIII, still a boy of eleven, to Philip's sister, Anne of Austria. The event inspired great hopes. The assassination of Henri IV two years earlier had shattered the dream that his continuing rule would usher in a new golden age for Europe marked by the peace and religious unity that he had brought to France. With these engagements, hope was briefly revived that the two great powers, the monarchy of France and the empire of Hapsburg Spain, would unite in a providential rule of peace.

It was in the Place Royale that the Bourbon court gathered to celebrate the auspicious event (see Fig. 41). A chivalric drama was enacted during three days, the *carrousel* of the Place Royale, in which two groups of knights battled to gain entry to the turreted Palace of Felicity, seat of the idyllic rule which, it was hoped, the marriages would bring about. The palace was "built . . . in France by the glorious work of the French Hercules Henry the Great," the author of the program, Vulson de La Colombière, explained, and "the Queen Mother and Regent desires to render it stronger than that which was built long ago in Athens to adore the same Divinity; she has used the cement of this double alliance which seemed certain to bring Europe an eternal peace and a perfect happiness." [119] By Chastillon's reckoning, 60,000 spectators witnessed the *carrousel* from the stands and pavilions surrounding the square, surely a grossly exaggerated figure. This pageant, which recalled the elaborate festivals of the Valois court, officially inaugurated the Place Royale, and for Parisians as well as others who were given a first glimpse of the new square in the numerous paintings and engravings of the royal ceremony, it marked the Place Royale as an aristocratic space.

In the following years, the square increasingly became the exclusive precinct of the nobility. It was here that noblemen practiced the equestrian arts, held tilting matches and jousts; in 1613 students of the royal instructor Antoine de Pluvinel performed an equestrian ballet, and Pluvinel illustrated his equestrian treatises with engravings of Louis XIII and his attendants at the square (Fig. 77). [120] Guidebooks and prints associated the Place Royale with these aristocratic entertainments, while the campaign for French silk came to an unnoticed end. When the obligation to maintain the manufacturing business terminated in 1615, Moisset immediately sold the *maison des moulins,* and his former partners replaced the silkworkers with rent-paying tenants in the houses north of the Place Royale (see Appendix A5).

The development of the area north of the square reinforced the aristocratic character of the neighborhood. The property at the end of the rue de Béarn, the street leading north from the Queen's Pavilion, was acquired in 1609 by the Minim order (see Fig. 73). The Minims had strong monarchical ties, counting the queen regent as well as several Place Royale property owners among their

Fig. 77. Crispin de Passe, tilting games at the Place Royale. Antoine de Pluvinel, *Maneige Royal,* 1623. (B.N. Est. Ke 7)

supporters.[121] The church was aligned with the central axis of the Place Royale, but it did not receive a proper facade until François Mansart designed one in 1657, which at last exploited the opportunity to view the church through the arches of the Queen's Pavilion. When work was abandoned in 1662, Mansart's monumental design was only realized up to the pediment of the first story. The facade was completed a decade later, after the architect's death, according to a modified design.[122] The convent was destroyed at the end of the eighteenth century (1793–98) in order to extend the rue de Béarn one block to the north.

Near the end of Louis XIII's reign, the Place Royale was permanently altered. In 1639, Cardinal de Richelieu placed an equestrian monument of Louis XIII in the middle of the square (see Fig. 69). The figure of the king, sculpted by Pierre II Biard, sat astride the horse that Daniele da Volterra had cast in 1566 for Catherine de' Medici's unfinished statue of Henri II.[123] The square yielded to the cult of the glorified king, yet the bourgeois character of the architecture was never entirely forgotten. Later in the century, prostitutes solicited customers under the arches of the Place Royale, and others used the gallery in more reputable ways that nonetheless showed they implicitly understood it was intended for commerce. In 1682, the noble residents, unhappy to see the public making use of the square as Henri IV had intended, created a private garden enclosed by a grill to which only they had keys. The Place Royale had become the privileged ground of the nobility, a space that segregated courtiers from the life of the city. By the end of the seventeenth century, Henri IV's plan for a square in which manufacturing and trade were encouraged by the crown was no longer even conceivable as his successors guided the absolute monarchy along an altogether different path, one that exiled the court from the capital and immersed it in a world of magnificence and ceremony at Versailles.

Renamed the Place des Vosges by Napoleon, the square has survived the centuries relatively unscathed, suffering only two major changes. The original equestrian monument, destroyed in 1793 during the French Revolution, was replaced in 1829 by a new statue of Louis XIII made by Dupaty and Cortot, and the small entrance pavilion at the northeast corner was demolished in 1825 to accommodate circulation across the north side of the square. In recent years, the Place des Vosges has again become a fashionable area, with the pavilions restored and the facades repointed. With shops and cafés now surrounding the square, it is not difficult to imagine it as the center of high-priced trade that Henri IV had envisioned.

CHAPTER THREE

THE PLACE DAUPHINE, PONT NEUF, AND RUE DAUPHINE

At the turn of the seventeenth century, the Ile de la Cité was one of the most active commercial districts in Paris. Booksellers, money changers, goldsmiths, and jewelers were concentrated on the island—on its shop-lined bridges and along the quais. The Cité attracted customers from all over Paris, in part because it was the administrative center of the capital. At the east end of the island were the cathedral of Notre-Dame and the general hospital, the Hôtel Dieu. At the west end were the courts, contained within a walled enclave known as the Palace because the Capetian kings had lived there long ago, before the Louvre was built. For the convenience of the judges, lawyers, and clerks who staffed the judicial administration, the Palace contained bookshops specializing in politics, law, and history, and banking offices where money was exchanged and other credit operations were performed. The Palace was also the meeting place of the Parlement of Paris, the political body responsible for registering the edicts of the king, and the home of the Parlement's president, Achille de Harlay. Beyond his house, at the very tip of the island, was a garden, partially enclosed by the Palace wall.

In March 1607, Henri IV gave the western tip of the island—from the garden to the Pont Neuf—to Achille de Harlay, who was in turn required to build the Place Dauphine. The first published report about the Place Dauphine appeared in the *Mercure françois* in its annals of 1608:

> [Henri IV] . . . had the Parc-Royal [Place Royale] designed to serve as a place of exchange or of brokerage [*place de change ou de Bourse*]; but being in one of the corners of the city and too far from the Palace where the bankers always have business after leaving the courts, this year he began to have the Place Dauphine built at the tip of the Ile du Palais [Ile de la Cité], and he has made a site which was essentially useless the most beautiful and useful spot in Paris . . .[1]

Although the description of the Place Royale was slightly inaccurate, the misstatement underscores the connection between money exchange, merchant banking, and the trade and manufacture of gold-threaded silk for which the first square was planned. The failure of the Place Royale had not vanquished the king's urban policies; it was the prelude to a second, more successful attempt to build a commercial square.

While the Place Dauphine fulfilled the king's urban and economic goals, embellishing the city while serving the predominantly merchant and artisan community, in the years thereafter architects and agents of the crown found little to admire at the square. They did not share Henri IV's commitment to mercantile and artisanal activity and considered the small-scaled brick buildings inappropriate for so prominent a site. Despite repeated calls for the demolition of the Place Dauphine that began in the late 1600s and continued over the next two centuries, it survived intact until the mid 1800s, when two ranges were destroyed. But over time, the condition of the square deteriorated sharply, partly as a consequence of its intensive use, and partly because the crown saw little benefit in improving buildings that failed to meet emerging standards of urban design.

The shabby condition of the buildings over the last two centuries partially explains why architectural historians, who traditionally favor more glamorous monuments, have ignored the square. What little has been written about the Place Dauphine concerns the role of Achille de Harlay: in 1911, Mallevoüe published the contract setting forth the terms of the king's donation, and in 1966, Babelon traced Harlay's initial sale of lots at the square. The design of the square and the aftermath of sale, the process of making the Place Dauphine, remain unexamined.[2]

The development methods tested at the Place Royale were adjusted at the Place Dauphine to enable merchants and artisans to build and occupy the shops and houses. The royal designers also demonstrated a growing interest in tying together different parts of the city, both visually and physically. Rather than viewing the Place Dauphine as self-contained, the designers joined the square into a network of interlocking elements with the Pont Neuf and the rue Dauphine, the Seine and the quais. The exterior facades of the Place Dauphine overlooked the busy quais, participating in splendid vistas, while the interior of the square formed an intimate and enclosed space. A masterful piece of urban design, the Place Dauphine was engaged in the surrounding fabric but unencroached upon by its traffic. It served as both a public monument for all of Paris and a space of privacy carved from the urban tissue.

THE PONT NEUF AND THE SITE OF THE PLACE DAUPHINE

For centuries, the kings of France cultivated a garden at the west end of the Ile de la Cité. At the tip of the island, inserted in the garden wall, was a pavilion called

Fig. 78. West end of the Ile de la Cité. c. 1500. *Très Riches Heures du Duc de Berry,* fol. 6. (Musée Condé, Chantilly; Giraudon/Art Resource) In the background are the Maison des Etuves, set in the wall, and the Palace.

Fig. 79. Olivier Truschet and Germain Hoyau, map of Paris (Basel plan), detail of the Ile de la Cité, before 1559. (Bibliothek der Universität Basel AA 124)

the Maison des Etuves overlooking two small islets in the river (Figs. 78, 79). In February 1578, Henri III had decided to build a new bridge, the Pont Neuf, which crossed the Seine 12 *toises* from the tip of the Cité, including one of the offshore islets on its path.[3] The gulf between the bridge and the Cité was filled in, and on that annexed land and on part of the garden, the Place Dauphine was built.[4]

The Pont Neuf had a double function. It was conceived as a means of entering the Cité from the west and of traveling between the Right and Left banks.[5] In particular, the bridge was intended to link the royal palace to the church of the Augustins where Henri III's confraternity, the Order of the Holy Spirit, was based. Three successive designs for the Pont Neuf were established during Henri III's reign, each one connecting the bridge to the island in a different way, each one affecting the site of the Place Dauphine. In order to understand the conditions of the site as well as the changes in the crown's urban strategy, the history of the Place Dauphine must begin with the Pont Neuf.

The king chose the original design for the bridge in February 1578. A surveyor's report the following month disclosed the project's three principal features, which are depicted in an anonymous sixteenth-century painting (Fig. 80).[6] First, the course of the bridge was to follow a straight line with eight arches across the north arm of the Seine, four arches across the south arm, and an intermediary platform on the island — the *terre-plein* — $28\frac{1}{2}$ *toises* wide. Second, unlike the other bridges in the city, which were all lined with buildings, the Pont Neuf was planned without any houses, promising an unobstructed view of the river. And third, a street was projected along the south side of the island running from the Pont Neuf to the Pont St. Michel.[7] The painting also depicts an elaborate superstructure with triumphal arches, obelisks, and pavilions; these elements, however, are not mentioned in the documents and may not have won the king's approval.[8] To prepare the site, experts recommended three measures: removing the smaller islet from the river; raising the level of the larger islet to the height of the bridge; and piercing the Palace wall and appropriating some of its property to build the raised street. The crown had no intention of developing the annexed land at the tip of the Cité. As the painting shows, this terrain was treated as interstitial space, a void traversed by the bridge and the road.

Soon after construction began on the southern piles, one of the builders of the Pont Neuf, Pierre des Isles, informed the supervisory commission that the

Fig. 80. Anonymous, project for the Pont Neuf, c. 1578. (Musée Carnavalet; Photographie Bulloz, Paris)

bridge should not cross the Seine in a straight line as planned. He argued persuasively that the bridge would better resist the river currents if its two sections were slightly angled, and following his suggestion, the commissioners decided in May 1578 to introduce a bend at the juncture with the island.[9] This decision seems to have provoked a reevaluation of other structural considerations. There are no records of the commission's proceedings during the following year, but when the minutes resume in June 1579, it is clear that other changes had been made in the design of the bridge.

The second design, which was finalized during the summer of 1579, entailed two crucial changes.[10] First, the distribution of arches was altered from eight and four to seven and five. There was no difficulty in implementing this change on the north side because construction was not yet under way. However, on the south side, where the four piles closest to the Left Bank were already built, the addition of a fifth arch meant cutting into the platform on the island. Consequently, the width of the *terre-plein* was reduced from 28½ *toises* to approximately 19 *toises*. The second major change was the addition of houses on the bridge.[11] This decision, which eliminated the most distinctive feature of the Pont Neuf, probably stemmed from the crown's unwillingness to sacrifice the prospective rental income.

The second design for the Pont Neuf initially guided construction on the island. The foundations of the *terre-plein* were completed by April 1581.[12] That summer, construction of the raised street began at the east end, near the Pont St. Michel. The course of the street as originally planned in 1578 had to be altered to accommodate the diminished width of the platform. The documents do not comment on this adjustment, but it seems that the street was simply shifted over to the platform, 9¼ *toises* to the north. Construction of the street proceeded from August 1581 through 1584, but the irregular payments to the mason during those three and a half years suggest that work advanced slowly.[13] How much was built is unclear, but the road certainly did not reach the Pont Neuf, as we can see in a drawing of 1583/84 which shows the platform of the bridge under construction but the tip of the island otherwise unaltered (Fig. 81).

The third scheme, which dates from 1584, only affected the island. In need of money to finish the bridge, the crown decided to sell the land at the tip of the Cité and to impose a building requirement on the purchasers. The king authorized the project in June 1584, before a specific street plan or house design was established:

> Specifications shall be established for each and every street which will
> be needed to go from the Pont Neuf to our Palace and to other places
> and locations in our city; and to make these streets and passages, demol-

Fig. 81. Anonymous, procession of Henri III, c. 1583/84. (B.N. Est. rés. Pd 29) The Pont Neuf is seen under construction from the Right Bank. The Maison des Etuves appears in the middle ground, and the church of the Grand Augustins on the Left Bank rises in the distance.

ish if necessary whatever is required of the houses assigned to the prebends of the canons of the Sainte Chapelle . . . , take their gardens as well as whatever amount of land is needed for these roads from our garden of the Bailliage and Maison des Estuves; . . . auction [the lots] to the highest bidder . . . with the requirement that the purchasers build houses within the time and according to the plans and designs to be stipulated by the commissioners so that the houses are uniform and alike, if possible, with the same street facade and front for the decoration of the street. . . . [14]

This plan involved quais on both sides of the island as well as other roads, as both the royal edict and the registration by the Parlement a month later make clear.[15] In the standard history of the Pont Neuf, Boucher incorrectly wrote that the scheme only involved the raised road on the south side of the island, failing to appreciate that an entirely new plan for the island was introduced in 1584.[16] The project envisioned by the crown in fact covered the entire tip of the Cité, the future site of the Place Dauphine.

The project proceeded haltingly. The canons of the Sainte Chapelle fought to preserve their garden, but two years later, the commissioners moved ahead. In

Fig. 82. Pont Neuf and Place Dauphine. Engraving by Israël Silvestre, c. 1660s. (B.N. Est. Ed 45)

July 1586, they commissioned a rendering of the project to be displayed during the public auction.[17] Then, the minutes drop all mention of the venture. The sale never occurred, blocked by the same political and economic pressures that soon brought construction of the bridge to a standstill. We have no record of the facade design or street plan proposed by Henri III's commissioners, but the possibility that they anticipated the Place Dauphine, that the design of the square was established in 1586, must be considered. Our only clue, the reference to streets and passages, "rues et passages," leads us to conclude that the crown had not designed a square, but a traditional sixteenth-century *lotissement* on a modified grid plan, similar to the scheme for the parc des Tournelles. Nevertheless, Henri III's project was an important precedent for the Place Dauphine, envisioning a residential development on the same site, with the same building type and the same formal device of uniform facades. But the Valois king lost the opportunity to embellish Paris. In 1588, the civil war brought an end to all building projects.

Henri IV's Plan for the Cité

A decade later, in February 1598, Henri IV announced his intention to complete the Pont Neuf, his first public building project in Paris. When construction resumed in 1599, the piles in the north arm of the Seine reached the springing of the arches, and the vaults on the south side were closed. It is unclear how high the platform on the island rose, but at least its foundations were built. Otherwise, the west end of the island was little changed: the recently annexed islet may have been partially terraced, but the Maison des Etuves was still standing and the walled garden still cultivated with flowers.[18] On the south side of the island, the raised street was only partially constructed, but its trajectory to the Pont Neuf was fixed.

Henri IV established a new scheme for the Pont Neuf and for the west end of the Cité. He decided to complete the bridge without any houses, to place a royal equestrian statue on the platform of the bridge, and to create the Place Dauphine (Fig. 82). These projects were not all established in 1599; they evolved during the next seven years with the Place Dauphine the last element to take shape. The open bridge, the monumental statue in a public location, the planned square: Henri IV was the first to realize each of these canonical forms in the capital, but the importance of his scheme was due not to the individual components but to their interaction. Together they inaugurated a new strategy of urban development.

The decision to complete the Pont Neuf without any encumbering buildings dated from the reopening of the chantier. When construction resumed in 1599 on the south arm of the bridge, the chief masons, François Petit and Guillaume Marchant, closed the basement spaces that were built during the reign of Henry III.[19] The new design was calculated to exploit the view of the Louvre, which Henri IV was in the process of enlarging. The bridge unleashed

Fig. 83. Stefano della Bella, view of the Seine from the Pont Neuf, 1646. (B.N. Est. Va 419j)

the eye to roam the city at large, to discover the river and its banks as an enticing spectacle. It opened up a new way of seeing Paris, a possibility appreciated by Jacques Du Breul in the 1608 edition of his history of the city, which called attention to the raised shoulders of the Pont Neuf from which "to see the river." [20] The Seine was now regarded not only as an artery of trade but as a sight to be admired. So, too, the quais—prized as landing docks for river traffic— were reappraised in visual terms, and they emerged as the most privileged location for monumental buildings in seventeenth-century Paris. Henri IV's Pont Neuf encouraged an aesthetic perception of the city—the river, the quais and the buildings. The view from the bridge became one of the highlights of Paris, lavishly praised in descriptions of the city and endlessly depicted by artists as a spectacle of urban beauty that is no less thrilling today (Fig. 83). [21]

The Pont Neuf was opened to traffic in 1604, although construction was not entirely finished until July 1606. [22] One building adorned the bridge, abutting the second arch from the Right Bank (Fig. 84). In 1604, the crown commissioned the Flemish engineer Jean Lintlaer to build a pump. It was housed in a three-story pavilion called the Samaritaine because of a sculptural relief of the good Samaritan, which associated the Biblical episode of Christian charity with the king's effort to provide the city with water. [23] The *Prévôt des marchands*

Fig. 84. Franciscus Hoiamis, map of Paris, detail, 1619. (B.N. Est. Va 212)

LA STATVE EQVESTRE DE HENRY LE GRAND SVR SON PIE-DESTAIL

HENRICO.
MAGNO.
U&c.

A' LA REYNE

Grande Reyne égale à ce Grand Roy, est par vous que reffeurit le L51 si vostre belle Florence choisi tant nostre belle Fleur, de grace ne dedaignez, ce reçeves portraict du portrait de l'unique chesf de vostre Ame: son vous a esté donné, l'autre vous est deub, car autre que vous rien est capable. Le bronze eternisera bien sa memoire dans les siecles, mais il ne peut le faire voir plus long qu'e son pourpris: Le papier plus autres bornes que l'Vnivers, il portera son Image par tout tant que son Nom est oüy.

Fig. 85. Pietro Francavilla and Pietro Tacca, equestrian statue of Henri IV on the Pont Neuf, c. 1614. Anonymous engraving. (B.N. Est. Va 224b)

described the crown's intentions in a declaration to the municipal government in 1601, emphasizing the king's concern for the well-being of Parisians:

> His Majesty announced his intention to spend his years in this city and live here like a true patriot, to make this city beautiful, splendid . . . and full of all the conveniences and ornaments that he possibly can. . . . His Majesty, having understood that, for lack of fountain water, many people are subjected to kidney stones [*maladies de grevelle*], desirous not only to protect us from our enemies but also to care for our health; having given us peace, [he] wants to embellish this city by completing the Pont Neuf and restoring fountains that once flowed. . . . In his words, he wishes to make this city an entire world and a miracle on earth, which certainly shows us a love that is more than paternal.[24]

To improve the water supply in the city, the crown reactivated several fountains. But Lintlaer's pump did not benefit the general public; via a reservoir in the cloister of St. Germain l'Auxerrois, it delivered water to the gardens of the Tuileries, serving only the king and the privileged few to whom he granted a special allotment.[25] Nevertheless, royal publicists effectively promoted the image of a populist king because his urban policies, however much they served the interest of the crown, were ultimately directed to a broader citizenry.

The second element of Henri IV's scheme for the Cité was the equestrian monument on the platform of the bridge. Commissioned by the queen from Giovanni Bologna in 1603/4, the statue was completed by Pietro Tacca and installed on the bridge in 1614 (Fig. 85).[26] It was the first large-scale royal monument in France to be placed in a public space, inspired by Bologna's earlier works for the Medici dukes in the Piazza della Signoria and the Piazza dell'Annuziata in Florence. Although the king was portrayed in modern armor with neither the laurel wreath nor mantle of a Roman general, as Louis XIV would don in his statues, the imperial associations of Henri IV's monument were nonetheless unmistakable. The inscription on the pedestal began *Errico IIII. Galliar. Imperat. Navar. Rex,* "To Henri IV, Emperor of the Gauls and King of Navarre." The four prisoners at the base of the statue and the reliefs on the pedestal — of Henri IV's great battles and his entry into Paris — were probably not planned until after the king's death, but they reiterate standard themes of his iconography: his military valor, the surrender of the enemy, and his restoration of peace.[27] When Henri IV's statue was unveiled in 1614, royal publicists compared the Bourbon king to a variety of Roman emperors, echoing the imperial imagery that was current during the last years of his reign, as we shall see in Chapter Six.[28]

We do not know when the crown decided to place the statue on the Pont Neuf. There is no evidence to support the prevailing view that this decision originated with Maria de' Medici, or even that it was made after she commissioned the monument.[29] It is entirely possible that there was an earlier plan for an equestrian statue on the bridge. A Dutch tourist, Arnold Van Buchel, saw the Pont Neuf under construction in September 1585, and in his travel diary he wrote, "I saw a statue of a horse that the king decided to place in the middle of the bridge, calling it the Pont de Valois . . ."[30] There is no corroborating evidence that Henri III entertained such a plan, but Catherine de' Medici's unexecuted project for an equestrian monument was certainly not forgotten by her son. In 1559/60, she commissioned an equestrian statue of Henri II for which only the horse was cast. It remained riderless in Rome until it was used eighty years later in the Louis XIII monument in the Place Royale, but a plaster mold was sent to the château of Fontainebleau and placed in the Cour du Cheval Blanc (Court of the White Horse), providing the court with its name.[31] In 1585, when Van Buchel heard rumors of a statue, the raised street on the south side of the island was aligned with the *terre-plein,* in accordance with the second scheme for the bridge. Even with houses on the two arms of the bridge, it is not inconceivable that a statue was planned for the platform. The street provided an axial view of the platform, a feature later exploited by Henri IV's architects.[32]

It is useful to consider the possibility that a project for a statue on the Pont Neuf predated Maria de' Medici's commission, if only to assess her role in the development of the Cité more carefully. The Medici queen has been credited for the conception of the *terre-plein* as well as the Place Dauphine, but these attributions are not based on concrete evidence. They spring from a misguided belief that Florentine culture exerted an inevitable and unmediated influence in France through the queen.[33] Medici traditions of patronage certainly exerted a general influence on the Bourbon king; the royal statue was a product of the Medici court and its artists, and Henri IV was surely aware of the new ducal foundation at the port of Livorno as he set upon remodeling Paris.[34] Yet Medici precedents do not account for the specific character of Henri IV's urbanism, which was shaped by his social policies and by the formal inventions of the royal architects.

In June 1603, when Petit and Marchant resumed construction of the road on the south side of the island, the quai des Orfèvres, the crown had not yet drawn up further plans for the island. By the time the quai was largely completed, in the winter of 1607, Henri IV had decided upon his next move: a square on the west end of the Cité.

The Design of the Place Dauphine

On 10 March 1607, the king gave President Harlay the western tip of the Cité, 3,120½ square *toises* (about 3 acres), extending from the garden to the Pont Neuf and from bank to bank. In exchange for the land, Harlay was required to execute a project in accordance with plans to be provided by Sully.[35] The project remained a mystery for another two months, until the crown established the name and design of the Place Dauphine. The name paid tribute to the dauphin, the future Louis XIII, whose birth in 1601 assured the continuation of the Bourbon dynasty. The king approved the design of the Place Dauphine in May 1607 and imposed a new condition on Harlay: the developer had to complete the square within three years. "My friend," the king wrote Sully on 13 May, "I send you this note to advise you that as soon as you have received it, you are to see the first president to settle the Place Dauphine according to the design that you showed me so that it is done in three years. If he does not want to do it, find someone else

Fig. 86. Vassallieu dit Nicolay, map of Paris, detail of the Place and rue Dauphine, 1609. (B.N. Est. rés. Hennin XV 1352)
Key: 1. Place Dauphine; 2. site of the Collège de France

Fig. 87. François Quesnel, map of Paris, detail of the Place and rue Dauphine, 1609. (B.N. Est. rés. AA 3)
Key: 1. Pont Neuf; 2. Place Dauphine; 3. rue Dauphine; 4. site of the Collège de France

who will undertake it, and tell him that he will profit from the land." [36] The king was offering Harlay a pot of gold. He could sell the building lots, transfer the construction requirement to the lot owners, and retain the revenue from the land sale.

None of the original drawings of the Place Dauphine survives, and we must rely primarily on later drawings to reconstruct the design. The three images from Henri IV's reign are all inaccurate, although they may reflect preliminary ideas for the square. The maps of Nicolay and Quesnel, published in 1609 before construction began, illustrate variant schemes (Figs. 86, 87). Nicolay was surely ill-informed in depicting a horseshoe-shaped square, but Quesnel conceivably recorded a preliminary project with an entrance pavilion on the Pont Neuf and individually roofed houses, both features of the Place Royale. The engraving after Chastillon correctly depicts the triangular form of the square but not the elevation. In the executed scheme, a doorway was framed by an arched shop-front on each side, whereas the engraving shows an A-B rhythm (Fig. 88). But Chastillon probably did not copy a discarded design; various distortions and inaccuracies in the engraving suggest that he simply took liberties with the elevation.[37] The most reliable evidence is provided by three measured drawings: a plan prepared in the studio of Robert de Cotte in 1685, and two plans by the Abbé Delagrive from the 1740s (Figs. 89–91).

The Place Dauphine had two components: a triangular square and a row of houses facing the base of the triangle. The row of houses extended uninterruptedly along a cross street (the rue de Harlay) and then turned onto the quais, wrapping around the perimeter of the Palace. The entrance to the Palace in the middle of the rue de Harlay, seen on the de Cotte and Delagrive plans, was only opened in 1671 to remedy a problem in the original design: the rue de Harlay buildings prevented direct circulation between the law courts and the square (see Figs. 89, 91). The enclosure along the rue de Harlay, correctly illustrated by Chastillon, confirms that the Place Dauphine was not conceived as a direct outlet for bankers upon leaving the Palace, contrary to the *Mercure françois* report (see Fig. 88).

The triangular shape of the square was suggested by the site, with the long sides of the triangle parallel to the diverging quais. Two entrances were opened along the central axis of the square: at the point of the triangle leading to the Pont Neuf, and at the midpoint of the base leading to the rue de Harlay. The square was otherwise enclosed by two continuous files of houses that formed asymmetric halves of the triangle.

The Place Dauphine was not an isosceles triangle, as is frequently stated, but a distinctly irregular triangle. Those irregularities, evident in the de Cotte

[127]

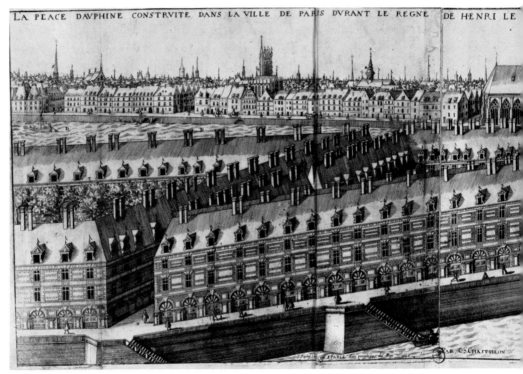

Fig. 88. Place Dauphine viewed from the Right Bank, 1607–15. Engraving after Claude Chastillon. (B.N. Est. rés. Ve 9)

and Delagrive plans, are still visible in the square today (see Figs. 89, 90). The southeast corner formed a more acute angle than the northeast corner; both segments of the southern half of the square were longer than those of the northern half; and the range of houses along the north quai—the quai de l'Horloge—was not uniformly wide, narrowing as it approached the Pont Neuf from inside the square. In addition, the south quai—the quai des Orfèvres—was wider than the north quai by approximately 1½ *toises*.[38]

The forces that produced the asymmetry of the square also produced an even more prominent result: the Place Dauphine was not aligned with the royal statue on the Pont Neuf. While the statue was centered on the *terre-plein,* it was approximately 3 *toises* south of the square's axis (Fig. 92). Consequently, the statue obliquely regarded the *place,* and only a partial view of the monument was possible from within the square (Fig. 93). Two of the best-informed historians of Paris, Henri Sauval and Jean-Baptiste Jaillot, criticized the misalignment.[39] Nevertheless, their comments have been overlooked by modern writers, convinced by idealized engravings that Henri IV's figure was placed on the axis of the square. Sauval offered two explanations for the misalignment in a passage

that deserves to be quoted at length, since no other attempt has been made to account for the placement of the statue:

> Both the sculptor and the mason unquestionably had very little skill to have so poorly positioned the pedestal and the statue that they can hardly be seen from within the Place Dauphine while the king views the entry [to the square] with a side glance and an evil eye. I am told that they erected the statue at the tip of the island, in the center of the area that separates the two bridges [i.e. the *terre-plein*]; and thus with respect to this irregularity, the fault lies with François Petit, supervisor of the Place Dauphine, for having made one of the quais much wider than the other, as a result of which the point of the *place* is not situated in the middle of the Ile du Palais. I grant that this explanation may defend them [i.e. the sculptor and mason], and besides it is the only one that can; nevertheless, it hardly suffices because they should have foreseen that the failure to place this statue at the entrance of the square deprived the bridge of an essential adornment. Indeed, given the condition that the tip of the Ile du Palais was then in, it would have been easy for them to establish its center where they wanted; and perhaps it is for this reason that Petit was not concerned about placing the point of the Place Dauphine exactly in the middle of the island.[40]

The first cause of the misalignment, Sauval supposed, was the unequal width of the quais, and for this, he blamed the sloppy work of the mason François Petit. But if without widening the island (for this is Sauval's initial premise), the placement of the square were simply shifted to the south by a *toise* so that the quais were equally wide, the axis of the square would still not intersect the statue. The misalignment could not be corrected simply by shifting the square due south, as Figure 94 demonstrates; it also would have been necessary to redesign the rue de Harlay entrance and to undertake major construction of the south quai.

[129]

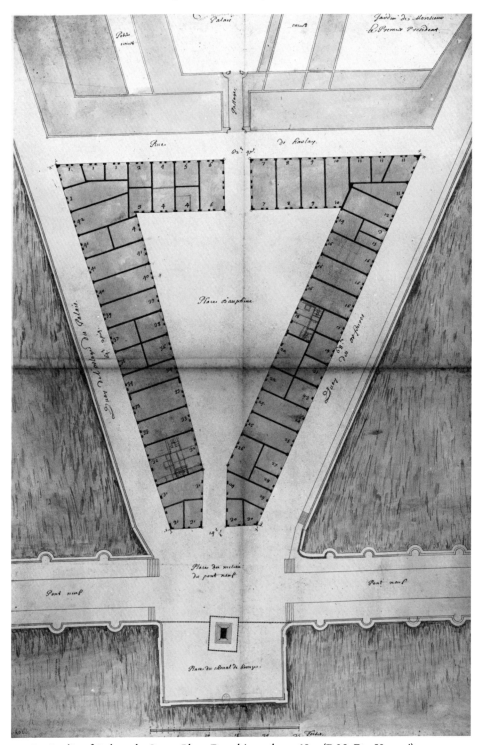

Fig. 89. Studio of Robert de Cotte, Place Dauphine, plan, 1685. (B.N. Est. Va 419j)

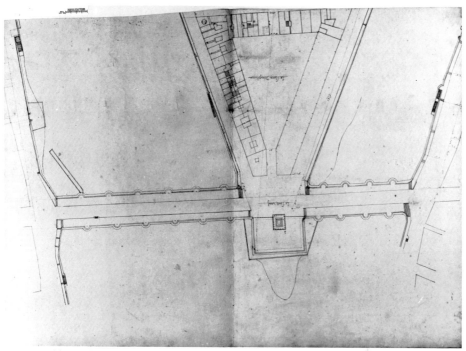

Fig. 90. Abbé Delagrive, Place Dauphine, plan (upside down), c. 1740s. (B.N. Est. rés. Ve 53h)

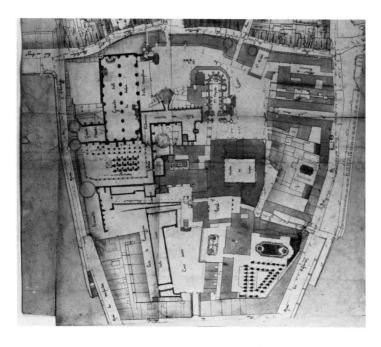

Fig. 91. Abbé Delagrive, Palace and rue de Harlay, plan, c. 1740s. (B.N. Est. rés. Ve 53j)

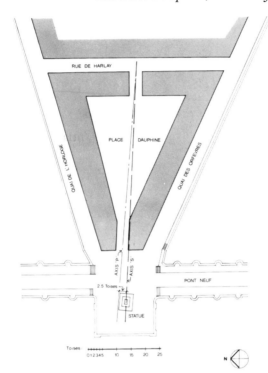

Fig. 92. Place Dauphine, plan showing misalignment of the statue and square. (Drawing by Julia Rogoff based on the 1685 de Cotte plan)
Key: Axis S: from the center of the statue on the *terre-plein* through the rue de Harlay entrance; Axis P: through the two entrances to the Place Dauphine

Fig. 93. View from the Place Dauphine to the statue of Henri IV. (Author)

As Sauval realized, the underlying problem was that the *terre-plein* was not centered with respect to the island. To bring them into alignment required the remodeling of either the island or the platform. The first option was to enlarge the island to the south; the architects would then have had to reposition the square and modify the Pont Neuf entrance in order to preserve its symmetry, as Figure 95 illustrates. Sauval did not consider this solution, perhaps because the work involved in rebuilding the quai des Orfèvres was so substantial.

The second option was to rebuild the *terre-plein*. The failure of the sculptor and mason to pursue this option was Sauval's second explanation for the misalignment, and on this point, Sauval was right. If the *terre-plein* were enlarged, the statue could have been aligned with the *place* while still remaining centered on its platform (Fig. 96). While changes to the *terre-plein* would have deformed the abutting arches of the Pont Neuf, the arches were irregular in size from the start. The arch on the south side of the island was deformed during the construction of the bridge (when the number of arches was changed from eight and four to seven and five); and according to the Delagrive plan, the arch abutting the north side of the island was also narrower than its neighbors (see Fig. 90). De Cotte pursued the second option when he proposed a new project for the site in 1685 (Fig. 97). Although he radically redesigned the buildings, de Cotte retained the axis of the rue de Harlay entrance from the original design; in order to align the equestrian monument with that axis, he extended the *terre-plein* to the south.

De Cotte's project suggests a third option which Sauval did not mention: entirely redesigning the Place Dauphine. If the square were reshaped and its central axis suppressed, the alignment of the statue would have posed no problem. Given the cost and difficulties involved in altering the site, the simplest solution certainly would have been to redesign the *place*. Yet Henri IV's architects rejected all of these alternatives; they made no attempt to modify the site or to redesign the square.

The misalignment did not result from ineptitude or carelessness, but from conscious choice. The axial relation between the statue and the square was simply not the paramount concern of Henri IV's architects. Unlike Sauval, they regarded the misalignment as an inoffensive feature and focused on other formal priorities. If we start with the premise that intentional design decisions produced the misalignment and geometric irregularities of the Place Dauphine, we can recognize what those priorities were.

Let us begin by asking why Henri IV's architects made the quais unequally wide, a question that takes us back to 1579 when the location and dimensions of the *terre-plein* were fixed. At that time, the *terre-plein* was not planned in relation

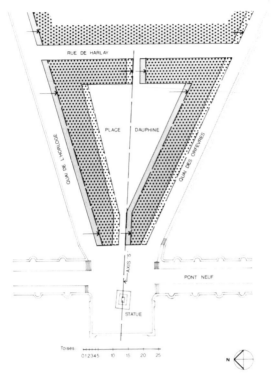

Fig. 94. Sauval's error: the Place Dauphine could not have been aligned with the statue simply by shifting the square to the south. (Drawing by Julia Rogoff based on the 1685 de Cotte plan)

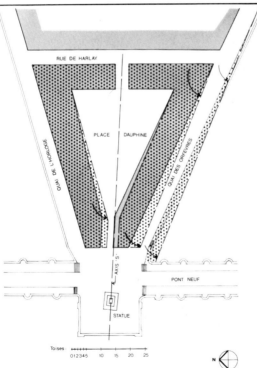

Fig. 95. Option I: realigning the Place Dauphine by enlarging the island. (Drawing by Julia Rogoff based on the 1685 de Cotte plan) The Place Dauphine could have been centered on the axis of the statue if the south side of the island were enlarged and the Pont Neuf entrance redesigned to maintain the symmetry of the facade.

to the west end of the island; the future site of the Place Dauphine was just a hole in the ground, as the Carnavalet painting illustrates (see Fig. 80). The *terre-plein* was conceived strictly in relation to the raised street, which later became the quai des Orfèvres; the perspective view from the quai to the platform was the important formal relationship. Even after the site of the square was filled in, the quai and the platform preserved the same formal relationship that had been established in 1579. Henri IV's architects wanted to exploit this feature of the site so that it was possible to view the royal equestrian monument the full length of the quai des Orfèvres. If the Place Dauphine were positioned so that the quais were equally wide, that view would be lost. On the other hand, if the quai des Orfèvres were slightly wider, the perspective view of the statue would be preserved. The view from the north quai was unaffected by this change, for in both cases, the statue was invisible almost the entire length of the quai (Fig. 98). Furthermore, the importance attached to the perspective view explains why the statue was angled toward the quai des Orfèvres, as seen on the de Cotte plan (see Fig. 89). As for the unequal width of the quais, it was only noticeable from the *terre-plein.* The de Cotte and Delagrive plans indicate that the architects masked the inequality at that spot by slightly widening the north quai where it joined the Pont Neuf (see Figs. 88, 90). Thus Henri IV's architects accepted the inequality of the quais, knowing that it could only be perceived in plan, in order to structure an urban experience: the experience of viewing the royal statue as one moved along the quai des Orfèvres.

What then accounts for the irregularities of the *place?* The square was formed by two superimposed geometries, both generated by the surrounding urban context: one by the shape of the island, the other by the Pont Neuf. The two long side ranges were parallel to the quais, and because the latter were not symmetric, neither were the sides of the square. The entrances to the square reflected a different set of considerations: the houses on the bridge and on the rue de Harlay were parallel to the Pont Neuf, the primary axis of circulation. The two incongruent geometries collided at the closed corners of the Place Dauphine and at the entrance on the bridge. The closed corners at the base of the triangle formed unequal angles, but the asymmetry presumably was tolerated because it was imperceptible from outside the square. At the highly visible main entrance to the square, however, the asymmetry would have been glaring. The architects corrected this by several local adjustments. They first established a symmetric facade on the Pont Neuf, which entailed widening the north quai, as mentioned above, so that the buildings appeared to be centered on the island. Then the architects opened a passageway into the square along the central axis of the Pont Neuf facade. But the side ranges obliquely intersected that axis such

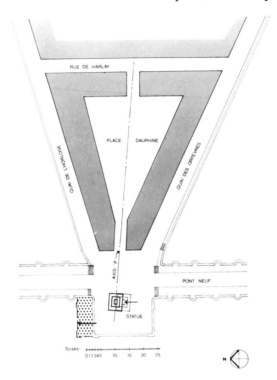

Fig. 96. Option II: realigning the Place Dauphine by enlarging the *terre-plein*. (Drawing by Julia Rogoff based on the 1685 de Cotte plan) The statue could have been centered on the axis of the Place Dauphine if the *terre-plein* were enlarged and the statue shifted to the north.

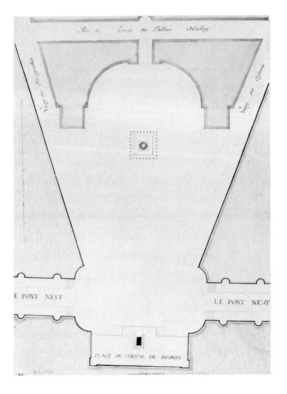

Fig. 97. Robert de Cotte, project for a monument on the site of the Place Dauphine, 1685. (B.N. Est. Va 226)

that the passageway was longer on the north side. In order to make the facades bordering the passageway equally long, the architects tapered the north range toward the Pont Neuf.

It was only within the square that the irregular geometry of the Place Dauphine was visible — the unequal corner angles and unequal length of the side ranges, if not the tapered north range. Once again, Henri IV's architects could have altered these features and formed an isosceles triangle within the square by appropriately aligning the interior facades. But they apparently attached more importance to maintaining regular housing lots and therefore made no attempt to disguise the irregular features of the square. The architects shaped the Place Dauphine from the outside in: first they established the orientation of the public facades overlooking the Seine; then they fixed the dimensions of the housing lots, which determined the alignment of the inner facades, those facing the interior of the square.

Henri IV's architects gave priority to the urban context. They abandoned the ideal figure of an isosceles triangle and shaped each side of the Place Dauphine in response to local site conditions. Rather than impose a unifying geometry on the design, the architects allowed different geometries to jostle with one another and handled each conflict differently. The south quai was widened to provide a perspective view of the statue, while symmetry was imposed on the prominent Pont Neuf facade, which required local adjustments to the north quai and north range. The resulting asymmetries and inequalities were accepted. From the world of the Renaissance with its respect for geometric purity, Henri IV's architects had traveled an enormous distance. They focused on the particular features of the site, on the experience of the passerby, on the urban dimension of design.

The argument that the Place Dauphine was finely attuned to its urban context is not inconsistent with the fact that the square formed an enclosed space. Its enclosure was not a means of disregarding the urban context, as some critics have concluded; it was, on the contrary, a subtle response to the city. The Place Dauphine was bordered by heavily traveled streets; the Pont Neuf and the quais had only just been built, but they were expected to be and indeed immediately became important arteries. With the monarch occupying and rebuilding the Louvre, the pressure of westward expansion was growing, and the Pont Neuf provided the westernmost link between the developing neighborhoods on both banks. The two new quais directed this traffic into the Cité: to the bustling commercial centers in the Marché Neuf, the Palace, and the shop-lined bridges; and to the institutions of civic life, the law courts, the cathedral, and the public hospital (Fig. 99). Henri IV's architects wanted to differentiate the

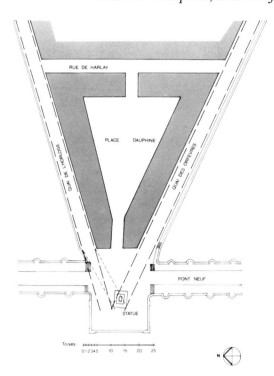

Fig. 98. Place Dauphine, sight lines from the quais to the statue. (Drawing by Julia Rogoff)

RUE DE HARLAY

QUAI DE L'HORLOGE

PLACE   DAUPHINE

QUAI DES ORFÈVRES

PONT NEUF

STATUE

Toises

0 1 2 3 4 5   10   15   20   25

N

character of the square from that of the surrounding streets. While the public facades participated in the hubbub of the quais and Pont Neuf, that tumult did not disturb the square.

The architects gave the Place Dauphine buildings this dual nature — public on one side, private on the other — in part through the design of the square's two entrances. At the Pont Neuf entrance, rather than have the side ranges spread apart at the threshold of the square, the end buildings tapered to create a narrow channel that separated the square from the bridge. This passage controlled physical access to the Place Dauphine, preventing Pont Neuf traffic from casually drifting into the square. Likewise, it controlled visual access, preventing comprehensive views of the space from the bridge. The location of the secondary entrance on the rue de Harlay cut the square off from primary roads. Rather than pierce the acute corners of the *place,* which would have put it in direct contact with the quais (as well as eliminating several irregular housing lots), the designers closed the corners and withdrew the entrance to a quieter secondary street, placing the opening in the middle of the square's east range (Fig. 100). The buildings bordering the circuitous route from the quai to the middle of the rue de Harlay made no architectural announcement of the entry; indeed, their uninterrupted uniformity minimized its importance. It should be noted that this entry was the one point from which it would have been possible to enjoy an axial view encompassing the square and the royal monument, had it been relocated on axis, yet the indirect approach to the rue de Harlay entrance as well as its unembellished architectural treatment make it clear that this possibility was not intended. Far from celebrating a privileged vantage point crucial to the perception and understanding of the Place Dauphine, the royal design masked the presence of the east entrance from outside the square.

Though buffered from the surrounding traffic, the square was nonetheless tightly bound to the neighborhood. As in the original scheme for the Place

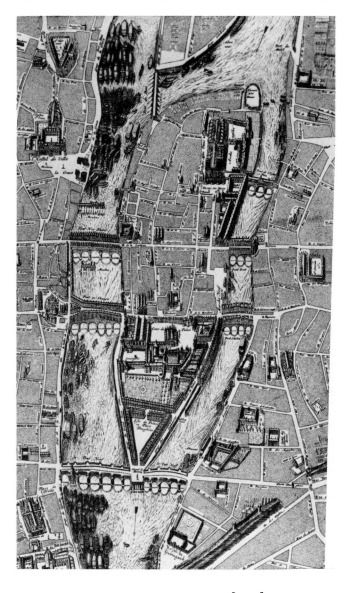

Fig. 99. Jacques Gomboust, map of Paris, detail of the Cité, 1652. (B.N. Est. Ve 31b)

Fig. 100. Place Dauphine, east range, before demolition in 1874. (B.N. Est. Va 226)

Royale, traffic entered the Place Dauphine along T-shaped axes that linked the square to the local streets. One approached the main entrance from a major artery—the Pont Neuf—which was perpendicular to the central axis of the square. Moving through the passageway, one entered the Place Dauphine on its central axis, marked at the far end by the second entrance. This axis of circulation abutted the houses on the rue de Harlay, which established the cross axis. Visually, the cross axis was unimportant, concealed as it was by the east side of the square, but it was asserted as an axis of circulation, with the rue de Harlay linking the two quais and providing a secondary approach to the square.

The effort to form an enclosed space at the Place Dauphine clarifies the misalignment of the equestrian monument and the square. The Place Dauphine and the royal statue were not harnessed to one regulating axis because they formed two independent spaces, as seventeenth-century guidebooks acknowledged in distinguishing between the Place Dauphine and the Place de Henri IV on the Pont Neuf.[41] The Place de Henri IV stood at the intersection of three major roads, an open space bustling with traffic. The Place Dauphine—that is, the interior of the square—formed a tranquil, enclosed precinct. The statue was not part of that interior space; it belonged to the *terre-plein,* to the Pont Neuf, and to the city at large.

Fig. 101. Place Dauphine viewed from the Pont Neuf. Engraving by Pérelle, c. 1650. (B.N. Est. Ee 76b)

Fig. 102. Place Dauphine viewed from the rue de Harlay. Engraving by Pierre Aveline, before 1722. (B.N. Est. Va 226)

Fig. 103. Anonymous, Place Dauphine, elevation, nineteenth century. (B.N. Est. Va 419j)

Fig. 104. Place Dauphine, houses facing the Pont Neuf. (Author)

Sauval could not accept the misalignment because he judged the Place Dauphine by different aesthetic standards than those of Henri IV's architects. Like other Frenchmen of his time, he valued axiality, symmetry, and ideal geometric forms. The aesthetic change that occurred between the reigns of Henri IV and Louis XIV is well illustrated in the seventeenth-century images of the Place Dauphine. Most later engravings distort the square, forcing the Place Dauphine to reveal itself through a perspective view that belies its form and

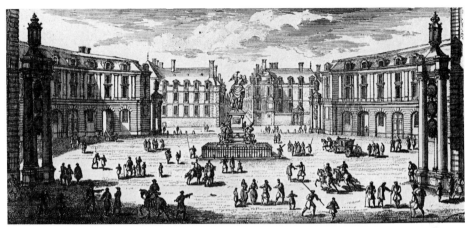

Fig. 105. Jules Hardouin Mansart, Place des Victoires, 1689. Anonymous engraving published by Jean Mariette, before 1714. (B.N. Est. Va 230e)

Fig. 106. Jules Hardouin Mansart, Place Louis XIV (Vendôme), 1699. Engraving by Pierre Aveline, before 1722. (B.N. Est. Va 234a)

urban posture. Pérelle's engraving, for example, exaggerates the central axis and reshapes the square as a rectangle (Fig. 101). Aveline, situating the viewer on the rue de Harlay, opened up the square by truncating the east range (Fig. 102). In both cases, the statue of Henri IV is placed on axis, correcting a misalignment that men of Louis XIV's age could only understand as the result of remarkable incompetence.

These distortions indicate how unaccommodating the Place Dauphine was to the axial structure and perspective view that artists later imposed on it with Procrustean rigor. The Place Dauphine was actually best appreciated through a sweeping vista from across the Seine. Silvestre and Chastillon captured this panoramic view encompassing quai, square, bridge, and statue (see Figs. 82, 88). The Place Dauphine revealed itself not from a fixed point, but through a series of changing views as one walked along the banks of the Seine and across the Pont Neuf. In this respect, we again encounter a departure from the Renaissance interest in structuring urban spaces by perspectival views and calculated vantage points. At the Place Dauphine, form was allowed to unfold through movement, and the space of the city was understood as a fluid sequence of possibilities.

We face the same uncertainties about the designer of the Place Dauphine as we did at the earlier square. Sauval attributed the project to François Petit; while Petit played a major role in the project, there is no evidence that his responsibilities exceeded those of a mason-contractor executing a scheme submitted to him.[42] The square bears a striking resemblance to the Place Royale, with respect to the elevation and building materials as well as the T-shaped axes of circulation (Figs. 103, 104). Above an arcaded ground floor were two stories and an attic lit by dormers in the roof, providing three floors for residential use above the street-level shops. The commercial arcade was dressed with stone; the upper wall was faced in brick with window surrounds, tablets, and quoins in stone, and the roof was covered with slate. The lively colors of the building materials again dramatized the simple decorative vocabulary of the repetitive facade. The similarities between the two royal squares suggest the participation of the same minds, and with the design for the Place Dauphine emanating from Sully's office, we can be confident that he relied on the royal architects.

Because the Place Dauphine marks the first joint appearance of a royal square and royal statue, it has been cast as the prototype of the French *place royale.* Yet it is crucial to distinguish Henri IV's squares from those of Louis XIV, the Place des Victoires (1689) and the Place Vendôme (1699; Figs. 105, 106). In certain respects, the earlier squares provided the developmental model used for the later ones: private owners were required to comply with a royal facade design, behind which they could build as they pleased. But otherwise, the squares are profoundly different. Louis XIV's squares were stages for a royal monument. The open ground of the Place des Victoires was, in effect, a large pedestal to accentuate the statue in the center; Hardouin Mansart proportioned the circular *place* and the facades to expose the effigy of the king to its best advantage. The Places des Victoires and Vendôme were conceived as voids, the evacuation of a spatial field to give priority to one object. The Place Dauphine did not focus attention on an object, external or otherwise. Of course, Henri IV's architects could not prevent later transformations of the square; in 1801, Napoleon had a commemorative statue of General Desaix placed inside the square (see Fig. 100). Nevertheless, the original planners designed the square so that its architectural properties gave no priority to any one spot. The space within the Place Dauphine was not a void; it was more like a large room with no roof.

In addition to these formal differences, the squares had different social and political objectives. Louis XIV's squares, surrounded by houses of the nobility, deified the king; they magnificently inscribed the cult of the monarch in the form of the city. The Place Dauphine and the Place Royale, as originally conceived, were planned as commercial and artisanal centers. Of course, Henri IV expected the economic prosperity of Paris to lend greater glory to his reign, but his sponsorship and close identification with commerce dramatically differentiated his urban policies from those of the Sun King. It is to the shop-keepers and craftsmen who developed the Place Dauphine that we shall now turn.

ACHILLE DE HARLAY AND THE DEVELOPMENT OF THE SQUARE

Achille de Harlay (1535–1616) was an unlikely candidate to develop the Place Dauphine. In 1607, he was seventy-one years old, living on borrowed time by seventeenth-century standards of life expectancy, and he had never built anything before. Nonetheless, the king gave Harlay the land in gratitude for his loyalty during the Wars of Religion and in deference to his long association with the site. Harlay's entire life was centered in the Palace, where he ascended the ranks of the Parlement of Paris, the most prestigious of the sovereign courts.[43] A second-generation gown noble who married well, Harlay was a magistrate *(conseiller)* in 1557 and assumed his father's position as deputy to the first president *(président à mortier)* in 1572. He then succeeded his father-in-law, Christophe de Thou, in 1582 as the first president, the chief justice of the Parlement, an office he did not relinquish until 1611. Throughout his tenure as first president, Harlay lived in the Hôtel du Bailliage at the western edge of the Palace, overlooking the future site of the square. Despite his advanced age, he accepted the charge of executing the Place Dauphine, stirred no less by the chance to embellish the capital than by the project's lucrative prospects. Even with the construction requirements, the land donation was regarded by the crown and by Harlay as an opportunity for considerable private gain. The growing demand for housing and the vigorous real estate market in the capital seemed to guarantee the project.

The three-year term for completion of the square began in May 1607. In the first year, Harlay took no action, probably waiting for the crown to prepare the site: the Maison des Etuves and the Palace wall had to be demolished; the sunken tip of the island had to be raised to the level of the bridge; and the quais had to be completed.[44] The south quai required no more than minor work, but the north quai was yet to be built.[45] On 14 August 1608, the crown awarded the masonry contract for the north quai to François Petit, who immediately began construction at the Pont Neuf end.[46] Two weeks later, Harlay began selling lots at the square, requiring the buyers to execute the royal design. Some of the lots he retained, financing his own construction of rental houses with the profits from the land sale. The work was executed in three stages: the sale of all but the corner lots at the Place Dauphine (1608–9); Harlay's construction of the houses on the rue de Harlay (1609–13); and the sale of the remaining land at the square and the lots backing onto the Palace along the quais (1611–16).

The triangular *place* had been divided into twelve lots, either by Sully or Harlay; by January 1609, Harlay had sold ten of those lots (Figs. 107, 108; also see Appendix B3). The two oddly shaped corner lots were not yet sold when Sully raised concerns about the Place Dauphine at a meeting of the state council, the *Conseil du Roi,* on 11 April 1609. According to the minister, Harlay was not complying with the royal design, a design which the king had approved a month earlier, in March 1609. The council gave Harlay another chance to consider his actions and "direct[ed] him to declare if he wants and intends to continue the necessary construction at the Place Dauphine according to the specifications and designs."[47]

We do not know what conditions Harlay failed to meet, and whether they related to the original 1607 design or perhaps to a modified scheme that Sully submitted to the king in 1609. Conceivably, Harlay's failure to sell the two corner lots caused the problem, but it is also possible that the dispute stemmed from a counterclaim asserted by Sully to some of Harlay's land. There is some evidence that Henri IV authorized his minister to construct buildings along the quais of the Cité, opposite the side ranges of the Place Dauphine, an episode that is discussed further below. If Sully devised this self-serving project in early 1609, it would certainly have elicited a protest from Harlay. He proceeded with the development of the Place Dauphine, but the conflict with Sully was to follow him to his deathbed.

Shortly after selling ten lots at the square, Harlay launched the second phase of the project: construction of eighteen houses on the east side of the rue de Harlay. He financed the project with the money he raised from the land sale, a total of 103,617 *livres.*[48] Most of the rue de Harlay houses backed onto his own residence, which may explain why he chose to retain control of this property. Building began in the spring of 1609 and ended in 1613, at which time the cross street was named in the president's honor (see Appendix B1).

Meanwhile, the lots abutting the Palace along the quais remained unsold. It was certainly not because of any difficulty in finding buyers. Perhaps Harlay wanted to retain all the property adjacent to the Palace and was simply waiting for his rue de Harlay houses to generate sufficient rental income to cover the building costs. But time was running out on the aged developer. Between 1611 and 1616, he sold the empty lots — the corner lots at the square and those abutting the Palace — with the last parcel, a small slot on the quai des Orfèvres, sold one month before Harlay's death (see Appendix B3).

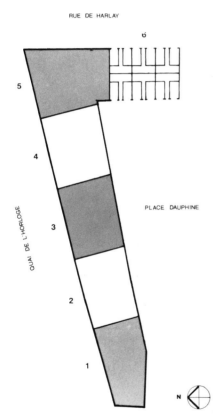

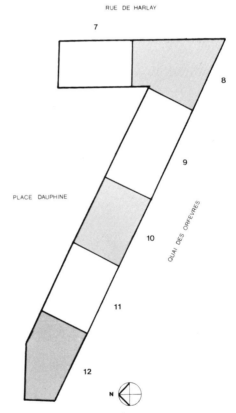

Fig. 107. Place Dauphine, north range, original lot division. (Drawing by Julia Rogoff based on A.N. F³¹ 94) Lot 6 illustrates the normative subdivision of a lot into six houses.

Fig. 108. Place Dauphine, south range, original lot division. (Drawing by Julia Rogoff based on A.N. F³¹ 94)

RUE DE HARLAY

Harlay hired François Petit (? – 1619), one of the most active masons in Paris, to build the eighteen houses on the rue de Harlay. In his official capacity as royal mason (*juré du Roi en l'office de maçonnerie*), Petit was involved in most of the municipal and royal projects during Henri IV's reign, serving as a contractor (*entrepreneur*), performing measured surveys (*toisés*), or completing technical reports (*expertises*). We know of only three private commissions, all from prestigious clients: in addition to his work for Harlay, he rebuilt the hôtel of Sébastien Zamet (1598), the king's banker, and constructed ten houses for the convent of the Augustins on the rue Dauphine (1608).[49] Petit's private practice was surely very active, but the full extent of his work will remain unknown until further discoveries are made in the notarial archives.

Harlay and Petit probably first met in connection with the Pont Neuf, a project with which both men had been involved since its inception. The president served on the royal commission which supervised construction, while Petit acted as a mason-contractor. Having relied on Petit for the Pont Neuf, the crown hired him to build the quai de l'Horloge in August 1608. Ten days later, the mason bought two Place Dauphine lots on the quai; they were the first lots that Harlay sold.[50] Petit's ingratiating purchase of this property and his long-term involvement in the development of the west end of the Cité must have promoted his candidacy as Harlay's mason.

The construction contract between Petit and the president was settled in the spring of 1609, and in August, Petit received a payment of 15,000 *livres* for his work during the summer.[51] The foundations were probably laid during this first year, and work on the facades was scheduled for the following season; Petit ordered 100,000 bricks and two tons of stone for delivery between April and August 1610.[52] A year later, carpenter Gilles Le Redde was instructed to do the carpentry work as soon as the masons finished.[53] Construction dragged on for nearly two more years; by 1612, six houses were finished, and the remaining twelve were completed in 1613 (see Appendix B1).

The building contracts do not provide sufficient information to extrapolate the total cost of construction, but given the cost of a similar house at the Place Dauphine (5,900 *livres*), we can estimate that Harlay spent roughly 106,000 *livres* to build the eighteen houses. The sale of Place Dauphine property, which brought in close to 104,000 *livres,* largely covered his building costs. The rue de Harlay houses generated 9,050 *livres* of rental income annually, a return on his investment of about 8.5 percent, assuming no debt financing was involved in the project.[54] Not only did the first president reap substantial financial benefit; he also had a street named in his honor and won credit for giving Paris a superb embellishment.

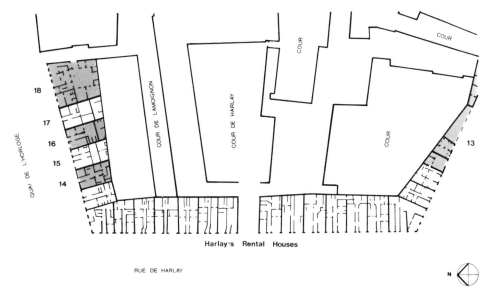

Fig. 109. Rue de Harlay, c. 1685. (Drawing by Julia Rogoff based on A.N. F³¹ 94) Numbered lots are identified in Appendices B3 and B4.

The houses on the rue de Harlay were probably identical in plan as in elevation, except for the corner buildings with two facades. The standard lot was approximately 4 *toises* wide (7.9 meters), half as wide as the Place Royale lots, and 6 *toises* deep (11.9 meters), with each house spanning two and a half bays. The only plan of these houses is the nineteenth-century cadastral plan, but by studying it in light of seventeenth-century descriptions, we can identify basic features of the original houses (Fig. 109). On the ground floor were two rooms, arcaded on the street and intended for commercial use, with a corridor in between leading to the court at the back of the house. The cadastral plan indicates that in some cases the staircase was situated at the end of the corridor, an unusual location for the stair, projecting into the courtyard and dividing it into two small sections. It would be tempting to suppose that this subdivision of the courtyard was a later modification, but some of the original leases describe the houses as having "two small courts," presumably to accommodate multiple tenants in the same house. Above the shops were two floors of apartment suites (bedrooms with adjacent antechambers) plus an attic room beneath the roof. This plan was typical of the Parisian bourgeois house, those Serlio recorded in his "casa al costume di franza," although the rue de Harlay houses did not include the two rear rooms shown in Serlio's larger project (see Fig. 63).

The majority of Harlay's tenants between 1611 and 1616 were merchants and artisans; there were several tailors, printers, and booksellers, along with a saddler, apothecary, joiner, and carpenter. Approximately a quarter were low-ranking courtiers, petty provincial magistrates, and minor judicial officers who worked in the adjacent law courts. Finally, there was a handful of widows living on modest inheritances of *rentier* income (see Appendix B2).

After Harlay's death, the buildings remained in his family, carefully maintained by the executor of his estate.[55] The houses were preserved intact until 1671, when the middle house was destroyed in order to provide access to the Palace. A taller, arched entrance pavilion was built which extended the central axis of the square and established a direct link between the courts and the Place Dauphine. Soon after this change, the great-grandson of the builder, Achille III de Harlay, sold the houses one by one during the 1670s and 1680s.[56]

THE CONSTRUCTION OF THE PLACE DAUPHINE

Property at the Place Dauphine was the most sought after in Paris, commanding far higher prices than land elsewhere in the city. In 1608, the lots at the square sold for 75 *livres* per square *toise* and those abutting the Palace on the quais for 72 *livres* per *toise.* Elsewhere in Paris, property could be bought on the rue Dauphine for 50 *livres* per *toise,* on the rue de Poitou—part of the Place de France development—for 11.4 *livres,* and at the Place Royale for less than 8 *livres.* The location of the Place Dauphine was ideal for commercial purposes, and thus commanded a substantial premium.

The procedures tested at the Place Royale were altered in four ways at the second square. First, the crown gave the entire site to one person rather than distributing the land among many recipients. Although this limited the opportunity for royal patronage, the reliance on Harlay—who functioned as a developer—effectively assured that the land would be used as residences by artisans and merchants, rather than the aristocracy.[57] Perhaps the crown also hoped that Harlay would personally build a large part of the square; by giving the developer sufficient land to generate substantial cash flow, the crown properly assumed Harlay might be more inclined to reinvest the money in large-scale construction.

Second, the royal architects defined a normative parcel of modest dimensions. When Marot engraved a plan of the square with uniform houses, he endowed the square with a regularity that it never possessed (Fig. 110); nevertheless, the plan elaborates an idea implicit in the original design. The elevation implied that a house spanned two and a half bays, 4 *toises* wide: a doorway with a mezzanine-level window above and an arch on each side. Each range had a depth of 8 *toises* and could accommodate two houses back to back, each one with

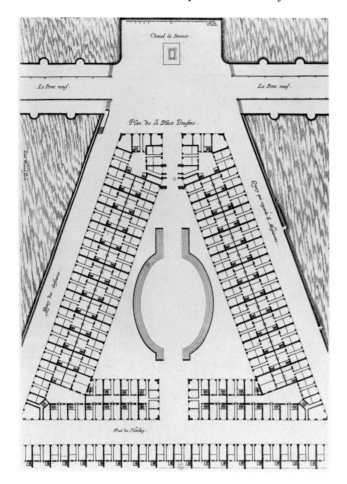

Fig. 110. Jean Marot, idealized plan of the Place Dauphine, *L'Entrée triomphante de Louis XIV et Marie Thérèse dans la ville de Paris,* 1662. (B.N. Est. Pd 43a)

a single brick-and-stone facade. Whereas the much larger Place Royale pavilions were suitable for either the aristocracy or wealthy artisans, there was no such ambiguity about the Place Dauphine buildings. These parcels, 4 *toises* square, were only fit for bourgeois housing.

Third, the crown allowed for flexibility with respect to the size of the individual houses. Subdivision was encouraged at the second square, and forty-five houses of varying sizes were built on the original twelve lots. The effect was to permit development consistent with the needs of individual craftsmen and merchants, and thus to enhance the financial viability of the project. Under these circumstances, the challenge was to devise a facade that could mask the irregularly sized houses behind it.

Fourth, unlike its counterpart at the Place Royale, the individual house at the Place Dauphine was subordinated to the overall unity of each range. In the skyline, a single roof covered an entire range, and the dormers, all with curved pediments, gave no hint of separate houses (see Fig. 103). While the facade implied that an individual house encompassed two and a half bays, various elements undermined the expression of this unit. A file of quoins demarcated the unit on the upper floors, yet this vertical line was not carried into the pier below; the entry bay and tablets above established a stronger vertical accent. Furthermore, on the ground floor, the uninterrupted stringcourse and the horizontal joints of the masonry visually detached the shops from the residential space above and emphasized the unity of the commercial arcade. At least in theory, property lines could be drawn anywhere without undermining the Place Dauphine facade.

By delegating responsibility for development to one individual, by defining a normative lot of modest dimensions, by encouraging a flexible subdivision of the land, and by emphasizing the collective identity of the square, the royal architects successfully targeted the square for a bourgeois constituency. Of the twenty-six people who built houses at the Place Dauphine and along the quais, more than half (14/26) were merchants and artisans: jewelers and goldworkers who previously lived on the nearby bridges; printers who had shops in the Palace; and craftsmen at the top rank of their professions, among them royal painter Jacob Bunel, royal marble cutter Robert Menart, royal violinist Grégoire Béthune, and royal mason François Petit. Most of the remaining property owners (10/26) were lawyers and minor court officers. Only a small minority (2/26) held high royal offices, confirming the lesson learned at the Place Royale that noblemen would be disinclined to invest in bourgeois rental property (see Appendix B3).

Nicolas de Harlay, sieur de Sancy, purchased one of the two lots facing Henri IV's equestrian monument (see Fig. 107, Lot 1). Sancy had served as Superintendent of both Finances and Buildings from 1594 to 1599 before being eclipsed by Sully. He was the cousin of Achille de Harlay, but this familial link probably had less bearing on his purchase than the square's association with the king, whom Sancy hoped to flatter by building the house opposite his statue.[58] Sancy was an experienced patron, having already built the château of Grosbois (1597), but he never built the house at the Place Dauphine. At first his building plans may have been obstructed by factors beyond his control; all construction on the north side of the square was delayed until approximately 1611 when the quai was finished. More important, the death of Henri IV in 1610 apparently dampened Sancy's enthusiasm. Not until August 1612 did he hire workers to excavate the site for the foundations.[59] One month later, the lot was seized by the Châtelet and sold by decree of the court to a strawman acting on behalf of

Jean de Ligny, treasurer of the *parties casuelles,* the office that collected proceeds from the sale of royal offices. The purchase price of 3,000 *livres* was further reduced by a penalty of 1,000 *livres* levied on Sancy; thus the lot that he had bought for 7,500 *livres* was resold four years later for a mere 2,000 *livres.*[60] But the low resale price resulted from the court-imposed settlement of a claim against Sancy and did not reflect the depreciated value of the land. De Ligny was the only nobleman to build at the Place Dauphine. The masonry contract he passed with René Fleury, published in Appendix B5, provides the most detailed description of the original building specifications.[61]

Land at the Place Dauphine was concentrated in the hands of merchants and artisans. Merchants and artisans owned approximately 776 square *toises* compared to 336 *toises* held by court officers, with the balance of 150 *toises* owned by de Ligny. The largest property owner was François Petit, Harlay's first customer, who bought two lots on the quai de l'Horloge in August 1608. In January 1609, friends of Petit, the wine merchants Guillaume Marrier and Philippe Chaillou, bought the two lots straddling the rue de Harlay entrance and hired Petit as their mason.[62] As construction was under way, probably in 1611, title to the property was transferred to Petit, although it is possible that he owned the lots from the start and simply had Marrier and Chaillou act as front men.[63] The mason now owned four lots at the square, but had only broken ground on the rue de Harlay lots. Unable to finance the necessary construction, Petit sold one of the lots on the quai de l'Horloge to the cloth merchant André Langlois in August 1613.[64] This transaction did not resolve his financial problems, and so he concluded a more lucrative arrangement a few months later. Petit found himself a rich wife, Marie Parque, daughter of one of the most prestigious notaries in Paris. According to their marriage contract, the mason could invade the couple's joint assets — that is, the bride's dowry — to finance construction of his houses at the Place Dauphine, while his wife was disallowed any future claim against the estate.[65]

Petit's speculative activity signals the rise of the entrepreneurial mason-builder in Henri IV's Paris. He owned almost a quarter of the square: three lots or approximately 300 square *toises*. On each lot, he built six houses, for a total of eighteen houses. His construction comes closest to realizing Marot's idealized plan of the Place Dauphine. Each house sat on a parcel 4 *toises* square; it had one wing with a brick-and-stone facade, two shops, and three residential floors above, and at the rear of the lot was a small courtyard, private in some cases and shared in others (Figs. 111, 112, Parcels 4, 6, 7). Some owners, such as Menart and his neighbor Antoine Mignollet, an innkeeper and wine merchant, put two such parcels back to back; their houses extended the full depth of the range with

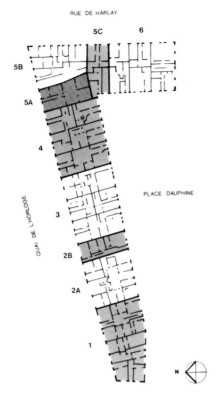

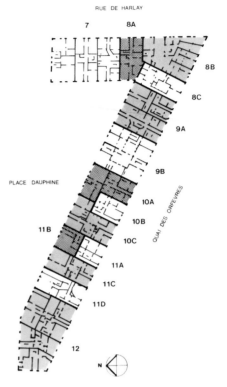

Fig. *111*. Place Dauphine, north range, subdivision of lots. (Drawing by Julia Rogoff based on A.N. F³¹ 94) Numbered lots are identified in Appendices B3 and B4.

Fig. *112*. Place Dauphine, south range, subdivision of lots. (Drawing by Julia Rogoff based on A.N. F³¹ 94) Numbered lots are identified in Appendices B3 and B4.

a wing on the quai and another on the *place,* a courtyard in between, and a connecting side wing (see Fig. 112, Parcels 11D, 11C).

But most owners disregarded the normative 4-*toise* dimension of the elevation when they subdivided the original lots; consequently, their facades did not achieve the perfect regularity of the royal design, as arches were contracted or expanded in order to make the appropriate sequence of openings fit across the width of the parcel. The case of Michel Deligny and Jean Laborie, who jointly bought the lot next to Sancy/de Ligny, is illustrative.[66] Deligny, a wood merchant, retained one quarter of the lot, a parcel approximately 3 *toises* wide (see Fig. 111, Parcel 2B). If the facade design were rigorously applied, a party wall would have abutted an arch and the windows above. Deligny's mason had no choice; he altered the dimensions of the arched openings, and according to the nineteenth-century cadastral plan, the house had a facade of one and a half bays. Although this plan postdates the original construction by two centuries, property lines at the Place Dauphine hardly changed over time, and the original bays probably survived as well. Laborie, a barrister representing the crown *(avocat au conseil privé du Roi)*, owned the adjoining three-quarters lot, with a width of approximately 9 *toises,* also incommensurate with the facade design (see Fig. 111, Parcel 2A). After adjusting the facade to accommodate the width of his parcel, his house must have read as a distinct five-bay unit, with a pair of arches on each side of the door. On his parcel of 75 square *toises,* he built two long *corps de logis* and two connecting wings around a court, creating the largest house at the Place Dauphine. While the regularity of the royal design was sacrificed, Laborie and his neighbors were able to build houses as large or small as they pleased.[67]

The crown remained entirely detached from the building process, providing no building incentives, subsidies, or tax abatements to the property owners. The only gesture of support was the waiver of mutation fees *(lods et ventes)* in a few instances.[68] The king did not even enforce the three-year building deadline, and when it expired in 1610, the Place Dauphine was far from completion. The houses on the north side of the square were only begun in 1611, probably due to construction of the quai, and the south range was rising at an uneven pace. Construction of the square was still incomplete when the statue of Henri IV was unveiled in August 1614; only with the closing of the gap at the southeast corner in 1616 was the Place Dauphine finally complete.[69] All told, it had taken nine years to realize the square. The preliminary preparation of the site, financial difficulties faced by some builders, perhaps Sully's disputed claim to the quais —all these factors had caused delays, which the crown took no action to mitigate.

Contrary to Sauval's claim, François Petit did not construct all of the houses at the Place Dauphine. Sauval's error is understandable, however, since Petit did build a great number — eighteen for Harlay on the rue de Harlay and eighteen for himself. Petit also acted as Harlay's factotum in matters relating to construction; it was the mason's task to notify the numerous property owners of the facade design and the alignments with which they had to comply. Thereafter, each property owner hired his own building crew and negotiated different payment schedules. Grégoire Béthune, violinist to the king, owned a standard parcel, 4 *toises* square, facing the quai des Orfèvres (see Fig. 112, Parcel 11A). His contractor, mason Jacques Le Redde, promised to build the house, cellar included, for 5,900 *livres.*[70] More frequently, owners negotiated separate contracts with each artisan. In these cases, the documentation is too spotty to calculate comparative costs for building an entire house; nonetheless, it is revealing to compare various rates for masonry work. Jean de Ligny, the wealthiest of the Place Dauphine *propriétaires,* paid his mason, René Fleury, at the flat rate of 9 *livres* 15 *sous* for each *toise* of masonry.[71] Germaine Durand, widow of sculptor Germain Pilon, paid Jean Gobelin 10 *livres* per *toise* of masonry plus an additional 120 *livres* for all projecting elements and moldings.[72] A different arrangement was used by Robert Menart, who established a tiered payment schedule: 15 *livres* per *toise* for the foundations, 12 *livres* per *toise* for the party walls, and 24 *livres* per *toise* for the facades, rates that demonstrate the high cost of complying with the royal facade design.[73]

Construction costs strained the resources of several property owners. Many borrowed money or disposed of other assets to raise sufficient cash, but these were the routine measures by which merchants and artisans engaged in small-scale entrepreneurial activity.[74] There were, however, some men who could not absorb the expenses. Claude Pothery, a provincial tax collector, was forced to suspend his building efforts when, at the request of his neighbors, his parcel was seized by the court and resold in September 1610.[75] In 1608, Pothery had paid 2,500 *livres* for his parcel, 4 by 8 *toises;* the new owner, Charles Beranger, tailor to Queen Marguerite, paid 4,700 *livres* for it. In two years, the value of the land had almost doubled. When royal marble cutter Robert Menart died in 1610/11(?), he had not yet paid all his building costs. His creditors, mostly the unpaid building crew, moved to have the house seized, forcing Menart's heirs to sell the building. It was bought by Germain Collier, counselor and secretary of the king, for 21,000 *livres,* with which Menart's debts were paid.[76] Estimating the cost of Menart's house at 14,500 *livres* (2,500 for the land plus 12,000 for construction, based on Béthune's price), it appreciated approximately 45 percent in three years.

The men who owned small quantities of land (less than 50 *toises* square) generally lived in their houses, while the larger land owners regarded the square as an investment, building several rental houses on each of their properties. Petit continued living in his old residence on the rue Montorgueil and rented his eighteen houses at the square to artisans, merchants, and some low-ranking officers from whom he collected rent of 7,200 *livres* annually. His houses facing the rue de Harlay rented for 350 *livres* a year while those on the quai and square cost 450 *livres,* reflecting the premium paid for these locations.[77] The most valuable commercial properties were the houses on the Pont Neuf. De Ligny charged 575 *livres* for a house with two shops facing the Pont Neuf.[78]

The other building on the bridge, on the south side, was owned by royal painter Jacob Bunel, who lived in the Grande Galerie of the Louvre.[79] Obviously, Bunel had no intention of living at the square, but he built a house to please his royal patron and to benefit from the profitable rental market in Paris. He built two houses at the Place Dauphine, each on plots of 50 *toises.* They were larger than the typical houses rented by artisans, and as a result, Bunel permitted subletting. He rented the house on the Pont Neuf to a prime tenant who in turn sublet the four ground-floor shops.[80]

From the moment the houses were completed, there was no lack of tenants. Prospering tradesmen of all sorts — goldsmiths, gem cutters, innkeepers, wine merchants, booksellers, a metalworker, leather gilder, and pin maker — made the Place Dauphine a thriving center of commercial activity, while minor court officers found housing conveniently located near the law courts. The success of Henri IV's second square was not achieved through the effort of wealthy nobles but of men with more limited means. Their participation testifies not only to the appeal of the square but to the growing value placed on investments in urban real estate. Yet the economic forces that had launched the Place Dauphine were soon to threaten its continuing success.

THE PLACE DAUPHINE THREATENED

Private speculation and commercial expansion, the forces that made the Place Dauphine possible, immediately jeopardized its architectural integrity. Powerful figures, hoping to follow Harlay's example in profiting from the alienation of royal land, greedily eyed the land along the quais bordering the square. According to testimony in 1623 of Pierre Perrot, the municipal solicitor, Henri IV had granted Sully the right to build shops on the river side of the quais, shops that would have obstructed views of the square.[81] The circumstances that induced the king to allow his favorite minister to spoil the impressive profile of the square remain unclear. The *Chambre des Comptes,* the court that reviewed fiscal edicts, revoked the donation to Sully in 1611, but the queen regent simply reassigned the same privilege to her ally, Pierre Jeannin, Controller-general of Finance.[82]

Experts hired by the municipality inspected the south quai in January 1612 in order to determine if navigation on the Seine would be hindered by projecting structures. It seems that construction on the north quai was not under consideration at this time. Although the experts concluded that it was technically possible to erect buildings from the Pont Neuf to the Pont St. Michel, Jeannin was stalled by opposition in other corners.[83] He was "contradicted and opposed by all the private residents of this city whose houses faced [the quai]," and was probably challenged as well by both Harlay and Sully with counterclaims to the same land.[84]

In November 1614, Sully renewed his fight, initiating litigation to claim the "gift made to him by His Majesty of the empty and vacant land, nooks and crannies which are or will be located in the roads [*voirie*] in the area of the Pont Neuf, the quais recently built, the Ile du Palais, and the Place Dauphine."[85] The appeal was evidently unsuccessful, and Sully resorted to extreme measures to press his claim. He harassed the aged Harlay on his deathbed, forcing the president to sign a document in which he surrendered his right to the property on the Cité. On 10 October 1616, Harlay dictated an affidavit "regarding the matter of M. de Sully":

> Monsieur Achille de Harlay . . . lying in his sickbed . . . has sworn and affirmed: . . . that Monsieur the duc de Sully on his own behalf has violently extorted from him [Harlay] a statement signed by the hand of Harlay prejudicial to the gift of the land in the Ile du Palais which had been made to Harlay by the late king . . . ; that Madame de Sully . . . begged him to sign the statement to please the sieur de Sully. . . . Monsieur Le Gras, treasurer of France, has since acknowledged . . . that the statement cannot be used against him [Harlay] or his heirs.[86]

Harlay died a fortnight later. His legatees retained the property on the rue de Harlay, and neither Sully nor Jeannin succeeded in gaining control of the quais.

Another campaign to exploit this land was waged from 1621 to 1623. After a fire destroyed the Pont au Change and the Pont Marchant on 24 October 1621, the displaced residents of the bridges sought the crown's permission to relocate on the quais of the Cité.[87] The municipality strongly objected to these requests on aesthetic grounds:

> The quais and adjacent areas must be preserved for the decoration of the city, health and salubrity of its residents, and because one of the most beautiful ornaments of this city is the Ile du Palais built as it is at present, endowed with spacious quais on both sides of the river on which no building can be raised without harming the structure and symmetry of the houses [of the Place Dauphine] which provide, in their present state, a pleasing prospect for views from the château of the Louvre.[88]

The spokesman for the city also reminded the crown that the quais were especially admired by foreign visitors. Persuaded by these arguments, Louis XIII proposed a compromise in 1623: he prohibited construction opposite the Place Dauphine but permitted new buildings east of the square. Nicolas Le Jay acquired the land as compensation for the destruction of the Pont Marchant, which he had inherited from his father-in-law, Charles Marchant. Le Jay built a row of twenty-nine houses of brick and stone running from the Pont St. Michel to the west end of the Palace wall, with a street-level arcade opening onto the new rue St. Louis (see Fig. 69).[89]

The first incursion on Henri IV's project took place in 1671 when the crown promoted the development of the area within the Palace behind the rue de Harlay houses. Louis XIV gave the president of the Parlement, Guillaume de Lamoignon, the surviving portion of the garden, the Jardin du Bailliage. In exchange, Lamoignon agreed to several building requirements: he opened the rue de Harlay entrance to the Palace, built four rows of shops around the Cour de Harlay, and erected a range of houses on the north side of the Cour de Lamoignon (see Figs. 91, 109).[90] The rue de Harlay was subordinated to the expansion of the Palace, adumbrating the transformation of the square in the nineteenth century.

The Place Dauphine was assaulted by changing aesthetic standards beginning in the late seventeenth century. The first signs of disfavor appeared in engravings where, as we saw, artists imposed symmetry and axiality on the square. By the eighteenth century, the Place Dauphine was considered expendable, an attitude no doubt encouraged by the ravages to Henri IV's design. Additional floors were built on top of most houses, new windows were pierced in the facade, and plaster patches scarred the walls of brick and stone. In the 1748 competition for a *place royale* dedicated to Louis XV, several submissions replaced the Place Dauphine with more monumental schemes, but most architects considered the site on the Cité insufficiently grand.[91] The Place Louis XV (de la Concorde) was ultimately built west of the Tuileries, and Henri IV's square was preserved for the time being.

Despite Henri IV's legendary populism, his bronze statue on the Pont Neuf shared the same fate of other royal monuments during the Revolution, and in 1792, his equestrian figure was destroyed. Appreciating the prominence of the site, Napoleon decided to erect an obelisk on the empty platform in 1809. Experts determined that the *terre-plein* had to be enlarged in order to support the weight of the obelisk. No sooner was this work begun than Napoleon was defeated and his obelisk abandoned.[92] In 1814, during Louis XVIII's reign, the crown commissioned a new equestrian statue of Henri IV from Frédéric Lemot. At this time, the enlarged platform was completed; it was lengthened westward but not made any wider. The statue was placed in the middle of the platform, 5 meters west of the first statue and consequently farther removed from traffic.[93] Situated on the same axis as the original monument, the nineteenth-century statue was also misaligned with the square, as it is today, obliquely positioned with respect to the entrance of the Place Dauphine.

The greatest threat to the square came in the mid-nineteenth century, when urban planners chose to sacrifice the commercial and residential life of the Cité in order to expand its administrative role. The decision in 1840 to enlarge the law courts led to the partial demolition of the square: in 1857–58, the houses built by Achille de Harlay on the east side of the rue de Harlay were razed; in 1874, the base of the triangle was destroyed to make way for the domineering facade of Duc's Palais de Justice.[94] The north and south ranges of the square today survive in a mutilated state. Only the houses facing the Pont Neuf, originally constructed by Jean de Ligny and Jacob Bunel, honor the original design, their brick-and-stone facades restored in 1945. Yet even as a ruin, the Place Dauphine preserves its dual character: a square of commercial appeal and urban prominence, of intimacy and tranquility.

THE RUE DAUPHINE

When Henri IV marched across the unfinished Pont Neuf in 1603, he found a rural, sparsely populated area surrounding the southern embankment—an environment hardly becoming to the majesty of his new bridge. Along the quai on the Left Bank rose two important buildings (see Figs. 86, 87). To the east was the church of the Augustins, where the royal confraternity—the Order of the Holy Spirit—gathered, the Parlement met on occasion, and the Estates General convened in 1614.[95] To the west was the Hôtel de Nevers, one of the most ambitious buildings undertaken during the reign of Henri III (see Fig. 49). In the early seventeenth century, the still unfinished structure was the residence of Charles de Gonzague, Prince of Nevers, Duke of Mantua, and founder of Charleville.[96] Between these buildings were two estates—a vast area of fields and gardens and sparsely scattered buildings spreading from the quai to the city wall—owned since the Middle Ages by the convent of the Grands Augustins and the abbey of St. Denis. Beyond the wall was the thriving faubourg St. Germain where in 1606, Queen Marguerite, the first wife of Henri IV, was building a palace opposite the Grande Galerie of the Louvre. Not only were the fields an unwelcome sight, but they blocked circulation between the bridge and the faubourg St. Germain.

By 1607, the crown decided to provide an outlet for the Pont Neuf on the Left Bank. This new street was an integral part of Henri IV's plan for the Cité, and the king called upon the commissioners of the Pont Neuf, headed by Achille de Harlay, to oversee the project. Through the joint efforts of the crown and private developers, the ecclesiastic domains were urbanized: the rue Dauphine extended the axis of the Pont Neuf across the Left Bank to a gate in the city wall, and the surrounding land was sold off for residential and commercial use.

Upon completion of the Pont Neuf, in March 1606, the abbey of St. Denis sold its estate on the Left Bank to a group of investors. The two buildings on the property, the Hôtel St. Denis and the maison de Chappes, had been used in the past by monks attending the university in Paris, but these buildings had been destroyed during the siege of Paris in 1590. Rather than repair them, the abbey decided to buy a dormitory elsewhere and to sell the land bounded by the city wall, the Pont Neuf, and the neighboring Augustin estate. The sale contract included one disclaimer: "In the event that for public convenience it is found necessary to build any street across the property, the buyer cannot appeal to the sellers for any compensation." [97] The abbey of St. Denis apparently anticipated the possible urban development of the land, but the monks did not want to take on the entrepreneurial role themselves. That role was assumed by three investors who paid 72,000 *livres* for the estate: Pierre Corbonnois, treasurer of France for Burgundy; Claude du Nesme, secretary of the king's chamber; and Nicolas Carrel, *bourgeois de Paris*.[98] Carrel acted as their representative in this and all subsequent transactions, leaving the names of his associates unmentioned and heretofore unpublished.

Nicolas Carrel earned his living from real estate speculation in Henri IV's Paris. In 1602, he joined a group of financiers in purchasing a tax farm, but thereafter his interest shifted to urban property.[99] He was to play an active role in the development of Henri IV's third square, the Place de France, purchasing a large tract with du Nesme on the rue d'Orléans (1,147 square *toises*) and two smaller lots with his brother-in-law Simon Coursin on the rues de Touraine and Bretagne.[100] Carrel revealed his ambitions in an undated proposal for a series of building projects submitted to Louis XIII.[101] Carrel volunteered to build a square called the Place de la Reine, Queen's Square, bordered by uniform buildings and a new mint at the end of the rue Dauphine; a navigable canal around Paris with four new ports; new fortifications from the Porte St. Denis to the Tuileries; and three additional city gates. As compensation, Carrel asked to be given large sections of the city wall and the surrounding territory. This proposal anticipates the speculative schemes of Louis Le Barbier during the 1620s and 1630s, in particular his development of the *fossés jaunes,* the land on the course of the demolished city wall in the neighborhood of Richelieu's Palais Cardinal.[102] Carrel was probably the underlying force in the rue Dauphine development, bringing Corbonnois and du Nesme in as his partners. There is no other trace of Corbonnois in contemporary documents, while we find du Nesme imprisoned in 1608 for falsifying documents during his tenure as a tax farmer in Poitiers a decade earlier.[103]

When the developers bought the abbey's estate in March 1606, the crown must have already decided to build the rue Dauphine, although a year passed before it actively pursued the project.[104] By the time of the first documented discussion of the rue Dauphine, in February 1607, the specifications of the street were determined. It was to be 5 *toises* wide, "in a straight line following and in alignment with the Pont Neuf going to the porte de Buci." The street was projected across property owned by the Augustins, who were forced to surrender a section of their garden and demolish a dormitory.[105] When, much to the amazement of the king, the monks objected to the expropriation of their land, Henri IV replied with worldly wisdom, "For goodness sake, Fathers, the profit you will make on the houses is well worth [your] cabbages."[106] In April 1607, the king's representatives reached an accord with the order. The Augustins deferred to "the king's desire to render the approach to the Pont Neuf easier for public convenience from the side of the convent of the Augustins" and accepted payment of 30,000 *livres* for 165 square *toises* of land, generous compensation at 182 *livres* per toise.[107] In addition, the crown agreed to build walls on both sides of the new road to enclose the Augustins' property as well as a subterranean passage to link the divided estate.[108]

After the crown settled with the Augustins, Carrel and his partners proceeded with the sale of their property, assured that the rue Dauphine, essential for their success, would be completed. Some of the developers' land was also taken for the rue Dauphine and for two small side streets, the rue d'Anjou to the west (today the rue de Nesle) and the rue Christine to the east, named after the king's children (Fig. 113; see Figs. 86, 87). Carrel expected the crown to indemnify him for this land and to pay for paving the new streets, but the crown thought otherwise and held the private developers responsible for the urban infrastructure: roads, paving, and city gate. In December 1608, the residents complained to the crown that the streets were left unpaved, and the king referred the matter to Sully, who as *Grand Voyer* was in charge of all roads.[109] Three months later, in March 1609, the royal council issued its verdict: the developers were ordered to pave the roads and to build a new gate in the city wall at the end of the rue Dauphine in accordance with specifications established by Sully.[110] The Porte de Buci had fallen into ruin during the occupation of Paris, and Sully saw an opportunity to have it rebuilt at private expense. We do not know whether Sully ever supplied a design, but Jacques Du Breul, who lived in the nearby abbey of St. Germain, reported in the 1612 edition of his guide that the Porte de Buci had been demolished and a new gate constructed, providing direct access to the faubourg St. Germain.[111]

The *lotissement* of the Hôtel St. Denis was conducted between June 1607 and May 1608, although several buyers may have staked verbal claims to the land in 1606 when Carrel originally acquired the estate from the abbey.[112] The

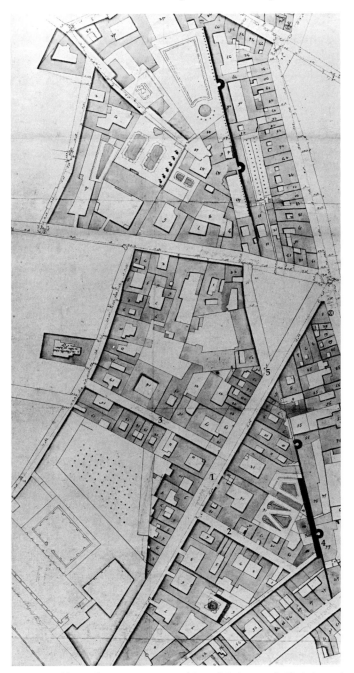

Fig. 113. Abbé Delagrive, rues Dauphine, d'Anjou, and Christine, plan, c. 1740s. (B.N. Est. rés. Ve 53j)
Key: 1. rue Dauphine; 2. rue d'Anjou; 3. rue Christine; 4. fragment of the city wall; 5. site of the seventeenth-century gate

Delagrive plan from the 1740s shows the area developed by Carrel: the land along the rue Dauphine between the convent and the city wall and along the two side streets (see Fig. 113). The rue d'Anjou abuts a narrow street (the rue de Nevers), which terminates at the city wall; this street was opened later in the seventeenth century and marks the western boundary of Carrel's property. Land was sold for 50 *livres* per square *toise* in parcels of various sizes, ranging from 23 to 143 square *toises.*

Henri IV had indicated his desire for uniform facades on the rue Dauphine in a letter to Sully in May 1607:

> Since I have been informed that work is beginning on the buildings on the new road that goes from the end of the Pont Neuf to the Porte de Buci, I wanted to send you this note to tell you that I would be very pleased if you would see to it that those who are beginning to build in the said street build the front of their houses all according to the same design, because it would be a beautiful ornament to see this street with a uniform facade from the end of the bridge.[113]

A masonry contract passed in June 1607 alluded to the possibility of forthcoming design specifications, advising the mason to comply "if it is advised and comes to pass that it is appropriate to build a facade of brick or something else for the wall facing the street." [114] A facade design for the rue Dauphine was never dictated by the crown, however, and buyers were merely required to build a house along the street. Here, as with the approach street to the Place Royale, the crown failed to take advantage of a valuable opportunity to embellish the city, evidence both of the limitations of Henri IV's urbanism and of its concentration on architectural projects growing out of more broadly conceived economic and social programs rather than decorative ensembles.

The development of the rue Dauphine was unimportant in terms of its architectural and urban design. There was no house design, no modeling of urban space. What distinguished the enterprise was the commanding role played by private investors. In previous *lotissements,* it was the crown that alienated its own land, or in the exceptional case of the Couture Ste.-Catherine, it was a church. In this instance, three private individuals bought land with the intention of reselling it at a profit, confident that the demand for real estate in Paris would make their investment a lucrative one. This speculative venture, as well as those undertaken by Captain Marchant and others we have already encountered in Henri IV's Paris, marks the appearance of private real estate investors as important players in the development of the city.

The profits of Carrel and his associates from the rue Dauphine project cannot be tallied because the operation remains only partially documented. The eight sales for which contracts have thus far been found produced about 34,000 *livres,* close to half of the cost of the land.[115] But many more lots were sold, and the developers also retained rental property that generated additional income. It seems more than likely that they at least recovered the initial investment.

The men who bought land on the rue Dauphine were almost entirely judicial or royal officeholders, who built houses in which they lived.[116] Only Corbonnois, du Nesme, and Carrel built rental houses. In 1607/8, Corbonnois and du Nesme jointly constructed at least four small houses as well as a larger hôtel, while Carrel and his brother-in-law built seven houses.[117] As the houses on the rue Dauphine were going up, Marguerite de Valois was building a new palace on the quai west of the Hôtel de Nevers, facing the Louvre, and her presence encouraged the residential development of the neighborhood.[118] The queen's contractor, master mason Jean Autissier, built a house for himself on the rue Dauphine and one for his neighbor, Samuel Menjot, a solicitor in the Parlement, collectively ordering materials for all three projects for delivery to the same site.[119]

As lawyers and royal officeholders built houses along the south end of the rue Dauphine, the Grands Augustins put up small shops at the north end of the street, near the Pont Neuf. In October 1607, the order hired François Petit to build new conventual buildings on the east side of the rue Dauphine, near the church, and a row of nine shops on the west side of the street.[120] Modest three-story buildings with ground-floor shops, they were rented to tradesmen and provided the monks with an annual income of 2,640 *livres,* far more than their cabbage, just as the king had expected.[121] The Augustins paid Petit 23,500 *livres* for his masonry work, and, ever eager to invest in the rental housing market, he bought a parcel on the rue Dauphine on which he built four small houses, abutting the walls of the convent.[122]

By projecting the axis of the Pont Neuf across the Left Bank, Henri IV instigated a process of development that transformed the area during the seventeenth century. The wall that separated the faubourg St. Germain from the city remained standing, but it was absorbed into the urban fabric; in 1607, the crown filled in the defensive ditch outside the wall and sold the land between the Portes de Buci and St. Germain for residential development.[123] The rue Dauphine brought the faubourg St. Germain into closer contact with the city. It was in this area that the nobility chose to build their hôtels in the following decades, that Maria de' Medici built her new residence, the Palais de Luxembourg, and that a speculative development was launched by Le Barbier on the grounds of Marguerite de Valois's unfinished hôtel. Although it was a modest project, the rue Dauphine stimulated the urban development of the Left Bank.

CHAPTER FOUR

THE HÔPITAL SAINT LOUIS

As soon as plans for the Place Dauphine were turned over to its developer, the crown launched a third major building project. In May 1607, Henri IV initiated construction of a plague hospital on the north side of Paris, where it survives to this day as the oldest functioning hospital in the city (Figs. 114, 115). The Hôpital St. Louis, built largely at royal expense from 1607 to 1612, was an unprecedented undertaking: it was the first monumental hospital in Europe for exclusive treatment of the plague. Hospitals in early modern Europe were charitable refuges, where the hungry and poor were fed and the seriously ill found compassion. But they did not offer the promise of restored health. Worst of all were plague hospitals, which bred contagion and condemned the sick to fatal reinfection. Plague hospitals were considered more deadly than the disease itself, and none who could afford private care at home, none who had rural property to which they might retreat would willingly enter a pesthouse. The Hôpital St. Louis was not intended to serve the nobility and the wealthy. It was for day laborers, shopkeepers, and craftsmen—those who had limited means and no land, and who constituted the vast population of Paris.

The founding of the hospital, then, was a grandiose act of charity. It associated Henri IV with the royal model of Christian devotion, Saint Louis. But if the crown wanted to bestow a benevolent gift upon the poor, why build a hospital to be used only during epidemics? Why not rebuild the dilapidated buildings of the general hospital on the Cité, the Hôtel Dieu? Furthermore, renovation of the Hôtel Dieu had the additional value of embellishing a site in central Paris, whereas the pesthouse was banished to the suburbs. The crown's priority was neither architectural embellishment nor the broader provision of medical services. Henri IV wanted to contain the plague's disrupting effects on Paris. He wanted to protect the life of the city. Though situated outside the walls, the Hôpital St. Louis was an essential element in Henri IV's urbanism.

During the second half of the sixteenth century, there were three major bouts of plague in Paris, in 1560–62, 1580, and 1594–96.[1] Beyond the thousands of people who died, mere rumors of the plague spread fear and unrest and threw the city into a spasm of social disorder. Panic-striken citizens invaded the countryside, escaping the infected air of the city. The population of Paris declined sharply, and the flow of essential goods and services into the city was

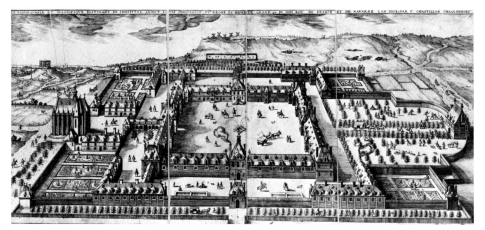

Fig. 114. Claude Vellefaux, Hôpital St. Louis, 1607–12. Engraving after Claude Chastillon, c. 1615. (B.N. Est. rés. Ve 9)

suspended. In 1604–6, rumors spread wildly that the plague had again struck the capital. Every death was attributed to the epidemic, but the city was so gripped by fear that few people noticed that the mortality rate remained at its normal level. "The fear in Paris was greater than the sickness," Pierre L'Estoile noted.[2] It was not a ravaging bout of plague that immediately inspired the founding of the Hôpital St. Louis; it was the social and economic dislocations that undermined urban order.

The Hôpital St. Louis has received little scholarly attention, although it is more thoroughly documented than any other monument built in early-seventeenth-century Paris. The organization of the workshop and building economy, changes in design and care of patients—all of these developments can be closely followed in the hospital's well-preserved archives, now held in the Archives of the Assistance Publique. The hospital is mentioned frequently in histories of epidemiology to illustrate attitudes toward the plague in early modern Europe, while art historians at most acknowledge it as an oddity for rejecting the plan of the prototypical Renaissance hospital, Filarete's Ospe-

Fig. 115. Hôpital St. Louis, aerial view. (Institut géographique nationale, Paris)

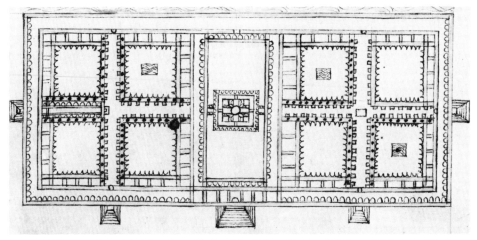

Fig. 116. Filarete, Ospedale Maggiore, Codex Magliabecchianus, fol. 82v. (Biblioteca Nazionale, Florence; Photo Donato Pineider)

dale Maggiore (Fig. 116).³ Even in discussions of Henri IV's patronage, the two royal squares have entirely overshadowed the hospital, which has been considered peripheral to the king's urbanism. This judgment results from the misperception of Henri IV's building program as a purely aesthetic enterprise rather than as an expression of broader objectives. It has been argued here that Henri IV's urbanism reflected policies of economic reform and political centralization that changed the requirements of the capital, both in terms of its function and its image. Viewed in the context of these larger concerns, the Hôpital St. Louis played a crucial role in Henri IV's planning of Paris.

URBAN DIMENSIONS OF THE PLAGUE

While the plague was understood first and foremost as a sign of God's wrath, the secular etiology attributed the disease to infected air, dirt, and vagrants. Medical authorities agreed that the pestiferous air of the city was the primary agent of contagion and advised city dwellers to take refuge in the unpolluted air of the country whenever the plague approached. "Truly the most excellent remedy that I can teach along with the ancients," wrote Ambroise Paré, surgeon to Henri III, "is to flee early and far from the infected location, to retreat to healthy air, and return very late, if it is possible to do so." ⁴ Paré's advice was followed, and each minatory hint of the plague produced a great exodus from Paris; the king, the Parlement, the municipal leaders, nobles, and bourgeois — everyone with rural property deserted the city. In 1580, the municipal government prohibited all judicial officers and notables from leaving Paris during the plague; three times this order was reiterated to no effect. "The majority of the residents of Paris with some means left the city," L'Estoile recorded in his journal, "and traders did not come for about six months, so that poor artisans and workers cried of hunger and played skittles on the Pont Notre-Dame and in many other roads in Paris, even in the great chamber of the Palace." [5] The city became a wasteland of the poor, the sick, and the criminal, sustained by the paltry harvests of urban gardens.

The flight from Paris spread panic and disease throughout the surrounding area. Neighboring towns imposed a blockade, refusing to deliver food and provisions to Paris or to admit travelers and goods from the capital for fear of contamination. [6] Indeed, the fate of Paris touched all of France, as the *Prévôt des marchands* of Lyon explained in a letter to his Parisian counterpart asking if plague had struck the capital: "Because we recognize that when finding the leader sick, all other parts will feel the effects, we must take precautions early because of the importance [to Lyon] of trade and travel to other countries." [7] Like the proliferation of domestic tolls and duties against which Laffemas railed, the plague fragmented the French economy. The economic and political network that bound the city to the countryside was severed as each town and village withdrew inside its own walls. The kingdom fractured into many little fiefs, rendering Paris powerless.

Medical authorities found another source of contagion in dirt and noxious vapors released by the earth. Nocturnal burials were recommended by the college of surgeons in 1606 "in order to remove the public's fear and to avoid the malign effluvia which arise from the opening of the ground." [8] Private households were fumigated with spices, and materials thought to breed infection were burned.

Yet these measures left the public domain unattended. As the city grew, the garbage and mud of unpaved streets received increasing attention, and doctors promoted street cleaning as a necessary measure against the plague. [9] Consequently, while paving had traditionally been the responsibility of the municipality, in 1602 the crown took charge of the matter. The king ordered Sully, in his capacity as *Grand Voyer*, to inspect the roads and prepare an inventory of the necessary repairs. His report does not survive, but Sully proceeded to establish a methodical program to clean, pave, and repair the streets in Paris, employing no less than eighty pavers during the spring and summer months. Large sums partially funded by a municipal tax were devoted to this project; in 1609, for example, 23,000 *livres* were spent on paving and 50,000 *livres* on street cleaning. [10] With this intensive effort to upgrade the streets, the king advanced three interlocking goals for the capital: the embellishment of Paris, some protection from the plague, and well-paved streets to serve the demands of trade.

Finally, it was widely believed that vagrants were agents of contagion. In the wake of Henri IV's entry into Paris came large numbers of poor and wounded seeking relief in the capital. War veterans won special treatment, and in 1597, Henri IV established a hospice for them called the Royal House of Christian Charity.[11] It was built on the same site in the faubourg St. Marcel and given the same name as a home for orphans founded by Nicolas Houël in 1578 under the patronage of Catherine de' Medici. Houël and his hospice were identified with the politics of religious unity, and it may well be that the Bourbon king wished to honor these associations in endowing a second House of Christian Charity for victims of the Religious Wars.[12]

War veterans, however, constituted only a small part of the immigration of the poor. Pierre L'Estoile estimated that in only three days in May 1595, 10,000 mendicants poured into Paris, and by the end of the month, the city was forced to close its gates to stop the unabating flood of beggars.[13] The municipality feared that this floating population would unleash an epidemic; when one broke out in 1596, the city leaders directed Captain Marchant to have his guards prevent any beggar from entering Paris.[14] In the public mind, a vagrant shed his susceptibility to contagion through a life of productive labor. In sixteenth-century cities throughout Europe, beggars had commonly been put to work on public projects, and this practice was continued during Henri IV's reign.[15] The poor were employed to terrace the site of the Hôpital St. Louis and to clean city streets.[16] But the humanist dimension of sixteenth-century poor-relief measures was now being eclipsed by the overriding importance of urban order. The beggar was losing his protected status as a Christian soul and appeared increasingly as a threat to the city. "Draw in the poor beggars, . . . find means of lodging them in some place," Nicolas Ellain urged in 1604, "and giv[e] them means to live without allowing them to run across the city."[17] This call for the physical containment of vagrants marked a fundamental change in the seventeenth-century response to vagabondage. Severe measures were passed in January 1606 to control vagrancy in Paris. It was decided to outlaw begging, mark the poor with a cross of red-and-yellow cloth worn on the right shoulder, require them to return to their native towns, and prohibit Parisians from lodging the poor for more than a single night; those who remained in the city would be fumigated and imprisoned. This legislation was the beginning of the human enclosure movement that was pursued more vigorously during the reign of Louis XIII.[18] It was in the context of this shifting attitude to the poor and the emerging strategy of containment that the Hôpital St. Louis was built.

Infected air, dirt, vagabonds — since the time of the Black Death they were thought to cause the plague. What had changed in early-seventeenth-century Paris, what provoked a different response from Henri IV, was the urban dimension of the plague. The disorder that accompanied the disease handicapped the authority of the crown and undermined the stability of the city and its surrounding regions. Henri IV's responses to the plague, no less than his mercantilist policies, were intended to create a more unified national economy, assure uninterrupted trade, halt the exodus from Paris, and protect the political authority of the capital. To anchor the monarchy in a safe haven and liberate Paris from the convulsive social and economic effects of the plague, if not from sickness and death, the king pursued a program of hospital reform with a new monumental plague hospital as its centerpiece.

TRADITIONAL RESPONSES TO THE PLAGUE AND HENRI IV'S REFORM

Paris was unequipped to defend herself against the plague. She had no pesthouse, no board of public health. The physical facilities, institutional procedures, and financial resources to handle the epidemic were all lacking; those shortcomings had been tolerated throughout the sixteenth century. Each time the prospect of the plague threatened, the municipal government had imposed a special tax to finance emergency measures, but the tax was an unreliable source of income at a time when citizens felt least committed to the city. Consequently, the Hôtel de Ville never had sufficient funds to respond adequately to the plague, and it invariably appealed to the Parlement of Paris, the governing body of the Hôtel Dieu, to assume responsibility for plague measures. The Parlement invariably refused financial aid, and the city, left with the burden, adopted whatever frugal measures its minimal resources would allow.

The municipality's primary goal was to sequester the sick. But sequestration was fiercely resisted by the infected, who legitimately feared their unprotected property would be pillaged and their lives even more seriously endangered by the ghastly conditions of the Hôtel Dieu and temporary pesthouses. Guards were posted at the doors of the Hôtel Dieu to block the sick from escaping without a health pass, and at the city gates to prevent those sent to makeshift facilities outside the walls from returning home. But it proved impossible to prevent the plague-stricken from circulating in the city. The municipal government relied on the existing network of local officials (*dixainiers, cinquantiniers, and quartiniers*) to identify the contaminated, evict them from their residences, and quarantine the houses, but the local officials generally refused the ominous task. A salaried public health officer (*prévôt de la santé*) was appointed for the first time during the epidemic of 1580, and three *prévôts* were employed in 1596. These were temporary measures, however, each of which was preceded by a struggle over financing and enacted in desperation at the last moment. The city could not even support a staff of specialized plague doctors and surgeons and asked the Faculty of Medicine to find four volunteers to treat the plague-stricken. With few doctors inclined to accept this dangerous charge, inexperienced apprentices were appointed with the promise of immediate promotion should they survive their service.[19]

The lack of a plague hospital further hindered the city. Those who could afford private care remained at home, by far the preferred alternative, while the majority of Parisians converged on the Hôtel Dieu, located beside the cathedral of Notre-Dame on the Cité (see Fig. 86). It consisted of three thirteenth-century buildings, unaltered since their construction, and one more modern wing, the Salle du Légat, built in 1531, which was used to isolate as many of the infected as the wing could hold.[20] The governors of the Hôtel Dieu estimated that 67,000 plague victims thronged to the hospital in 1562, 20,000 in 1580, and 10,000 to 12,000 in 1596, all crammed into the small, medieval rooms on the Cité.[21] The surplus mingled with regular patients in the other, overcrowded rooms, propagating yet more contagion. Apart from the appalling conditions in the Hôtel Dieu, municipal leaders feared that the whole city was imperiled by containing the contagion in the very heart of Paris.

The necessity of building a plague hospital was recognized during each epidemic, but as each episode subsided, the urgent need for a pesthouse abated. In 1515, the governors of the Hôtel Dieu sought permission to build a two-story wing across the Seine to isolate the contagiously ill. The municipality objected, fearing interference with river traffic, the commercial lifeblood of the city. The archbishop also objected, not wishing to discourage the healthy members of his flock from attending the cathedral. The combination of municipal and clerical opposition forced the Hôtel Dieu to drop the project.[22] Thereafter, it was understood that the sick had to be removed from the city. During the cholera epidemic of 1519, the Hôtel Dieu appealed to François I to build a plague hospital just beyond the Tour de Nesle on the south bank of the river (quai Malaquais), where in Henri IV's day Queen Marguerite built her palace. François I promised 10,000 *livres* for the hospital, a row of six uniform buildings was planned, and the first stone was laid in June 1520.[23] A few months later, with no funds forthcoming from the crown, construction was halted. François I had changed his mind and no longer wanted a pesthouse so close to the Louvre.[24]

In the absence of any other facilities, the sick continued to converge on the Hôtel Dieu, and in 1548, the governors, hoping to relieve their overcrowded

Fig. 117. Rémond Constant, Ex-voto of Claude Beaujean, 1631. (Musée Lorrain, Nancy; Photo Gilbert Mangin)

facilities, requested permission from the city to quarantine plague victims in city-owned houses on the Petit Pont. "The Hôtel Dieu is situated in the middle of the city," the municipal leaders replied, "like the heart in the middle of a man, such that bad air within it can infect the rest of the body, and all the parts and places of this city; and so if it were permitted to undertake the expansion, it would be adding wood to fire, poison to poison." [25] The only acceptable alternative was to expel the infected beyond the walls where, in the absence of a permanent pesthouse, the municipality erected compounds of tents and huts, usually made of wood or canvas, which were burned when the epidemic passed. An ex-voto painted by Rémond Constant in the late 1630s depicts the makeshift huts erected outside Nancy during the plague of 1630, typical of those used throughout France during the sixteenth and seventeenth centuries (Fig. 117). [26]

The epidemic of 1580 provoked another muncipal effort to build a plague hospital. A site isolated from suburban settlements was chosen, the plain of

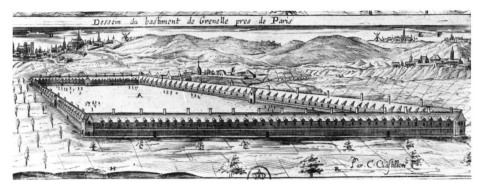

Fig. 118. Grenelle pesthouse, 1580. Engraving after Claude Chastillon. (B.N. Est. rés. Ve 9)

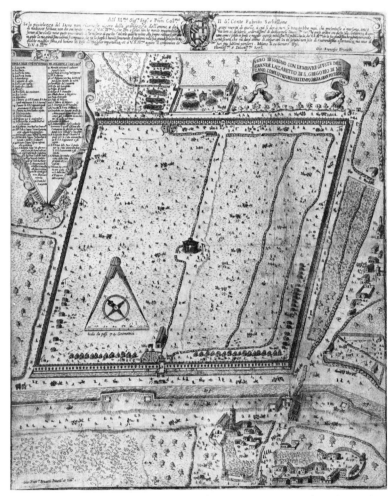

Fig. 119. Lazzaretto di San Gregorio, Milan, 1488. Engraving by Giovanni Brunetti, 1632. (Civica Raccolta Stampe A. Bertarelli, Castello Sforzesco, Milan)

[174]

Grenelle, west of the faubourg St. Germain where the Hôtel des Invalides was built a century later, and construction of a pesthouse began in 1580. Once again the special plague tax levied on Parisians failed to generate sufficient funds; the hospital was not completed, and in 1589, the Duke of Mayenne, the leader of League-occupied Paris, ordered his troops to destroy the Hôpital de Grenelle and pillage its materials for guardhouses around the city walls.[27] From an engraving after Chastillon and a contemporary description by Pierre Fayet, a judicial clerk, we learn that the short-lived hospital consisted of four connecting wings enclosing a large rectangular courtyard, 96 by 52½ *toises* (190m by 104m) (Fig. 118).[28] The Grenelle pesthouse was modeled after the Lazzaretto di San Gregorio (1488) in Milan, the largest permanent plague hospital before the Hôpital St. Louis.[29] Most earlier pesthouses were simply abandoned leper houses, which may in part explain the continuing use of individual cells in the plague hospital at Milan. Occasionally, new buildings were constructed to isolate victims of the plague; the first Italian city to do so was Venice in 1403, and the first French city was Bourg-en-Bresse in 1472, but these were simple structures of a single block. There was nothing to compare to the scale of the Lazzaretto di San Gregorio (Fig. 119). The engraving made by a lucky survivor in January 1631 shows a vast rectangular court (370m by 378m; 187 by 191 *toises*) with a chapel in the center surrounded by 288 adjoining cells; when they were fully occupied, huts of wood and straw were erected in the courtyard. According to a witness, the population reached 16,000 during the great plague of 1630.[30] Unlike the Lazzaretto with its individual cells, the hospital at Grenelle had open ranges with axial pavilions providing access to the central courtyard, features that reappear at the Hôpital St. Louis.

When the plague struck in 1596, Paris again had no alternative to the overcrowded halls of the Hôtel Dieu and the straw huts outside the walls. The responsibilities shunned by the municipal government fell to the Hôtel Dieu, with money coming neither from the city nor the crown. Pressed to its limits, the Hôtel Dieu installed recuperating patients in two houses in the faubourgs.[31] But this measure did nothing to ameliorate the larger problems posed by the plague, problems that Henri IV was less willing to tolerate than his predecessors because of his aspirations for Paris. In 1606, the cycle was repeated for the last time. When a mild epidemic touched Paris, the city purchased two houses in a sparsely settled quarter southeast of the city, the faubourg St. Marcel, to hold the overflow of patients from the Hôtel Dieu.[32] The ghastly conditions at the Hôpital St. Marcel, as the houses were somewhat grandly called, became notorious. "The plague-infected moved . . . to the faubourg St. Marceau are so badly treated, to the point that they are left to die of hunger and their days numbered, that they are compelled to escape," L'Estoile reported in August 1606. "They put up huts in the fields . . . , spreading out wherever they can to the great detriment of the public and infection of the poor, who for lack of police are forced to suffer the worst extremes of the world." [33] The leaders of the Hôtel de Ville appealed to the crown to rectify the conditions at the Hôtel Dieu and the "great disorders" resulting from the absence of an isolated pesthouse, and they requested that responsibility for the plague be turned over to the Hôtel Dieu. This time the governors of the Hôtel Dieu accepted the responsibility. They recommended a reform program to the crown, and the Hôtel Dieu's proposals were endorsed by the king and promulgated in a royal decree of May 1607.[34]

The edict of 1607 restructured the response to the plague in seventeenth-century Paris. First, the edict transferred jurisdiction over plague-related issues from the municipality to the Hôtel Dieu. The financial burden was similarly shifted from the city to the crown, which allocated a portion of its revenues from the salt tax to finance the various reforms.[35] Since the early sixteenth century, when the chapter of Notre-Dame voluntarily ceded control of the hospital, the administration of the Hôtel Dieu had been in the secular hands of the Parlement of Paris. While appointments to the board of governors were nominally made by the Hôtel de Ville, they were in fact controlled by the Parlement, so that the Hôtel Dieu constituted an independent secular institution closely tied to the crown. Thus the plague reform was another instance of royal interests gaining greater control over Paris, in this case at the invitation of the municipal government.

Second, the edict established a permanent administration of public health officials. The health officers included two full-time *prévôts de santé* and four policemen (*archers*) to identify the infected and transport them to the pesthouses, a staff of doctors and nurses to work in the hospitals, and two barber-surgeons to treat patients remaining in private residences. Finally, the king provided royal funds for hospital construction. The governors of the Hôtel Dieu were instructed to repair their medieval buildings, which experts had cited as being on the verge of collapse in 1601.[36] Funds were also allocated to the governors for three other hospitals, including a new pesthouse to be built on the north side of the city.[37]

This reform was shaped by the eight governors of the Hôtel Dieu. Two of the governors were representatives of the bourgeois, and the remainder were judicial magistrates and royal officeholders. At the time the plague reform was planned, the governing body included two active participants in the crown's building program: Achille de Harlay, appointed in 1587, and silk investor Pierre

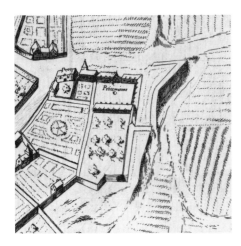

Fig. 120. François Quesnel, map of Paris, detail of the Petites Maisons, 1609. (B.N. Est. rés. AA 3)

Fig. 121. Hôpital St. Marcel, site plan, c. 1620. (Archives de l'Assistance Publique de Paris, plan 201)

Sainctot, appointed in 1606.[38] The edict demonstrates a familiarity with the plague measures adopted by other European cities, and especially the public health bureaus operating in Italy. Permanent health boards had been established in Venice in 1486 and in Florence in 1527; and by the second half of the sixteenth century, every major Italian city had a board regulating all aspects of sanitary life.[39] Paris had been backward compared to these cities in terms of establishing a public health administration, but there had been no precedent for Henri IV's building program. The crown transformed a purely administrative reform into an architectural enterprise that changed the image of Paris.

The royal edict identified three sites to be used for hospitals. First, the Petites Maisons was an abandoned hospice for the deranged, which had been built in the faubourg St. Germain in 1557.[40] The crown provided 24,000 *livres* to convert the Petites Maisons into the renamed Hôpital St. Germain, which was to be used as a shelter for poor invalids (Fig. 120).[41] Second, southeast of the city, on the future site of the Val-de-Grâce, were two houses which the city had bought prior to the edict in 1606 and renamed the Hôpital St. Marcel. The Hôtel Dieu upgraded the facility, which had so appalled L'Estoile, by establishing new procedures for patient care and undertaking limited repairs.[42] A site plan from about 1620 shows a long, narrow building for the sick set in the middle of a large tract of land, a cemetery in one corner of the enclave, a kitchen nestled in another, a service court with a chapel added in 1620, and a second wing along the street for the hospital staff (Fig. 121).[43]

The Hôpital St. Marcel was typical of pesthouses: modest buildings without any architectural significance whatsoever, casually distributed in an open plot of land. But the third hospital called for in the royal decree was a major new project to be built in northern Paris. The decision to elevate the trivial requirements of a pesthouse into the monumental Hôpital St. Louis reveals the mark of Henri IV's urban planning.

THE DESIGN OF THE HÔPITAL ST. LOUIS

The site chosen by the governors of the Hôtel Dieu for the new plague hospital was outside the city walls between the Porte St. Martin and the Porte du Temple (Figs. 122, 123).[44] It was easily accessible from the city yet safely removed from any suburban settlement. The property was straddled by two major roads, to the west by the rue faubourg St. Martin (the primary north-south artery in Paris which led to Meaux), and to the east by the rue faubourg du Temple (which ran from the Place de Grève to Belleville). The Porte du Temple, which had been closed for forty years, was rebuilt by the city (1605–7) and reopened in 1607, thus assuring easy access to the new hospital.[45] Yet topographical factors isolated the site despite its proximity to Paris. There were marshlands to the south, and the hill of Montfaucon to the north, with its dreaded gallows and fetid garbage dump (the future site of the parc des Buttes-Chaumont). The combination of both isolation and proximity to Paris commended the location, at least in terms of urban planning considerations.

Salubrity was clearly a secondary concern, since the site failed to offer the healthful environment normally associated with hospitals. After an inspection in May 1607, two doctors hired by the Hôtel Dieu concluded that no more

Fig. 122. Vassallieu dit Nicolay, map of Paris, detail of the Hôpital St. Louis, 1609. (B.N. Est. rés. Hennin XV 1352) The hospital is labeled "Maison des pestiferez."

Fig. 123. François Quesnel, map of Paris, detail of the Hôpital St. Louis, 1609. (B.N. Est. rés. AA 3)

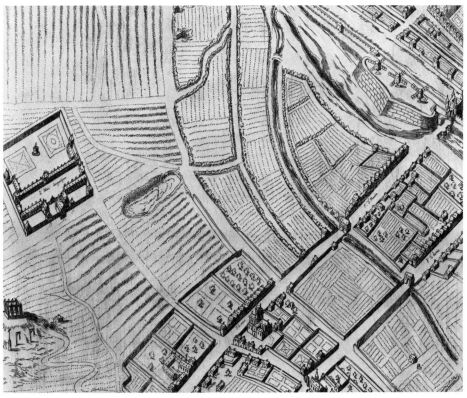

fitting location could be found, but they overlooked two conspicuous problems.[46] First, the putrid stench from the waste dump at Montfaucon was widely considered a source of the plague, causing such experts as Nicolas Ellain to warn that Paris was vulnerable to the plague from the north, "especially from the side of the Temple and St. Martin when the wind blows, sending this bad air in the city."[47] Perhaps ancient notions of the linkage between wind directions and health determined the perfect alignment of the hospital with the northeast axis of the compass, a decision that has no evident topographical cause. But the orientation of the hospital had no mitigating effect on the winds. The construction crew at the Hôpital St. Louis found the smells so offensive that they threatened to desert the project in 1608.[48] The Hôtel Dieu repeatedly pressed the municipality to remove the waste from the site "due to the stench that fills the Hôpital St. Louis," but the city took no action, and the Hôtel Dieu was forced to hire a private guard to prevent further dumping at Montfaucon.[49] Second, the hospital had difficulty in obtaining sufficient supplies of water, an extraordinary oversight since by 1607 an abundant water supply was considered essential to a hospital. Indeed, hospitals were usually situated near rivers, as with the Hôtel Dieu on the banks of the Seine, or provided with a moat, as at the Lazzaretto di San Gregorio and the Ospedale Maggiore in Milan. The decision to build the Hôpital St. Louis far from the Seine or any other assured water source confirms the secondary importance accorded patient health and the greater weight given to broader urban considerations — specifically, achieving the delicate balance between isolation and proximity to Paris.

The relative inattention paid to the needs of the patients, however, did not hinder the crown from capitalizing on the memory of an exalted benefactor of the sick and afflicted. In early 1608, the hospital, or *maison de santé* (house of health) as it was called until then, was named in honor of Saint Louis. The dedication carried political resonances that contemporaries could not fail to appreciate. Saint Louis (1226–70) was the royal model of Christian charity and devotion. The original founder of the Hôtel Dieu, the Hôpital des Quinze Vingts, and numerous other charitable foundations, he had died of the plague while fighting the Crusades in Tunis. The Hôpital St. Louis associated the devout saint with the Bourbon king whose Christian faith was still questioned by many Frenchmen. It also reiterated the political legitimacy of Henri IV, whose claim to the throne was based on his distant descent from Saint Louis. The plague hospital demonstrated Henri IV's rightful claim as *Rex Christianissimus,* the Most Christian King.[50]

The king selected the hospital design without any delay in May 1607. The governors of the Hôtel Dieu sent their colleague Pierre Sainctot to Fontainebleau "to deliver to the king . . . several plans for the building of the *maison de santé* to know which of them His Majesty finds agreeable."[51] It is striking that a group dominated by high-ranking nobles chose the merchant Sainctot to be its representative at the court. Sainctot had been to Fontainebleau in 1604 to discuss the royally sponsored silkworks, and now, in the spring of 1607, he and his partners were again negotiating with the crown about the silk business and the transformation of the Place Royale. Perhaps the governors expected Sainctot to receive a more favorable reception because of his leadership in another project so important to the king. Sainctot remained more closely involved with the hospital than any other governor throughout the building process; he frequently visited the construction site and attended official inspections. It is not known how many designs Sainctot originally carried to Fontainebleau, but while he was at court, two additional plans were sent to him from Paris.[52]

Sully inscribed the king's approval on the winning scheme (Fig. 124). "The king, having seen the three plans which were shown to him of the *maison de la Santé,* has ordered that the present one be followed. Executed at Fontainebleau by the *Grand Voyer* of France Maximilien de Bethune."[53] This drawing, the only one for Henri IV's Parisian buildings that survived to modern times, vanished from the Archives of the Assistance Publique between 1937 and 1950. Now known only from photographs, the plan is amplified by the masonry specifications published on 1 June 1607, when the Hôtel Dieu invited bids for the contract.[54] The original design was subsequently modified due to practical considerations that emerged during construction. Those changes are described in later contracts and in inspections of the finished work, and a metalworker employed at the hospital in 1681 was thoughtful enough to make a plan that explained how all the buildings were used (Fig. 125).[55] With these documents, we can trace the development of the building's monumental form.

The hospital occupied a large rectangular field, roughly 27 acres in area, with two hemicycles projecting from the short sides, to the left and right on the plan (see Fig. 124). The entire enclave was surrounded by a wall with guardhouses at each of the four corners and an entry pavilion along the central axis, at the bottom of the plan, through which the sick entered the hospital. The axial pavilion on the far side of the enclave was not originally planned as an entryway, but the design was soon modified to provide access to a cemetery planned north of the hospital.[56]

Within these walls, the buildings were situated so as to maximize the distance between the infected patients and the staff. The sick were confined to their own precinct at the center of the complex: four ranges enclosing a courtyard, the *cour des malades,* 50 *toises* square (99 meters square). A chapel had originally been planned in the center of the courtyard; it was replaced by a fountain, and a simple altar was installed in the lower left pavilion of the quadrangle. The ranges were modulated by a series of projecting elements, each expressing a different interior use of space. Corner and axial pavilions projected outside the quadrangle while inside the courtyard were large axial pavilions for the staircases; smaller units at the midpoint of each half-range for chimneys and wash basins; and L-shaped corner elements for toilets (Figs. 126, 127). The ranges rose two unequal stories and were topped by a steeply pitched timber roof pierced by dormers. The ground floor interior was divided by a row of piers supporting groin vaults; it formed a closed, cellar-like space, while the much taller upper floor was bathed in light from the long windows and dormers (Figs. 128, 129).

Since only the upper floor was to be used for patients, circulation between the courtyard and the second floor was an important consideration. In the original design, the four axial pavilions housed a pair of single-return flights, an arrangement that blocked direct passage between the quadrangle and the exterior (see Fig. 124).[57] In 1611, the masons were instructed to tear down the stairs in

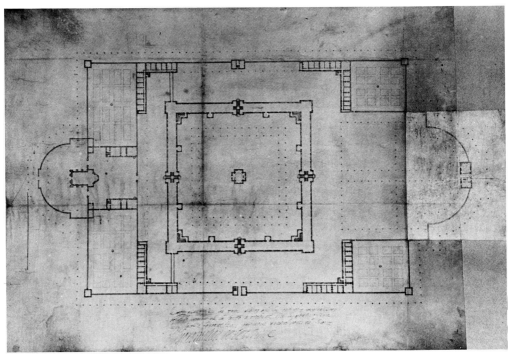

Fig. 124. Hôpital St. Louis, plan signed by Sully, 1608. (Archives de l'Assistance Publique de Paris)

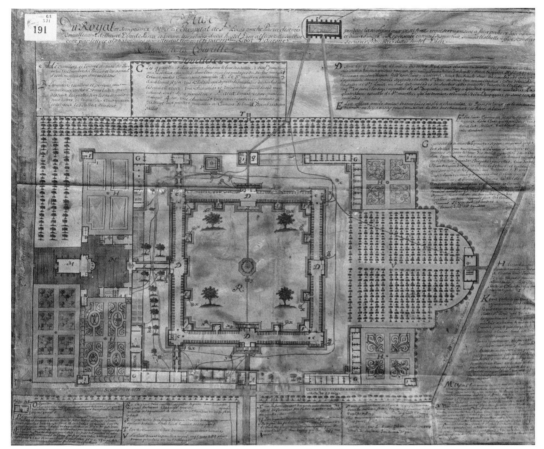

Fig. 125. Robert Davesne, Hôpital St. Louis, plan, 1681. (Archives de l'Assistance Publique de Paris, plan 191)

the north and south pavilions (at the top and bottom of the plan) and to rebuild them according to a new design.[58] Now the patient began his climb to the sick wards by an exterior staircase with two converging flights. The elevated landing left room below for a vaulted passageway through the pavilions (Fig. 130). The modified stairs differentiated the north and south pavilions, slightly accentuating the axis by which the plague victims would make their journey from the city to the hospital, and for the unlucky ones, beyond to the cemetery.

Outside the quadrangle, bracketing its corners, were four L-shaped buildings. They were divided into individual rooms, each heated by a chimney (see Fig. 130). The two L-shaped buildings on the right side, the *logis des bourgeois,* were intended for patients able to pay for private rooms. The two on the left were for the staff of the hospital: priests, doctors, surgeons, and an apothecary in

Fig. 126. Hôpital St. Louis, view of the southeast range, 1909. (B.N. Est. Va 291)

Fig. 127. Hôpital St. Louis, view of the courtyard. (Author)

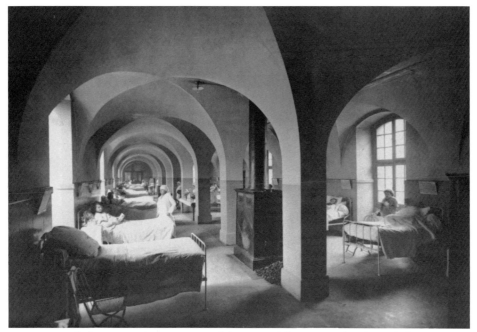

Fig. 128. Hôpital St. Louis, interior view of the ground floor, 1937. (Archives de l'Assistance Publique de Paris)

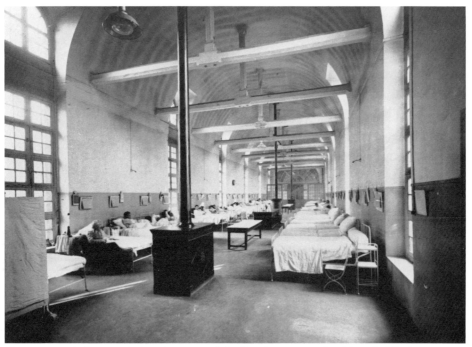

Fig. 129. Hôpital St. Louis, interior view of the first floor, 1937. (Archives de l'Assistance Publique de Paris)

one, nuns and female servants in the other.[59] Each of the L-shaped buildings bordered a kitchen garden, which supplied the hospital with food and herbs. The residences of the hospital staff were linked to the corner pavilions of the quadrangle by two closed passageways; as a result of design changes in 1608, the galleries were raised above an open arcade on ground level so that the staff had direct access to the upper floor of the sick wards.[60]

At the sides of the hospital enclave, two hemicycles were planned with buildings on the lateral axis of the complex (see Fig. 124). On the right side, beyond a field of elm trees, was a pavilion for the governors of the Hôtel Dieu. On the left side was a church. During the course of construction, the semicircular wall was eliminated and the nave elongated by an additional bay, projecting the building in the public domain, as Israël Silvestre's view reveals (Fig. 131, see Fig. 130). These changes made it clear that the church was not restricted to the hospital community but was open to the city at large. The governors of the Hôtel Dieu clarified its public function because the church's success in collecting donations and raising funds for the hospital depended on its ability to draw a large following. The same concern prompted the king's request in 1608 that the pope grant the hospital church full indulgences on the feast day of St. Louis, a request that was granted later that year.[61]

The church belonged to the public sector of the Hôpital St. Louis. Gates on both sides of the nave led to the service court. The bakery and kitchen were installed in the side wings; the two small pavilions were originally used by porters and later enlarged as stables.[62] During construction, it was decided to isolate the healthy workers and churchgoers from the plague-infected by closing off the service courtyard from the sick wards. Opposite the apse, a pavilion was built with two flanking staircases that led to the kitchen and bakery (see Figs. 124, 125). By building a two-story gallery between the pavilion and quadrangle, the architect devised a system for transporting food and other provisions from the service buildings to the patients while limiting contact between the two communities.[63]

The same formal vocabulary, materials, and scale that we have seen at the two royal squares characterized the Hôpital St. Louis. Except for the stone church, the buildings were faced in brick with quoins, stringcourses, and dormers in stone.[64] The quadrangle superficially recalls the Place Royale in that one passed through an axial entry pavilion, similar to the King's Pavilion, to discover an enclosed square surrounded by uniform buildings of brick and stone. But the Place Royale design was far more skillful, achieving a refined balance between its planar facade and the volume of the roofs. At the hospital, the

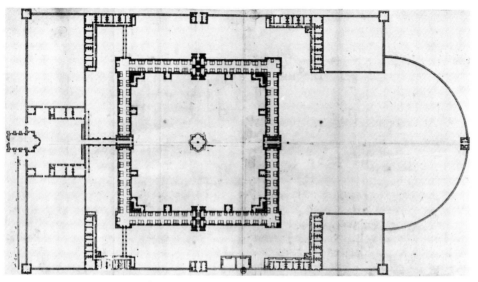

Fig. 130. Anonymous, Hôpital St. Louis, plan, seventeenth century. (B.N. Est. Va 291)

Veuë de l'Eglise de l'Hospital de Sainct Louis basti hors la porte du Temple par Henry quatriefme pour la commodité et le foulagement de ceux qui font attaquez de la maladie.

Fig. 131. Church of the Hôpital St. Louis. Engraving by Israël Silvestre, c. 1650–55. (B.N. Est. Va 291)

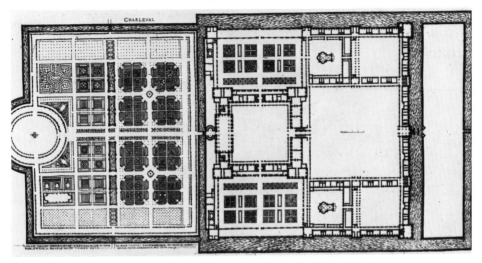

Fig. 132. Jacques Androuet Ducerceau, château de Charleval, plan. Engraving by Jacques Androuet Ducerceau, *Les plus excellents bastiments de France,* 1576–79. (B.N. Est. Ed 2a)

volumes were poorly proportioned and the roofs awkwardly combined. These weaknesses eliminate the possibility that the hospital was designed by royal architects Ducerceau and Métezeau.

The basic scheme of the quadrangle, a square courtyard surrounded by buildings of uniform height with corner and axial pavilions, derived from a form of château common in the sixteenth century. Examples of this model included Lescot's design for the Louvre and Ducerceau's Charleval (Fig. 132; see Fig. 10). Several other features suggest that the architect of the Hôpital St. Louis studied the French château. For example, the exterior staircase, which at the hospital provided access to the sick wards, was used to take the château owner from the *piano nobile* to his garden. The governors' pavilion set in a semicircular wall, *en théâtre* according to the documents, combines two motifs: the curved garden wall as at the Tuileries (see Fig. 11) and the pavilion *en théâtre* as in Ducerceau's project for a palace, dating from the 1570s (Fig. 133). Finally, the three galleries providing covered passage between the service buildings and the quadrangle derive from the nobleman's gallery, which in its primitive state was used strictly for circulation. Ducerceau illustrates a more elaborate example in the château of Maulnes (Fig. 134).

If the quadrangle reflects the planning tradition of the sixteenth-century château, the small Latin-cross church takes us far from the Valois court and French Renaissance architecture. The facade of the church was treated as a field

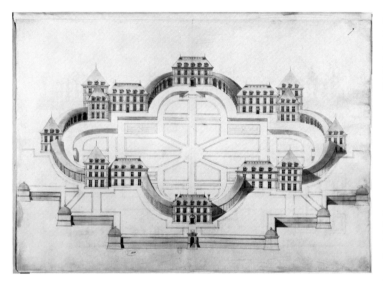

Fig. 133. Attributed to Jacques Androuet Ducerceau, project for a palace. (B.N. Est. rés. Ed 2p)

Fig. 134. Château de Maulnes. Engraving by Jacques Androuet Ducerceau, *Les plus excellents bastiments de France,* 1576–79. (B.N. Est. Ed 2)

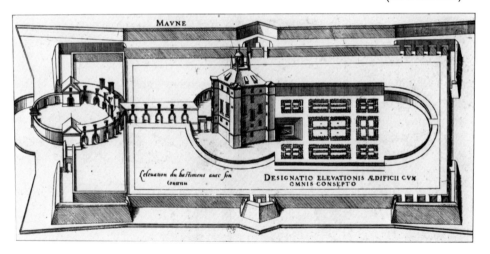

of sculptural decoration, with statues of the king and queen filling the niches beside the entrance, and the royal arms and an inscribed marble tablet honoring Henri IV placed above the door (Fig. 135).[65] The entrance was framed by an attenuated arched molding, with an oculus opening above it in the gable. This high curve at first recalls François Mansart's later Church of the Visitation (1632), yet the difference between these examples reveals how removed the hospital church was from principles of classical design (Fig. 136). Mansart's arch

Fig. 135. Church of the Hôpital St. Louis, 1909. (B.N. Est. Va 291)

is the semicircular extension of a classical cornice resting on the piers of the porch; at the church of St. Louis, the arched molding is only a decorative device with no reference to the structure of the wall. The gabled facade has a Flemish ancestry that is confirmed in the lateral elevation and its massive buttresses. An architect steeped in French Gothic traditions would probably not have divided the nave elevation with a bold stringcourse that truncated the windows and destroyed the vertical accent. At the Hôpital St. Louis, we are in the presence of an architect of Flemish roots, schooled in brick-and-stone construction, in French château planning, and in the architecture of Henri IV.

This man was Claude Vellefaux (15? – 1627/29), whose present obscurity hardly corresponds to his prominence in early-seventeenth-century Paris. Born in the Franche-Comté, then part of the northern empire of the Spanish Haps-burgs, the young Vellefaux would have been exposed to the Flemish culture that filtered through the southern Netherlands. He reached Paris during the 1580s, and by the time he was granted letters of naturalization by Henri IV in 1600, he was already one of the leading masons in Paris.[66] One of the city's four expert-masons, he was involved in numerous municipal projects, among them construction of the Porte St. Germain (1599) and the Chapelle du St. Esprit in the Hôtel de Ville (1608). By 1610, he was the surveyor for both the abbey of

LE FAMEVX FRONTISPICE DV TEMPLE DE S.^{te}MARIE
Situe à Paris Rue Saint Antoine du deſſeing de Manſart

Fig. 136. François Mansart, Church of the Visitation, 1632. Anonymous engraving. (B.N. Est. Va 251g)

St.-Germain-des-Prés and the Prince de Conti, two of the most powerful patrons on the Left Bank where Vellefaux lived.[67] Vellefaux was kept busiest in his role as building supervisor of the Hôtel Dieu, a position he held from 1602 until his death.[68] Whenever it was necessary to repair their dilapidated facilities, the governors relied on Vellefaux to produce the plans, prepare specifications, and undertake the masonry work, although the advice of other prominent masons was solicited on occasion. When Henri IV instructed the governors of the Hôtel Dieu to design a new pesthouse, they naturally turned to their chief mason.

Vellefaux was controller of the building project, *Contrôleur de la maison de la santé*, a job that required him to visit the site twice a day, enforce the design, measure the completed masonry work (*toisé*), and occasionally pay the workers. For this he received a monthly salary of 100 *livres*.[69] On 27 November 1607, the minutes of the executive committee of the Hôtel Dieu record a payment for other work:

> The Company delivered payment order to Claude Vellefaux, sworn master mason for the sum of 257 *livres* 3 *sols tournois* as reimbursement for what he paid to those who helped him make the drawing and model in elevation of the *maison de la Santé* . . . , and for the cost of food incurred several times when the sworn masons inspected the masonry work that was done in the said building, and [for] other expenses . . .[70]

To a modern reader, this passage leaves open the possibility that Vellefaux was only the draftsman and not the author of the plan. That interpretation reflects the view held by several modern historians, who point out that he is always identified in the documents as a mason.[71] But in early-seventeenth-century French architectural practice, the same individual was normally responsible for drafting, designing, and building, thus it is likely that Vellefaux executed all of these tasks. The documents are more explicit in other passages: masons are instructed to ornament the church following "the design made by Vellefaux," to build the governors' pavilion "according to the design he submitted," and to follow his designs for the remodeled staircases and fountain.[72] While the documents never explicitly call him an architect, the evidence suggests that Vellefaux was the designer of the Hôpital St. Louis. The point is important because the distinction between the architect-designer and mason-builder was not firmly established for several decades; designing functions and manual labor were, to a large extent, still connected in the architectural culture of France before the founding of the Royal Academy in 1671.

Vellefaux's scheme departed from all precedents in hospital design. He rejected the model of Filarete's Ospedale Maggiore as well as the ideal projects he may have seen, such as Jacques Androuet Ducerceau's schemes for a circular hospital (see Fig. 116).[73] Vellefaux did learn from the Grenelle pesthouse, which he must have seen during its brief existence in the 1580s (see Fig. 118). Both plague hospitals had large courtyards surrounded by two-story buildings with axial and corner pavilions. Both had open wards, rejecting the model of the famous lazaretto in Milan, which was planned like a Carthusian cloister with separate cells for the patients. But both the Grenelle pesthouse and the lazaretto confined all of their services within a single courtyard, offering Vellefaux no guidance on how to accommodate the many facilities at the Hôpital St. Louis— sick wards, kitchen, bakery, laundry, stables, pharmacy, lodgings for the staff, and meeting place for the administrators. His challenge was to integrate the multiple elements of the project while restricting contact between the healthy and the sick.

We have already seen that the sixteenth-century château was a reference point for the design of specific elements of the hospital, but Vellefaux also used it as a model for the organization of the entire complex. The Hôpital St. Louis, like a château, combined several components: service court, main court, church, and garden. In a château designed on a regular plan, such as the elder Ducerceau's colossal palace of Charleval, these elements were arranged along a central axis: forecourt, court of honor, and garden, with service areas discreetly located to the side (see Fig. 132). Reading the plan of the Hôpital St. Louis across the lateral axis, we find a similar sequence of spaces: service court, quadrangle, and garden. Even the placement of the L-shaped buildings echoes the detached pavilions at the corners of a moated platform, such as those built for Henri IV and Gabrielle d'Estrées at Montceaux (before 1600). But the lateral axis survives in the hospital only as a formal reference; as an axis of circulation, it has been suppressed because of the overriding need to isolate the plague-striken. There were three separate entrances to the hospital preserving the independence of each precinct within the enclave: the public entrance to the church and service court to the west, the entrance for the sick to the south, and the private entrance for the governors of the Hôtel Dieu to the east.

In short, Vellefaux recomposed the traditional elements of château design to satisfy the need for isolated precincts within the compound. The result was not only a highly original hospital, but a project of such grandeur that visitors commonly mistook its function. "At first one would take this house for a true royal palace, and more for a place of pleasure than a retreat of the plague-striken," read the caption added to Chastillon's engraving of the Hôpital St. Louis in 1641. The Englishman Peter Heylyn had a similar reaction in 1656; it is "a house built quadrangular wise, very large and capacious; and seemeth to such a stand afar off it (for it is not safe venturing nigh it or within) to be more like the Palace of a king, than the King's Palace itself."[74]

BUILDING AND OPERATING THE HOSPITAL

Henri IV had laid the first stone of the Hôpital St. Louis on 13 July 1607; five years later, the hospital was complete. Given the delays caused by a severe winter that damaged the masonry of the church, late design changes that required some rebuilding, and ongoing financial disputes with masons, it was built with remarkable speed. The masonry contract was originally awarded to a team of inexperienced masons who had substantially underbid their competitors.[75] Quickly discovering that they could not afford to work at the rate of 9 *livres* 15 *sols* per square *toise,* they resigned from the project. The governors replaced them with a more seasoned team of masons, Perceval Noblet and his brother Louis, Sébastien Jacquet, and Antoine Desnotz, who were paid at the rate of 11 *livres*.[76] But a year later, they too asked to terminate the contract. The governors of the Hôtel Dieu refused, and the masons struggled on for another year before trying once again to unburden themselves of the job. This time the governors consented, inviting other contractors to take over. When none would accept the job for less than 15 *livres,* the governors agreed to renegotiate with the Noblet brothers and a new rate of 13 *livres* 10 *sols* was established.[77] Recalling the rate of 24 *livres* paid for the Place Dauphine facade, it would seem that the hospital's long walls of brick and stone raised construction costs beyond the expectations of the masons.

Construction began with the church and proceeded eastward. When the masons reached the quadrangle, they feared that "because of the length of the wings and without the reinforcement of *dosserets* and buttresses [*contrepiliers*], the vaults might push out and buckle the walls . . . ," and so experts were consulted to determine if it was necessary to buttress the ground-floor vaults.[78] The stone quoins were thinly cut and, like the brick, only dressed the facade, playing no structural role in strengthening the wall of rubble. Nonetheless the experts concluded that buttresses were not needed. When the dauphin visited the building site in August 1609, he saw half of the hospital completed, a phase that is captured in the maps of Nicolay and Quesnel, inaccurately in the former case (see Figs. 122, 123). A year later, construction had advanced to the east range of the quadrangle; by 1611, the quadrangle was closed, and all the peripheral buildings were completed. The only remaining work involved the projects that were modified during the construction process: the galleries, the axial pavilion in the service court, and the remodeled stairs in the quadrangle. But for a few finishing touches, the Hôpital St. Louis was completed in June 1612.

To bring this project to completion within five years required a large building crew and a constant flow of money. Du Breul estimated two to three hundred men were working on the hospital. His figure is probably inflated, even if it included the day workers on poor-relief dispatched by the municipality to terrace the site and the fifty masons and unskilled laborers that Vellefaux hired to lay the water pipes.[79] The building accounts provide no tally, but even with a more prudent estimate of 150 workers at the height of construction, the Hôpital St. Louis was, after the Louvre, the largest building site in Paris.

The governors calculated the total cost of building the Hôpital St. Louis at 679,068 *livres*. More than half of that sum, 383,283 *livres,* went to the masons (see Appendix C). Among the other items listed in the inventory of construction costs was 5,900 *livres* paid to "sieur Vellefaux sworn mason for having made the designs of the building and carried out the supervision," at a rate of 100 *livres* per month for fifty-nine months; the architect was not compensated specifically for the design of the hospital. The royal revenues drawn from the salt tax covered only 40 percent (268,000 *livres*) of the building expenses, according to an appeal from the governors to the crown for additional funds. Louis XIII granted their appeal by renewing in perpetuity a part of the salt tax, which had originally been assigned to the Hôtel Dieu only for a short term.[80] The documents do not indicate the ultimate financial burden borne by the Hôtel Dieu. What is most surprising about the cost of the Hôpital St. Louis is not the large sums spent by the crown and the Hôtel Dieu (nearly 700,000 *livres*), but rather that the investment was made for a hospital to be open only during times of plague. The expense underscores the importance of the monumental plague hospital as a symbol of the security and stability of Henri IV's Paris.

The Hôpital St. Louis was initially kept empty for four years, and then was used only to accommodate the surplus of patients at the Hôtel Dieu, still straining in its medieval quarters. An outbreak of plague in 1618 put the pesthouse to its first test. The original plan had anticipated the installation of the plague-stricken on only the upper floor, elevated above the humid, telluric vapors suspected of escaping from the ground and aggravating contagion. This policy was not followed during the first period of occupancy. The infected were placed on the ground floor and the recuperating patients on the upper level, segregated by sex; a cemetery was opened north of the hospital for the deceased.[81] This arrangement was altered during subsequent epidemics, with the ground floor used for kitchens, and the sick and the recuperating all on the upper floor but confined to different ranges. Every patient at the Hôpital St. Louis had his own bed, which in and of itself represented an improvement; in 1632, 260 beds were filled, and the hospital reached its capacity of 900 in 1679.[82]

In the absence of comparative mortality figures, we cannot know whether the plague-stricken had a greater chance of survival at the Hôpital St. Louis than might otherwise have been the case. In any event, the reputation of the hospital was not sufficiently compelling to tempt any patients able to afford private rooms, and the two L-shaped buildings intended for that purpose were filled with doctors, embalmers, and other health officers. The Hôpital St. Louis was used steadily between 1618 and 1636, though not exclusively by plague victims. It was then closed for many years, reopening briefly in 1651/52 and in 1670 for victims of scurvy, followed by short periods of operation during the last quarter of the century. Between 1612 and 1700, the hospital was open for no more than twenty-six years, primarily because the number of epidemics in seventeenth-century France had diminished.

From the point of view of the royal and municipal authorities, the success of the Hôpital St. Louis depended less on curing the sick than on confining them. By this standard, Henri IV's plague reform and the hospital that was the centerpiece of that effort proved to be effective. An administration of public health officers policed the city, rounded up the infected, and delivered them to the pesthouse, where the sick were enclosed. The Hôpital St. Louis was the city's defense against the plague; even empty, the building represented insurance against urban disorder. Mathieu Merian's view of Paris, engraved in 1616, expressed the symbolic importance of the hospital (Fig. 137). The king, queen, and their attendants overlook the city from the hills of Belleville, and between the royal couple, in the middle ground, lies the Hôpital St. Louis, the most prominent monument in the urban landscape. Martin Zeiller included a similar view of Paris in his *Topographia Galliae* (1655), "Paris as it was seen in 1620," with the monumental hospital spreading before the city in miniature (Fig. 138).

Fig. 137. Mathieu Merian, view of Paris from the north, 1616. (B.N. Est. rés. Hennin XX 1798)

Fig. 138. Martin Zeiller, view of Paris from the north, c. 1620 (B.N. Est. rés. Hennin XXI 1886)

The Hôpital St. Louis relieved the walls around Paris of their prophylactic role. With the infected enclosed in the pesthouse, the ramparts were no longer needed to stop the sick who would not be parted from their family or their property from reentering the city. At the same time as the hospital eliminated the sanitary function of the wall, Sully was fortifying the boundaries of France, thus depriving the bastions of their strategic value as well. The walls of Paris became vestigial, losing both their functional and symbolic value as the constituent element holding Paris together. Henri IV's urbanism had moved Paris toward becoming an open city, a city whose boundaries no longer needed to be marked.

Likewise, within the walls, a new order was being forged that gave unity to the loose patchwork of parishes. In terms of social organization, the new squares and hospital served not one neighborhood but the entire city. In terms of physical organization, the buildings were designed on a larger scale than Paris had ever before seen, an urban scale opening up great vistas and revealing the landscape of the city as a spectacle to behold.

The advocates of hospital reform at the end of the eighteenth century were impressed by the functional organization of the Hôpital St. Louis. They admired the construction of a single floor in the wards that prevented contagious patients from being stacked above each other, the tall windows that allowed the "morbid atmosphere" to escape, and the enclosing wall and double ring of courtyards that isolated the hospital from the city. Tenon, writing in 1788, found the Hôpital St. Louis fit as a facility for contagious diseases, "because it partakes of a hospital, lazaretto and prison." [83] His principal complaints concerned the absence of partition walls in the sick wards, allowing infection to circulate freely from one wing to the next, and the shortage of drinking water. The emphasis on the hospital's functional structure by men of the Enlightenment overlooked the atrocious conditions which the Englishman John Howard, moved by a different reforming spirit, could not ignore. "The Hospitals of Saint-Louis and the Hôtel-Dieu for the sick, are the two worst hospitals that I ever visited," he wrote in 1792. "The Hospital of Saint-Louis stands out of the city. There is a considerable ascent to the wards, and there is no floor over them. They were dirty and noisy, and in many of the beds there were three patients. These two hospitals are a disgrace to Paris . . ." [84]

Various proposals were made to enlarge the Hôpital St. Louis, beginning with Louis XVI's finance minister Necker in 1780, who submitted a broad reform that would have substantially altered the seventeenth-century buildings. The Hôtel Dieu objected to the plan, arguing that the hospital was "a masterpiece of this type, which one could not touch without spoiling it."[85] The hospital was preserved, although nineteenth- and twentieth-century structures have encroached upon the old pesthouse. Some of the seventeenth-century buildings have been destroyed, some survive in a radically remodeled state, and nearly all the brick has been replaced by plaster.[86] But even in this degraded state, one recognizes the grandeur of the old plague hospital — part palace, part prison.

CHAPTER FIVE

UNFINISHED PROJECTS: THE PLACE DE FRANCE AND COLLÈGE DE FRANCE

By 1609 Parisians were beginning to see the results of Henri IV's urbanism. The Pont Neuf and Grande Galerie of the Louvre were completed, and construction of the Place Royale, Place Dauphine, and Hôpital St. Louis was well advanced. Two city maps publicizing the king's buildings and offering a global image of Henri IV's Paris were published that year. These accomplishments encouraged the king to pursue his building program. A northern gallery between the Louvre and the Tuileries was under discussion, and in the last months of 1609, the crown plotted two more projects: a square in northeast Paris and a royal college in the university district, on the Left Bank. Construction of the square and college was about to begin when the king was assassinated on 14 May 1610. Without Henri IV and his administration, the royal commitment that was needed to realize these projects was lost.

THE PLACE DE FRANCE

Only one sizable tract of agricultural land remained within the walls on the Right Bank. Between the Porte du Temple and the Place Royale lay approximately 25 acres of kitchen gardens and orchards known as the couture du Temple (see Fig. 71). The property was owned by the priory of the Temple, an enclave of buildings on the rue du Temple where the Parisian chapter of the Knights Hospitaler of St. John of Jerusalem had been installed since the twelfth century. The Temple had leased the *couture* to gardeners, but the rising real estate market in Henri IV's Paris convinced the order that it would be more profitable to sell the land for construction. The mother house in Malta approved the sale in May 1607, and the following December, the priory appointed representatives to discuss the enterprise with the crown, "to learn its desire and direct people to establish the design, plan, and order of streets." [1]

Initially the crown attached no importance to the development of the couture du Temple. By 1608 Sully, in his capacity as *Grand Voyer*, established an unambitious street plan, recorded in an undated drawing in the Archives Nationales. The plan projected four concentric rings and three radial streets, each

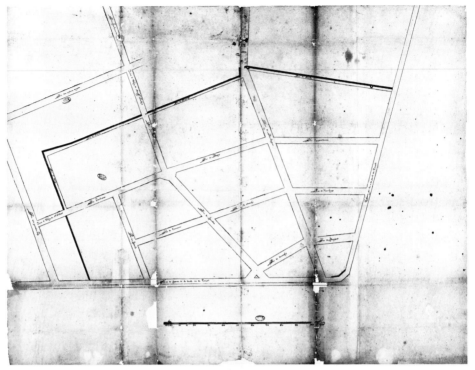

Fig. 139. Couture du Temple, first street plan, here dated 1608. (A.N. S5063 A; Service Photographique des Archives Nationales)

named after one of the provinces of France (Fig. 139). The fan shape of the scheme was determined by the course of the open sewer that demarcated the northern boundary of the site; after running parallel to the west range of the Place Royale, the sewer followed the curving trajectory of Charles V's wall to the Porte du Temple (see Figs. 70, 71). The new roads were to be linked to existing ones; the rue de Poitou cut through a garden to connect with the rue Pastourelle, and the rue d'Orléans was to join the rue des Quatre Fils. But the new streets did not extend to the primary roads on the Right Bank, the rue du Temple and the rue St. Martin. Sully projected a series of local streets, contained by the irregular boundaries of the couture du Temple and serving only that neighborhood.

The Temple concluded preparations for the sale in 1608. An agreement was reached with the gardeners to compensate them for the loss of their plantings. After the harvest, the site was cleared and surveyed; in December 1608, the land was sold at auction.[2] On the third day of bidding, the Temple accepted the terms of Michel Pigou, an obscure *bourgeois de Paris* who offered to buy the entire

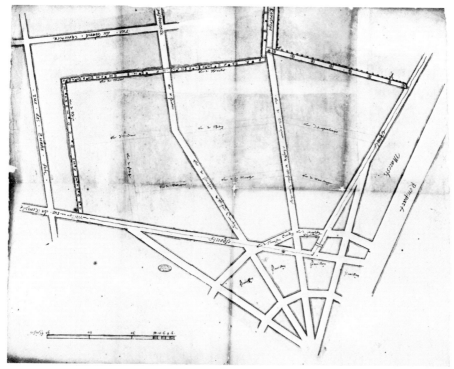

Fig. 140. Couture du Temple, revised street plan, here dated 1609. (A.N. S5063 A; Service Photographique des Archives Nationales)

tract for 52,000 *livres,* including 8,000 *livres* for the gardeners. In addition, Pigou agreed to build and pave the roads dictated by Sully's plan and to pay the Temple 600 *livres* in *cens,* the annual dues claimed by a seignorial land owner. The *cens* would be collected from forty houses to be built in the *couture.* Although Pigou was named in all the contracts, he was acting on behalf of a group of investors: Claude du Nesme and Nicolas Carrel, the developers of the rue Dauphine; Paul Aymeret, *maître ordinaire* in the *Chambre des comptes;* Paul Nivelle, *controleur des guerres,* and his nephew, publisher Sébastien Cramoisy; Charles Margonne, *commissaire des guerres,* and François Rousselet, former Controller-general of the fortifications of Picardy.[3] Margonne and Rousselet had participated in the auction and backed out after Pigou made his offer; these facts raise suspicions that the men had secretly maneuvered to keep the bidding down.

The crown approved the sale to Pigou in January 1609, but months passed without the developers taking any action.[4] It seems that the delay was caused by the *Grand Voyer,* who was reconsidering his street plan for the couture du Temple. The limited scope of the 1608 plan effectively meant surrendering an

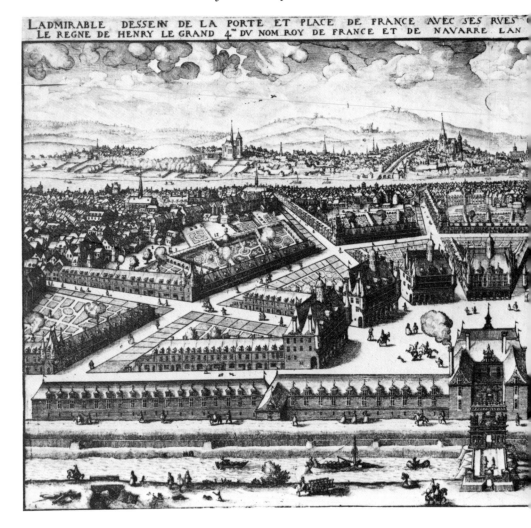

LADMIRABLE DESSEIN DE LA PORTE ET PLACE DE FRANCE AVEC SES RVES
LE REGNE DE HENRY LE GRAND 4.me DV NOM ROY DE FRANCE ET DE NAVARRE LAN

opportunity to embellish the city; a year later, the crown reversed itself and decided to use the *lotissement* to subsidize a new public amenity. In an edict dated 6 October 1609, the king announced his intention "to reclaim the 25 *arpents* of land or thereabouts purchased by Pigou from the Commander of the Temple on which His Majesty intends to build streets and houses and other buildings for the decoration of his good city of Paris, most of which will be built with money provided by His Majesty for this purpose." 5 The revised design failed to incorporate plans for a square and city gate; only "streets and houses and other buildings" were projected, as we can see from a second, undated drawing in the Archives Nationales detailing the crown's second scheme (Fig. 140). The crown enlarged the site by annexing the land lying between the sewer and the ram-

ONSTRVIRE ES MARESTX DV TEMPLE A PARIS DVRANT SIX CENS ET DIX PAR CLAVDE CHASTILLON CHAALONNOIS

Fig. 141. Claude Chastillon and Jacques Alleaume, Porte and Place de France, 1610. Engraving after Chastillon, 1615. (B.N. Est. rés. Ve 9)

parts, and extended the radial streets to the ramparts. Symmetric houses were probably planned for these streets ("cymetrie" is written in the two middle streets), and pavilions for the four large blocks north of the sewer. But there is no indication of a square in either the drawing or the edict of 6 October 1609.

Within the next month, royal engineers Claude Chastillon and Jacques Alleaume established the final design for a new square and city gate, the Place and Porte de France.[6] According to Chastillon, Sully brought the engineers to the *couture* and had them draw a plan for the square in situ. The design is recorded in an engraving and description of the project by Chastillon, published in 1615, in an appeal to Louis XIII to bring it to completion (Fig. 141).[7] The engraving depicts a strictly geometric composition with eight radial streets, double the number in the 1609 plan. The engineers must have taken over additional land between the rue Vieille-du-Temple and the ramparts to accommodate the left part of the square, but the generalized topography in Chastillon's engraving does not clarify the precise location of the square. This design did not require the crown to take over the *couture* as the 1609 edict had anticipated. The square proper was carved from the annexed land without invading the Pigou property, and the developers agreed to sell the housing lots with the stipulation that the owners build in accordance with the royal design.[8] The Porte de France was placed at the radial point of the composition, in the middle of a long market hall. Bordering the semicircular *place* were seven uniform buildings, their elevation mirrored in the city facade of the Porte de France. The radial streets intersected a ring road 40 *toises* beyond the square, with each corner marked by a turreted building and all the streets lined by uniform houses.

The square was conceived as a monumental entry to Paris. Placed about midway between the Portes St. Antoine and du Temple, the new gate was aligned with the road to Meaux. In Chastillon's print, the traveler crossed the canal, passed through the triumphal arch and *porte*, and upon entering the square faced a choice of eight routes into the city. Whereas the Place Royale and Place Dauphine were enclosed squares situated in the midst of the urban fabric, Chastillon and Alleaume designed the Place de France as a permeable space to accommodate its function as a gateway to the capital. Their concern was circulation, and they drew upon their expertise in military architecture, where it was common to use the radial plan to link the center of a citadel directly to the bastions. Chastillon shows his straight and relatively wide streets (6 *toises*) yielding to the narrow, winding ones of the existing fabric. The 1609 plan indicates where some of the links were planned (see Fig. 140): the radial street near the scale bar fed the rue Vieille-du-Temple; the rue de Poitou, after a slight change in direction, joined the rue Pastourelle which abutted the rue du Temple; and the rue de Bretagne led to the rue de la Corderie. The design strategy is clear: knit the new to the old with minimal disturbance to the Right Bank. Instead of extending the trajectory of the new streets through blocks of the old city, traffic was funneled indirectly from the square to the primary axes of the Right Bank, and obliged to follow the meanderings of local streets. The Place de France was the first of Henri IV's projects concerned with open circulation, but the logic of the design was constrained by the refusal to tamper with the existing fabric as the avenues of the Place de France petered out upon contact with the old city.

As an entryway to the city, the Place de France engaged the city wall as well as the interior streets, but Chastillon excluded the walls from his view (see Fig.

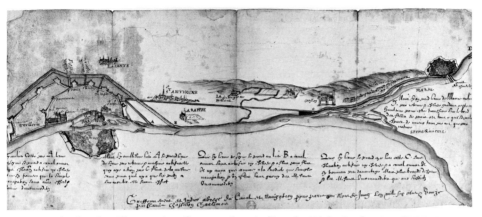

Fig. 142. Claude Chastillon, project for a canal encircling the Right Bank, 1615. (B.N. Est. rés. Ve 53d)

141). They were located on the far side of the canal. Gatehouses were normally set in the ramparts and restricted access to the city, yet the Porte de France was detached from the wall and played no defensive role. The market hall also failed to limit entry to the city. The length of the building was motivated by aesthetic considerations; according to Chastillon, the market was designed to prevent Parisians within the square from seeing the irregularities of the ramparts. Furthermore, while the hall has no entrances on the quai, one can enter the city simply by walking around either end of the building, as several travelers prepare to do in Chastillon's print. In short, the Porte de France was purely a ceremonial entrance.

Chastillon's engraving implicitly suggests a significant shift in the way the enclosure was conceived. In the foreground of his print, the engineer illustrated a project to transform the *fossé,* the ditch bordering the city side of the wall, into a navigable canal. With the general decay of the fortifications, the *fossé* had become a convenient but obnoxious dumping ground. In 1603, Henri IV had converted the section between the Seine and the Porte St. Antoine into a canal.[9] Since that time, the crown had received various proposals to extend the canal so that it fully encircled the Right Bank, including an unusually ambitious project in 1611 from Nicolas Carrel, developer of the rue Dauphine.[10] The canal was intended to facilitate the delivery of river cargo, increase the water supply, and service the street-cleaning program. Chastillon submitted his own project in 1615. In the only surviving autograph drawing by Chastillon, he analyzed four possible engineering solutions (Fig. 142). Options A, B, and C are open canals fed by the Seine and serve no function other than navigation. He recommended option D, a canal fed by the Marne, because it descended from higher ground, an advantage in dredging the channel, clearing sewage, pumping fountains, and supplying power. Chastillon depicted the city's defenses sandwiched between two canals, one in the *fossé,* corresponding to the Place de France engraving, and another lying beyond the ramparts. The canals did not supplant the ramparts, but they transformed that no-man's-land into a functional space of quotidian life and signaled the diminished strategic value attached to the city wall. By disarming the fortified zone, Chastillon's project redefined the boundary of Paris and helped make it possible to conceive of an open city, as Paris became in the 1670s when the walls were demolished.

Like the other royal squares, the Place de France was also programmed for a social purpose; it was intended as a seat of the royal administration, with the Grand Conseil installed in the buildings bordering the square.[11] The Grand Conseil was the sovereign court which handled issues relating to office-holding as well as matters referred by the Conseil d'Etat. This judicial body was undoubtedly selected to confer prestige upon the new neighborhood, although it is difficult to imagine the court's willing transfer from the Cité to the northern perimeter of the city. With the presence of the Grand Conseil and the street names invoking all parts of the realm, the Place de France was an emblem of the centrality of Paris, seat of the crown, within the French state. But the symbolism was imposed on the square after the fact. It did not generate the design, for the structure and names of the streets were already established in the 1608 plan, prior to any thought of the square. Nor did the political symbolism circumscribe the purpose of the square. As the market and the shops and houses on the side streets attest, the Place de France was not planned exclusively, nor even primarily, as a representational space of royal power, as were the *places royales* of Louis XIV. Henri IV's third square was planned as a social unit serving a new neighborhood and the city as a whole.

It is somewhat surprising that Sully chose Chastillon and Alleaume rather than royal architects Ducerceau and Métezeau to design the Place de France. Sully's choices were military engineers who, to the best of our knowledge, had no experience in civil architecture. Chastillon's career will be discussed in the next chapter. Alleaume (dates unknown) was renowned as a mathematician; his treatise on perspective and surveying, *La Perspective speculative et pratique,* was published posthumously in 1643. He taught at the national military academy of the United Provinces sometime between 1605 and 1608, and it is said that Maurice of Nassau was his student in mathematics. Upon returning to France, Alleaume was granted an apartment in the Louvre by Henri IV and was appointed royal engineer in Picardy in 1612.[12] Most likely, the *Grand Voyer* originally called upon the engineers to plan the roads in the *couture,* a task appropriate to their profession, and retained their services as the project evolved. Chastillon and Alleaume prescribed brick-and-stone construction for the square but the buildings otherwise departed from the royal style, with the corner turrets, elongated towers, and awkward twinning of hipped roofs drawing on a medieval vocabulary. Chastillon's authorship of these pavilions should put to rest any lingering suspicions that he designed the Place Royale and Place Dauphine. In terms of both architectural and urban design, the Place de France embodied values different from those of the two earlier squares. These disparities in approach remind us that Henri IV's urbanism did not devolve from one global plan, but was fashioned piecemeal over time by various minds.

In November 1609, the crown ordered the gardeners to vacate the hemicycle by the following April.[13] The crown presumably intended to begin construction soon after the deadline, but the king's death in May brought an end to the project. Neither the queen regent nor Louis XIII took an interest in the Place de France, and the development of the couture du Temple was completed without any further effort to realize Henri IV's scheme. The *lotissement* of the *couture* proceeded from October 1609 through 1612.[14] The contracts that were passed in 1609 and 1610 specify compliance with the royal design, but the clause was thereafter dropped. Lots were sold at prices ranging from 8 to 17 *livres* per square *toise,* well above the purchase price of close to 3 *livres* per *toise*.[15] In 1615, the crown granted three residents permission to establish a market in the new neighborhood, which grew as the large parcels controlled by the original partners continued to be subdivided until 1630.[16] Today the rues de Poitou and Bretagne remain the only vestige of Henri IV's design for the Place de France.

THE COLLÈGE DE FRANCE

The Left Bank was home of the university and the Sorbonne. These institutions had contributed to the stature of Paris across Europe, and while Henri IV had no interest in classical learning, he understood the value of this enterprise in the profile of a capital city. Henri IV's construction of the Collège de France "will prove in the future," wrote royal historiographer Jean de Serres, "that the king, more than any of his predecessors, favored the sciences, . . . filled the colleges, and continually worked to renew the famous Athens of France, the University of Paris, . . . the queen of the academies of Christianity."[17]

The program of the royal college was formulated originally by François I in 1530 with plans for a "college of the three languages" in the Hôtel de Nesle, where professors would give public lectures at the crown's expense. Professors of Greek, Hebrew, and Latin were appointed by the king, but the college was not built.[18] To accommodate the fledgling institution, Henri II leased two medieval buildings, the Collèges de Cambrai and de Tréguier, located on the rue St. Jean de Latran (today the rue des Ecoles) at the corner of the rue St. Jacques. This was the site on which Henri IV envisioned the Collège de France and on which it stands today (see Figs. 86, 87).

Sixteenth-century colleges were appendages to the university system and lacked the authority to grant degrees to graduating students.[19] The typical college had emerged in the medieval period as a pension for poor students, who were supported by private benefactors. In the early sixteenth century, there were nearly forty colleges in Paris, but during the second half of the century as the weak French economy eroded charitable funds, many colleges were forced to close. Colleges assumed a pedagogical function in the sixteenth century when they were taken over by humanist reformers promoting a new curriculum in Latin and Greek grammar. This association of the college with classical education underlay François I's conception of the Collège de France. The institutional history of the Parisian college is well illustrated by the Collège de Cambrai.[20] Founded in the late thirteenth century by the archbishop of Cambrai to provide board and instruction to six poor boys, the enterprise was subsidized in the following centuries by renting rooms to other students. Subsequently the crown, in need of a venue for its professors, took over the building for classes on the classical languages, supplemented in the course of the century by studies on medicine.

In late 1609, Henri IV decided to replace the dilapidated medieval structures with a new royal monument. The *Mercure françois* reported that Sully inspected the site on 23 December 1609 in the company of several dignitaries and reviewed plans for a college with four lecture rooms, apartments for the professors, and the royal library.[21] The royal library was then housed at Fontainebleau, and the crown had plans to transport its collection of books and manuscripts to the capital. This interest in the royal library, which surely did not emanate from the king personally, may well have been promoted by Isaac Casaubon, the royal librarian from 1604 until 1610. Casaubon certainly had cause to focus on the Collège de France; as royal professor of Greek, he could expect to teach and reside in the new building. In conjunction with the construction program, the king also assured the continued funding of the royal professors through the issuance of a bond for 30,000 *livres*.[22] It has been argued in a recent history of French universities that the crown extended its power into the administration and curriculum of the university during the sixteenth century, and that Henri IV contributed to this movement by appointing a commission in 1595 to draw up new regulations for the faculties, which the crown

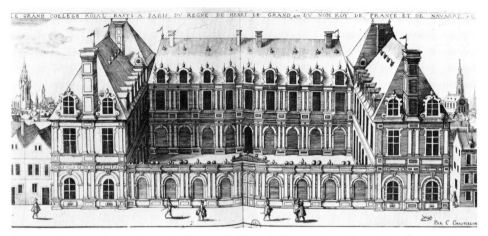

Fig. 143. Attributed to Salomon de Brosse, Collège de France, 1610. Engraving after Claude Chastillon, 1612. (B.N. Est. rés. Ve 9)

endorsed in 1600.[23] But his decision to build the Collège de France was not primarily conceived as an element in the crown's centralizing educational policy. Rather, it was rooted in the traditional model of the humanist prince committed to learning, and in the crown's ongoing effort to improve the city.

The building contracts were passed in February 1610, and their specifications are accurately recorded in Chastillon's engraving of the royal college (Fig. 143).[24] Three wings opened onto a courtyard (12 by 18 *toises*), which was enclosed along the rue St. Jean de Latran by a wall. In the main block were the professors' apartments, facing the rear, and in the side wings were ground-floor lecture rooms, with the library above. Reproducing the hôtel plan on a larger scale, the college stepped back from the street, seeking the tranquility provided by a forecourt, and it turned away from the busier rue St. Jacques, preserving the orientation of the original buildings. The concentrated ornament on the wall was the only nod to the city. With no further attempt to engage the urban fabric, to carve a public space before the royal monument, the Collège de France was the least ambitious of Henri IV's designs.

Nevertheless the lavish architectural decoration of the building, atypical of Parisian colleges, clearly expressed the royal status of the Collège de France. The fleurs-de-lys on the wall enclosing the courtyard were only the most obvious sign of the crown's patronage. As in Henri IV's other public buildings, the walls were to be built of brick and the ornament of stone. The two most important facades — the street elevation and the main wing on the courtyard — were to be decorated with a superimposed order of paired Ionic pilasters, except the end bays, where single pilasters were planned.

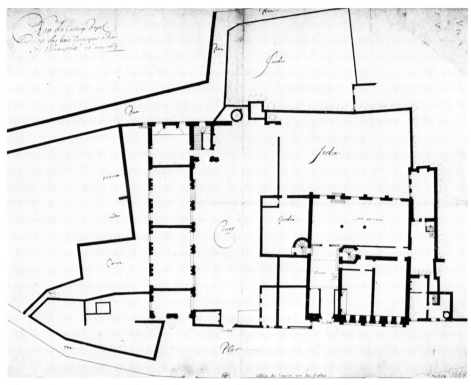

Fig. 144. Anonymous, Collège de France, site plan, 1664. (B.N. Est. Va 259h)

Although the documents do not identify the architect, these architectural details suggest that Salomon de Brosse designed the Collège de France. Rosalys Coope noted formal similarities to de Brosse's superimposed order at Bléran-court and his single corner pilaster at the Parlement of Rennes.[25] The college also anticipates the use of coupled pilasters at the Luxembourg Palace by de Brosse. The only other architects in Henri IV's Paris capable of endowing brick-and-stone construction with the classical order demonstrated at the Collège de France were the designers of the Place Royale. But the case for de Brosse is reinforced by the fact that a man identified as "Brosse" made the first and highest bid for the masonry contract: 25 *livres* per cubic *toise* compared to the winning bid of 14 *livres* by mason Claude Monnard. This "Brosse" presumably was Salomon — his son Paul must still have been a teenager — and surely he would not have sought to build the work of another architect.[26] Furthermore, Sully had recently shown his respect for de Brosse by hiring him in 1607 to design the buildings in Henrichemont.

Ground was not yet broken at the time of the regicide, at least in part because no agreement had been reached with the owners of the two colleges. In

July 1610, the crown purchased the Collège de Tréguier, which stood on the eastern half of the site; it was then demolished, and the first stone of the Collège de France was laid by Louis XIII on 28 September. In 1612, the crown bought the Collège de Cambrai and agreed to pay the pensions of three students who would continue to live at the college.[27] By this time, the east wing of the Collège de France was well advanced, but the crown thereafter lost interest in the project. In 1613 the masons complained that not even a quarter of the building was erected.[28] A plan of the royal college in 1664 shows that only the east wing had been built, while the Collège de Cambrai continued to occupy the west side of the site (Fig. 144). This drawing was made in connection with a project for the completion of the royal college, but it was never executed.

Another royal college was under construction in 1664: the Collège des Quatre Nations. Although Cardinal Mazarin financed the college and defined its activities, the Collège des Quatre Nations had the official status of a royal foundation. By comparison with this grand, domed building opposite the Louvre on the Left Bank, Henri IV's college appears extremely modest. The Collège de France, however, was planned simply to advance the academic standing of the foundation, not as a prominent urban monument. By contrast, Louis XIV's advisors consciously sacrificed educational considerations to embellish the area of the royal palace. The Collège des Quatre Nations did not offer the academic program proposed for the earlier college; that goal was not accomplished until the Collège de France was completed by Chalgrin in 1774.

But the legacy of Henri IV's urbanism is revealed in the urban design of the Collège des Quatre Nations: the building accepts geometric irregularities in deference to the surrounding streets, it responds to distant vistas, and it participates in the magnificent panorama encompassing the Seine, the Louvre, the Pont Neuf, and the Place Dauphine. In short, despite the limitations of the Collège de France from an urbanistic perspective, the architectural achievement represented by the Collège des Quatre Nations was a natural extension of Henri IV's urban vision.

CHAPTER SIX

THE IMAGE OF PARIS: MAPS, CITY VIEWS, AND THE NEW HISTORICAL FOCUS

Throughout the preceding chapters, bits of information were extracted from the maps by Nicolay and Quesnel to reconstruct the form of Henri IV's Paris. The maps were consulted for documentary purposes. But maps do not objectively reproduce a topographical reality; they interpret it subjectively through pictorial and verbal descriptions.

Cartographic history traditionally has focused on issues pertaining to the documentary value of maps — their accuracy, methods of construction, and genealogy. In recent years, however, a small but growing number of scholars have turned to maps as a subject of cultural history and probed their ideological and symbolic content.[1] That is the aim of this chapter: to reinstate the varied topographical texts of Henri IV's Paris in their political and cultural context and to decipher their symbolic representations of the city.

Sixteenth-century France had not fostered the topographical arts: mapmaking was a marginal enterprise, the topographical view a rarity, and architectural guidebooks nonexistent. These genres began to show new signs of life during Henri IV's reign. In 1609, Nicolay and Quesnel published two large wall maps of Paris, the first entirely new maps of the city in nearly eighty years. Claude Chastillon drew Henri IV's buildings in Paris and other sites throughout the realm, compiling a vast collection of topographical views. And from the monastic library of St.-Germain-des-Prés, Father Jacques Du Breul introduced a new way to narrate the history of Paris based on the topography of the city. By artistic and scientific criteria, the French examples were backward compared to contemporary work in Italy, Germany, and the Netherlands. Consequently, historians of art and cartography have largely ignored the contributions of Nicolay and Quesnel, Chastillon, and Du Breul.

But if these men did not reshape their disciplines in a European context, nevertheless their work represented a significant shift in French culture. It signaled a growing interest in the physical form of the city, an interest sparked by Henri IV's urbanism. The royal building program in Paris and the king's broader centralizing policies played a crucial role in the emergence of the topographical arts in France.

MAPMAKING IN SIXTEENTH-CENTURY FRANCE

France played little part in the great advances made in European cartography during the second half of the sixteenth century. The index of contributors to Abraham Ortelius's great world atlas in 1570 lists eighty-seven mapmakers, only nine of whom were Frenchmen. Philip II charted the Hapsburg Empire, commissioning city plans of the Spanish Netherlands from Jacob van Deventer in 1558 and views of Spanish cities from Anton van den Wyngaerde in the 1560s.[2] Queen Elizabeth recognized the political value of Christopher Saxton's county maps of England (1574–78), begun by private initiative, and engraved them at her expense.[3]

But in France, there was no comparable effort. Unlike the other monarchs of sixteenth-century Europe, the Valois kings displayed little interest in mapmaking, whether for decorative, military, or political purposes. The Valois court included a royal geographer, an office held by Jean Jolivet during the reign of François II and by Nicolas de Nicolay under Henri II, but their cartographic activity for the king was limited to isolated sheet maps.[4] Without royal patronage, French mapmaking remained the preserve of a handful of scholars who were sustained by their contacts with foreign cartographers and publishers.

Even the private market for French mapmaking was limited. While the trade in single-sheet and larger wall maps thrived in sixteenth-century Italy, it barely existed in Paris. There was, however, genuine demand in France for the leading foreign atlases and cosmographical books. The two greatest sixteenth-century atlases—the *Theatrum Orbis Terrarum* by Ortelius, first published in 1570, and the *Civitates Orbis Terrarum* by Braun and Hogenberg, appearing two years later—were quickly available in French translations, which went through multiple printings.[5] Popularized versions came from the presses of Lyon; their publication in Lyon, rather than Paris, indicates that early French atlases owed less to the crown than to the European contacts of the Lyonnais economy.[6] These atlases stimulated rising curiosity about French geography, a demand which the French publishers Nicolas Chesneau and Michel Sonnius sought to meet by hiring royal historiographer François de Belleforest to revise Münster's atlas. His *Cosomographie universelle* appeared in Paris in 1575, with the first of its three volumes devoted entirely to France.[7] Whereas Münster had published three maps of French territory, Chesneau and Sonnius had fifty-nine, forty of which they commissioned.

The growing interest in French geography, in conjunction with royalist pressures for national unity during the religious wars, produced the first atlas of France: Maurice Bouguereau's *Le Théâtre françois,* published in Tours in 1594.[8]

Le Théâtre françois contained twenty maps of the provinces of France, each accompanied by a brief history of the region. Bouguereau used whatever maps were already available (copying mostly from Ortelius and Mercator), had them all reengraved on copperplates, and appealed to his readers to supply additional maps for future publications "for the love and decoration of your country."

The copperplate engraving was done by Gabriel Tavernier, a Protestant artist who had settled in Paris after the Hapsburg attack on Antwerp in 1573.[9] When the League occupied Paris, Tavernier fled to Tours, where Henri IV's court and the Parlement of Paris ruled in exile from 1589 to 1594. French engraving was undeveloped compared to the Flemish school, and the arrival of Protestant émigrés such as Tavernier introduced France to the highest level of copperplate engraving. In this instance, Bouguereau indicated that the rare opportunity to employ a highly skilled engraver had prompted him to produce the atlas.

Le Théâtre françois was a political manifesto for Henri IV, to whom the atlas was dedicated. Indeed, Bouguereau's workshop was a center of anti-League activity in the exile capital: he published part of the *Satyre ménippée,* a widely read satire of the League, and he conceived the atlas as a weapon of the royalist party. In the preface to the atlas, Bouguereau condemned the League and "the open war against the king under the pretext of Catholic union, which is ruining the French monarchy to the sound of Spanish trumpets." With large parts of France in rebellion, Bouguereau planned the atlas to demonstrate the full territorial extent of the king's authority. "What principally led me to this work," Bouguereau wrote, "was so that on the subject of each province, I might note for the records of immortality the valorous acts (as well as the piety and mercy) of our great Hercules, Henri de Bourbon IV."[10] The atlas included Lorraine, even though it was an independent state, because its ruler, Charles de Lorraine, had been allied with the League and defeated by Henri IV. The atlas was not yet finished when Paris surrendered to the king in 1594. Maps of Normandy, the Ile-de-France, and Champagne were missing, but Bouguereau published it anyway to celebrate the political and religious reunification of France under the Bourbon king. Bouguereau closed his preface with an entreaty: "Let the Heavens send us peace under [Henri IV's] reign, for all to have only one God, one King, one Faith, and one Law."[11] These words, which we will find again on Quesnel's map, had become the slogan of the royalists as they sought to link religious unity and the preservation of the French monarchy.

Bouguereau also understood that maps were useful in the exercise of royal power. He suggested that they be used by soldiers for military purposes, by royal treasurers for tax collection, and by merchants for trade. For the maps to be

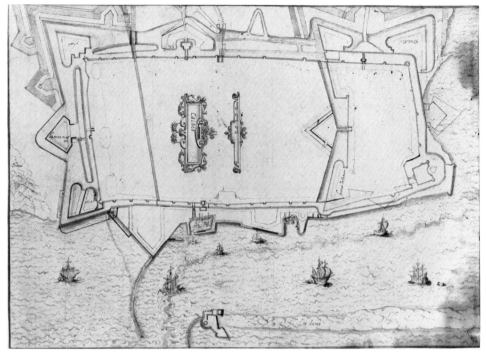

Fig. 145. Jean Errard, Calais, plan of fortifications, c. 1602. (British Library Add. ms. 21,117, fol. 21)

effective as Bouguereau suggested, the crown had to have some degree of centralized control over defense, taxation, and commerce. *Le Théâtre françois* adumbrated both the symbolic and the practical importance of mapmaking to Henri IV's program of national unification. From the beginning of his reign, the claims of royal power were inscribed in topographical images and in the enterprise of mapmaking.

Henri IV's Program of National Defense and the Mapping of France

Despite the broad reach of his building program in Paris, Henri IV ignored the city's walls, battered though they were by years of siege warfare during the occupation of the League. Even in 1590, before the most difficult battles for the capital had been fought, the pope's engineer, Filippo Pigafetta, noted how poorly the city was defended; in some places, he wrote, Paris was protected by no more than a ditch and terraced heaps of garbage.[12] Historically, walls had been as crucial to the identity of a city as to its defense, yet this traditional feature of urban life received no attention from Henri IV.[13]

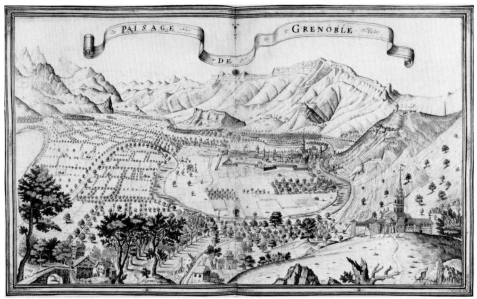

Fig. 146. Jean de Beins, view of Grenoble, c. 1604. (British Library Add. ms. 21,117, fols. 49v–50)

There were perceived tactical reasons not to rebuild the bastions. Walls "give occasions to the possessors to rebell and usurpe," Robert Dallington commented, as "these fortie yeeres troubles in France do testifie."[14] Machiavelli had argued against fortifications a century earlier, and his point was echoed by Dallington in 1604: "It is judged by the wisest, that in great kingdomes, such as France, no places should be fortified but the frontiers: after the example of Nature, who armeth the heads and heeles of Beasts, but never the Bowels nor middle part. For indeede the strength of a Countrey consists not in walled townes, but in united hearts of the people."[15] The argument that Paris could be left exposed, however, is only fully understandable in the context of the crown's policy of national defense.

Henri IV defended Paris not by building walls around the city, but by raising fortifications along the French borders. The Valois kings had made efforts to fortify border sites, but their citadels were not intended to supplant the walls encircling Paris and other inland cities. In strategic terms, sixteenth-century France was organized as a collection of self-contained cities surrounded by vast amounts of unprotected, open lands. Henri IV's transfer of the defenses that had protected Paris to the boundaries of the realm was central to his effort to unify the country. Underlying his program of national defense was a conception of France as a single, integrated network. By neglecting the walls of Paris, the king signaled a change in the role of the city: from an essentially autono-

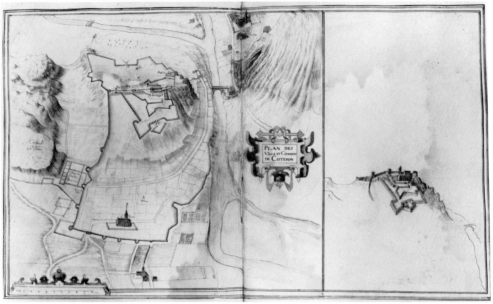

Fig. 147. Jean de Beins, Cisteron (Sisteron, Provence), c. 1608/9. (British Library Add. ms. 21,117, fols. 80v–81)

mous medieval municipality, albeit dominated by the king, Paris was to be the capital of a centralized state.

The program of national defense was carried out by Sully in his capacity as Superintendent of Fortifications.[16] During the sixteenth century, the crown had established a centralized administration to oversee fortifications. But it proved ineffectual, in part because fiscal control was never wrested from local authorities, and in part because the crown, spent by the civil wars, failed to build any fortifications after 1550. Sully altered this fractured, underfinanced structure in three ways. First, he reformed administrative procedures, bringing the financing, planning, building, and maintenance of fortifications under the rigorous control of the crown. Second, he allocated greater sums from the royal treasury than the crown had ever before spent on fortifications. Third, Sully formed a corps of royal engineers, which was responsible for fortifying and mapping the boundaries of France.[17]

Sully dispatched a royal engineer and draftsman (generally, an apprentice engineer) to each of the frontier provinces. The engineers had three responsibilities: determining the defensive requirements of the region and designing the necessary fortifications; maintaining the bridges and roads (the *voirie*); and mapping the territory. They pursued these projects with remarkable results. By 1609, the royal engineers had built twenty-eight new citadels—Henri IV's bastions still survive in several towns including Amiens, Doullens, and Sisteron

—and modernized a great many others. The engineers sent Sully annual reports about the regional roads, allowing him to supervise the formation of a national road network from Paris. And they produced a collection of manuscript maps, some of which David Buisseret rediscovered in 1964 in the British Museum. This was the first campaign to map the territory of France, and it highlights the importance of military engineering to the development of seventeenth-century French cartography. Both enterprises were substantially advanced by the centralization of the French state.

The maps were made for functional, nondecorative purposes; they were manuscript documents with privileged information about French fortifications used for strategic planning. A visual inventory of French strongholds was created with citadel plans, such as the drawing of Calais by Jean Errard, royal engineer in Picardy (Fig. 145).[18] Cities were depicted in stereographic and bird's-eye views, as in the stunning renderings of Grenoble and Sisteron by Jean de Beins, the royal engineer in Dauphiné (Figs. 146,147).[19] Like the other regional maps, the map of Chastelet by Jean Martellier, the assistant engineer in Picardy, depicted roads and rivers, defenses and passes (Fig. 148). When de Beins was ennobled in 1611, the royal edict commended his "art in fortifying all kinds of sites and making all kinds of plans and maps, general as well as particular, to lodge and defend an army."[20] With the maps commissioned by Sully, military strategists could plot the itinerary of an army and identify routes of supply and transport. But the maps did more than facilitate centralized military planning. The increasingly detailed information about French geography permitted the crown to move toward the core elements of the modern centralized state: control over taxation, commerce, roads, boundaries, and the very image of France.

Sully's regional maps demarcated for the first time the boundaries of France.[21] On Martellier's maps of Picardy, a broken line marks the frontier with the Spanish Netherlands (see Fig. 148). De Beins delineated the boundary between France and Savoy, and Chastillon, the royal engineer in Champagne, traced the boundaries of Lorraine and the Franche-Comté. That blurred zone where the language and culture of different countries overlapped was replaced by abstract lines on Henri IV's map. The invention of the boundary line satisfied both the linear vocabulary of the engraver and the crown's political objectives.

As the mapping enterprise was under way, Sully considered decorating the Petite Galerie of the Louvre with maps of France. He discussed his idea with the cartographer Antoine de Laval, who had a splendid map collection that interested Sully. Laval discouraged Sully and recommended instead the historical program which the minister executed, as we have seen.[22] Perhaps Sully was

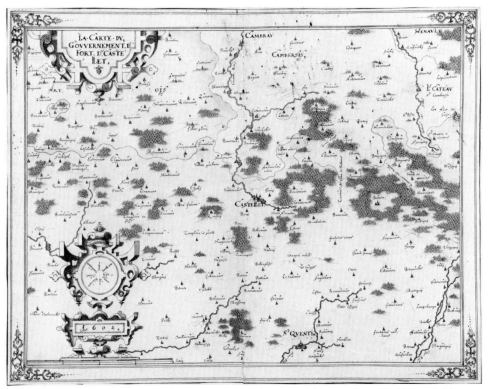

Fig. 148. Jean Martellier, map of Castellet (Chastelet, Picardy), 1602. (British Library Add. ms. 21,117, fol. 18v)

inspired by the *Galleria delle carte geografiche* in the Vatican palace; his brother, Philippe de Béthune, had served as the French ambassador to Rome and may well have described the regional maps, city views, and battle scenes painted for Gregory XIII in 1580/81.[23] But Sully need not have had a specific model, for decorative map cycles were commonly found in sixteenth-century princely palaces.[24] In the context of Henri IV's program of national defense and the royal mapping campaign, Sully's proposed map gallery in the Louvre underlines the closer relationship being forged between the capital and the periphery.

Although the military maps were guarded as secret documents and hidden from public view, the process of drafting those maps had an indirect influence on public consciousness. The mapping enterprise gave royal engineers Nicolay and Chastillon the training and experience that equipped them to depict Henri IV's Paris. Through their mapping expertise and through the city they portrayed, the images of Nicolay and Chastillon embodied the centralizing policies of the crown.

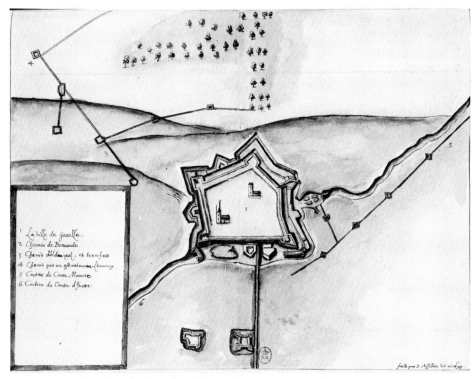

Fig. 149. Vassallieu dit Nicolay, plan of Groenloo, c. 1597–98. (B.N. Est. Vx 27)

NICOLAY'S MAP OF PARIS

One of the two maps that best captured Henri IV's ambitions for Paris was the work of Benedit de Vassallieu dit Nicolay, a military engineer first mentioned in the royal accounts of 1585. Unfortunately, very limited biographical information on Nicolay is available today.[25] During the 1590s, he served in Henri IV's artillery and developed an expertise in mobile artillery. A trip to Flanders is suggested by Nicolay's undated plans of six Flemish citadels, where the armies of Spain and the United Provinces clashed in 1597 and again in 1605–6. Among the plans was a drawing of Groenloo, which shows bastions and trenches, troop positions and major land features (Fig. 149). It was probably sketched in situ shortly after the 1597 battle. At that time, France was allied with the United Provinces — an alliance that ended a year later — and Nicolay may have joined the French attack on the Spanish supply road to Flanders.[26] In 1604, Sully commissioned him to map the coasts and fortifications of Normandy, Brittany, and Poitou; none of these drawings survives.[27] Nicolay succeeded Louis de Foix as royal engineer in Guyenne in 1609, an office he retained through at least 1614, after which Nicolay disappears from the documents. In 1613, Nicolay wrote a treatise on the transport and firing of artillery, an expertise, like cartography, that required a mastery of triangulation to calculate distances and angles of fire (Fig. 150).[28] The frontispiece illustrates the tools with which the military engineer exercised his skills in warfare and mapmaking: the torch and grenade to fire the smoking canons; the compass and straight rule to plan the siege, design the fortress, and draft the plan.

Nicolay's bird's-eye view of Paris, which spread across four sheets, altogether $2\frac{1}{2}$ feet high by $3\frac{1}{4}$ feet wide, offered an entirely new picture of the city (Fig. 151).[29] Earlier maps of Paris were nearly identical: mapmakers had updated the image by inserting recent buildings but the basic image, first outlined in the early sixteenth century, was left unchanged.[30] Nicolay abandoned the sixteenth-century prototype; he altered the pictorial conventions and surveyed the city anew. The improved accuracy, three-dimensional appearance, and innovative decoration of Nicolay's map immediately distinguished it from all earlier maps of Paris. Nicolay's manuscript drawings do not foreshadow the aesthetic quality and rich iconography of his Paris map; for these features, credit must go to the anonymous engraver, possibly Léonard Gaultier (1561–1641), one of the most skilled copperplate engravers in Paris. Gaultier's hand appears visible in the royal portrait in particular, which bears a striking resemblance to Gaultier's frontispiece to *Les Paralleles de Cesar et de Henry IIII* by Antoine de Bandole, also engraved in 1609 (Fig. 152).[31]

Gaultier frequently worked with the publisher Jean Le Clerc (1560–1621/22), who is prominently named on the map. A strong supporter of Henri IV, Le Clerc escaped to Tours when Paris was occupied; there he joined forces with the local royalist publisher, Bouguereau, and worked on his atlas.[32] Le Clerc subsequently specialized in printed maps; he acquired Bouguereau's copperplates and produced a more comprehensive French atlas, *Le*

Fig. 150. Vassallieu dit Nicolay, frontispiece of his *Recueil du reiglement general de l'ordre et conduitte de l'artillerye*, 1613. (B.N. Ms. fr. 592)

Fig. 152. Léonard Gaultier, frontispiece of Antoine de Bandole, *Les Paralleles de Cesar et de Henry IIII*, 1609. (B.N. Est. Qb 1609)

Théâtre géographique du royaume de France, the first of its numerous editions appearing in 1619.[33] Le Clerc published Nicolay's map to publicize the newborn splendor of Paris, "so that each and everyone knows the excellence of this great city, [and so] that foreigners may admire her."[34] For the benefit of non-Parisians, the map was accompanied by brief remarks about the city's monuments, which an otherwise unknown author named Etienne Cholet compiled from sixteenth-century guides.[35] The map was reprinted in 1614 with an enlarged text rededicated to Louis XIII, but we know nothing about the number of maps published or their geographic distribution. Large wall maps have been especially vulnerable to destruction, and therefore we can draw no conclusions from the rarity of the map today.[36]

Nicolay's surveying skills were easily transferred from the battlefield to the city. He probably first established a ground plan, measuring distances both by pacing and by triangulation. In essence, the surveyor established a measured baseline, projected a triangle from the end points of the baseline toward a

Fig. 153. Philippe Danfrie, drawing the plan of a fortress with a *graphomètre, Declaration de l'usage du graphomètre,* 1597. (B.N. Imp. rés. V2037)

third topographical mark, and determined the length of the two remaining sides of that triangulated space with trigonometric calculations based on the corner angles. The mapmaker would then sketch individual buildings and superimpose these views on the ground plan. This procedure had not changed during the preceding half-century; taking triangulated measurements only became easier with the invention of new surveying instruments, such as the *graphomètre,* which Philippe Danfrie invented in 1597 (Fig. 153).[37]

Nicolay succeeded in correcting two distortions in the sixteenth-century views of Paris. First, although the city is seen from a bird's-eye view in earlier maps, important buildings are depicted in elevation, for example, the Bastille at the top of the Braun plan (Fig. 154). Second, Braun did not maintain a consistent aerial perspective; the area at the top of the map, theoretically most distant from the viewing point, is tilted toward the picture plane. As a result, distances are distorted and all monuments appear the same size; the Bastille is as large as the Louvre, at the bottom of the Braun plan, even though the palace is closer to the viewer. Nicolay adhered to his vantage point with greater fidelity. He depicted the buildings from an aerial perspective rather than in elevation, and he allowed the city to recede somewhat from the picture plane. Nicolay took advantage of this backward tilt and the steep, raking vantage point to accentuate the city's three-dimensional space. The streets are pressed into the background, and the

Fig. 154. George Braun, map of Paris, 1572. (B.N. Est. Va 212)

buildings projected in sharp relief so that the city appears as a sculptural object with a crusty, uneven surface.

Nicolay intensified the three-dimensional pictorial effect through selective distortions. He enormously exaggerated the height of buildings; the King's Pavilion at the Place Royale, for example, is pictured as a towering six stories tall. He represented the thicket of narrow medieval alleys as a system of wide

and capacious streets, and he enclosed the Right Bank with modern angled bastions. Not only were the ramparts a fiction, but the faubourgs were far more densely settled than the map indicates. Ever since the reign of Henri II, the crown had unsuccessfully attempted to limit suburban growth, in part because many faubourgs belonged to seignorial estates and were outside the crown's juridical and economic control. Instead of showing this formless suburban sprawl, Nicolay gave the Right Bank a fixed shape and stripped the outlying land of all but the monuments.

It was Nicolay's symbolic objectives, not cartographic advances, that account for the way in which he structured the image. First, Nicolay abandoned the east-west orientation of the earlier maps of Paris (see Figs. 151, 154). Turning the compass about 45 degrees counterclockwise, his view overlooks the city from the northwest. The river no longer functions as a static, vertical axis but cuts a supple, diagonal path across the map. This shift was more than a formal adjustment to animate the composition. By reorienting his map, Nicolay represented the actual course of the Seine as it wound through the Ile-de-France. In sixteenth-century views, the Seine had been an abstracted compositional element; he presented it as a geographical fragment that implicitly situated Paris within a larger territory.

Yet Nicolay did not extend this logic by positioning the city as it would be on a national map, with north located at the top. Rather, he reversed north and south, turning Paris upside down as it were, and placed the city so high on the picture plane that the densest regions of suburban development — the fau-

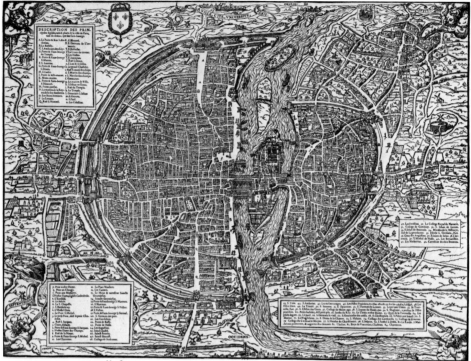

Fig. 155. François Belleforest, map of Paris, *Cosmographie universelle,* 1575. (B.N. Est. Ve 31a)

bourgs St. Marcel and St. Victor on the Left Bank — were pushed off the top of the map, while a swatch of undeveloped land remained at the bottom. The rationale for this apparently awkward treatment was to feature the royal palace in the foreground. The diagonal thrust of the Seine leads us down the map, until the bend in the river and the canal fix our eyes on the Tuileries gardens and royal palace. The implicit linkage between the palace and the municipal emblem in the corner suggests the identification between the crown and the city.

While the orientation of Nicolay's view subtly connected Paris to the larger region outside the city and associated it with the seat of royal power, the ornamental elements explicitly linked the map with the reign of Henri IV. In the upper left corner, a banner balanced on the fleurs-de-lys of the royal crown names the city and dedicates the map to the king, whose arms appear below: *Portrait de la Ville, Cité et Université de Paris avec les Faubours di celle dédié au Roy.* Although earlier maps of Paris carried the royal arms, none was inscribed with a dedication to the king; Nicolay was the first to state the royal mission of the city so boldly. In the lower left corner, measuring instruments — compass, surveyor's folding rule, and scale bar — appear beside the royal printing privilege.

The scale is in *toises,* the local Parisian unit which the crown promoted as a national standard. Because of the diversity of regional units of measurement, Jacques Androuet Ducerceau had defined the royal standards at the beginning of his model books. In Henri IV's France, the scale in *toises* and the printing privilege were resonant signs of the royal power which regulated the production and signification of Nicolay's map. The city's emblem, we have seen, fills the lower right corner; in all earlier maps of Paris, such as the one by Belleforest, the municipal arms were located in the more prominent upper register, paired with the royal arms (Fig. 155). Nicolay displaced the city's shield to the lower register, and in its more visible traditional position he set a framed image of the king, an element never before seen on a plan of Paris.

This portrait casts Henri IV as a Christian emperor, honored for his clemency and his valor (Fig. 156). The theme is introduced in the inscription above the portrait:

Fig. 156. Vassallieu dit Nicolay, map of Paris, detail of Henri IV, 1609. (B.N. Est. rés. Hennin XV 1352)

Fig. 157. Boscoreale silver cup, Venus offers Victory statuette to Augustus, first century A.D. (Private collection; Musée du Louvre, *Le Trésor d'orfèvrerie romaine de Boscoreale,* 1986)

Fig. 158. Boscoreale silver cup, Submission of the barbarians to Augustus, first century A.D. (Private collection; Musée du Louvre, *Le Trésor d'orfèvrerie romaine de Boscoreale,* 1986)

Nec Pietate Fuit, Belli nec Maior in Armis, "There was no greater in piety nor in weapons of war." Henri IV, wearing modern armor and a laurel wreath denoting his imperial rank, rides triumphantly on a rearing horse caparisoned with fleurs-de-lys. The battles are literally behind the soldier-king; his most precious victory, the capture of Paris, is loosely suggested by the scene in the background, where troops gather outside a city on a riverbank. A maiden draped in fleurs-de-lys, the personification of France, faces the king; she offers him a ship with full-blown sails, the emblem of Paris. At his feet, among the defeated soldiers, one kneeling rebel begs the pardon of the king. Henri IV responds to the offering of the maiden and the entreaty of the soldier with an outstretched right hand.

This scene combines three conventional motifs in Roman imperial art: the emperor's military triumph, the submission of his defeated enemies (*submissio*), and his clemency (*clementia*). These scenes are succinctly illustrated on the Boscoreale cup, a silver piece from the first century A.D., which celebrated the virtues of Augustus.[38] While the cup was unknown in the seventeenth century — it was not excavated until 1894 — the iconography is typical of the imperial Roman art that the French engraver would have seen. On one side of the cup, Venus gives the seated Augustus a Victory statuette, the trophy for the emperor's defeat of the barbarians (Fig. 157). The gift is paralleled on Nicolay's map where the maiden representing France presents the symbol of Paris to Henri IV. But unlike Venus on the Boscoreale cup, France holds her right hand to her heart, a gesture symbolizing Catholic faith, according to Ripa.[39]

In the second scene on the Boscoreale cup, the barbarians appeal for mercy from Augustus; he responds with the sign of clemency, an outstretched, open right hand (Fig. 158). On the map, Henri IV answers the rebel's plea with the same imperial gesture. The significance of the outstretched hand is underlined by two other equestrian portraits of the king; in Gaultier's frontispiece and in an engraving after Antoine Caron, the king grips a staff to denote his sovereign power (Fig. 159; see Fig. 152). Although the gesture of clemency is taken from the language of ancient Roman art, it acquires a religious meaning on Nicolay's map. After capturing Paris, Henri IV pardoned the rebels who occupied the city; at a time when the king's heretical past created enormous political difficulties, royalists eulogized the pardon to create the image of a devout Christian king. With imperial and Christian iconography, Nicolay's map represents Henri IV as Emperor of France, rewarded for his victory with the submission of Paris.

Yet the imperial tropes refer to Paris as well. Its role as the capital of France is elaborated in other ornamental features, which compare Henri IV's Paris to Augustus's Rome. This parallel is introduced in the quatrain by Julien de Fonteney directly below the royal portrait: "During the reign of this great king, very clement, very valiant, very just, Paris is as Rome was under Augustus, the wonder of the world."[40] The very qualities praised by Fonteney — clemency, valor, and justice — are those that Augustus singled out in describing his ascension to imperial rank in the *Res Gestae*:

In my sixth and seventh consulships, when I had extinguished the flames of civil war . . . I was given the title of Augustus by decree of the senate, . . . and a golden shield was placed in the Curia Julia whose inscription testified that the senate and the Roman people gave me this in recognition of my valor, my clemency, my justice and my piety.[41]

Like Augustus, Henri IV ended civil wars, brought peace to Gaul (26th act), and, most important, rebuilt the capital (20th act).

In the map's dedication, the publisher Le Clerc extolled the royal building program which made Paris "a second Rome." "You [Henri IV] have so embellished and enriched [Paris] with sumptuous buildings and superb structures," Le Clerc wrote, "that she is now much more grand, more beautiful,

Fig. 159. Gilbertus Vaenius after Antoine Caron, Henri IV, 1600. (B.N. Est. N2)

Fig. 160. Anonymous, Jeton de prévôté, obverse, 1606. Legend: MARMOREAM RELINQVET LVTETIA. (B.N. Médailles armoire 8, tiroir 265, no. 32)

more opulent, and more magnificent than she ever was before, and you can truthfully say that having found her built of plaster, you will leave her to posterity made entirely of stone and marble."[42] Le Clerc paraphrased Suetonius's famous homage to Augustus: "Aware that the city was architecturally unworthy of her position as capital of the Roman Empire . . . ," the Roman historian wrote, "Augustus so improved her appearance that he could justifiably boast: 'I found Rome built of bricks; I leave her clothed in marble.' "[43] Finally, the Augustan iconography was extended to the making of the map itself. As Augustus had his empire surveyed by Agrippa, so the Bourbon king had France charted by a corps of military engineers. Beneath the royal portrait, Henri IV's Agrippa is named: the topographer and engineer Vassallieu dit Nicolay (see Fig. 156).[44]

Royalist imagery had shifted during the last years of Henri IV's reign from national to imperial models, from the Gallican Hercules to the French Augustus. Augustus was the preferred imperial model because of the analogies suggested by Henri IV's building program. The words of Suetonius became a frequent refrain in royalist imagery and literature, as these two examples illustrate. On a commemorative medal commissioned in 1606 by François Miron, the *Prévôt des marchands,* the legend "MARMOREAM RELINQVET LVTETIA" frames a view of the Cité (Fig. 160).[45] And in a funeral address for the king, André Laval delivered these words: "It could indeed be said of his [Henri IV's] city, that our Augustus found it made of plaster and left it all in marble, just as the other did [in Rome]."[46]

The imperial imagery provided a broader historical context and rationale for Henri IV's centralizing policies. It was difficult for a Frenchman to imagine France as a centralized state and Paris as its center. But the Augustan imagery assimilated the unfamiliar idea of a centralized state; Paris could be conceived as a capital city by casting it as the new Rome. "The other cities of this realm regard Paris as their elder," the royal historiographer André Du Chesne wrote in 1609; they "submit to her actions, serve her goals, and revere her as the queen and mistress of the cities of France. What Pliny said of Rome . . . is as true of

Paris, which is our French Rome and which yields nothing to the old Rome."[47] On one level, the Augustan iconography offered an historical precedent for Henri IV's kingship, defining his urbanism and mapmaking as the traditional manifestations of an imperial grandeur. On another level, the imperial references explained the emerging role of Paris vis-à-vis France. To borrow the formulation of Suetonius, the map tells us that Henri IV rebuilt Paris to make her worthy of her new position as the capital and symbol of the centralized French state. Through the familiar idea of imperium, the map represented the nascent changes in the political and symbolic function of Paris.

Nicolay's map of Paris is a condensed image of the crown's overarching policy goals. Through the program of national defense, the crown enabled Nicolay to develop his mapping expertise. The map publicized Henri IV's building program, picturing the new embellishments. And the decoration and formal structure of the map identified Paris as the seat of the king and capital of his realm. Nicolay's Paris is the spatial representation of royal power.

QUESNEL'S MAP OF PARIS

With no prior cartographic experience, François Quesnel (1544/5–1619) embarked on his mapping venture from the world of court painting. Quesnel succeeded François Clouet as the favorite portraitist at the late Valois court, serving Charles IX and Henri III, who named him royal painter (see Fig. 4).[48] As the prestige of portraiture waned during Henri IV's reign, Quesnel turned to other genres. The Bourbon court prized his tapestry cartoons and ceremonial decorations, which are known today only from engraved copies. Though Henri IV did not renew Quesnel's appointment as royal painter, the artist remained active at the court; he prepared decorations for Maria de' Medici's entry into Paris and depicted the coronation of Louis XIII, works that drew special praise later in the century from the Abbé de Marolles, a respected collector.[49]

Quesnel's map was far larger than any earlier printed view of Paris. A bold effort for a novice, it spread across twelve sheets and measured nearly 5 feet square, three times larger in surface area than Nicolay's map (Fig. 161).[50] As its size suggests, Quesnel conceived the mapping project as akin to the practice of mural decoration in which he was grounded. Whereas Nicolay came to the city view from the domain of military engineering and surveying, Quesnel proceeded from the artistic tradition of large-scale encomiastic decoration. These were the two approaches to topographical art in early-seventeenth-century France, when the city view was beginning to emerge as an independent genre in French art.

Fig. 161. François Quesnel,
map of Paris, 1609. (B.N. Est.
Ve 31a, plates 13 and 13bis.
The distortions in this
composite image derive from
the original photographs
supplied by the Bibliothèque
Nationale.)

PL. XIII.

The decision by the inexperienced Quesnel to try his hand at mapmaking may have been stimulated by the example of another royal artist, Etienne Dupérac, who had published large maps of ancient Rome (1574) and modern Rome (1577), which he dedicated to Henri III. After living in Italy for about twenty years, Dupérac returned to Paris in 1578. From 1595 until his death in 1604, he was attached to Henri IV's court, where he surely met Quesnel.[51] Besides Dupérac's work at the Tuileries palace, little is known about his years in France, and Dupérac's influence on late-sixteenth-century French art and architecture remains unexplored. When Jacques Androuet Ducerceau published *Les Edifices antiques romains* with a map of ancient Rome in 1584, he indirectly acknowledged Dupérac's work as his model.[52] Presumably Ducerceau was not the only French artist inspired by Dupérac's maps. It is quite conceivable that this multifaceted artist, steeped in the vibrant Roman culture of the *veduta,* reinforced the budding topographical interests of Henri IV's artists, Quesnel among them. Dupérac's wall map of modern Rome did not provide Quesnel with a formal or iconographic model, but it offered the painter a distinguished precedent for his equally large map of Henri IV's Paris.

Quesnel made the map at his own initiative and without any royal subsidy.[53] Since engraving twelve large copperplates was a costly project, Quesnel requested an exclusive royal patent, which would at least protect his investment against pirated copies. The crown granted a printing privilege in January 1608, but that could not prevent Le Clerc from publishing a rival map. To deter prospective copyists, Quesnel included a lengthy excerpt from the royal printing privilege at the bottom of the map.

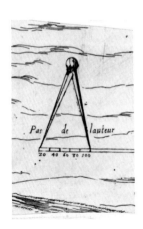

Fig. 162. François Quesnel, map of Paris, detail of scale, 1609. (B.N. Est. AA 3 rés.)

The copperplates were engraved by Pierre Vallet, whose monogram VLJ appears below the patent. Vallet was also attached to the Bourbon court, holding the post of embroiderer to the king (*brodeur ordinaire du roi*). Of his engraved oeuvre, only one other signed work survives: a volume of etchings illustrating the flowers that had been cultivated on the site of the Place Dauphine in the Jardin du Bailliage.[54] Vallet did no more than engrave the plates; Quesnel published the map and probably designed the decoration. Quesnel wanted it to enable "foreigners who have not seen her [Paris] to behold the marvels" built by Henri IV. Whether the map reached a foreign audience, we do not know. By virtue of its size, Quesnel's map must have fetched a higher price and

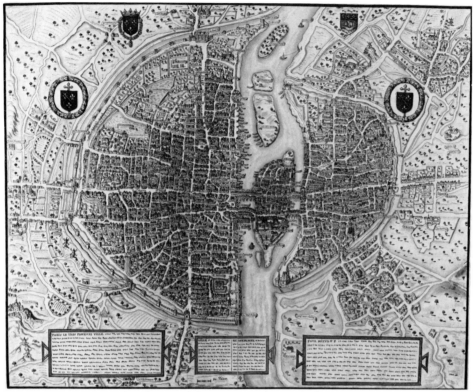

Fig. 163. Anonymous, reduced copy of the Tapestry plan made for François-Roger de Gaignières, c. 1680s. (B.N. Est. Va 419j)

had a more limited distribution than Nicolay's. Today the map in the Bibliothèque Nationale is the only known surviving copy.

Given Quesnel's inexperience as a mapmaker, he achieved a remarkable degree of accuracy in depicting the city's monuments. Appreciating the rising standards of cartographic precision, Quesnel emphasized his "exact observation of all dimensions and measurements." He, too, made a measured survey of the city, using a scale based on his own footstep, the "pas de l'auteur" seen at the bottom of the map (Fig. 162). While surveying normally involved pacing, Quesnel's failure to translate his footstep into a standardized measurement suggests his inexperience as a surveyor. Those architectural features that he included were delineated with greater accuracy than on Nicolay's print, but most buildings were schematically drawn and failed to convey an illusion of three-dimensional monumentality. Quesnel also flattened the terrain, rendering the suburban fields, for example, as an abstracted linear patchwork. While this gives large parts of the map a dissatisfying blankness, the abstracted fields present an inconspicuous ground that highlights the dense architecture of the city. Quesnel shows no familiarity with the art of the Netherlands, either its landscape tradition or its mapping culture. But the apparently archaic features of Quesnel's map are not the signs of a provincial artist.

Quesnel took the sixteenth-century views of Paris as his guide in order to exploit the powerful political credibility attached to the local pictorial tradition. Among the earlier maps of Paris, there was only one large wall decoration, and it may have served as Quesnel's particular point of reference: a tapestry measuring approximately 16¼ feet wide by 13 feet high (5m by 4m).[55] As the most prized representation of the city — at least among the ruling elite — the tapestry gave Quesnel an obvious model to emulate. But because it was tainted by antiroyalist associations, it also carried a political symbolism that Quesnel would have wished to reshape. The tapestry was destroyed during the Revolution, but a reduced, watercolor copy made in the 1680s for François-Roger de Gaignières probably provides a faithful record of it (Fig. 163).[56] While picturing Paris in about 1535, the tapestry was woven sometime between 1569 and 1588. The patron was Cardinal Charles de Bourbon (1523–90), a leading cleric at the late Valois court whose escutcheon is paired with the royal and municipal arms.[57]

Charles de Bourbon presided over numerous abbeys, including the powerful abbey of St.-Germain-des-Prés, where he lived after 1562; the tapestry probably hung in the new abbatial palace, built by the cardinal in the 1580s. Cardinal de Bourbon served as lieutenant general of Paris on several occasions (1551, 1557, 1562, and 1577), overseeing the city for periods of up to five months when the king was absent. His political fortunes were to rise and eventually fall on the basis of one simple fact: the cardinal was the only Catholic member of the Bourbon family. Charles de Bourbon was the uncle of Henri IV but allied with the Guises in their revolt against the crown. When his nephew, then the Protestant king of Navarre, emerged as the successor to Henri III, Catholic partisans promoted Cardinal de Bourbon as the rightful heir to the French throne. In 1584, a secret treaty which recognized the cardinal as the next king, Charles X, was concluded between the Guises and the Spanish king, Philip II, and ratified by the pope. Henri III arrested the cardinal in 1588, and he spent the last two years of his life in prison. The tapestry then entered the collection of the Guise family, where it remained during the seventeenth century. While the tapestry was undoubtedly woven before Charles de Bourbon's candidacy for the throne became an issue, it was later identified with the League. Throughout Henri IV's battles to secure the throne, the rebel leaders owned the most famous image of Paris.

Quesnel repossessed this image in a political sense by adapting the decorative devices of the tapestry to the royalist cause. He retained the placement of the royal and municipal arms at the top of the map, giving visual parity to crown and city.[58] At the bottom of the tapestry were three unornamented, rectangular panels with texts on the founding of Paris, its institutions and geography.[59] Quesnel copied the simple linear frames, although he altered the composition. Perhaps he even placed the scale bar at the bottom of his map, separated from the compass rose, because it has an analogous spot on the tapestry. Though the tapestry does not include the wind gods that fill the corners of Quesnel's map, they do appear on several other Paris maps, for example the Basel, St. Victor and Belleforest plans which also bear the text panels and municipal arms in the upper register (Figs. 164, 165; see Fig. 155). In short, Quesnel's formal references to a local pictorial tradition reinforced the map's political message, a message that emphasized Henri IV's continuity and fulfillment of a French royal tradition.

Quesnel highlighted this tradition in the abbreviated history of Paris contained in the panel on the right side of the map (Fig. 166). It begins: "The city of Paris was founded, according to some, by a king of the Celts named Luce, from which the name Lutece comes. . . . Others insist she was built by a Gaul named Paris."[60] This statement is noteworthy because it omits a third account of the founding of Paris: the theory of Trojan origins, which the Basel plan recounted, for example.[61] According to the Trojan theory, Aeneas was joined by another survivor of Troy, a man named Francion, who crossed the Rhine and eventually founded Paris. This mythical theory had appeal, to classicists in particular, because it gave Paris an ancestry as venerable as Rome's. By the mid-sixteenth century, however, it was thoroughly discredited as a literary invention with no basis in historical fact. Yet this does not fully explain Quesnel's omission, since he reported the equally unsupported Celtic theory of the city's origins.

Quesnel rejected the Trojan theory precisely because it implied a common ancestry for the French and Romans, whereas the Celtic and Gallic theories postulated origins independent of Rome, origins from which distinctive French cultural and legal traditions developed. The map lists the kings and institutions embodying that tradition. Clovis made Paris the capital, Pepin created the Parlement, Charlemagne founded the university, and Philippe Auguste instituted the municipal government and gave the city its arms. "But Henri IV," Quesnel concluded, was "the most illustrious of any of these predecessors as much for his endless, beautiful buildings which this map represents as for his wise laws which are faithfully guarded and respected to the honor and glory of His Majesty."

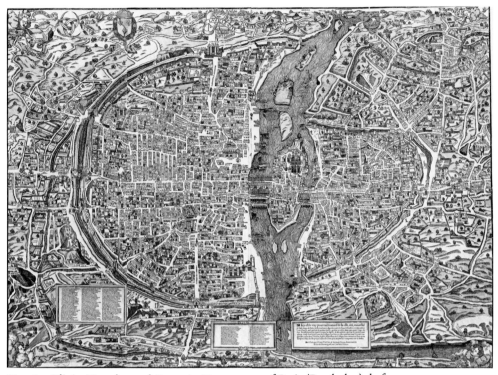

Fig. 164. Olivier Truschet and Germain Hoyau, map of Paris (Basel plan), before 1559. (Bibliothek der Universität Basel AA 124)

Fig. 165. Attributed to Jacques Androuet Ducerceau, map of Paris (St. Victor plan), c. 1550/51. (B.N. Est. rés. AA 6)

Quesnel detailed Henri IV's accomplishment more fully on the left side of the map, in the dedication addressed to the Bourbon king:

> You . . . regenerated, rebuilt, and perfected Paris after having rescued her by your invincible valor from the extremes to which she had been reduced. You were long destined to be the Perseus of France, and your care and attention has made [Paris] preeminent among the cities of the world, so that no signs of the past difficulties disfigure her. You have so magnificently decorated and embellished her that Paris is now comparable only to herself for the number of buildings, houses, palaces, churches, hospitals, colleges, streets, bridges, fountains and gates of which she is composed, such that she is at present more like a large province than a city.[62]

The self-referential aspect of this account is distinctive; whereas Nicolay likened the city to Augustan Rome, Paris was utterly unique in Quesnel's eyes. This disavowal of Rome as a paradigm and emphasis on an independent French standard were facets of Gallicanism, the political theory that provides the interpretive key to Quesnel's map.

The doctrine of Gallicanism began to develop in the thirteenth century as a rationale for the crown's control over the French Catholic church.[63] Because the king's power was vested in him by God—coronation was a sacrament, performed in the Cathedral of St. Denis—royal jurists argued that the king was the pope's equal. Originally limited to ecclesiastical matters, Gallicanism was more broadly applied to political matters during the civil wars, when royalists exploited the Gallican emphasis on the king's sovereign and sacerdotal power in defending the beleaguered monarchy. They advocated religious and political unity, subordinating the religious conflict to the higher cause of preserving royal power. After Henri IV ended the wars, royal jurists again resorted to Gallican theory to justify the rise of the absolutist state.

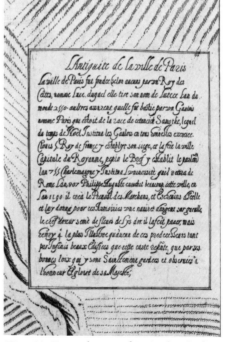

Fig. 166. Quesnel, map of Paris, detail of "The Antiquity of the City of Paris," 1609. (B.N. Est. rés. AA 3)

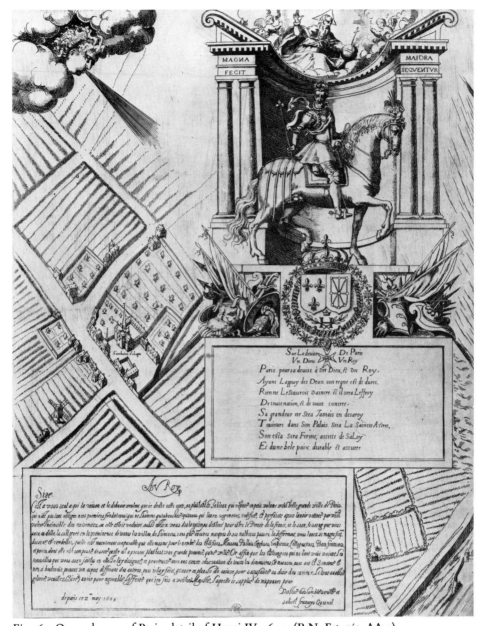

Fig. 167. Quesnel, map of Paris, detail of Henri IV, 1609. (B.N. Est. rés. AA 3)

It was in this political context that Quesnel constructed his image of Henri IV's Paris with the Gallican themes of unity, divine kingship, and indigenous French traditions.

In the upper left corner, an equestrian Henri IV, holding the royal staff, is framed by a rounded niche. The inscription in the entablature predicts greater

Fig. 168. Mathieu Jacquet dit Grenoble, equestrian relief of Henri IV for the Belle Cheminée, Fontainebleau, 1597–1601. (Réunion des Musées Nationaux)

Fig. 169. Quesnel, map of Paris, detail of Faith and Law, 1609. (B.N. Est. rés. AA 3)

things to come from a reign that has already achieved greatness: *Magna Fecit Maiora Sequentur* (Fig. 167). The portrait is a reversed copy of the Belle Cheminée (1597–1601) at Fontainebleau, a marble relief commissioned by Henri IV from Mathieu Jacquet dit Grenoble (Fig. 168).[64] Through this reference to Jacquet's sculpture, Quesnel discreetly pays homage to the king's patronage of the arts. Above the niche, the bearded figure of God holds a cross and globe, signs of the dominion of Christianity. He blesses the king, who is supported from below by the royal arms and trophies of war. Henri IV appears as the intercessor between the divine and secular order, between religion and the French state. On the right side of the map, the arms of Paris are framed by personifications of Faith, who holds the cross, and Law, who holds the Mosaic tablets (Fig. 169). Victory stands above the municipal shield, and from her trumpet issues the proclamation: *Talem Nec Proferet Aetas,* "Time will not alter his Fame."

The two pairs of figures — God and King, Faith and Law — illustrate the Gallican motto that heads the verses directly below: *Un Dieu, Un Roy, Une Foy, Une Loy,* "One God, One King, One Faith, One Law." This was the royalist rallying cry during the second half of the sixteenth century. It was invoked by Michel de L'Hospital, the chancellor of Catherine de' Medici, by the Gallican jurist and historian Etienne Pasquier, by Bouguereau in his atlas, and by Henri IV's solicitor Antoine Loisel (1556–1617), a leading Gallican jurist who had represented the king in negotiations for the surrender of Paris.[65] "Let us all unite together in recognition that we are subjects of the same king," Loisel appealed in a speech published in 1605, " . . . and let us take for our motto that of our fathers and ancestors, let us all live at last under one God, one King, one Faith, one Law."[66]

By the time Quesnel's map was published in 1609, the Gallican vision had incorporated an imperial strain. There were hopes that Henri IV would forge a new era of religious and political unity in Europe. The verse below the royal portrait alludes to that hope (see Fig. 167):

> Paris has for its motto one God and one King,
> Having the support of both, his reign will endure.
> Nothing will conquer him and he will be the terror
> Of every nation, and of every country.
> His grandeur will never be in disorder,
> Holy Astrea will always be in his palace.
> His state will be strong, supported by the Law
> And by a beautiful peace, enduring and assured.[67]

Henri IV's reign is identified with the rule of Astrea, the virgin queen who inaugurates a universal Golden Age in Virgil's Fourth Eclogue. Frances Yates has shown that in the ceremonial art of the Elizabethan and Valois courts, Astrea symbolized the desire for religious harmony.[68] Quesnel's verse anticipated the fulfillment of this promise, with every nation respecting Henri IV's rule of law.

Moreover, the map gives a precise geographical focus to Astrea's return; the Gallican vision is to be realized in Paris. Below the city's arms, the poem promises an age of peace and concord if Paris honors the famous watchword — one God, one King, one Faith, and one Law.[69] Paris is represented as the privileged site of Gallican unity forged by Henri IV. Quesnel translated the idea of Paris as the royal capital into the imagery of Gallicanism, as Nicolay had done with the imperial iconography of Augustan Rome. Drawing from the two currents in royalist ideology — the Gallican and the Roman — the maps presented the city as the vehicle of a political order which ultimately implied the domination of Europe.

CHASTILLON'S VIEWS OF PARIS

Claude Chastillon (1559–1616) joined the military entourage of Henri de Navarre in the early 1580s, and as king, Henri IV rewarded Chastillon with the posts of royal topographer in 1591 and royal engineer in 1595.[70] Chastillon made frontier maps which the king used in 1598 to plan new fortifications.[71] This effort was the prelude to Sully's comprehensive mapping campaign, beginning

Fig. 170. Henri IV's siege of Montmélian, 1600. Engraving after Claude Chastillon. (B.N. Est. rés. Ve 9)

after 1600, when Chastillon was responsible for his native province of Champagne. An expert in waterworks, Chastillon canalized a river in Poitou in 1605, finished the lighthouse of Cordouan in 1606, designed a bridge in Rouen in 1608, and planned a canal around Paris in 1611, as noted above. Despite his wide-ranging travels, Chastillon maintained an active presence in the capital, keeping a pied-à-terre in his Place Royale house. In addition to designing the Place de France, Chastillon contributed to the decorations for the queen's coronation in 1610.

It was Chastillon's job as royal topographer to record the battles waged by Henri IV's troops. These scenes, such as the engraving of the royal victory at Montmélian in Savoy in 1600, nurtured Chastillon's interest in landscape and topography (Fig. 170). His professional development was not unique in this respect. Claude Lorrain and Jacques Callot also built careers involving both military and topographical views. But the examples of these great artists should not obscure the fact that the less accomplished battle scenes made by Henri IV's engineers — Chastillon and de Beins in particular — stimulated the development of the topographical view in France.[72]

Chastillon's topographical drawings reveal his immense visual curiosity, observant eye, and accurate hand. In crisscrossing France with the royal army, Chastillon drew all the major buildings and cities he passed. Only the royal châteaux were excluded, probably because they were the focus of Ducerceau's *Les plus excellents bastiments de France* (1576 – 79); Chastillon evidently intended his volumes on French topography to complement Ducerceau's work. Chastillon's volumes were unfinished when he died in 1616. His work was compiled in a formless compendium of 550 images by the publisher Jean Boisseau, and the first posthumous edition of Chastillon's *Topographie Françoise* appeared in 1641.[73] But Chastillon probably had not planned one mammoth volume. The varied subject matter and format of the engravings suggest that he was working on individual thematic works focusing on battles, châteaux, provincial cities, and the French capital.

To find a French precedent for Chastillon's interest in the urban landscape, one must go back to illuminated medieval manuscripts where the changing seasons were illustrated by pictures of urban sites. An example would be the view of the Palace on the Cité in the Duc de Berry's Hours (see Fig. 78). But there was no precedent for a topographical volume devoted to Paris. The preference of the Valois court for hunting grounds and country estates, its patronage of a seignorial rather than urban culture, and its lack of interest in Paris, may account for this phenomenon. There is no more stunning example of the bias against urban topography than Ducerceau's views; while the gardens and fields surrounding country châteaux are often shown, the plates of the Louvre and Tuileries palaces reveal nothing of their urban setting.

Chastillon's interest in Paris was clearly sparked by Henri IV's building program. He began the *Topographie Parisienne,* as I shall call it, in 1609, at the height of the royal building program. In the next six years, he recorded eleven Parisian monuments, including all of Henri IV's buildings, except the Louvre.[74] The *Topographie Parisienne* also included three late-sixteenth-century hôtels (the Hôtels de Nevers, d'Angoulême, and de Mayenne) and two older monuments (the Temple and the Roman ruins at the Hôtel de Cluny). Not all of the plates were originally made for the *Topographie Parisienne.* The prints of the Place Royale and Place de France were distributed as single sheets accompanied by explanatory texts; the other engravings do not all have the same format. Yet given his generally unsystematic approach, Chastillon's thoroughness in depicting Henri IV's projects is noteworthy.

Whereas Ducerceau limited his focus to building design, Chastillon was interested in the city as a whole — its monuments, ceremonial life, and broader architectural landscape. He depicted important urban ceremonies in two plates:

the ceremonial fire of St. Jean, a municipal ritual held in front of the Hôtel de Ville, and the royal *carrousel* of 1612 in the Place Royale (see Figs. 5, 41). Most of Chastillon's images included a panoramic view of Paris at the horizon line. Beyond the Place Royale, we see the spires of dozens of churches all the way to Montmartre on the distant hilltop; beyond the Hôtel de Nevers, we see the plague hospital of Grenelle, the châteaux of Meudon and Madrid, and numerous villages (see Fig. 49). With the impetus provided by Henri IV's urbanism, Chastillon became the first artist to record systematically the topography of Paris.

By the mid-seventeenth century, French topographical artists such as Silvestre and the Pérelle family were unsurpassed in Europe. Given their accomplishments, it is easy to forget that the topographical view had only just emerged as a genre in French art. But the focus on urban culture, first manifest in Chastillon's drawings, was set in motion by Henri IV's building program.

THE RISE OF TOPOGRAPHICAL HISTORY

The history of France was rewritten during the second half of the sixteenth century. Historians skeptically measured the legends of the past against the unyielding test of documentary proof. They studied legal charters and foundation letters, applying juridical and philological methods to French history. The new history, which emerged during the civil war when the monarchy came under attack, had a political purpose: to prove that French law derived its authority from the king. As the historiographical studies of Claude Dubois, George Huppert, Donald Kelley, and J.G.A. Pocock have underscored, the new history not only affirmed the French monarchy but also contributed to the formation of a French national consciousness.[75] The newly energized concern for the national past extended to the history of cities.

The period from the late sixteenth century through Henri IV's reign spawned a proliferation of local history books, the titles of which almost invariably included the word *antiquitez*.[76] One of the more popular publications, for example, was André Du Chesne's *Les Antiquitez et recherches des villes, chasteaux, et places plus remarquables de toute la France,* which first appeared in 1609; by 1631, it had gone through six editions.[77] Lacking the modern connotation of ancient monuments, *antiquitez* referred to the historic deeds of kings and venerable institutions of the monarchy, as in Quesnel's description of the antiquities of Paris. The *antiquitez* books were simply dynastic chronicles, recounting in chronological order the glorious deeds of kings, their derivative authorities, and royal institutions. The city only surfaced as the occasionally visible setting of political events. Topographical history, a history of physical environments, had not yet emerged as an independent genre.

Nowhere was the merger of local and dynastic history more evident than in the books on Paris. The point of departure was an encomiastic pamphlet written by a Parisian bookseller, Gilles Corrozet, in 1532, *La Fleur des antiquitez, singularitez, et excellence de la noble et triomphante ville et cité de Paris.* "To illustrate the very noble and invincible Gallican and French nation," he explained, "I will succinctly describe the names of the princes and successors directly descended from Francus."[78] Over the next sixty years, Corrozet's book was handed down to three successive authors—Nicolas Bonfons, his son Pierre, and Jacques Du Breul; each renamed the book, inflected the message in response to changing political conditions, and greatly expanded the scholarly content.[79] Pierre Bonfons's 1605 edition met the standards of the new history, both in his research methods and overt Gallican politics.[80] Three years later, Du Breul published a revised edition, *Les Antiquitez et choses plus remarquables de Paris,* substantially enlarged by legal documents and ancient titles.[81] Although the editions from Corrozet and Du Breul are generally called guidebooks, the term is a misnomer. They were not intended for the traveler. They were not about the physical fabric of the city; alphabetical lists of streets, churches, and colleges were included not to orient the visitor but to demonstrate the magnitude of Paris.

However, Du Breul made a crucial innovation in his revised edition of 1612, *Le Théâtre des antiquitez de Paris,* by abandoning the chronological order that had been the organizing principle of all earlier books.[82] His book was structured in accordance with topography, following the location of buildings rather than the chronological sequence of their foundation. Du Breul (1528–1614), a Benedictine monk, was in charge of the abbey's archives at St.-Germain-des-Prés. After years in provincial outposts, he had been recalled to Paris in 1594, and there he wrote his books on Paris as well as Latin treatises on the history and ceremonies of the Benedictine order.[83] Du Breul was eighty-four when *Le Théâtre* was published. Bound to the abbey by old age and monastic habits, the monk relied on the footwork of younger friends and on the research of canons, who consulted the archives in private libraries on his behalf. The result was a massive tome of 1,343 pages in quarto, a monument to antiquarian passion.

Le Théâtre is divided into four sections—Cité, Université (Left Bank), Ville (Right Bank), and the rural diocese—and each section follows a geographical sequence. On the Ile de la Cité, Du Breul's narrative begins at the east end and moves consistently westward, from the cathedral of Notre-Dame to the Place Dauphine. Geography was less rigorously respected when Du Breul reached the Right and Left banks, where the imperatives of institutional and dynastic history compete with topography for control of the narrative sequence. Even so, Du Breul follows logical itineraries. The section on the Right Bank, for example, jumps from the Louvre to the Place Royale before circulating in the neighborhood from the Bastille to the Arsenal to the Châtelet; it closes by discussing the city gates in order from east to west.

Unless Du Breul had an extraordinary geographic memory, he must have worked from a map of Paris. He adopted the topographical structure soon after his 1608 edition, and in revising the text between 1609 and 1612, this exhaustive scholar surely consulted the new maps of Henri IV's Paris published in 1609. Du Breul had also undoubtedly seen the tapestry map during the lifetime of its original owner, Cardinal de Bourbon. Du Breul had been closely associated with the cardinal for twenty-six years; in homage to his long-standing protector, Du Breul dedicated *Le Théâtre* to the cardinal's nephew, François de Bourbon, the Prince de Conti. But it is not known whether the tapestry map was still hanging in the abbey of St.-Germain-des-Prés in the early seventeenth century. Whether it was the Nicolay or Quesnel map in particular, a map of Paris almost certainly was instrumental in Du Breul's topographical reordering of the history book. From his perch in the monastic library, city maps made it possible for him to see Paris in terms of its topography rather than its institutions.

Yet Du Breul's reorganization did not affect the content of *Le Théâtre;* the book was still fundamentally conceived as an institutional history. It is understandable that the book did not comment on architecture. Old age precluded Du Breul from touring the monuments of Paris, and the materials available in his cloistered library were limited to charters, titles, books, and maps. But by giving the narrative a topographical order, Du Breul registered the growing awareness of the city as a physical object, a level of awareness raised by maps and indirectly by Henri IV's urbanism.

With *Le Théâtre des antiquitez,* topographical history in France took its first step away from the dynastic chronicle. But topographical history did not emerge as a discrete and distinctive genre until 1684, when Germain Brice published the first book devoted to the architecture of Paris, *Description nouvelle de ce qu'il y a de plus remarquable dans la ville de Paris.* This guidebook manifests changes instigated at the beginning of the seventeenth century when Henri IV's urbanism, the city views of Nicolay, Quesnel, and Chastillon, and Du Breul's history book all focused attention on the topography of Paris.

CONCLUSION

I am a Frenchman only by this great city: great in population, great in the felicity of her situation, but above all great and incomparable in variety and diversity of the good things of life; the glory of France, and one of the noblest ornaments of the world."[1] Provoked by the League's control of Paris, Michel de Montaigne had written these words in the late 1580s. The importance of Paris — its central role in the political order of the French state and in the definition of French national identity — were not inventions of Henri IV. They were long-established premises of French history and culture, the values that moved Montaigne to fear for his country when Paris was attacked. "I warn her [Paris] that of all parties the worst will be the one that throws her into discord."

But Henri IV reached the throne at a time when the allegiance of Paris, the monarchy, and French unity itself were threatened from within as never before. His administration remade the political and cultural order, and Paris was the crucible in which this enterprise was forged. That transformation was a means toward a broader political end: rebuilding and representing the renewed power of the crown, the power of France.

Henri IV was no different from his predecessors in regarding Paris as a domain of royal power. A century earlier, Louis XII had sponsored the Pont Notre-Dame, and François I had built the Hôtel de Ville as homages to the royal affiliation of Paris. But while the Valois kings regarded the city as an important setting of royal ceremony and a deserving recipient of royal beneficence, Paris was only one of many movable locations of the court.

For Henri IV, the court and the city were inextricably linked. He not only made Paris the home of the crown and growing numbers of royal officers; he treated Paris as the testing ground and model for the full range of his policies and patronage. His building program aimed to strengthen the city's economic base, meet the needs of an urban citizenry, and promote the institutions of urban culture. He constructed manufacturing workshops, squares for artisans and merchants, spaces for promenading, a plague hospital for the poor, and a royal college. It was not difficult for royal publicists to represent these accomplishments as signs of the king's genuine concern for his subjects.

The unveiling of Henri IV's equestrian monument on the Pont Neuf in 1614 set off a new round of eulogies to the Bourbon king. One such pamphlet by the doctor and architectural writer Louis Savot reviewed the king's public works.

[Henri IV] began to build a royal college in Paris, offering larger wages
than in any other university to draw the greatest men in the world
there. For the ease and prosperity of commerce, he attracted to his realm
the finest artisans from foreign countries to establish silk manufacturing
and other foreign crafts, because more than 6 million *livres* were annually exported from France; for the same reason, he rebuilt the bridges
which the wartime fury had demolished, built several new ones, leveled
roads, restored the old streets, and made new ones. Recognizing that
buildings were the eternal monuments of a prince's grandeur and the
power of his riches, an occupation for various artisans and a livelihood
for an infinity of poor laborers and manual workers who, for lack of
being occupied, become idlers, vagabonds, and thieves, he spent more
than 8 million *livres* on buildings: namely, he built the Pont Neuf in
Paris, the canal de Briare, the tower of Cordouan, Montceaux, the
Grande Galerie of the Louvre, the Hôpital St. Louis, Place Royale, Place
Dauphine, rue Dauphine, as many streets in the marais du Temple as
there are provinces in France, the great college of la Flèche, a part of the
Arsenal, the Louvre, and the best of the Tuileries, Saint-Germain-en-
Laye, Verneuil, and Fontainebleau.[2]

Savot mentioned projects outside of Paris and beyond the scope of this book. At
St.-Germain-en-Laye, Henri IV completed the Château Neuf, which Philibert
Delorme began for Henri II, and created a terraced garden with grottoes and
elaborate automata. At Fontainebleau, he added the Cour des Offices and Porte
Dauphine, and remodeled the Cour Ovale and the gardens. He also financed the
work carried out at the château of Verneuil, a gift to his mistress Henriette
d'Entragues, and at the château of Montceaux, a gift to the queen. The Cordouan lighthouse in the mouth of the Gironde river and the Jesuit college in La
Flèche, to which he promised his heart, were his only major buildings outside
the Ile-de-France, excluding the frontier fortifications which Savot failed to
mention. As the châteaux and gardens indicate, Henri IV did not neglect the
traditional forms of royal patronage, but Paris was his primary workshop.

No master plan guided the royal building program. Rather, it evolved
during seven years of intensive activity, from 1603 to 1610. Nor did the program
follow a consistent progression. Rather, varying approaches to urban design
were tested by different architects, whose identities have been merged into that
of the king and his indispensable minister Sully. For example, planning ideas
introduced in the Louvre in 1603 were explored in the Place Royale and further
elaborated in the Place Dauphine, while the Place de France followed a different direction. Yet the projects flowed from a coherent strategy, a strategy that
can be defined in part by examining what Henri IV chose *not* to do.

First, the royal building program made no attempt to renovate the old city. Indeed, throughout the *ancien régime,* historic Paris remained largely untouched, belying the myth of the monarch's unlimited power to implement urban designs. The refusal to demolish whole blocks of the old city accounted for the crown's persistent failure to clear the courtyard between the Louvre and Tuileries, or to create a monumental forecourt east of the palace. The *grand dessein* was to remain unrealized until Baron Haussmann — guided by modern notions of urban beauty, security, and hygiene — destroyed large parts of central Paris during the third quarter of the nineteenth century. Henri IV's urbanism was confined to empty sites: the Place Royale was built on the abandoned grounds of the Hôtel des Tournelles, the Place Dauphine on a garden, the Place de France on fields, and the Hôpital St. Louis outside the walls. His projects consumed the undeveloped land within the walls, and the city was embellished by knitting the new to the old.

Nor did Henri IV's urbanism restructure the street system. Through the writings of Sigfried Giedion and Lewis Mumford, we have come to see the avenue as the paradigmatic element of Baroque urban planning, as in the Rome of Sixtus V. During his brief reign as pope (1585–90), Sixtus V projected a network of streets that stretched across Rome.[3] His avenues crossed hills and valleys, linking the basilicas through a city-wide system of roads. By this standard, Henri IV's urbanism was deficient, for he failed to pierce avenues across the capital. The Place de France was the only project that treated circulation through the city as a central design priority, and even this project entailed no city-wide streets. The pope was no more willing than Henri IV to demolish the historic city center, but Rome had a unique resource: vast amounts of unsettled land inside the city walls. Sixtus V confined his efforts to undeveloped land at the fringe of the city; his roads tackled the deserted landscape while the medieval and Renaissance fabric remained untouched. Paris, however, was bursting inside its ramparts, and road construction on a scale comparable to that in Sistine Rome would have required the large-scale expropriation and demolition of private property.

Yet the building programs of Sixtus V and Henri IV were determined by underlying social policies, not by conditions of urban density. The pope's program, shaped by the legacy of Rome's Christian topography, was conceived in terms of circulation; it was destined for the pilgrim. Henri IV's program was conceived in terms of functional spaces; it was devoted to the daily activities of Parisian residents. Henri IV's urbanism placed greater importance on the formation of architectural spaces promoting social and economic programs than on movement through the city. He did not meet the standards of Sixtus V, but the king was guided by a different approach to urban planning.

On the other hand, it would be incorrect to conclude that the king's architects were entirely uninterested in problems of circulation, and that the enclosed squares were planned as autonomous ornaments. The squares were structured by axes of circulation that linked them to major roads: the Place Royale to the rue St. Antoine and rue des Franc Bourgeois, the Place Dauphine to the Pont Neuf and quais of the Cité. Rather than pierce wide avenues through the city, Henri IV's architects made minor incisions in the old city to provide access to new buildings. The architects adjusted the squares to the surrounding fabric; the buildings absorbed the contingencies of the urban context through local symmetries and irregular geometries. This malleable process of design represented an alternative to the ideals of Renaissance and Baroque planning, where the order of the city was regulated through axial compositions and perfect geometric forms.

Finally, Henri IV's architects did not perceive Paris as an organic whole; intervention in one part was generally not considered in relation to the functioning of the entire city. Yet as the royal building program developed, it implicitly demonstrated a growing recognition of Paris as a unified entity, both in the design and program of the buildings. In formal terms, the king's architects introduced an urban scale of design; that is, the size and form of buildings were designed to be seen from afar. The *grand dessein* of the Louvre and the Place Royale formed spaces that were scaled in relation to the city. All Parisians were invited to promenade in the first royal square, the largest built space they had ever known. The Grande Galerie, Pont Neuf, and Place Dauphine were designed as parts of a grand panorama, as sights to be viewed from a distant point and as platforms from which to survey the city. The buildings were composed as parts of an urban landscape, and the visual delight arising from this spectacle marked an emerging urban aesthetic, an aesthetic which valued the medley of the city's sights. In programmatic terms, the royal projects were not intended to serve merely the local parish but the city at large: the Place Royale was planned as a recreational space and as a center of the luxury trades for all Parisians; the Hôpital St. Louis had the purpose of protecting the entire city from upheavals caused by the plague. The civic identity of the *bourgeois de Paris* remained tied to his parish, but Henri IV's urbanism inserted a network of monuments and places that reached beyond the neighborhood and belonged to all of Paris.

Measured in terms of stylistic influence, Henri IV's urbanism was of little consequence. It directly influenced only the new towns of Henrichemont

(1606) and Charleville (1608), founded respectively by Sully and by Louis de Gonzague, Duke of Nevers. The Place Ducale at Charleville, designed by Clément Métezeau, closely echoed the Place Royale. Gonzague's project also included a hospital and a hospice, where orphans were taught a trade, components modeled after the royal enterprise. The influence of the Place Royale can also be traced to Covent Garden, which was begun in London in 1630 and designed by Inigo Jones. But the squares in Charleville and London returned to the Renaissance type of town square. Each incorporated a monumental building — a ducal palace in Charleville, a church in London — in the designs, whereas the Bourbon model boldly adopted an unmonumental architecture. With the classicizing taste of the second half of the seventeenth century, Henri IV's buildings found few admirers; the brick-and-stone construction was devalued, the absence of axial planning faulted. The social content of Henri IV's urbanism was all but forgotten, his effort to forge an alliance between court and commerce having failed. The case of the Place Royale was premonitory; the monied classes were unwilling to invest in manufacturing, and the wealth of Paris was instead devoted to royal offices, tax farms, and seignorial estates.

An immediate consequence of Henri IV's urbanism was the rise of Parisian real estate developers: land speculators such as Nicolas Carrel, and developers of rental housing such as Charles Marchant and François Petit. During the reign of Louis XIII (1610–43), the crown ceded all initiative to private investors, who were responsible for the development of three neighborhoods: the Ile-St.-Louis, the last tract of empty ground within the walls; the site of Queen Marguerite's palace on the south bank of the Seine, opposite the Grande Galerie; and the quartier Richelieu, north of the cardinal's palace.

Whereas Henri IV regarded Paris not only as the locus of the court but as the primary vehicle for implementing the policies of the crown, his successors displayed far less interest in the capital city. Louis XIII was merely uninterested in Paris; Louis XIV came to loathe it and transferred the court to Versailles. However, his minister, Jean-Baptiste Colbert, who subscribed to an imperial model of kingship, pursued several building projects to immortalize the absent king. As a result of Colbert's efforts, the Cour Carrée and Tuileries were completed, four triumphal arches with reliefs celebrating the virtues and conquests of the king were erected, and the ramparts encircling Paris were destroyed. Henri IV's building program had already deprived the walls of their role in terms of defense, sanitation, and civic identity. By the 1670s, they were manifestly obsolescent, and Colbert had them replaced by a tree-lined boulevard, making Paris the first open city in Europe.

In the course of the century, Paris had shifted from a collection of neighborhoods held together by the circuit of walls to a physical network anchored by its own internal order. Henri IV's urbanism had set this trajectory in motion, but the separation of the court from the capital and the imperial model of urbanism that prevailed during Louis XIV's reign ran against the core of Henri IV's policies. In a famous memo of 1669, Colbert noted his ideas for Paris: "The Louvre to continue everywhere. Arch of Triumph for conquests of land. Observatory for the Heavens. Pyramids, difficulty in executing them. Grandeur and Magnificence."[4] The urban order of the city was of no interest to the crown. Paris served to provide testimony to the monarch's glory.

The crown's transformed vision of the city was embodied in the royal squares of Louis XIV, the Place des Victoires and the Place Louis XIV (Vendôme). The primary purpose of these squares was to frame the effigy of the king in a firmly aristocratic precinct. It was as if the content of Henri IV's squares — their artisanal and mercantile character, their modest architectural profile, their formation of a space for myriad public uses — were extracted, leaving simply uniform facades fronting building lots. Into this empty shell, Louis XIV's architect Hardouin Mansart injected the imperial dream: enduring stone, ennobling orders, a royal statue, a space of deference and of awe. Grandeur and magnificence, the goals set by Colbert, were fulfilled in Louis XIV's *places royales*.

Henri IV had tried to build a different type of city. Where Louis XIV's Paris was aristocratic, honorific, and grandiose, Henri IV's buildings reached across social divisions and advanced the crown's key objectives: promoting domestic manufacturing, linking the court with commerce, and establishing Paris as the focal point of a unified French state.

A Note on the Transcriptions

In transcribing seventeenth-century French documents in the appendices and Notes, I have followed the guidelines set forth by Bernard Barbiche in "Conseils pour l'édition des documents français de l'époque moderne," *GBA* 96 (July–August 1980): 25–28. The original spelling has been respected. Although accent marks are almost universally absent from the documents, some accents have been added: the cedilla (ç), the "é" to distinguish a tonic from an atonic "e" at the end of a word ("payé" but "croisee"), and the "à" (in this case, I depart from Barbiche who advises against the "à"). Punctuation has also been inserted.

ABBREVIATIONS, MEASURES, AND CURRENCY

ABBREVIATIONS

A.N.	Archives Nationales, Paris
A.S.	Archives de la Seine, Paris
BHVP	Bibliothèque Historique de la Ville de Paris
B.N. Est.	Bibliothèque Nationale, Cabinet des Estampes, Paris
B.N. Ms.	Bibliothèque Nationale, Département des Manuscrits, Paris
BSHAF	*Bulletin de la Société de l'Histoire de l'Art français*
BSHP	*Bulletin de la Société de l'Histoire de Paris et de l'Ile-de-France*
CVP	*Commission du Vieux Paris, Procès-verbaux*
Du Breul	Jacques Du Breul, *Le Théâtre des antiquitez de Paris* (Paris: 1612)
EPHE	*Ecole Pratique des Hautes Etudes, IVe Section, Annuaire*
Félibien	Michel Félibien and Guy-Alexis Lobineau, *Histoire de la ville de Paris,* 5 vols. (Paris: 1725)
GBA	*Gazette des Beaux Arts*
JSAH	*Journal of the Society of Architectural Historians*
Lasteyrie	R. de Lasteyrie, "Documents inédits sur la construction du Pont-Neuf," *MSHP* 9 (1882): 1–94
Lettres missives	J. Berger de Xivrey and Jules Guadet, *Recueil des lettres missives de Henri IV,* 9 vols. (Paris: 1843–76)
Mallevoüe	F. de Mallevoüe, *Les Actes de Sully passés au nom du Roi de 1600 à 1610* (Paris: 1911)
Min. cent.	Minutier central des notaires de Paris, Archives Nationales
MSHP	*Mémoires de la Société de l'Histoire de Paris et de l'Ile-de-France*
Plumitif	Plumitif concernant le Pont Neuf, 1578–1605, A.N. Z1F/1065
Registres	*Registres des délibérations du Bureau de la Ville de Paris,* 19 vols. (Paris: 1883–1958)
Sauval	Henri Sauval, *Histoire et recherches des antiquités de la ville de Paris,* 3 vols. (Paris: 1724)

MEASURES		CURRENCY	
1 *Pouce*	= 2.7 cm.	1 *Sol*	= 10 *Deniers*
1 *Pied*	= 12 *Pouces*	1 *Livre Tournois*	= 20 *Sols*
1 *Toise*	= 6 *Pieds*	1 *Ecu*	= 3 *Livres*
1 *Toise*	= 1.98 m.		

Although the value of the *livre* cannot be translated into 1991 dollars, the following food prices may give some context to the various costs cited in the text. In 1608, Henri IV purchased one hundred eggs for 45 *sols*, a rabbit for 12 *sols*, a small bass for 18 *sols*, and half a kilo of beef for 2 *sols* 9 *deniers*; these prices may be higher than those at market. A *setier* (1.56 hectoliters) of the finest wheat was sold at Les Halles in 1607–8 for approximately 10 *livres*.

(Sources: Micheline Baulant and Jean Meuvret, *Prix des céréales extraits de la Mercuriale de Paris (1520–1698)*, 2 vols. (Paris: 1960); Pierre Couperie, "L'alimentation du XVIIe siècle: les marchés de pourvoierie," *Annales ESC* 19/3 (May–June 1964): 467–79; Robert Le Blant, "Marchés de pains, de viandes et de poissons pour Henri IV, 21 décembre 1607," *Bulletin philologique et historique (jusqu'à 1610) du Comité des travaux historiques et scientifiques*, 1969, 685–96.

APPENDIX A: THE PLACE ROYALE

1. Construction of the Silkworks (1604)

a. Roofing contract: 3 August 1604.

"Furent presents en leurs personnes Cuny Bracony et Nicolas Hullot, maistres couvreurs de maisons en ceste ville de Paris y demeurans, scavoir led. Bracony rue au Maire, parroisse St. Nicolas des Champs, led. Hullot rue Vannerye, parroisse St. Gervais, tant en leurs noms que comme eulx faisans et portans fortz de Marin Moreau et Françoys Cocquelle, aussy maistres couvreurs de maisons à Paris, . . . lesquels ont recogneu et confessé avoir promis et promectent . . . à nobleshommes [blank], à ce present et acceptant, de couvrir de neuf, bien et deuement au dire d'ouvriers et gens à ce cognoissans, tant de thuille que d'ardoize sellon ce que leur sera commandé par led. sieur Parfaict et lesd. sieurs susnommez, les bastiments et edifices que lesd. sieurs font faire de neuf dans le parc des Tournelles. Et pour ce faire, commencer à y travailler si tost et incontinant qu'il y aura charpenterie faite, continuer avecq bon nombre d'ouvriers sans discontinuer, . . . [et] fournir par lesd. entrepreneurs . . . [toutes] matieres necessaires. . . . Ce marché fait moyennant et à raison de six livres dix sols tournois pour chacune toise desd. ouvrages tant de thuille que d'ardoise et seront thoisez aux us et coustumes de Paris. Et sur lesquels ouvrages, lesd. entrepreneurs ont confessé et confessent avoir eu et receu desd. sieurs Sainctot, Parfaict, Lumague et Le Camus par les mains dud. sieur Lumague . . . la somme de mil livres tournois. . . . Faict et passé en l'etude de Contesse, l'un des notaires soubsignez, l'an mil six cens quatre, le troisiesme jour d'aoust apres midy. Led. Bracony a dict ne pouvoir quant à present signer à cause du tremblement de ses mains.

[Signatures:] Nicolas Hullot, [Claude] Parfaict."

Archives Nationales, Minutier central CVIII 34bis, no. ii^{c}iiii^{xx}.

b. Specifications and contract for joinery work: 2 September 1604.

"Devis des ouvrages de menuyserye qu'il convient faire de neuf dans le parc des Tournelles de ceste ville de Paris pour la construction de douze maisons, chacune de XIIII à XV thoises de long sur XXI piedz de large dans oeuvre, avecq ung pavillon de quatre thoises sur cinq thoises dans oeuvre pour Messieurs les entrepreneurs des manufactures de soye ordonnez par le Roy nostre sire, le tout suyvant les articles cy apres declarez.

Premierement, fault faire des huys d'en bas qui auront sept piedz deux poulces de hault et quatre piedz quatre poulces de largeur et de deux poulces d'espoisseur le tout ou environ, ambouttez par les deux boutz, jointz et bien collez avecq des clefs et des languettes dans lesd. jointz, de bon bois de chesne secq et loyal de Montargis; vallant chacun desd. huis seize livres dix sols tournois.

Item, fault faire des huis des chambres de six piedz ou environ de haulteur et trois piedz de large et d'ung pousse et demy d'espoisseur aussy ou environ, ambouttez par les

[259]

deux bouts, bien collez avecq des clefz dans les joints, de bon bois comme dessus; vallant chacun huict livres tournois. Et s'il en convient de plus grande ou plus petitte de la mesme espoisseur pour servir en lieux suyvant la baye qui se fera, seront payez à prorata dud. prix de huict livres.

Item, fault faire les huis surplus des garderobbes qui auront ung poulce d'espoisseur et de six piedz de hault et de deux piedz et demy de large, collez et ambouttez par les deux bouts, le tout de bon bois; vallant chacun cent sols tournois.

Item, fault faire les croisees qui auront sept piedz et demy de hault et quatre piedz et demy de largeur, garnye chacune croisee d'un grand chassis dormant . . . ; vallant chacune desd. croisees dixneuf livres dix solz tournois. . . .

Item, fault faire les fenestres aux lieux ou l'on travaillera qui se coulleront avecq deux coulisses, une en hault et l'autre en bas pour fermer la baye moictié par moictié, lesquelles fenestres auront ung poulce d'espoisseur d'assemblaiges avec des panneaux à reyneure en facon de lambris et auront de hault sept piedz et demy et quatre piedz dix poulces de largeur pour les deux costez; vallant chacune baye douze livres tournois. Et s'il en convient de plus grandes ou plus petittes seront payés à prorata dud. prix de douze livres tournois. . . .

Furent presents en leurs personnes honnorables hommes Christofle Mauré et Hugues Le Roy, maistres menuysiers à Paris demeurant, scavoir led. Mauré rue Neuve, parroisse St. Medericq, et led. Le Roy rue Cossonnerie, parroisse St. Eustache, lesquels ont volontairement recogneu et confessé avoir promis et promectent l'un pour l'autre . . . à [blank] de faire et parfaire bien et deuement au dire d'ouvriers et gens à ce cognoissans tous et chacunes les ouvraiges de menuiserie mentionnez au devis cy dessus escript sellon et au desir dud. commis; travailler incessament, continuer sans discontinuer, et le tout rendre faict et parfaict au plustost qu'il faire se pourra. Et pour ce faire, fournir tous le bois qu'il conviendra. . . . Ceste promesse ainsy faicte moyennant et aux prix portez par chacune des articles du devis cy dessus escript. . . . Sur lesquelz ouvrages, lesd. Mauré et Le Roy confessent avoir eu et receu desd. sieurs susnommez par advance la somme de six cens livres tournois. . . . Faict et passez en estude desd. notaires l'an mil six cens quatre, le second jour de septembre avant midy.

[Signatures:] Parfaict, Mauré, Hugues Le Roy."

Archives Nationales, Minutier central CVIII 34bis, no. iii^{c}xvi.

c. Specifications and contract for metalwork: 4 September 1604.

"Devis des ouvrages de serrurerye qu'il convient faire pour Messieurs Sainctot, Parfaict, Camus, et Lumague au bastiment qu'ilz font faire dans le parc des Tournelles.

Premierement fault fournir tout le gros fer avec boulons, cloudz, crampons, et treillis s'il en fault, lesquels treillis ceux qui auront cinq piedz de hault auront deux traversiers, et ceux qui en auront neuf auront trois traversiers. Lesquelz ouvrages seront payez au cent, pour chacun cent huict livres tournois.

Item, fault faire les ferrures des portes à deux manteaux, garnie chacune de deux gondz, deux bandes à crosses, sondez au collet, garniz de clouds . . . et d'une grand ferrure à tour et demy ouvrant dedans et dehors, garnye de trois clouds à teste carree et escusson, deux gros verrous rondz garnis de leur vertevelles à gaches, une barre de fer . . . garnye de son moraillon et serrure et une boucle pour tirer la porte. . . . Pour chacune desquelles portes ferrés comme dict est sera payé sept livres dix sols tournois.

Item, seront faits les ferrures des portes des chambres qui seront garnies chacune de deux pantures, deux gondz, une serrure à tour et demy aveq deux verrous platz et la main pour tirer. Pour chacune desquelles portes sera payé cent dix solz tournois.

Item, fault ferrer les portes des garderobbes et aisements qui auront chacune des pantures, des gondz, un loquet et son verrou. Pour chacune desquelles et pour toutes celles qui seront ferrez de mesme, sera payé trente solz tournois.

Item, fault ferrer les croisees à six panneaux pour chacune desquelles sera fourny vingt quatre fiches et huict pattes à chacun chassis avec les verroux sur targettes dorez et etamez. Pour chacune desquelles sera payé cent dix solz tournois. Et pour les autres croisseez et chassis qui seront à moindre nombre de panneaux sera payé à prorata desd. cent dix sols.

Item, fault ferrer les portes des caves qui auront chacune une serrure à bosse garnye de son verrou, deux pantures, et deux gondz. Pour chacune desquelles sera payé soixante solz tournois.

Et outre seront fournies toutes les verges des vitres. Pour chacune desquelles sera payé sept livres dix solz tournois.

Furent presents en leurs personnes Esme Cresson et Jacques Guellard, maistres serruriers à Paris y demeurant, scavoir led. Cresson rue Geoffrey Lasnier, parroisse St. Gervais, et led. Guellard rue de Jouy, parroisse Saint Paul, lesquelz ont recogneu et confessé avoir promis et promectent l'un pour l'autre . . . à [blank], à ce present et acceptans, de faire et parfaire bien et deuement au dire d'ouvriers et gens à ce cognoissans toutes et chacunes les ouvrages de serrurerye mentionnez au devis cy dessus escript. . . . Pour ce faire, fournir tout le fer qu'il conviendra, . . . commencer à travailler sans discontinuer lundi prochain, et le tout rendre fait et parfaict au plustost que faire se pourra. . . . Faict et passé en estude desd. notaires l'an mil six cens quatre, le quatriesme jour de septembre apres midy.

[Signatures:] Parfaict, Esme Cresson, Guelart."

Archives Nationales, Minutier central CVIII 34bis, no. iii^{c}xxiii.

d. *Masonry contract for the* bastiment des moulins: *10 December 1604.*

"René Girault, masson demeurant à Paris, rue des Petitz Lions, parroise St. Sauveur, confesse avoir promis et promect par la presente à Guillaume Pingard, Jehan Poussart, Jacques Le Redde et Baltazard Monard, tous maistres massons à Paris y demeurant, lesd. Poussart et Monard à ce present, de faire et parfaire la massonerie de trois lucarnes et sallies, architraves, frontons, clefs, entablemens et appuidz, et desd.

lucarnes, cuillies et enduictz dedans et dehors; ensemble de faire les entablemens; et en chacune desd. lucarnes, faire huict consoles semblables à celles qui sont du costé de la rue St. Anthoine; cuillir l'entablement et massonner les pierres desd. entablemens, le tout bien et deuement au dire d'ouvriers et gens à ce cognoissans, au bastimens qui ce faict de neuf au parc des Tournelles appellé le bastiment des moullins. A commancer ausd. ouvraiges dans lundy prochain venant, et contynuer sans aulcune discontinuation luy avec ung autre masson et deux maneouvres. Ceste promesse faict moyennant la somme de quarente deux livres tournois, asscavoir: trente deux livres tournois que led. Girault dict avoir avecq Pierre Deschamps, aussy masson, cy devant trop receuz par les mains du sieur Parfaict, marchant drappier, par quictance signé dud. Girault datté du cinquieme des present mois et an, montant cinquante une livres tournois, et promectant d'acquiter led. Girault envers led. Parfaict des LI livres tournois, sur les ouvraiges de massonerie mentionnez en certain marché faict soubz les soings desd. Girault et Deschamps en datte du vingt deuxiesme novembre dernier passé; et dix livres tournois que lesd. Poussart et Monard promectent payer aud. Girault ou au porteur à en fin de la perfection desd. lucarnes. Et moyennant ce, lesd. Poussart et Monnart consentent et accordent que led. marché susdatté demeure nul, et comme tel l'en rendre aud. Girault pour en avoir par luy son recours aller contre led. Deschamps ainsy qu'il verra estre à faire. . . . Faict et passé en estude de notaires l'an mil six cens quatre, le dixieme jour de decembre apres midy, et ont signé la presente:

Rene Girault, J Poussart, B Monnard, Derossignol [notaire], Biard [notaire]."

Archives Nationales, Minutier central CV 293.

2. Construction of the North Range of Pavilions (1607–8)

a. Building specifications prepared by Sully: no date.

"Devis des pavillons qu'il convient construire en la place Royalle en la partye de Septentrion au lieu ou maintenant est basty le corps de logis des Manufactures et sur le mesme allignement aboutissant sur icelle place.

Et premierement, en la susdicte partye de septentrion de ladicte place Royalle et au lieu susdict se construiront huict pavillons, ayans chacun huict toyses de longueur sur quatre toyses cinq piedz de largeur, le tout hors oeuvre.

Plus ung aultre pavillon aussy de huict toises de longueur sur six toises deux piedz de largeur, le tout hors oeuvre, lequel pavillon sera au milieu des huict susdictz et sera directement opposé au Pavillon du Roy qui est de present basty en icelle place en la partye de Midy.

Tous lesquelz neuf pavillons sur leurs allignemens contiendront ensemble pareille longueur que les neuf aultres qui leur sont directement opposez en ladicte partye de Midy. Savoir en tout la quantité de soixante et douze toises, longueur et largeur, bornée pour la quadrature de ladicte place, et dont les deux extremitez desdictz neuf pavillons à bastir doibvent se rapporter justement et à l'eraze des pavillons à present ja bastiz de partye d'orient que d'occident pour fournir l'angle droict.

Lesquelz pavillons de ladicte partye de septentrion, il y en aura les huict qui auront pareille longueur, largeur, haulteur et mesures semblables en toutes dimentions, soit estages, ouvertures de fenestres, proportion de toictures, et persés par le dessoubz en leurs longueurs d'une gallerye d'arcades publicque et commune pour aller à couvert soubz iceulx. Le tout sera de mesme ordre, cimestrye et architecture, et generallement de semblables matereaulx, et en un mot pour ressembler en tout et par tout aux pavillons bastiz en la partye de Midy ou ilz sont directement opposez.

Se fera l'aultre gros pavillon estant au milieu des huict susdicts avec pareille cimestrye, ordre et architecture, mesmement voulté et percé et repercé en deux sens d'arcades, et de semblables matereaulx, haulteur, largeur, et longueur que le pavillon du roy qui est à present tout construict en ladicte place au costé de Midy auquel il doibt estre en toutes partyes esgal et proportionné et directement opposé.

Desquelz pavillons cy dessus, voicy les mesures abregees. Le pavillon à bastir à l'egal de celluy de Roy:

     Sa longueur sera de huict toises.

     Sa largeur sera de six toises deux piedz.

     La haulteur du premier estage du rez de chaussée aura vingt trois piedz.

     La haulteur du second et principal estage aura quinze piedz.

     La haulteur du troisiesme estage d'entablement aura treize piedz.

     Sur ce dernier estage s'esleveront les lucarnes, en toute haulteur jusques à l'entablement cinquante et ung piedz.

Les huict autres pavillons à bastir auront chacun de longueur huict toises, largeur quatre toises cinq piedz.

La haulteur du premier estage du rez de chaussée sera douze piedz quatre
   poulces.

La haulteur du second estage aura treize piedz et demy.

La haulteur du troisiesme estage aura unze piedz et deux poulces.

L'exaussement de l'entablement aura de haulteur ung pied et dix poulces.

Sur lequel exaussement s'esleveront les lucarnes et oues,

   en toute haulteur trente huict piedz dix poulces."

Archives Nationales, 120 AP 49 f31–33.

b. Carpentry contract: 28 February 1607.

"Furent presents en leurs personnes Jehan Vivier, maistre charpentier à Paris, et Jehan de La Roue, son beaupere, aussy charpentier demeurant à Paris, rue Neufve pres le parc royal, parroisse Sainct Paul, lesquelz de leurs bons grez et volontez ont recongneu et confessé avoir promis et promectent l'un pour l'autre . . . à nobles hommes Pierre Sainctot, Jehan Andre Lumague et Claude Parfaict, bourgeois de Paris y demeurant, tant en leurs noms que comme eulx faisans et portans fortz de leur compaignie, lesquels sieurs Sainctot, Lumague et Parfaict à ce present et acceptans esd. nommez, de faire et parfaire en les maisons du parc royal les ouvrages qui ensuivent, le tout bien et deuement au dire d'ouvriers et gens à ce cognoissans, asscavoir: de desmolir la charpenterie de six maisons estant dans le parc royal du costé du pavillon Royal, et auparavant que faire lad. desmolition, de prendre le bois par compte à la piece et icelluy garder et soigner en sorte qu'il n'y arrive aulcune perte vif. . . . Lad. desmolition faicte, restablir et remectre en oeuvre ledict bois es lieux et endroictz et en telle facon qu'il leur sera commandé par lesd. sieurs ou l'un d'eux. Et faire des crouppes aux boutz des logis qui seront refaictz aux endroictz qui seront par lesd. sieurs advisez. Esquels logis lesd. Vivier et de La Roue feront toute la charpenterie qu'il conviendra et les sera commandé par lesd. sieurs Sainctot, Lumague et Parfaict. Faire ce aveq bois qui aura, comme dict est, esté desmoly sans qu'ilz y puissent employer autre bois ny mesme de bois neuf san l'expres commandement desd. sieurs Sainctot, Lumague et Parfaict. . . . Et pour faire tout ce que dessus, commancer à travailler des le jour de demain et travailler sans discontinuer avec nombre d'ouvriers sufisans. Et sy en lad. besongne tout led. bois desmoly n'estoit employé, lesd. Vivier et de La Roue seront tenuz rendre le surplus selon le compte qui en aura esté fait comme dict est auparavant lad. desmolition. Ce marché faict moyennant et à raison de soixante six livres tournois pour chacune cent dud. bois qui aura, comme dict est, esté remis en oeuvre à compter apres lad. besongne faicte au compte des marchans; que pour ce, les. sieurs Sainctot, Lumague et Parfaict esquelz nommez en ont promis, seront tenuz, promectent et gaigent rendre, bailler et paier chacun en soy lesd. Vivier et de La Roue ou au porteur, et ce au feur et ainsy qu'ilz seront lad. besongne; et apres icelle parfaicte et ou il en auroit du bois neuf employé, ils en seront payez selon qu'il en sera arbitré à l'amyable entre lesd. parties. . . . Fait et passé double scavoir par lesd. sieurs

Sainctot et Lumague en leurs hotelz, et par led. sieur Parfaict et lesd. Vivier et de La Roue en estude des notaires soubsignez en l'an mil six cens huict, le vingthuictiesme jour de febrier avan midy.

[Signatures:] Sainctot, Parfaict, Lumague, Jehan Vivie [sic], J de Laroue, Contesse [notaire], Herbin [notaire]."

Archives Nationales, Minutier central CVIII 37, no. lxxix.

c. Masonry contract: 8 March 1608.

"Devis des ouvrages de maçonnerie qu'il convient faire pour Messieurs de Moisset, Sainctot, Lumague, Camus, et Parfaict en la place royalle pour refaire les bastimens qui sont en la face du pavillon royal en la mesme forme, façon et structure qu'est led. pavillon et les bastimens joignant icelluy.

Premierement, fault desmolir de fondz en comble soixante quatre thoises de longueur des bastimens ou sont à present les Manufactures estant en lad. face du pavillon royal, mectre les desmolitions à part, et rendre place nette.

Item, fault faire les vuidanges des terres massives, trenchez et rigolles pour faire pavillons doubles suivant le desseing qui en sera baillé et paraphé par lesd. sieurs.

Item, fault faire tous les murs dans les fondations de pierre de plastre dure, maçonnés de chaux et sable jusques à trois piedz prez du rez de chaussee; et au dessus de trois piedz, de moillon de Charenton ou Vaugirard, maçonnez de chaux et sable jusques au rez de chaussee. Lesd. espoisses des murs seront assavoir: le mur du costé de la place Royalle aura en fondation trois piedz et demy jusques au rez de chaussee; et audessus du rez de chaussee, les pierres porteront deux piedz et un quart qui seront de pierre de Cliquard . . . jusques sur les arcades, et audessus desd. arcades vingtdeux poulces en diminuans sur retraicte jusques à l'entablement.

Item, fault faire le mur de la gallerie qui aura deux piedz en fondation, et au dessus du rez de chaussee aura vingt pouces; seront faictz les piedz droictz de pierre de Cliquard . . . ; et les voulsures et arcades qui seront tant dedans le corps de la gallerie que au dehors seront faictz de pierre de St. Leu aveq brique.

Item, fault faire le mur qui separe les deux pavillons qui aura deux piedz et demy en fondation, et deux piedz jusques au premier estaige, et au dessus à vingt deux pouces en diminuant d'estage en estage. Et seront faictz des jambes soubz poultres . . .

Item, fault faire le mur du costé de la court de pareille espoisseur et en la mesme forme qui est à present icelle de Monsieur de La Salle.

Item, fault faire les murs de refan separant les pavillons de deux piedz en fondation, et au dessus du rez de chaussee de vingt pouces en diminuant jusques en hault.

Item, fault faire les murs de clostures qui seront de douze piedz en fondation plus ou moings s'il y besogne, et de deux thoises de hault, sans y comprendre le chapperon qui auroit d'espoisse par bas deux piedz du rez de chaussee en hault vingt poulces, garnies de jambes espassez de neuf piedz en neuf piedz, et de cinq piedz en cinq piedz des marches

[265]

parpines ensemble deux assizes de pierre par bas, parpine entre deux, une maçonnez à trois piedz prez du rez de chaussee de pierre de plastre, chaux et sable, et le reste de bon moislon de Vaugirard ou Charenton.

Item, fault faire les voulsures des caves de bon moislon maçonné de plastre, et faire des chesnes es endroitz des jambes soubz poultres; remplir les reins de moislon de plastre dur, maçonnez de chaux et sable.

Item, fault faire les planchers, cloisons, lambris, manteaux de chemineez et enduitz suivant le desseing qui en sera baillé par lesd. sieurs et non autrement.

Item, fault faire les thuyeaux de chemineez jusques à la hauteur du comble du plastre, et le surplus d'en hault de bricque.

Item, fault faire les aires des planchers du premier estage de petit carreau à six pandz, ensemble les monteez, le tout maçonné de chaux et sable.

Tous lesquelz ouvrages de maçonnerie seront faitz selon et conformemant le plan qui en sera comme dict est baillé par lesd. sieurs pour faire lesd. bastimens par le devant, conformés au bastimen dud. pavillon Royal et des maisons joignantes icelles et par derriere à l'egal de celle dud. sieur de La Salle.

Et seront lesd. ouvrages thoisez aux uz et coustumes de Paris fors et reservé qui ne sera rien thoisé, prisé, estimé ni evalué pour les plaintes, sallies, ornemens, moulloures, lucarnes et entablemens tant dehors que dedans, fors les cheminees, le tout neantmoings faict suivant le desseing qui en sera baillé par lesd. sieurs et selon qu'il est cy dessus dict.

Prendre l'entrepreneur toutes les desmolitions à son profict desquels il en emploira ce qu'il sera ordonné par lesd. sieurs susnommez ou l'un d'eux.

Furent present en sa personne honnorable homme Baltazard Monnard, maistre maçon à Paris demeurant rue des Juifs, parroisse Sainct Gervais, lequel a recongneu et confessé avoir promis et promect à nobles hommes Pierre Sainctot, Jehan Andre Lumague, Nicolas Camus et Claude Parfaict, tous bourgeois de Paris y demeurant, à ce present et acceptans, de faire et parfaire bien et deuement au dire d'ouvriers et gens à ce cognoissans tous et chacunes les ouvrages de maçonnerie mentionnez au devis cy dessus escript. . . . Commancer à travailler des le jour de lundy prochain et continuer sans discontinuer jusques à perfection aveq bon nombre d'ouvriers sufisans. Fournir de pierre, plastre, moilon et toutes autres matieres à ce necessaire, peyne d'ouvriers, et rendre place nette. Ce marché faict moyennant et à raison de huict livres tournois la thoise desd. ouvrages, thoisez selon qu'il est dict par led. devis, laquelle somme luy sera payee au feur et à mesure qu'il fera lesd. ouvrages, et ce par lesd. sieurs susnommez, chacun pour soy. Outre la somme de quatre mil six cens dixneuf livres quatorze solz tournois que led. Monnard a cy devant receu desd. sieurs susnommez depuis le septieme septembre jusques au XVII decembre ensuivant gvi^c sept [1607], laquelle somme lesd. sieurs luy ont delaissee . . . en consideration et rescompense de la lourde besongne qu'il convient faire suivant led. marché au grand pavillon et de ce qu'il convient desmolir et restablir en icelluy à cause de ce qui a esté gasté et partie geleez. Et outre est le present marché faict a condition expresse que led. Monnard ne pourra prendre aucuns hasteliers ni faire maçonnerie pour autres personnes que pour lesd. sieurs jusques à ce que

lesd. ouvrages seront parfaicts à peyne de tous despenses, dommages et interestz. . . .
Fait et passé double scavoir par led. Monnard en estude et par lesd sieurs en leurs hostelz
à Paris, l'an mil six cens huict, le huictieme jour de mars apres midy.

[Signatures:] Lumague, Sainctot, Parfaict, Nicolas Camus, B Monnard, Herbin
[notaire], Contesse [notaire]."

Archives Nationales, Minutier central CVIII 37, no. iiii^{xx}vii.

d. *Contract for the purchase and delivery of stone: 19 March 1608.*

"Estienne Allart, voicturier par eaue demeurant à Paris, rue des Jardins, parroisse St.
Paul, confesse avoir promis et promect en la presente à Baltazard Monart, maistre maçon
à Paris, à ce present et acceptant, de luy fournir et livrer toute la pierre de moillon que
led. Monart aura . . . pour la construction des bastimens qu'il a entrepris faire au parc
Royal. A icelluy moislon livrer et thoiser dedans led. parc aux frais et despens dud. Allart
hormis le thoisé qui sera aux despens dud. Monart; et d'icelluy moislon en livrer aud.
Monart par chacune sepmaine la quantité de quinze thoises ou plus si faire se peult,
pourveu qu'il puisse voicturer par eaue sans aucun peril et que le temps soit propre à ce
faire, bon moislon loyal et marchand. Ceste promesse faicte moyennant et à raison de
treize livres tournois pour chacune toise dud. moislon, lequel prix led. Monart promect
payer aud. Allart en fin de chacune sepmaine pour ce qu'il aura livré. Et ou led. Allart ne
pourroit livrer du moislon à cause de l'intempery du temps que pourroit arriver, en ce cas
sera permis aud. Monart de prendre dud. moislon d'autres personnes jusques à ce que le
temps sera propre pour faire la voicture d'icelluy. . . . Faict et passé en estude l'an mil
six cent huict, le dix neuviesme jour de mars. . . .

[Signatures:] B Monnard, Groyn [notaire], Biard [notaire]."

Archives Nationales, Minutier central CV 300.

3. The Royal *Lotissement* and Redistribution of Empty Lots

The crown donated the lots at the Place Royale to the men listed on the left side of this chart. Dashed lines demarcate the boundaries of the empty lots, which were in most cases one pavilion wide. Many recipients sold their empty lots; the new owners, those who built the mandated pavilions, are listed on the right side of the chart. Solid lines demarcate the boundaries of the houses that eventually were built. Dimensions are given in *toises* (t), *pieds* ('), and *pouces* ("). Roman numerals refer to documents in the Archives Nationales, Minutier central; other documents were published in Mallevoüe, *Les Actes de Sully* (Paris: 1911).

No. of Pavilions	Width/ Length	Original Recipient	Title	Date of Donation Document	Date of Transfer Document	Second Owner	Title	Purchase Price (livres)	No. of Pavilions
EAST RANGE									
1	7t2'8" 22t	LAFFEMAS, Barthélemy	*Contrôleur du commerce*	4.VI.1605 Mallevoüe	17.VII.1607 A.N. E14A f63	MARCHANT, Louis	Royal carpenter	Royal Gift	1
1	7t2'8" 24t	d'ANGENNES, Nicolas	*Chevalier des ordres du Roi*	6.VI.1605 Mallevoüe	17.VII.1607 A.N. E14A f63	FONTAINE, Jean	Royal mason	Royal Gift	1
1	7t2'8" 25t	CHEVALIER, Nicolas	*Président-Enquêtes Parlement*	6.VI.1605 Mallevoüe					1
1	7t2'8" 27t2'	FELISSAN, François	*Contrôleur gnl. taillons-Soissons*	6.VI.1605 Mallevoüe	27-XII.1605 XIX 354	DROUIN, Barthélemy	Carpenter	House plus 1,200 livres	1
1	7t2'8" 29t3'	RIBAULD, Antoine	*Intendant-Finances*	6.VI.1605 Mallevoüe	28.I.1606 III 462ter	RIBAULD, Antoine			1¼
1	7t2'8" 31t	JEANNIN, Pierre	*Conseiller du Roi*	6.VI.1605 Mallevoüe					
1	7t2'8" 33t	LA FOND, Etienne de	*Intendant-Meubles*	4.VI.1605 Mallevoüe	28.I.1606 III 462ter	CASTILLE, Pierre de	*Maître des requêtes*		1¼
1	7t2'8" 34t5'	CHASTILLON, Claude	*Royal Engineer*	4.VI.1605 Mallevoüe					1
1	7t2'8" 36t	FOURCY, Jean de	*Intendant-Bâtiments*	4.VI.1605 Mallevoüe	? ?	LE REDDE, Antoine	Carpenter	?	1
SOUTH RANGE									
1	17–21t 27t	ARNAULD, Issac	*Conseiller du Roi*	4.VI.1605 Mallevoüe					1
1	8t 9" 21t4'	REGNOUART, Noël	*Secrétaire-chambre du roi*	4.VI.1605 Mallevoüe					1
1	8t 9" 22t	MASSY, Daniel de	*Lieutenant-Bastille*	5.XII.1605 Mallevoüe	5.XII.1605 III 462ter	COIN, Jean	Mason	850	1
1	8t 9" 22t	FOUGEU d'ESCURES, Pierre	*Intendant-Turcies*	4.VI.1605 Mallevoüe					1

Appendix A: The Place Royale

No. of Pavilions	Width/Length	Original Recipient	Title	Date of Donation Document	Date of Transfer Document	Second Owner	Title	Purchase Price (livres)	No. of Pavilions
1	8t / 6t	King's Pavilion							1
1	8t / 22t	BOUHIER, Jacques	Maître d'hôtel du Roi	1.VII.1605 Mallevoüe	8.VII.1606 LXVIII 86	COLLANGES, Philippe	Secrétaire du Roi	1,200	1½
1	8t / 22t	FOURCY, Jean de	Intendant-Bâtiments	?.VIII.1606 III 462ter					
1		LE GRAS, Simon LE GRAS, Nicolas	Trésorier gnl.	? ?	14.VII.1606 ?	LE GRAS		?	1½
1	8tl' / 20t2'	CAILLEBOT, Louis and Louis de (frères)	Lieut. Gardes du Roi Capt. Gardes du Roi	17.VII.1607 CXVII 469					1
WEST RANGE									
1		FOUGEU d'ESCURES, Pierre	Intendant-Turcies	10.III.1607 CXVII 469;					2
1		FOUGEU d'ESCURES		A.N. X1A/8646 (copy)					
1	7t2' / 26t	FOUGEU d'ESCURES			23.III.1607 CXVII 469	LOMENIE François de	Secrétaire des finances	?	1
1	7t4'	FOUGEU d'ESCURES			3.IV.1607 CXVII 469	PÉRICARD Jean	Conseiller du Roi	1,200	2
1	7t4'	FOUGEU d'ESCURES							

No. of Pavilions	Width/ Length	Original Recipient	Title	Date of Donation Document	Date of Transfer Document	Second Owner	Title	Purchase Price (livres)	No. of Pavilions
1		MARCHANT, Charles	*Capitaine-Archers de la Ville*	Early 1607 ?					1¼
1		MARCHANT							1¼
1		MARCHANT							1
1		MARCHANT							1
NORTH RANGE									
1	8t / 32t	LUMAGUE, Jean-André	Banker-merchant	8.I.1609 LXXXVI 185					1
1¼	12t / 32t	PARFAICT, Claude	Merchant	8.I.1609 LXXXVI 185					3/4
1¼	12t / 32t	SAINCTOT, Pierre	Merchant *Conseiller de la Ville*	8.I.1609 LXXXVI 185					3/4
2¼	8t / 6t2' / 12t / 32t	MOISSET, Jean	*Receveur des rentes Secrétaire du Roi*	2.X.1608 XC 168					1¼
1¼	12t / 32t	PARFAICT, Guillaume	*Contrôleur gnal.du Roi*	8.I.1609 LXXXVI 185					2¼
1	8t	CAMUS, Nicolas	Banker	8.I.1609 LXXXVI 185					1¼

4. Index of Construction Contracts and Other Documents by Owner

Abbreviations

A.N.   Archives Nationales
A.P. H.D.   Archives de l'Assistance Publique, Fonds Hôtel Dieu
A.S.   Archives de la Seine
BHVP   Bibliothèque Historique de la Ville de Paris
Lods   Waiver of mutation fees (*lods et ventes*)
Terrier   Tax declaration (*Papier Terrier du Roi*); date of earliest statement is given.
Roman numerals refer to documents in the Archives Nationales, Minutier central.

The nineteenth-century plans reproduced in Figures 171–74 vary in some respects from the original seventeenth-century property lines.

EAST RANGE (Fig. 171) ——————————————————————

   1. *MARCHANT, Louis* (1 pavilion)
     Masonry: CV 300, 9 June 1608
     Joinery: XIX 359 f130, 21 April 1608
     Lease: CXVII 471 f366, 16 June 1609
     Terrier: A.N. Q1/1099 34A, 27 Jan. 1672

   2. *FONTAINE, Jean* (1 pavilion)
     Masonry: CXVII 469 f477, 24 Aug. 1607; CV 300, 9 June 1608

   3. *CHEVALIER, Nicolas* (1 pavilion)
     Sale: LIV 508, 17 Oct. 1626

   4. *DROUIN, Barthélemy* (1 pavilion)
     Receipt for payment by Felissan: XIX 355 f164, 21 March 1606
     Leases: CVII 104 f337, 26 Nov. 1610, and f369, 16 Dec. 1610
     Sale by heirs: CVII 119 f328, 1 Dec. 1622

   5. *RIBAULD, Antoine* (1¼ pavilions)
     Purchase of de La Fond's lot and subdivision with Castille: III 462ter, 28 Jan. 1606
     Lods for subsequent owner: A.N. Z1F/560 f200v, 23 June 1613
     Castille received the lot of his father-in-law, Jeannin, as a gift and then purchased Etienne de La Fond's adjoining lot jointly with Ribauld for 1,290 *livres*. Castille and Ribauld subdivided the land so that each had 1¼ pavilions.

   6. *CASTILLE, Pierre de* (1¼ pavilions)
     Purchase of de La Fond's lot and subdivision with Ribauld: III 462ter, 28 Jan. 1606
     Maintenance of roofs: XC 185, 27 May 1620

   7. *CHASTILLON, Claude* (1 pavilion)
     Payment of carpenters: XIX 383 f67, 21 May 1616
     Leases: CXVII 470 f431, 25 Aug. 1608; CV 316, 3 May 1614

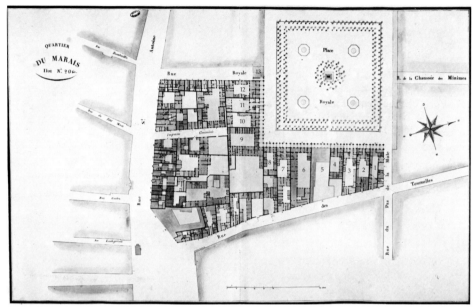

Fig. 171. Place Royale, east and south ranges, cadastral plan, Atlas Vasserot, c. 1830–50. (A.N. F³¹ 87, Ilot 20bis)

Sale: XLV 22, 21 Feb. 1617
Terrier: A.N. Q1/1099 34A, 15 May 1636

8. *LE REDDE, Antoine* (1 pavilion)
Masonry: CV 313, 5(?) June 1613 (partially destroyed)
Sale of property to finance construction: XIX 358 f361, 9 Nov. 1607
Sale of rear portion of lot: CV 313, 15 May 1613
Terrier: A.N. Q1/1099 34A, 20 Dec. 1667

SOUTH RANGE (Figs. 171, 172) ──────────────────────

9. *ARNAULD, Isaac* (1 pavilion)
The crown gave the lot to Arnauld and his brother-in-law Hilaire Lhoste, who
renounced any interest in property: III 462ter, 21 Jan. 1608.
Purchase of stone: CV 295, 18 Oct. 1605
Payment of mason: CXV 18, 5 Jan. 1608
Sale: A.S. 4 AZ 1153, 14 April 1612

10. *REGNOUART, Noël* (1 pavilion)
No documents found.

11. *COIN, Jean* (1 pavilion)
Sold by 1608 to Pierre Chastellain

[273]

Purchase of additional land (Chastellain): CV 300, 22 March 1608
Specifications for stables (Chastellain): CVIII 37 f167, 14 May 1608

12. *FOUGEU, Pierre* (1 pavilion)
    Masonry: XXXIX 38 f223, 17 March 1606
    Toisé: BHVP Ms. C.P. 3365 f17v, 10 Dec. 1607
    Metalwork: XXXIX 39 f193, 29 Dec. 1607
    Carpentry: BHVP Ms. C.P. 3365 f30, 27 March 1608
    Sale of house to Jean Phélypeaux: BHVP Ms. C.P. 3365 f63, 10 March 1608
    Leases: XIX 369f106, 15 April 1608; BHVP Ms. C.P. 3365 f88–99, 21 Nov. 1611, 29
        Nov. 1616, 11 Nov. 1620

13. *The King's Pavilion*
    Masonry: Mallevoüe 158, 1 July 1605
    Carpentry: Mallevoüe 160, 1 July 1605
    Budget: A.N. 120 A.P. 49, Voirie 1607 f29
    Sale: A.N. Q1/1234, 10 May 1674

14. *COLLANGES, Philippe de* (1½ pavilions)
    Purchases of additional land: III 462ter, 12 Dec. 1606; CXV 17, 17 Sept. 1607
    Masonry: LXII 45, 18 Nov. 1609
    Inventory after death: CV 590, 31 Jan. 1637

15. *LE GRAS, Nicolas and Simon* (1½ pavilions)
    No documents found.

16. *CAILLEBOT, Louis and Louis de, frères* (1 pavilion)
    Payment for leadwork: XCVI 4 f45, 24 July 1610
    Settlement with convent of Ste. Catherine: A.N. ZIF/565f82, 14 July 1615

WEST RANGE (Fig. 172) ——————————————————————————

17. *FOUGEU, Pierre* (2 pavilions)
    Masonry: CVIII 43 f56, 25 Feb. 1611
    Painting: CVIII 48 f235, 19 Sept. 1614
    Sale: CXV 87, 7 March 1644
    Inventory of titles: BHVP Ms. C.P. 3442, after 1644

18. *LOMENIE, François de* (1 pavilion)
    Masonry: CVIII 36 f203, 12 May 1607
    Lease: CVIII 43 f283, 2 Sept. 1611

19. *PÉRICARD, Jean* (2 pavilions)
    Provision of wood: CV 170, 26 May 1607
    Roofing: CV 170, 1 June 1607
    Joinery: CV 170, 13 June 1607
    Metalwork: CV 171, 8 Aug. 1607

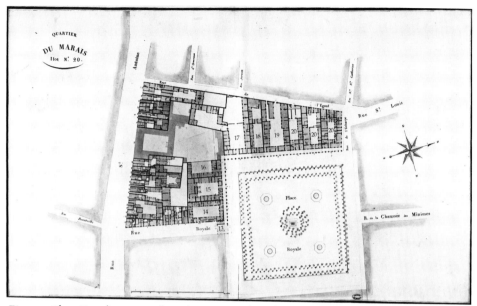

Fig. 172. Place Royale, west and south ranges, cadastral plan, Atlas Vasserot, c. 1830–50. (A.N. F³¹ 87, Ilot 20)

> Plasterwork: CV 174, 13 June 1608
> Paving: CV 175, 21 July 1608
> Loan for construction: XIX 361 f45, 14 Feb. 1609
> Lease: LXII 46, 25 Aug. 1610

20. *MARCHANT, Charles* (4 pavilions: 1 1-pav. house and 2 1½-pav. houses)
> Masonry: XIX 355, 4 April 1606
> Purchase of slate: XIX 367, 12 April 1607
> Purchase of additional land from Fougeu: CXVII 469 f236, 14 April 1607
> Roofing: XIX 357, 17 May 1607
> Carpentry: XIX 358 f311, 14 Sept. 1607
> Joinery: XIX 358 f368, 13 Nov. 1607
> Purchase of rubble: CXV 18, 24 and 25 Feb. 1608
> Division of Marchant's estate: CVIII 57 f206, 7 May 1618
> Leases by heir: CVIII 54 f20, 13 Jan., and f183, 14 June 1617
> Seizure of one house: A.N. T 209 1, 31 March 1628
> Sale of one house by subsequent owner: A.N. T 1051 73.815, 24 May 1667

NORTH RANGE (Figs. 173, 174) ————————————
See Appendix A2.

21. *LUMAGUE, Jean-André* (1 pavilion)
> Carpentry: CVIII 37 f345, 8 Nov. 1608; CV 301, 22 Nov. 1608
> Subdivision of property among Lumague's partners: CXII 258, 10 Jan. 1609

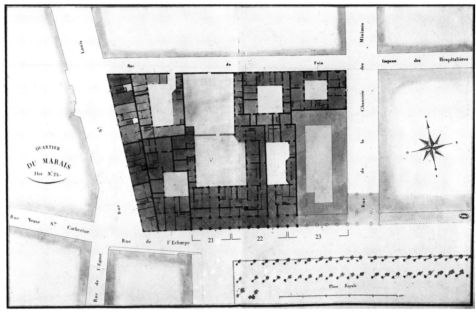

Fig. 173. Place Royale, north range west of the Queen's Pavilion, cadastral plan, Atlas Vasserot, c. 1830–50. (A.N. F^{31} 87, Ilot 24)

Joinery: CXII 260, 18 March 1610
Glazing: LXII 46, 19 March 1610
Leases: CXII 273, 23 May 1617; CXII 283, 6 April 1622
Sale: CXII 299, 22 Aug. 1630
Terrier: A.N. Q1/1099 34A, 20 Dec. 1667

22. *PARFAICT, Claude* (1¼ pavilions: 2 ¾-pavilion houses)
Carpentry: CVIII 37, 19 May 1608
Metalwork: CVIII 37, 8 Aug. 1608
Joinery: CVIII 37, 28 Aug. 1608
Chimney mantels: CXV 20, 16 April 1609
Metalwork: CVIII 41 f302, 20 Aug. 1610; CVIII 57 f93, 21 March 1618
Leases: CVIII 43 f292, 18 Sept. 1611; CVIII 47 f185, 4 June 1613; CVIII 50 f187, 23
    July 1615; CVIII 54 f126, 10 April 1617; CVIII 57 f135, 14 May 1618
Sale: CVIII 61 f205, 20 June 1620; copy A.P. H.D. 60.350
Appraisal of houses: CVIII 64(2) following f237, 19–22 Sept. 1623
Sale by heirs: CVIII 64(2) f166, 13 Aug. 1624; copy A.P. H.D. 60.350
Inventory after death: CVIII 64(2) f237, 13 Dec. 1624
Terrier: A.N. Q1/1099 34A, 11 April 1681

23. *SAINCTOT, Pierre* (1¼ pavilions)
Leases: LXXXVI 187, 22 Aug. and 6 Sept. 1611; LXXXVI 225, 10 and 12 Feb. 1618
Will: LXXXVI 261, 27 May 1639

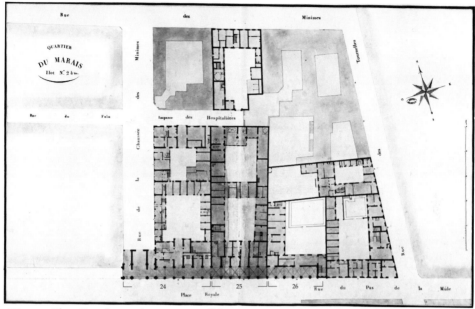

Fig. 174. Place Royale, north range east of the Queen's Pavilion, cadastral plan, Atlas Vasserot, c. 1830–50. (A.N. F^{31} 87, Ilot 24bis)

Sale by heirs: CVIII 87 f83, 26 March 1641

Terrier: A.N. Q1/1099 34A, 12 May 1681

24. *MOISSET, Jean* ($2\frac{1}{2}$ pavilions, including the Queen's Pavilion)

Masonry: XC 172, 2 March 1612

Provision of wood: XC 172, 8 March 1612

Provision of stone: XC 172, 21 April 1612

Staircase: XC 173, 15 May and 4 Sept. 1613; XIX 380 f204, 11 Sept. 1613; XC 173, 22 Oct. 1613

Leases: XC 174, 31 Oct. 1614; XC 178, 5 Feb. 1618

Terrier: A.N. Q1/1099 34A, 9 Sept. 1681

25. *PARFAICT, Guillaume* ($1\frac{1}{2}$ pavilions)

Masonry: CVIII 43 f176, 28 May 1611

Survey (*toisé*): CVIII 43 f177, 28 May 1611

Painting: CVIII 43 f178, 30 May 1611

Paving: CVIII 43 f180, 31 May 1611, and f188, 8 June 1611

Chimney mantels: CVIII 43 f223, 15 July 1611

Carpentry for stables: CVIII 47 f216, 17 July 1613

Masonry for stables: CVIII 47 f231, 27 July 1613

Leases: CVIII 45 f223, 27 June 1612; CVIII 47 f183, 3 June 1613; CVIII 48 f135, 6 June 1614; CVIII 52 f203, 5 Oct., and f230, 4 Nov. 1616; CVIII 59 f159, 10 May 1619; CVIII 62(4) f127, 22 April 1622

[277]

Sale by heirs: CVIII 68(5) f139, 5 June 1630
Terrier: A.N. Q1/1099 34A, 23 Aug. 1669

26. *CAMUS, Nicolas* (1 pavilion)
Receipt for payment of rent: XCVI 8bis, 10 Oct. 1620
Terrier: A.N. Q1/1099 34A, 24 Dec. 1667

5. The Houses on the Rue des Minimes

The leases and sale contracts listed below concern the houses built and owned by the silk investors on the rue de Vitry, later renamed the rue des Minimes, seen in Figure 73. Although the king required them to rent the houses free of charge to silk artisans through 1615, the owners did not fully comply with the royal stipulation; those leases involving silk artisans are indicated. Unless otherwise noted, all documents are from the Archives Nationales, Minutier central.

A. *Lumague, Jean-André*
    11 Sept. 1614, CXII 268
    11 Nov. 1614, CXII 268
    22 May 1617, CXII 273

B. *Sainctot, Pierre*
    No documents found.

C. *Parfaict, Claude*
    6 Oct. 1610, CVIII 41
    1 Sept. 1611, CVIII 43   silk artisan
    4 Sept. 1612, CVIII 45
    25 May 1613, CVIII 47
    6 Mar. 1614, CVIII 48   silk artisan
    22 Dec. 1615, CVIII 50   silk artisans
    12 Jan. 1616, CVIII 52
    10 Feb. 1618, CVIII 57
    4 Apr. 1618, CVIII 57
    29 Dec. 1618, CVIII 57
    8 Mar. 1619, CVIII 59   silk artisan
    9 Jan. 1620, CVIII 61
    20 Feb. 1621, CVIII 62(2)
    11 Mar. 1621, CVIII 62(2)
    6 Aug. 1622, CVIII 62(4)

D. *Parfaict, Guillaume*
    23 Sept. 1609, CVIII 39   silk artisan
    26 Aug. 1611, CVIII 43   silk artisan
    24 Sept. 1614, CVIII 48

E. *Camus, Nicolas*
   14 May 1616, LXXXVI 223
   3 Dec. 1616, LXXXVI 223
   15 June 1622, LXXXVI 229
   Sale:
   8 Jan. 1628, A.N.S 6184

F. *Sainctot, Pierre*
   30 Sept. 1622, LXXXVI 229
   Sale to the Hôpital de la Charité Notre-Dame for 24,000 *livres*:
   3 Sept. 1626, LXXXVI 233

G. *Lumague:* Residence for Spinners (*Logement des filleuses*)
   21 July 1614, CXII 268
   Sale to the Hôpital de la Charité Notre-Dame for 8,000 *livres*:
   11 Sept. 1629, A. N. S 6148

H. *Moisset, Jean: Maison des Moulins*
   10 Oct. 1615, XC 175   silk artisan
   Sale:
   15 July 1616, XC 176; copy B.N. Ms. fr. 26313 f55
   30 Sept. 1616, XC 176
   According to these documents, the *maison des moulins* consisted of "un grand corps
   d'hostel, escalier au milieu, galleries et autres bastiments aux deux costés dud. logis,
   cave, court, jardin, puis, porte cochere sur lad. rue des Tournelles et issue par le
   jardin sur une rue [Roger Verlomme] conduisant à la rue neuve du grand pavillon de
   la place Royalle aux Minimes [rue de Béarn]."

6. Silk Production on the Rue des Minimes: Lease of a House to a Silk Artisan, 26 August 1611

"Furent presens en leurs personnes noble homme Guillaume Parfaict, conseiller du Roy et controlleur general de la maison de sa majesté, demeurant rue des Mauvaises Parolles, parroisse Sainct Germain l'Auxerrois, d'une part, et Anthoine Besson, maistre ouvrier en draps d'or, d'argent et de soye en la ville de Lyon ainsi qu'il a faict apparoir par le certificat qu'il en a faict faire par les presents jurez dud. mestier aud. Lyon . . . inseré en fin des presentes, led. Besson demeurant à present dans l'enclos de la Trinité de ceste ville de Paris, d'autre part, lesquelz de leurs bons grez et volontez ont recongneu et confessé avoir faict et accordé entre eulx ce qui ensuit. C'est asscavoir que led. Parfaict logera gratuitement Besson par l'espace de quatre annees entieres et consecutifves qui commenceront du jourdhuy et finiront à pareil jour mil six cens quinze, en une maison scize au parc des Tournelles du costé de la maison de Monsieur de Vitry ou soulloit cy devant demeurer Roch Cobert[1] pour jouir et occuper en icelle des deux chambres basses attenant à la montee et la bouge derriere icelle, ensemble de la grande boutique haulte et logement en galletas qui sont au dessus, sans pour ce cy payer par led. Besson aulcun loier. . . . Et quant aux deux autres chambres basses qui sont d'un costé à la batterie de l'or et d'autre à une allee estant à l'opposite de la porte de Monsieur de Vitry, elles sont reservees par led. sieur Parfaict pour y loger telles personnes que bon luy semblera . . .

Recongnoissant led. Besson luy avoir esté baillé par led. sieur Parfaict et avoir en la possession en lad. maison tous les mestiers qui avoient esté baillez aud. Cobert . . . ensemble les ustancilles et equipages servant ausd. mestiers pour faire ouvrages de draps de soye, selon que lesd. mestiers, ustancilles et equipages sont au long contenus et declarez par le rapport et proces verbal faict d'iceulx par le commissaire Fizeau et le sieur Lancy, marchans à ce commis et nommez par monsieur le lieutenant civil en datte du [blank]. Lesquels mestiers led. Besson sera tenu faire travailler dans la grande boutique dud. logis d'estoffes de diverses sortes à la façon d'Italye des largeurs portees par des ordonnances et des façons qui se trouveront à la vente les plus commodes. . . . Et pour les mestiers qui sont à la boutique haulte, les pourra monter et faire travaller de toutes et telles autres estoffes que bon luy semblera de grande et petite navette ainsi qu'il advisera pour en faire son proffict. Et pour cest effet, led. Besson pourverra de soyes et autres choses necessaires . . .

Et pour donner plus de moyen aud. Besson de travailler et faire travailler ausd. ouvrages, led. sieur Parfaict luy a presentement payé, baillé et presté la somme de trois cens livres tournois . . . et luy promect encores prester et paier dans six sepmaines autres trois cens livres tournois, faisant lesd. deux sommes ensemble six cens livres tournois que led. Besson emploiera, mais il promect en achapt de soies et autres estoffes et choses necessaires à sond. mestier. Et lesquelz six cens livres tournois il sera tenu rendre et restituer aud. sieur Parfaict en fin desd. quatre annees sans aulcun proffict ni interest.

Pourra led. Besson vendre et debiter pour son compte et à son proffict soict au comptant ou à tenue selon ce qu'il advisera bon estre les estoffes qui seront faictes et travaillees sans que led. sieur Parfaict soict tenu de luy fournir autre chose que le contenu cy dessus. En fin desquelles quatre annees sera tenu led. Besson rendre et restituer aud. sieur Parfaict les meubles, mestiers et unstancilles . . . et sans que pendant led. temps led. Besson en puisse disposer au prejudice dud. sieur Parfaict et autres associez ausd. manufactures.

Joira led. Besson des privilleges accordez par le Roy ausd. manufactures. Et pour en faire jouir à l'advenir les compaignons et apprentis qui travailleront soubz luy, il tiendra registre des noms et surnoms des ouvriers et du lieu de leur naissance pour en fin de chacune annee en bailler le memoire . . . aux sieurs Sainctot et Claude Parfaict nommez par sa majesté pour cest effect. . . . Faict et passés en estude des notaires l'an mil six cens et unze, le vingtsixiesme jour d'aoust avant midy et ont signé . . .[2]

Parfaict, Besson, Contesse [notaire], Contesse [notaire]."

Archives Nationales, Minutier central CVIII 43, f ii^{c}lxxix.

1. House leased to Roch Cobert, "maistre ouvrier en draps d'or, d'argent et de soye," by Guillaume Parfaict: Min.cent. CVIII 39, f iii^{c}iiii^{xx}x, 23 Sept. 1609.
2. Inserted before the signatures is a copy of Besson's certification of his standing as a master silk artisan by the guild masters of Lyon.

APPENDIX B: THE PLACE DAUPHINE

1. Rue de Harlay: Construction Contracts (1609–11)

a. Payment for masonry work: 14 August 1609.

"Pardevant les notaires et gardenottes du Roy nostre Sire en son Chatelet de Paris soubzsignez fut present en sa personne honnorable homme François Petit, juré du Roy en l'office de massonerie, demeurant à Paris, rue de Montorgueil, parroisse St. Eustache, lequel a volontairement confessé avoir eu et receu de Messieur Achilles de Harlay, chevallier, conseiller du Roy en ses conseilz d'estat et privé, et premier president en sa cour de Parlement, la somme de quinze mil livres tournois sur et tant moings des ouvrages de massonnerie et tailles faites et à faire pour led. seigneur en la place Daulphine size en l'isle du Pallais. . . . Faict et passé avant midy en estude des notaires et gardenottes soubzsignez l'an mil six cens neuf, le quatorziesme jour d'aoust et a signé

F Petit, Leboucher [notaire], Lusson [notaire]."

Archives Nationales, Minutier central LXXVIII 184.

b. Purchase of bricks: 12 March 1610.

"Fut present en sa personne Gilles Gaultyer, marchand bourgeois de Paris et y demeurant sur le quay des Ormes, parroisse St. Paul, lequel volontairement a confessé et confesse avoir vendu et promect garantir de toute revendication à honnorable homme François Petit, juré du Roy en l'office de massonnerye à Paris et y demeurant, rue de Montorgueil, parroisse St. Eustache, à ce present et acceptant, la quantité de cent milliers de brique de l'eschantilon de huict poulces de longueur, quatre poulces de large, et deux poulces d'espoisseur, bien cuitte, bonne, loyalle et marchande, que led. Gaultyer promect fournir et livrer aud. Petit ou au porteur à l'isle du Pallais de ceste ville de Paris; apres descharger du costé du grand cours, assavoir: vingt milliers dedans le dernier jour d'avril prochain, pareille quantité ung mois prochain apres ensuivant, et ainsy contynuer led. fournissement de pareille quantité de moys en moys consecutives apres ensuivant jusques en fin de lad. livraison. Ceste vente faicte moyennant et à la raison de dix livres dix sols tournois pour chacun millier de lad. brique. Que pour ce led. Petit en promect et gage bailler et payer aud. Gaultyer ou au porteur au feur et à mesure qu'il fera lad. livraison dont led. Petit sera tenu faire le deschargement à ses frais et despenses. . . . Faict et passé double en l'estude des notaires soubzsignez le vendredy apres midy, douziesme jour de mars gvi^c dix et ont signé

Gaultier, F Petit, Lesemelier [notaire], Le Camus [notaire]."

Archives Nationales, Minutier central LIX 42 fol. ii^{c}lxix.

c. Purchase of stone: 18 March 1610.

"Fut present en sa personne Estienne de La Fontaine, . . . lequel a confessé et confesse avoir vendu et promect garantir de toute revendication à honnorable homme

François Petit, juré du Roy es oeuvres de massonnerye à Paris y demeurant rue de Montorgueil, parroisse St. Eustache, à ce present achepteur, la quantité de deux mil tonneaux de pierre doulce de Saint Leu, bonne, loyalle et marchande, que led. de La Fontaine sera tenu et promect fournir et livrer dans les batteaux que led. Petit envoiera sur la riviere au port dud. Sainct Leu, asscavoir: mil tonneaux dans le jour et feste de Pentecoste prochain, et le surplus dans deux mois apres led. jour. Sans pouvoir led. de La Fontaine vendre aulcune pierre à personnes quelzconques synon apres le fournissement et livraison de toute lad. pierre dessus vendue. La voicture de laquelle se fera aux frais dud. Petit. Ceste presente vente et marché faictz moyennant le prix et somme de vingt deux sols pour chacun tonneau de lad. pierre. . . . Et en faveur du present marché, led. de La Fontaine promect et oblige bailler et fournir aud. Petit ou au porteur dans lesd. batteaulx que voictureront lad. pierre la quantité de cinq cens de fagotz, fasson de sentier, et cinq cens de fallourdes, et ce dans led. temps du fournissement de lad. pierre. . . . Faict et passé en l'estude des notaires soubsignez, jeudy avant midy, dix-huictieme jour de mars gvi^c dix et ont signé

F. Petit, de La Fontaine, Lesemelier [notaire], Le Camus [notaire]."

Archives Nationales, Minutier central LIX 42 fol. ii^ciiii^{xx}i.

d. *Purchase of wood beams: 1 January 1611.*

"Furent presents en leurs personnes Philippe Pemalle et Jean Mahou, marchans de boys et voicturiers par eaus demeurant à Houercourt pres St. Dizier en Champagne estans à present à Paris, . . . lesquelz volontairement ont recongneu et confessé, re-congnoissent et confessent avoir vendu et promectent l'un pour l'autre . . . à honno-rable homme François Petit, juré du Roy en l'office de massonerie à Paris y demeurant rue de Montorgueil, parroisse St. Eustache, à ce present et acceptant, la quantité de vingt cinq poultres de boys de chesne, bon, loyal et marchan, chacun depuis vingt cinq jusques à trente piedz de long et de quinze, seize, dixsept et dixhuict poulces de grosseur. Et icelles poultres telles que dessus promectent et s'obligent lesd. Pemalle et Mahou . . . fournir et livrer aud. Petit ou au porteur en ceste ville de Paris en l'isle Louvier aux frais et despens d'iceulx Pemalle et Mahou . . . dedans le premier jour de febvrier prochain ou au plus tard dedans le dernier dud. moys, pour tout delay à peyne de tous despens, dommages et interetz. . . . Ceste vente de tous ce que dessus moyennant et à la raison de deux cens livres tournois pour chacun cens de tous led. boys cy dessus. . . . Faict et passé double en l'estude desd. notaires soubsignez samedy apres midy, premier jour de janvier, l'an mil six cens unze et ont signé

F Petit, J Mahou, Philippe Pemal, Lesemelier [notaire], Le Camus [notaire]."

Archives Nationales, Minutier central LIX 43, f1.

e. *Carpentry contract: 20 June 1611.*

"Fut present en sa personne Gilles Le Redde, maistre charpentier à Paris, demeu-rant rue du Petit Muscque, parroisse Sainct Paul, lequel a volontairement promis et promect à Monsieur Charles de Harlay, chevallier, sieur de Dolot, demeurant en l'hostel du baillage du pallais à Paris, au nom et comme soy faisant et portant fort de Monsieur Achilles de Harlay, chevallier, conseiller du Roy en ses Conseilz d'estat et privé, à ce present et acceptant, de faire bien et deuement au dire d'ouvriers et gens à ce congnoissans tout le reste des ouvrages de charpenterie qu'il convient faire aux maisons scizes en l'isle du palais appartenant aud. sieur de Harlay et suivant le dessaing qu'il luy en sera donné par led. sieur de Dolot, et travailler ausd. ouvrages suivant les massons. Ceste promesse et marché faict moiennant et à raison de trois cens livres tournois pour chacun cent de bois mis en oeuvre, duquel bois led. Le Redde ne sera payé que ce qui se trouvera mis en oeuvre tant pour les grosseurs que longuers. Et les solives seront espassees esgallement tant plain que vidde, et ou il se trouvera que lesd. solives soient espassees plus pres que tant plain que vuide, ne luy en sera rien paié du surplus qui se trouvera en oeuvre suivant led. dessaing. Lesquelz trois cens livres pour chacun cent de bois en oeuvre led. Sieur de Dollot au dict nom a promis bailler et payer aud. Le Redde ou au porteur au feur et à mesure qu'il travaillera ausd. ouvrages. . . . Faict et passé en l'hostel dud. sieur de Dolot cy dessus declaré l'an mil six cens onze, le vingtiesme jour de juing apres midy et ont signé

G Le Redde, C de Harlay, Le Boucher [notaire], Lusson [notaire]."

Archives Nationales, Minutier central LXXVIII 186.

2. Rue de Harlay: Tenants of Achille de Harlay (1611–16)

Several tenants were widows; the profession of their husbands, if known, is given in parentheses.

DATE/ DOCUMENT (Min.cent.)	TENANT	PROFESSION	PRIOR PARISH/ ADDRESS	RENT (livres)
31.V.1611 LXXVIII 186	Aubert, Catherine	Widow	St. Eustache	600
8.VI.1613 LXXVIII 188	Aubert, renewal			500
1.VI.1611 LXXVIII 186	Fleuret, Jean	*Bourgeois de Paris*	St.-Jean-en- Grève	600
1.VI.1611 LXXVIII 186	Bouynaul, Jean	*Avocat*	St. Eustache	600
1.VI.1611 LXXVIII 186	Puy, Anne du	Widow (*gentilhomme, chambre du Roi*)		600
8.VI.1612 LXXVIII 187	Magdelaine, Henri de la	*Ecuyer*	St. Sulpice	600
29.VIII.1612 LXXVIII 187	Gay, Paul du	*Secrétaire du Roi,* Navarre	St. Honoré	600
3.IV.1613 LXXVIII 188	Pasquier, Pierre	Master cloth dyer	Cité	500
23.IV.1613 LXXVIII 188	Bourdin, Nicolas	Bookseller	Cité	500
3.V.1613 LXXVIII 188	Bouriquant, Fleury	Printer-bookseller	St. Hillaire	500
4.IX.1616 LXXVIII 204	Bouriquant, renewal			
10.VI.1613 LXXVIII 188	Cartiret, Barthélemy	*Bourgeois de Paris*	St. Jacques	500
10.VI.1613 LXXVIII 188	Guydon, Isaac	*Conseiller du Roi*	St. Méderic	500
13.VI.1613 LXXVIII 188	Cathernie, Jean	Barrelmaker	Pont aux Marchands	500
19.VI.1613 LXXVIII 188	Menessier, René	Tailor	Cité	500

Appendix B: The Place Dauphine

DATE/ DOCUMENT (Min.cent.)	TENANT	PROFESSION	PRIOR PARISH/ ADDRESS	RENT (livres)
3.VII.1613 LXXVIII 188	Doussin, Pierre,	Archer	not in Paris	500
	Guillaume, Didier	Merchant	Cité	
31.VII.1613 LXXVIII 188	Panze, Antoine	Bourgeois de Paris	St.-Germain-l'Auxer.	500
13.VIII.1613 LXXVIII 188	Lebeuf, François	Ecuyer		500
7.IX.1613 LXXVIII 188	Alyot, Nicolas	Bourgeois de Paris	St. Paul	500
11.IX.1613 LXXVIII 188	Ferrier, Hierosme	Ex-provincial magistrate		500
11.IX.1613 LXXVIII 188	Bernard, Nicolas	Master tailor	St.-Germain-l'Auxer.	500
4.VII.1616 LXXVIII 204	Bernard, renewal			500
9.IX.1613 LXXVIII 188	Champion, François	Master saddler	Ste.-Croix-de-la-Breton.	500
17.IX.1613 LXXVIII 188	Besnard, Antoine	Wine merchant	St. Sauveur	500
19.XI.1613 LXXVIII 188	Verryer, Claude	Widow	St.-André-des-Arts	500
3.II.1614 LXXVIII 189	Mollignay, Jacques	Master tailor	St.-André-des-Arts	600
20.IV.1614 LXXVIII 189	Bourdeaux, Jean de	Printer-bookseller	St.-Germain-le-Vieil	500
	Millon, Jean	Printer-bookseller		
26.V.1614 LXXVIII 189	Barbier, Damien	Tailor	St. Eustache	500
7.VI.1614 LXXVIII 189	Chermays, Louis de la	Craftsman	Cour du Palais	500
8.VII.1614 LXXVIII 189	Dore, Pierre	Master joiner	St.-Jacques-du-Hault-Pas	500
28.VIII.1614 LXXVIII 189	Froment, Jean	Master apothecary	St. Sulpice	500

Appendix B: The Place Dauphine

DATE/ DOCUMENT (Min.cent.)	TENANT	PROFESSION	PRIOR PARISH/ ADDRESS	RENT (livres)
23.IX.1614 LXXVIII 189	Venes, Jean	*Avocat*	St. Eustache	500
31.III.1615 LXXVIII 90 First floor sublet:	Allain, René	Officer, royal household	Marché Neuf	500
27.VI.1615 LXXVIII 90	Beguin, Jean	Royal almoner	St.-Germain-l'Auxer.	165
20.V.1615 LXXVIII 190	Regonnier, Jacques	*Procureur*		500
7.XI.1615 LXXVIII 190	Desperon, Louise, &	Widow (*procureur*)	St.-Nicolas-des-Champs	500
	Rocher, Judicz	Widow (prov. notary)	St. Paul	
4.X.1616 LXXVIII 204	Bailleul, Pierre de	Surgeon	Cité	450
8.X.1616 LXXVIII	Couppe, Anne	Widow	St. Sulpice	500

Tenants by Profession (including renewals):

Merchants, Craftsmen, and *Bourgeois de Paris*	23/	56%
Minor Officeholders	11/	27%
Widows	7/	17%
Total	41/	100%

3. Harlay's *Lottissement*: Land Sales at the Place Dauphine and on the Quais

Achille de Harley sold lots at the Place Dauphine to the individuals listed in this appendix. Several buyers sold their lots before completing the mandated houses of brick and stone; they are identified by an asterisk. A corresponding asterisk appears before the data on the subsequent owners, who ultimately built the houses. Lot numbers refer to Figures 109, 111, and 112. Roman numerals refer to documents in the Archives Nationales, Minutier central.

LOT	SALE DATE	NAME	PROFESSION	PRIOR PARISH/ ADDRESS	AREA (toises)	PRICE (livres)
PLACE DAUPHINE						
1	12.IX.1608 LXXVIII 183	*Sancy, N. Harlay de	Royal minister	St. Eustache	100 +	7,500
*	19.IX.1612 LIV 494 n. 503	Ligny, Jean de	Officer, royal treasury	St.-Jean-en-Grève		3,000
2A	23.IX.1609 LXXVIII 183	Laborie, Jean	*Avocat*	St. Eustache	75	5,625
2B	23.IX.1609 LXXVIII 183	Deligny, Michel	Merchant	St.-Ger.-l'Auxer.	25	1,875
3	28.VIII.1608 LXXVIII 183	*Petit, François	Royal mason	St. Eustache	100	
*	16.VIII.1613 LIX 45	Langlois, André	Draper	St. Eustache	112	562 in *rente*
4	28.VIII.1608 LXXVIII 183	Petit, François			100	
5A	20.IX.1613 LXXVIII 188	Breteau, Jean	Goldsmith	Pont au Change	c. 41	3,014
5B	26.XI.1613 LXXVIII 188	Fillassier, Pierre	Goldsmith	Pont au Change	c. 77	5,862
5C	3.X.1613 LXXVIII 188	Poullet, Nicolas	*Procureur*	St. Eustache	c. 36	2,680
6	24.I.1609 LXXVIII 184	*Chaillou, Philippe	Merchant	St. Sauveur	100	7,500
*	c. 1611–12	Petit, François				?
7	24.I.1609 LXXVIII 184	*Marrier, Guillaume	Merchant	St. Sauveur	100	7,500
*	c. 1611–12	Petit, François				?
8	30.V.1611 XXIX 163	*Gillot, Jacques	Canon, Ste. Chapelle		110	Gift
*A	27.XI.1614 LXVI 30	Virlorjeux, Jean	*Greffier de Bourbonnais*	St.-Ger.-l'Auxer.	c. 35	2,538
*B	28.XI.1614 LXVI 30	Ferrier, Hierosme	Ex-provincial magistrate	Cité	60	4,200
*C	12.XI.1614 LXVI 30	Le Gaigneur, Etienne	Court clerk [*greffier*]		34	2,460

LOT	SALE DATE	NAME	PROFESSION	PRIOR PARISH/ ADDRESS	AREA (toises)	PRICE (livres)
9A	10.IX.1608 LXXVIII 183	*Langelier, Abel	Publisher-bookseller	Ste. Chapelle	50	3,750
9B	10.IX.1608 LXXVIII 183	Pepin, François	*Greffier*	St. Paul	50	3,750
*A	By 1613	Chevalier, Jacques	Magistrate	?	50	
10A	7.I.1609 LXXVIII 184	Montel, Olivier	*Avocat*	St.-Ger.-l'Auxer.	c. 39	2,950
10B	7.I.1609 LXXVIII 184	Belot, André	*Procureur*	St.-Ger.-l'Auxer.	c. 21	1,600
10C	7.I.1609 LXXVIII 184	Bacher, Baudouin	Jeweler	St.-Ger.-l'Auxer.	c. 39	2,950
11A	25.IX.1608 LXXVIII 183	*Pothery, Claude	Tax farmer, Normandy	St.-Ger.-l'Auxer.	c. 33	2,500
11C	25.IX.1608 LXXVIII 183	Mignollet, Antoine	Wine merchant	St. Sulpice	c. 33	2,500
11D	25.IX.1608 LXXVIII 183	Menart, Robert	Marble cutter	St.-Ger.-l'Auxer.	c. 33	2,500
*B	20.IX.1610 LIV 253	Beranger,ª Charles	Tailor	St.-Ger.-l'Auxer.	c. 16	2,700
*A	20.IX.1610 LIV 253	Bethune, Gregoire	Royal violinist	St.-Ger.-l'Auxer.	c. 16	2,000
12	24.X.1608 LXXVIII 183	Bunel, Jacob	Royal painter	Louvre	100	7,500
QUAI DES ORFÈVRES						
13	19.IX.1616 LXXVIII 204	Bonigalle Thomas de	Bailiff [*huissier*]	Palace	c. 33	2,400
QUAI DE L'HORLOGE						
14	11.VII.1609 LXXVIII 184	Durant, Germaine	Widow	Cité	24	Exchange
15	20.IX.1613 LXXVIII 188	Bethune, Gregoire	Royal violinist	St.-Ger.-l'Auxer.	c. 32	2,295
16	20.IX.1613 LXXVIII 188	Leger, Quentin	Royal violinist	St.-Jacq.-la-Bouch.	c. 36	2,550
17	20.IX.1613 LXXVIII 188	Delart, Claude	Solicitor [*procureur*]	St.-André-des-Arts	c. 38	2,778
18	11.XII.1613 LXXVIII 188	Voisin, Daniel	*Secrétaire du Roi*	Palace	101	6,588
19	17 July 1612 LXXVIII 187	Barbier, Guillaume	Merchant	St.-Jacq.-la-Bouch.	c. 6	450

Place Dauphine Builders by Profession

PROFESSION	NUMBER		AREA (sq. *toises*)
Craftsmen and Merchants	12	46%	c. 833
Judicial Personnel	11	38%	c. 452
Nobles	2	12%	c. 200
Widows	1	4%	c. 24
TOTAL[b]	26	100%	

a. On 17 March 1609 (LIV 250), Pothèry sold half of his parcel — the half facing the square (11B) — to Beranger for 1,250 *livres*. But Beranger had not yet paid for his half-lot in 1610, when Pothery's entire parcel was seized at the request of his neighbors Menart and Mignollet. At that time, Beranger purchased the entire parcel for 4,700 *livres*, and resold the half-lot facing the quai (11A) to Béthune for 2,000 *livres* (LIV 253, 20 Sept. 1610).

b. This tally does not include the three men who began houses but did not finish them — Chaillou, Marrier, and Pothery; nor does it include Barbier because he was not required to comply with the royal facade design. Although Petit and Béthune built houses on more than one lot, each man has been counted only once.

4. Index of Construction Contracts and Other Documents by Owner

Abbreviations
A.N.   Archives Nationales
A.S.   Archives de la Seine
Lods   Waiver of mutation fees (*lods et ventes*)
Terrier Tax declaration (*Papier Terrier du Roi*); date of earliest statement is given.
Titles Property titles inventoried during the Revolution
Roman numerals refer to documents in the Archives Nationales, Minutier central. Lot numbers refer to Figures 109 and 111, 112.

NORTH RANGE (Fig. 111) ——————————————————————

1. LIGNY, Jean de
   Excavation of foundations by prior owner (Sancy): LIV 479, 19 Aug. 1612
   Purchase of lot from Sancy: LIV 479, 22 and 24 Oct. 1612
   Masonry: LIV 480, 30 April 1613 (see Appendix B5.)
   Metalwork: LIV 480, 14 May 1613
   Carpentry: LIV 480, 18 May 1613
   Roofing: LIV 481, 26 Nov. 1613
   Leases: LIV 484, 23 March and 12 May 1615; LIV 490, 5 April 1618
   Other building contracts mentioned in de Ligny's inventory after death: LIV 494, 1619–20

2A. LABORIE, Jean
   Subdivision of lot with Deligny: LXXVIII 183, 23 Sept. 1608
   Terrier: A.N. Q1/1099 25B, 19 Oct. 1671

2B. DELIGNY, Michel
   Subdivision of lot with Laborie: LXXVIII 183, 23 Sept. 1608
   Lods: A.N. Z1F/560 f148v, 31 March 1610
   Roofing: LIX 44 f267, 5 March 1612
   Lease: XLI 105, 31 Aug. 1641
   Terrier: A.N. Q1/1099 20, 1 Dec. 1667

3. LANGLOIS, André
   Purchase of lot from Petit: LIX 45, 16 Aug. 1613
   Lease: LXVI 30, 30 Oct. 1614
   Titles: A.S. DQ10 126/3169, 1607–1790

4. PETIT, François
   Leases: LIX 47 f211, 17 Feb. 1615, f317, 10 March 1615, f459 and f471, 7 April 1615; LIX 53, 4 Feb. 1619

5A. BRETEAU, Jean
   Terrier: A.N. Q1/1099 25B, 28 Nov. 1667
   Titles: A.S. DQ10 121/2883, 1613–1790

5B. *FILLASSIER, Pierre*
Terrier: A.N. Q1/1099 25B, 18 May 1626

5C. *POULLET, Nicolas*
No documents found.

6. *CHAILLOU, Philippe; PETIT, François*
Petit gained possession of the lot in c. 1611–12.
Stone cutting (Chaillou and Marrier): LIX 42 f312, 16 April 1610
Metalwork (Chaillou): LIX 43 f103, 20 Jan. 1611
Leases (Petit): LIX 44 f424, 4 April 1612, f648, 29 May 1612; LIX 45 f119, 29 Jan. 1613; LIX 46 f790, 12 June 1614; LIX 47 f63, 13 Jan. 1615, f315, 10 March 1615; LIX 52 f154, 7 Feb. 1618, f654, 5 May 1618

SOUTH RANGE (Fig. 112) ——————————————————

7. *MARRIER, Guillaume; PETIT, François*
Petit gained possession of the lot in c. 1611–12.
Metalwork (Chaillou and Marrier): LIX 43 f103, 20 Jan. 1611
Leases (Petit): LIX 44 f364, 23 March 1612; LIX 45 f281, 4 March 1613; LIX 49 f349, 26 May 1616

8A. *VIRLORJEUX, Jean*
Purchase of lot from prior owner (Gillot): LXVI 30, 27 Nov. 1614
Titles: A.S. DQ10 99/1592, 1613–1792

8B. *FERRIER, Hierosme*
Purchase of lot from prior owner (Gillot): LXVI 30, 28 Nov. 1614

8C. *LE GAIGNEUR, Etienne*
Purchase of lot from prior owner (Gillot): LXVI 30, 12 Sept. 1614
Titles: A.S. DQ10 99/1592, 1613–1792

9A. *CHEVALIER, Jacques*
Lods: A.N. Z1F/563 f62v, 5 May 1618
Division of property among heirs: LXVI 89, 9 March 1641

9B. *PEPIN, François*
Lods: A.N. Z1F/563 f89v, 25 May 1609

10A. *MONTEL, Olivier*
Subdivision of lot with Belot and Bacher: LXXVIII 184, 4 Jan. 1609
Lods: A.N. Z1F/563 f164, 6 June 1609
Titles: A.S. DQ10 93/1254, 1607–1792

10B. *BELOT, André*
Subdivision of lot with Montel and Bacher: LXXVIII 184, 4 Jan. 1609

10C. *BACHET, Baudouin*
Subdivision of lot with Montel and Belot: LXXVIII 184, 4 Jan. 1609

11A. *POTHERY, Claude; BETHUNE, Gregoire de*
Subdivision of lot with Mignollet and Menart: LXXVIII 183, 25 Sept. 1608
Agreement concerning party wall (Pothery, Beranger, and Mignollet): XCIX 90,
   22 Oct. 1608; LXVI 22, 29 May 1609
Seizure of lot from Pothery and purchase by Béthune: LIV 253, 20 Sept. 1610;
   LXXVIII 187, 3 July 1612
General construction contract: LIV 253, 13 Oct. 1610
Masonry: LIV 254, 20 April 1611 and 7 May 1611
Sale: LXVI 70, 15 Dec. 1634
Titles: A.S. DQ10 98/1529

11B. *BERANGER, Charles*
Purchase of lot from prior owner (Pothery): LIV 250, 17 March 1609
Purchase renegotiated after Pothery's lot seized: LIV 253, 20 Sept. 1610
Masonry: LIV 250, 17 March 1609

11C. *MIGNOLLET, Antoine*
Subdivision of lot with Pothery and Menart: LXXVIII 183, 25 Sept. 1608
Agreement concerning party wall (Pothery, Beranger, and Mignollet): XCIX 90,
   22 Oct. 1608; LXVI 22, 29 May 1609
Dispute with mason: XXIX 161, 7 Sept. 1609; LXVI 23, 16 Sept. 1609

11D. *MENART, Robert*
Subdivision of lot with Mignollet and Pothery: LXXVIII 183, 25 Sept. 1608
Foundations: XLII 48 f352, 27 Dec. 1608
Loan to finance construction: LXVI 24, 28 June 1610
Lods: A.N. P 2670 f57v, 30 May 1609; J. Guiffrey, *Nouvelles archives* (Paris: 1873),
   230.
Sale: XLI 56, 5 Feb. 1613
Payments to craftsmen: XLI 56 f34, 7 Feb. 1613, f47, 13 Feb. 1613, f74, 4 March
   1613, f158, 18 May 1613
Titles: A.S. DQ10 124/3021, 1613–1792

12. *BUNEL, Jacob*
Loan to finance construction: XCVI 4 f70, 26 March 1611
Leases: VI 282, 17 March and 13 June 1611; XLII 53 f465, 7 Dec. 1613
Sale: LIV 56 f698, 3 June 1622
Lods: A.N. Z1F/567 f50, 8 June 1622
Terrier: A.N. Q1/1099 30, 17 June 1667
Titles: A.S. DQ10 127/3196 and 93/1254, 1608–1792

QUAI DES ORFEVRES (Fig. 109) ———————————————————
13. *BONIGALLE, Thomas de*
Terrier: A.N. Q1/1099 30, 6 July 1655

QUAI DE L'HORLOGE (Fig. 109) ——————————————————————

  14. *DURANT, Germaine*
      Masonry: VI 282, 14 June 1611; VI 287, 15 July 1613
      Leases: VI 287, 26 Oct. 1613; VI 293, 24 Sept. 1616
      Titles: A.S. DQ10 98/1529
  15. *BETHUNE, Grégoire de*
      No documents found.
  16. *LEGER, Quentin*
      Terrier: A.N. Q1/1099 25B, 15 Dec. 1667
  17. *DELART, Claude*
      No documents found.
  18. *VOISIN, Daniel*
      No documents found.

5. Masonry Contract for a House Facing the Pont Neuf: 30 April 1613

"Devis des ouvrages de maçonnerie et pierre de taille qu'il convyent faire de neuf au bout de la place Daulphine à l'alignement du Pont Neuf pour le parachevement et contynuation d'ung bastyment encommencé de ses fondations appartenant à Monsieur de Lygny, tresorier des parties casuelles.

Premierement, sera achevé de lever la fondation des murs quy font la fassade des troys costez, ensemble le grand mur separant la moyctyé de la place et trois autres murs de reffan encommencez quy seront eslevez de leurs espoisses jusques au rez de chaussee, maçonné de bon moellon, chaulx et sable. Et faire aud. rez de chaussee le nyveau et araze aulx murs et fassades dud. logis pour poser les premyeres assises de pierre de taille de Clicquart portant parpain entre deulx d'une, et faire retraicte sur lesd. fondations. Et au dessus desd. assises sera erigé les huisseryes, grandes arquades, et pillyers d'icelles quy seront de pierre dure jusques à la hauteur de l'imposte des arquades. Et les claveaulx des huisseryes et voulsures desd. arquades seront de pierre de St. Leu. Et au dessus desd. voulsures sera erigé les chesnes de pierre pour porter les croisees, ensemble les tables et plinthes de relief qui seront de pierre de St. Leu. Et lesd. fassades seront aornés de maçonnerie de bricque, et le derriere desd. fassades sera maçonné avecq moellon, chaulx et sable. Et faire les entablementz et lucarnes desd. fassades de pierre de St. Leu, aornez de leur architecture, forme, façon et simmetrye que les autres maisons quy sont faictes. Et faire les deux coings dud. bastyment du costé du pont quy seront eslevez de quartyers de pierre dure de Clicquart jusques à haulteur des impostes des arquades de lad. fassade et le dessus de St. Leu avecq lyaison.

Sera vuydé et fouillé le reste des vuydanges et terres massyves qu'il sera necessaire d'oster pour faire les caves dont les voultes seront maçonnee de moellon et plastre. Et remplyr les reins d'icelles voultes de maçonnerie. Et faire la maçonnerie des enduitz des murs encommencez quy seront faictz de plastre, et les descentes de caves seront faictes de marches de pierre de taille de bas clicquart, poser sur les voultes de maçonnerie en bourceau. Et paver les petittes couches avecq pavé de grez, chaulx et sable, et donner les pentes.

Sera fondé le reste des murs de reffen quy seront fondé jusques à vif fondz. Et pour ce faire, sera vuidé les terres de trenchees et rigolles pour fonder les murs quy seront maçonnez avecq moellon, chaulx et sable, et eslever lesd. murs jusques au haut et leur donner finict de part de d'autre.

Sera fait la maçonnerie des planchers et aires dud. logis dont les deux premyers seront maçonnez avecq petit carreau de terre cuite à six pans, chaulx et sable, et les autres de maçonnerie de plastre. Et faire tous les lambris avecq plastre, cloud et latte. Et les cloisons seront faictes de charpenterye et maçonné avecq plastre et plastras et enduits des deulx costez. Et les escallyers et montés dud. logis seront faictes de charpenterye et maçonné de plastre.

Sera fait la maçonnerie des thuyeaulx et mantheaulx de chemynés quy seront faictz de maçonnerye de plastre. Et lesd. thuyeaulx seront maçonnez de brique depuis le dernier plancher de pareil desseing que les autres.

Seront faites les fossez des privez et faire la vuydange des terres massyves, trenchees et rigolles pour faire les fondations d'icelles, lesquelles seront maçonnés avecq bon moellon, chaux et sable, et les voultes d'icelles avecq moellon et plastre, et les reins d'icelle voultes de maçonnerie, et les chaulsés et sieges d'icelles fossés seront contynuez d'estage à autre de maçonnerie de plastre.

Tout ce qui est dessus sera fait bien et deuement au dire d'ouvryers, expers et gens à ce cognoissans suyvant le plan quy en a esté faict et conformement à l'architecture et simmetrye des fassades des autres maisons voisines. Et pour ce faire, l'entrepreneur fournira de touttes choses à ce necessaire: eschaffaulx, engins, grais, chasbles, chariages de pierre de taille, moellon, chaux, sable et plastre, bricque, cloud et latte, petit et grand carreau de terre cuite, et pavé de grez, de peyne d'ouvryers. Mener les gravoys aulx champs, et rendre place nette, et s'ayder de quelques mathieres et ustancilles qui sont sur les lyeux.

Tous lesquelz ouvrages de massonerie seront thoisez à thoise courante et bout avant et lesd. terres massyves, trenchees et rigolles thoisez à deux cens seize pieds par thoise. Le tout moyennant prix et somme de neuf lyvres quinze sols tournois pour chacune thoise desd. ouvrages cy dessus, lesquelles se commenceront dans lundy prochain et y travailler sans discontynuer avecq bon nombre d'ouvryers lesquelz seront payez au feur et à mesure qu'ils en feront. Et led. entrepreneur ne sera point tenu de la garendy des fondations encommencés, et en cas que lesd. fondations ne se trouve bonnes et suffisantes en faisant lesd. ouvrages, led. entrepreneur sera tenu les reprendre en le payant d'icelle.

Plus se fera la maçonnerie de deux puitz selon le plan quy seront maçonnez avecq bon moellon et plastre . . .

Honnorable homme René Fleury, maistre maçon à Paris y demeurant rue des Lyons, parroisse de Sainct Paul, confesse avoir promis et promect à noble homme Jehan de Ligny, seigneur de Rentilly, conseiller, secretaire du Roy et de ses finances, tresorier des parties casuelles de sa Majesté, demeurant en ceste ville de Paris rue de Paradis, parroisse de Sainct Jehan en Greve, . . . de faire et parfaire bein et deuement ainsy qu'il appartient au dire d'ouvriers et gens à ce congnoissans tous les ouvrages de maçonnerie mentionnez au devis ci devant escript de la main dud. Fleury en une place appartenant aud. sieur de Ligny en l'isle du Pallais. Ce marché faict moiennant et à raison de neuf livres quinze sols tournois pour chacune thoise, lesd. ouvrages thoisez ainsy qu'il est porté aud. devis, que led. Sieur de Ligny fault luy payer au fur et à mesure qu'il travaillera auxd. ouvrages. . . . Faict et passé double apres midy en la maison dud. sieur de Rentilly, l'an mil six cens treize, le mardy xxxe et dernier jour d'apvril et ont signez:

De Ligny, Fleury, Le Normant [notaire], Haultedesens [notaire]."

Archives Nationales, Minutier central LIV 480.

APPENDIX C: THE HÔPITAL SAINT LOUIS:
Construction Costs

The governors of the Hôtel Dieu prepared the following summary of building costs in c. 1616. While sums were expressed in Roman numerals, I have transcribed them in Arabic numerals. They are calculated in *livres* (*l*), *sols* (*s*), and *deniers* (*d*).

"Estat de la despence faicte pour le bastiment des hospitaulx de St. Louis, St. Marcel, et de l'Hostel Dieu et d'autre despence faicte en consequence de l'entreprise desd. bastiments le tout suivant l'edict du Roy du mois du mars mil six cens sept . . .

Bastiment de l'hospital St. Louis

Achapt de places à bastir 6,746*l*

Massonnerie faicte par les sieurs Noblet, Jacquet et Desnotz, entrepreneurs dud. bastiment. 339,552*l* 16*s* 10*d*

Autre massonnerie faicte par le sieur Gamart 195*l*

Autre massonnerie paiee au sieur Vellefaulx 43,535*l* 10*s*

Charpenterie paiee au sieur de La Champagne 1,161*l*

Autre charpenterie faicte par les sieurs Le Redde et Defosses entrepreneurs. 109,730*l* 10*s*

Couverture 37,895*l* 15*s* 1*d*

Plomberie 37,768*l* 15*s*

Menuiserie 20,591*l* 6*s* 6*d*

Serrurerie 30,822*l* 10*s*

Vitrerie 3,680*l* 14*s* 1*d*

Vuidange et remplage du terre pour rendre la place niveau 17,397*l* 8*s*

Vuidange du terre et trenchees pour la fontaine 6,664*l* 3*s* 6*d*

Pompe faicte au grand puisart pour la conduite des eaues 2,000*l*

Ouvrages de fondeur 1,982*l* 19*s* 6*d*

Ouvrages de pavé de grais 7,124*l* 8*d*

Ouvrages de tailleur de marbre et sculpteur. 786*l*

Ouvrages de painture 1,225*l*

Achapt d'ormes plantez à diverses fois tant au dedans dud. hospital que hors iceluy et pavement faict aux manoeuvres qui ont faict les trenchees pour les planter 1,536*l*

Frais et mises communes composés de l'achapt des ornements d'eglise, de quelques modelles tant de carte qu'en painture du bastiment dud. hospital dont deux ont esté donnez au roy et un autre à la royne Marguerite; recompenses donnez à plusieurs parties pour trenchees et regardz faictz au dedans et à travers de la terre pour le passage des eaues; vin des manoeuvriers qui ont travaillé aud. hospital; aumosnes faicte à une pauvre femme de laquelle le mari auroit esté tué aud. bastiments, et à un pauvre homme qui seroit tombé du hault d'iceluy;

frais du thoiser et paiement faict aux jurez qui ont visité led. bastiment et autres frais durant led. bastiment qui n'ont point ce chapitre
paié 2,773*l* 3*s* 8*d*
Appointemens paiez au sieur Vellefaux juré masson pour avoir faict les
desseings dud. bastiment et faict le controlle d'iceluy depuis le premier
jour de Aoust mil vi^c sept jusques au dernier jour de Juin mil vi^c onze
qui sont quatre ans onze mois à raison de douze cent livres par an cy. . .5,800*l*[sic]
Somme des parties du present estat . . . . .679,068*l* 13*s* 11*d*"

Archives de l'Assistance Publique, Fonds Hôtel Dieu 8.64.541, excerpt.

APPENDIX D: CHARLES MARCHANT

Charles Marchant (†1610), Captain of three musketry companies of the Paris militia (*Capitaine des trois compagnies de trois cents archers, arquebusiers, et arbalestres*), was the largest developer of rental housing in Henri IV's Paris. In prior centuries as well, there was probably no equal to him in the French capital. His most celebrated project was the Pont aux Marchands (or Pont Marchant), a bridge that spanned the north arm of the Seine between the rue St. Denis on the Right Bank and the clocktower of the Palace on the Ile de la Cité (Fig. 76). The captain began the bridge in 1598, following the collapse of the Pont aux Meuniers two years earlier, and completed it in 1608.[1]

Three *toises* wide at street level, the Pont aux Marchands was straddled by fifty-one houses painted in multi-colors, each with a shop sign representing a different bird. The two-story houses were built in two sizes: the larger ones were five *toises* deep—the same depth as a typical pavilion at the Place Royale—and rented for 450 *livres,* while the smaller ones, of unspecified dimensions, rented for 300 *livres.* The tenants were merchants and artisans: hatters, glovers, jewelers, and lacemakers.[2] Marble reliefs with figures of the king and queen were displayed in the middle of the bridge, and tablets inscribed with Latin verses honoring the captain hung at each embankment. During its brief existence—the bridge was destroyed by fire in 1620—the Pont aux Marchands was considered a "singular and exquisite work," in the words of Pierre de L'Estoile, "adorned with a great many beautiful and superb buildings, and an embellishment to this great city."[3]

Marchant attached great importance to this project, not only as a business venture but as a personal contribution to the city he had faithfully served as a militia officer and municipal leader for many decades. The bridge was not yet finished in 1606 when Marchant, severely ill, drafted a short will with only five bequests. He donated bonds to the church of St. Paul and the church of St. Gervais, where he asked to be buried. He gave half of his property to his son, and he left money to the carpenters at work on the bridge. After the bridge was completed, Julien was to be paid 1,200 *livres* and another fellow 500 *livres.* The testament ends with Marchant's final wish: he asked that the bridge be finished as speedily as possible.[4] The captain fulfilled his own wish; he survived the illness and lived to complete the Pont Marchant, as he spelled it.

As a privately financed public embellishment, the Pont aux Marchands was without precedent in Paris. Marchant assumed the entirety of the building costs; the crown merely waived the tariffs on wood used in construction and instructed the *prévôt* to provide Marchant with a storage and work site.[5] Construction was directed by carpenter Julien Pourrat, the man affectionately mentioned by his first name in Marchant's will. Marchant had launched the carpenter's career. He financed Pourrat's training and gave him free lodgings, an annual salary of 100 *livres,* and a wage of 20 *sols* for every working day.[6] The captain employed Pourrat on a full-time basis. Finally, Marchant nominated

Fig. 175. Signatures of Captain Charles Marchant, at left, and carpenter Charles Marchant, at right. (A.N. Min. cent. XIX 355, 4 April 1606; Min. cent. CVII 85, 16 March 1605)

him to the post of *maître des oeuvres de charpenterie de la ville,* an office which Pourrat obtained in 1612. Evidently the captain controlled the succession of the office, but this privilege was generally granted to the officeholder. Was Captain Marchant also a high-ranking carpenter?

This question reopens a historical debate concerning the identity of Charles Marchant. A man named Charles Marchant did, in fact, serve as *maître des oeuvres de charpenterie* until his death in 1610. While nineteenth-century writers and Dumolin believed that there was only one Charles Marchant, Lambeau and Babelon maintained that the captain and the carpenter were two different individuals. The fact that no documents have yet been found which identify Marchant by both titles suggests that they were indeed separate figures. Yet both the captain and the carpenter lived on the rue Ste. Catherine in the parish of St. Paul, and both died in 1610. Their signatures bear a striking resemblance (Fig. 175). Furthermore, the captain had strong ties to the carpentry profession: he selected the next *maître des oeuvres de charpenterie,* and he acted as his own contractor, an undertaking rarely assumed by an amateur. The captain's career as a housing developer may well have emerged from an expertise in carpentry, just as François Petit's construction of rental housing evolved from his work as a mason. While this evidence is inconclusive, it prods us to reconsider the two Marchants and, more broadly, the relationship between the building crafts and real estate development in seventeenth-century Paris.

No one in Henri IV's Paris owned more residential property than Captain Marchant. In addition to the fifty-one houses on the Pont aux Marchands, he owned three houses at the Place Royale (formed from four pavilions), a house on the rue des Minimes, eight other houses on the Right Bank, and a garden and plaster-kiln in the Marais.[7] He collected rent from at least sixty houses in Paris, fifty-five of which he built. In 1605, the captain passed a long-term lease with the Hôpital St. Gervais for 6 *arpents* of land north of the Place Royale, between the rues St. Claude and St. Gilles.[8] According to Sauval, Marchant intended to build rental housing on this estate, but the project did not advance because Marchant was already overextended by his other real estate transactions.[9] Outside of Paris, Marchant owned a house with vineyards in the village of Sceaux and the seignorial estate of Chambuisson near Fontenay-en-Bois, which covered 1,300 *arpents.*[10] The captain also financed other building projects. According to statements by his heirs, he had loaned 150,000 *livres,* in part to the king for repairs to the

Pont au Change, and in part to the abbey of St.-Germain-des-Prés for construction of the abbatial palace.[11] It is not known whether the captain was related to the architect of that palace, Guillaume Marchant.

On the entrance to one of his Place Royale houses, Marchant placed a portrait of Henri IV. Like the king he loyally served, Captain Charles Marchant played a pioneering role in the development of Paris.

NOTES

Introduction

1. On Henri IV's claim to the throne and the challenges to the Salic Law, see Roland Mousnier, *The Assassination of Henry IV* (London: 1973), 106–16.

2. The representation of Henri IV as the Gallic Hercules is discussed by J.-P. Babelon, "Architecture et emblématique dans les médailles d'Henri IV," *Revue de l'Art* 58–59 (1983): 29–30; Frances Yates, *Astraea. The Imperial Theme in the Sixteenth Century* (London: 1975), 208–14; Françoise Bardon, *Le portrait mythologique à la cour de France sous Henri IV et Louis XIII* (Paris: 1974); Corrado Vivanti, "Henri IV, the Gallic Hercules," *Journal of the Warburg and Courtauld Institutes* 30 (1967): 176–97. The program of the royal entry in Avignon in 1600, devised by André Valladier, elaborated the theme of Henri IV as the Gallic Hercules: Valladier, *Labyrinthe royal de l'Hercule Gaulois triomphant* (Avignon: [1601]).

3. Henri IV's political weaknesses are emphasized in Mark Greengrass, *France in the Age of Henri IV: The Struggle for Stability* (London: 1984).

4. Richard Bonney, "Absolutism: What's in a Name?" *French History* 1/1 (March 1987): 93–117. The theory of fundamental law and constitutional monarchy is discussed in Nannerl Keohane, *Philosophy and the State in France* (Princeton: 1980); William Church, *Constitutional Thought in Sixteenth-Century France* (Cambridge, Ma.: 1941).

5. Roger Mettam, "Historians and 'Absolutism': The Illusion and the Reality," *Power and Faction in Louis XIV's France* (Oxford: 1988), 44, 37. Mettam is reacting to the scholarship of the past twenty years which has stressed the importance of Henri IV's rule in the formation of the absolutist monarchy: David Buisseret, *Henry IV* (London: 1984); David Parker, *The Making of French Absolutism* (New York: 1983); Bernard Barbiche, *Sully* (Paris: 1978); Buisseret, *Sully and the Growth of Centralized Government in France, 1598–1610* (London: 1968); Buisseret, "A Stage in the Development of the French Intendants: The Reign of Henry IV," *The Historical Journal* 9/1 (1966): 27–38; J. Russell Major, "Henry IV and Guyenne: A Study concerning the origins of Royal Absolutism," *French Historical Studies* 4/4 (Fall 1966): 363–83; Mousnier, *Assassination of*

Henry IV. These studies had, in turn, revised the view of Henri IV as a conservative ruler who preserved the structures of the Valois monarchy.

6. Roland Mousnier, *La Vénalité des offices sous Henri IV et Louis XIII,* 2nd ed. (Paris: 1971).

7. Sully's activities are documented in F. de Mallevoüe, *Les Actes de Sully passés au nom du Roi de 1600 à 1610* (Paris: 1911), and in his papers deposited at the Archives Nationales, A.N. 120 AP, catalogued in Robert-Henri Bautier and Aline Vallée-Karcher, *Les Papiers de Sully aux Archives Nationales* (Paris: 1959). On Sully's activities: Barbiche, *Sully*; Buisseret, *Sully and the Growth of Centralized Government;* Barbiche, "Henri IV et la surintendance des bâtiments," *Bulletin Monumental* 142/1 (1984): 19–39; M. Boutet, "Sully Grand Voyer de France," *Urbanisme* 75 (Feb. 1942): 61–69. Although Maximilien de Béthune was not awarded the title of Duc et Pair de Sully until 1606, I consistently refer to him by the more familiar name of Sully.

8. The administrative procedures established by the *Grand Voyer* were set forth in an edict dated 13 January 1605: A.N. E8A f7, published in Mallevoüe, xxxi–xxxiii. The annual budgets of the *Grand Voyer* document the building undertaken by the crown on the roads, bridges, and quais in Paris; they are among Sully's papers at the Archives Nationales (A.N. 120 AP).

9. For contemporary descriptions of Paris during the occupation of the League and following Henri IV's entry, see: Martin Huber, "Paris sous la Ligue," *Art de France,* 1964, 104–15; Albert Gérard, "La révolte et le siège de Paris en 1589," *MSHP* 33 (1906): 65–150; Thomas Platter, "Description de Paris (1599)," *MSHP* 23 (1896): 167–224; Gaston Raynaud, ed., "Paris en 1596. Récit de F.-G. d'Ierni," *BSHP,* 1885, 164–70; A. Dufour, "Histoire du siège de Paris sous Henri IV en 1590 d'après un manuscrit," *MSHP* 7 (1880): 175–270; Filippo Pigafetta, *Relatione dell'assedio di Parigi* (Rome: 1591), and in French translation, "Relation du siège de Paris par Henri IV," *MSHP* 2 (1875): 1–105.

10. There are no reliable population figures. According to one visitor, Francesco Gregory d'Ierni, the population of Paris dropped from

600,000 before the civil war to 350,000 in 1596: Raynaud, ed., "Paris en 1596. Récit de F.-G. d'Ierni," 169. The papal engineer Filippo Pigafetta estimated the population was 400,000 in 1590: Pigafetta, *Relatione dell'assedio,* 26.

11. Construction of the Porte de la Tournelle, also called the Porte St. Bernard, was financed by the crown: A.N. E11A f31, 8 July 1606. The masonry contract is published in *Registres* 14:146–48, 12 Feb.–3 March 1607.

12. Sully passed a contract to terrace the site on 19 March 1603: Mallevoüe, 269–70. A year later, he engaged Louis Routard, an artillery guard at the Arsenal, to build and maintain the playing field at his own expense; in exchange, Routard was allowed to use the playing ground, which was otherwise reserved for the king. The contract called for two rows of elm trees and a third file of either elm or mulberry trees: Mallevoüe, 22–23, 6 March 1604. The municipality disputed the crown's claim to the land on the grounds that the city controlled the banks of the Seine, but the complaint had no effect: *Registres* 14:202–4, 17 Dec. 1609; 14:409, 12 Jan. 1610; A.N. Z1F/561 f35, 28 Oct. 1614.

13. On the port and quai St. Paul: A.N. E7A f318, 21 Aug. 1604; A.N. E11B f187, 19 Aug. 1606; A.N. 120 AP 38 f4, 1605; A.N. 120 AP 39 f8, 1606.

14. The paving program will be discussed in Chapter 4. The extent to which Sully enforced the building regulations is unclear; the ban on timber construction in particular was certainly violated with some frequency. Building regulations were enacted throughout Henri IV's reign: A.N. E4A f369, 20 Aug. 1602; A.N. X1A/8646 f339, July 1609; A.N. E23A f203, 1 Aug. 1609. The medieval regulations are discussed by Simone Roux, "La Construction courante à Paris du milieu du XIVe siècle à la fin du XVe siècle," *La Construction du Moyen Age,* Actes du congrès de la Société des historiens médiévistes de l'enseignement supérieur, June 1972 (Paris: 1973), 185–86.

15. "Ceste-cy particuliere est pour vous dire des nouvelles de mes bastimens et de mes jardins et pour vous asseurer que je n'y ay perdu le temps depuis vostre partement. A Paris vous trouverés ma grande galerie qui va jusques aux Tuileries parachevee, la petite [galerie] doree, et les tableaux mis dans les Tuileries; un vivier et force belles fontaines, mes plans et mes jardins fort beaux; la place Royale qui est pres la porte St.-Anthoine, et les manufactures, des quatre parts les trois faictes et la quatrieme sera

achevee l'annee prochaine; au bout du Pont-Neuf une belle rue qui va jusques à la porte de Bussy faicte, et les maisons d'un costé et d'aultre sinon faictes du moins elles le seront avant la fin de l'annee prochaine; plus de deux or trois mille ateliers qui travaillent ça et là pour l'embellissement de la ville, sy qu'il n'est pas croyable comme vous y trouverés du changement": *Lettres missives* 7:219–20, 3 May 1607.

16. Robert Dallington, *The View of Fraunce* (London: 1604; reprint, London: 1936), G4–G4v.

17. On Sully's architectural projects: Barbiche et al., *Histoire de Sully-sur-Loire* (Roanne: 1986); Barbiche, *Sully,* 170–85; Anne Albert, *Sully à Rosny-sur-Seine* (Bonnières-sur-Seine: 1975); Rosalys Coope and Catherine Grodecki, "La création d'Henrichemont," *Cahiers d'archéologie et d'histoire du Berry* 41 (June 1975): 21–48; Rosalys Coope, *Salomon de Brosse and the Development of the Classical Style in French Architecture from 1565 to 1630* (University Park, Pa.: 1972), 44–46.

18. After his fall from power in 1611, Sully wrote his memoirs as a personal apologia. He exaggerated his authority and distorted his original views to align them with the subsequent course of events: *Sages et royales Oeconomies d'Estat,* 2 vols., ed. Michaud and Poujoulat (Paris: 1837). A modern edition has been partially completed: *Les Oeconomies royales de Sully,* 2 vols., ed. David Buisseret and Bernard Barbiche, t. 1 (1572–1594), t. 2 (1594–1599) (Paris: 1970–88). For an appraisal of Sully's role in the royal building program: Raymond Kierstead, *Pomponne de Bellièvre. A Study of the King's Men in the Age of Henry IV* (Evanston: 1968), 121; D. Buisseret, "The Legend of Sully," *The Historical Journal* 5/2 (1962): 181–88.

19. Cited by Mousnier, *Assassination of Henry IV,* 193. The study of Miron by his descendant, A. Miron de L'Espinay, *François Miron et l'administration municipale de Paris sous Henri IV de 1604 à 1606* (Paris: 1885), inflates Miron's importance and attributes to the municipality a degree of independence that it did not possess. Nevertheless, Miron was an energetic *Prévôt* and inspired two contemporary panegyrics: N. Fardoil, *Remerciment à Monsieur Myron* (Paris: 1606); *La Prévosté des Marchans* (Paris: 1605). On the municipal government during Henri IV's reign: Robert Descimon, "L'échevinage parisien sous Henri IV (1594–1609)," *La ville, la bourgeoisie et la génèse de l'état moderne (XIIe–XVIIIe siècles),* Actes du colloque de Bielefeld,

ed. Neithard Bulst and J.-Ph. Genet (Paris: 1988), 113–50; Henri de Carsalade Du Pont, *La Municipalité parisienne à l'époque d'Henri IV* (Paris: 1971).

20. In June 1605, Marin de la Vallée, *juré du Roi en l'office de maçonnerie,* was contracted to complete construction of the facade of the Hôtel de Ville. The remaining work entailed rebuilding the "grande salle" (1607–9), constructing a pavilion above the Chapelle du St. Esprit on the north side of the Hôtel de Ville (1609), and adding a wing behind the chapel (1618–28): *Registres* 14:105–6, 143–45, 230–31, 360–64; Carsalade Du Pont, *Municipalité parisienne,* 236–42.

21. The appreciation of real estate in seventeenth-century Paris is analyzed in Emmanuel Le Roy Ladurie, ed., *La Ville classique,* Histoire de la France urbaine, vol. 3 (Paris: 1981), 142–44; E. Le Roy Ladurie and Pierre Couperie, "Le mouvement des loyers parisiens de la fin du Moyen Age au XVIIIe siècle," *Annales ESC* 25/4 (1970): 1002–23; Pierre Goubert, "Economie et urbanisme en France dans la première moitié du XVIIe siècle," *L'Urbanisme de Paris et l'Europe 1600–1680,* ed. Pierre Francastel (Paris: 1969), 37–45.

Chapter 1: The Louvre

1. Cited by Adolphe Berty et al., *Topographie historique du vieux Paris,* vol. 2 (Paris: 1866), 59 (hereafter cited as Berty).

2. Délégation à l'Action Artistique de la Ville de Paris, *L'Enceinte et le Louvre de Philippe Auguste* (Paris: 1988). The history of the Louvre is surveyed in Délégation à l'Action Artistique de la Ville de Paris, *Le Louvre et son quartier. 800 ans d'histoire d'architecturale* (Paris: 1982); Christiane Aulanier, *Histoire du palais et du musée du Louvre,* 10 vols. (Paris: 1948–71); Berty, vols. 1 and 2, *Région du Louvre et des Tuileries* (Paris: 1866–1868).

3. *Registres* 2:17–18, 24 March 1528. On François I's construction at the Louvre: Bates Lowry, "Palais du Louvre 1528–1624. The Development of a Sixteenth-Century Architectural Complex," Ph.D. diss., University of Chicago, 1956 (hereafter cited as Lowry); Louis Batiffol, "Les premières constructions de Pierre Lescot au Louvre d'après de nouveaux documents," *GBA* 1930/2: 276–303; Louis Hautecoeur, "Le Louvre de Pierre Lescot," *GBA* 1927/1: 199–218; Batiffol, "Le Louvre et les plans de Lescot," *GBA* 1910/1: 273–98.

4. Sebastiano Serlio, Bk. VI, Project X, f70–73, Avery Architectural and Fine Arts Library, Columbia University, N.Y.; Project XXII, f66v–73, Bayerische Staatsbibliothek, Munich. Claude Perrault made the first documented reference to a design by Serlio for the Louvre: Perrault, *Les dix livres d'architecture de Vitruve* (Paris: 1673), Preface. On Serlio's project: Introduction by M.N. Rosenfeld in Sebastiano Serlio, *On Domestic Architecture* (New York: 1978), 60; André Chastel, "La Demeure royale au XVIème siècle et le nouveau Louvre," *Studies in Renaissance and Baroque Art presented to Anthony Blunt* (London: 1967), 80–81; Marco Rosci, *Il trattato di architettura di Sebastiano Serlio* (Milan: 1967), 80–81; Lowry, 106–33; William Bell Dinsmoor, "The Literary Remains of Sebastiano Serlio," *Art Bulletin* 24 (1942): 150–52.

5. Catherine Grodecki, "Les marchés de construction pour l'aile Henri II du Louvre (1546–1558)," *Archives de l'art français* 26 (1984): 19–38. It is debated whether the decision to quadruple the Cour Carrée was made in 1551 or at a later date. Lescot's plan of 1551 does not survive, but the changes made immediately pursuant to it involved the redistribution of interior space in the west range of the Cour Carrée. It has been convincingly argued that the changes in plan and circulation anticipated the reconstruction of the south wing and the extension of the west range to the north: Lowry, 30–45.

6. Anthony Blunt, *Philibert de l'Orme* (London: 1958), 91–107. There is an illuminating analysis of the ways in which Ducerceau's engravings distorted Delorme's designs in Françoise Boudon and Jean Blécon, *Philibert Delorme et le château royal de Saint-Léger-en-Yvelines* (Paris: 1985), 105–20.

7. On the Petite Galerie of Charles IX: Sauval, 2:37.

8. Lowry, 70–71. The idea of a gallery connecting two distant buildings ultimately derived from Bramante's scheme to join the Vatican Palace to the Belvedere. According to Berty, the decision to build the river gallery was made in 1566. This date is based on a reference to a gallery near the Seine in the minutes of the city's building commission, the *Bureau,* on 21 July 1566: "le Roy a mandé . . . de faire clorre de grosse maconnerye la seconde descente approchant du port St. Nicolas devant les clostures du Louvre, à l'endroict d'un gallerie que Sa Majesté a ordonné estre faicte en ce lieu"; quoted by Berty, 1:258–259. This date

has implications for the redesign of the Tuileries which are discussed in the following note.

9. Lowry argues that the decision to extend the Tuileries palace to the river followed from the planning of the river gallery in 1566; consequently, the extension of the Tuileries was planned in 1566 or shortly thereafter. The implication is that Delorme, who lived until 1570, executed the changes in his original design, that the crown instructed him to abandon the courtyard scheme and devise a new project for a single-range building. Delorme described the Tuileries palace, his last building, with great pride in the *Premier Tome*. It surely would have been a bitter disappointment and source of great resentment if his royal patron had compelled him to redesign the palace during construction; yet he makes no reference to this event in his writings. It is far more likely that Delorme's scheme was modified after his death in 1570, when Bullant assumed control of the Tuileries palace. I do not believe that Charles IX's plan for the royal palaces was finalized in 1566. Rather, it evolved over time: first he decided to build a gallery along the Seine, in about 1566; four to five years later, after Delorme's death, he decided to join the Tuileries to the gallery; then the Huguenot massacre on St. Bartholomew's Night and the outbreak of the religious wars in 1572 forced the king to shelve his ambitious plan. In conjunction with construction of the Tuileries palace, Charles IX enclosed the Tuileries garden by a wall and built a connecting gate on the quai, the Porte de la Conférence. This enclosure was begun in 1566 at the request of the queen mother, who wanted her palace better defended. The construction did not affect the Portes Neuve and St. Honoré. Dumolin incorrectly stated that Charles IX rebuilt these gates 950 meters west of their original location: *Etudes de topographie parisienne*, 3 vols. (Paris: 1929–31), 2:114. As numerous seventeenth-century engravings confirm, the two gates remained aligned with the wall of Charles V.

10. Berty, 1:271–73.

11. A detailed chronology of Henri IV's construction is provided in Jean-Pierre Babelon, "Les Travaux de Henri IV au Louvre et aux Tuileries," *MSHP* 29 (1978): 55–130. Documents concerning Henri IV's construction are published in Louis-Henri Collard and Edouard-Jacques Ciprut, *Nouveaux documents sur le Louvre* (Paris: 1963) (hereafter cited as Collard); Mallevoüe, 103–44. In the late 1590s,

Henri IV had the walls of the Galerie des Cerfs at Fontainebleau decorated with views of his buildings. They were subsequently buried beneath later decorations, and the painting of the Louvre was only rediscovered in 1862. Although only fragments survived, the view of the Louvre generally corresponds with Destailleur 147. Berty published an engraving of the painting in its unrestored state (2:97–99), which is far more reliable than the overly restored painting in situ at Fontainebleau. L. Gouvenin, "La Galerie des cerfs au palais de Fontainebleau et l'architecte Paccard," *Annales de la société historique et archéologique du Gâtinais* 1 (1883): 33–42.

12. Lowry, 14.

13. Henri III commissioned a design for the chapel from Baptiste Androuet Ducerceau. Masonry contract for the chapel, 26 February 1580: Collard, 46–49.

14. This description is based on a mimeographed information sheet prepared by the archaeologists in charge of the excavation and distributed at a tour of the Friends of the Tuileries on 21 October 1989. I would like to thank Emmanuel Jacquin for inviting me to participate in this event.

15. Although the platform was not begun, the retaining wall was repaired: Min. cent. XIX 331 f124, 16 Jan. 1595.

16. Boullet's work was severely criticized by Sauval, 2:54. On Boullet: Babelon, "Travaux de Henri IV au Louvre," 70.

17. "Devis des ouvrages de massonerye de pierre de taille qu'il convient faire pour le Roy nostre sire en son bastiment des Thuilleries pour reddiffier de neuf une gallerye joignant le corps d'hostel dud. bastiment tirant en longeur depuis le grand pavillon [de Bullant] jusques contre l'escallier [de Delorme]." Contract passed with Pierre Guillain and Robert Marquelet, 24 May 1594: Min. cent. XIX 329 f140. Masonry contract for the terrace overlooking the western gardens and for chimney mantels, 12 March 1601: Min. cent. XIX 343 f41. No contract for work on the Bullant pavilion has been found. In 1868, before the building was destroyed, Berty reported that the initials HM appeared on the chimneys and niches. The attic of the Delorme wing was decorated with the same ciphers, indicating that Henri IV undertook this work after his marriage to Maria de' Medici: Berty, 2:93.

18. Contract with royal sculptor Barthélemy Prieur, 12 October 1594: Min. cent. XIX 330. The royal ciphers on the court facade of the

west wing disclose the chronology of the decorative work: K (Karolus) for Charles IX, H for Henri III, and HB (Henri de Bourbon) for Henri IV.

19. Carpentry contract for the roof of the Petite Galerie, 9 October 1596: Min. cent. XIX 334 f299. Two weeks later, the municipality gave carpenter Charles Marchant permission to assemble the frame on the grounds of the Arsenal: *Registres* 10:317, 21 Oct. 1596.

20. Sauval, 2:37. Sauval's text does not in fact refer to Jean Coin but to an unknown mason named Plain. There is, however, no doubt that the mason in question was Coin.

21. Sculpture contracts with Mansart, 13 December 1601 and 15 December 1602: Collard, 51–52.

22. Sauval, 2:40.

23. Masonry contract for the Grande Galerie, 14 January 1595: Min. cent. XIX 331 f6. Only Fournier is named in this contract, but he formed an association with the other masons one day earlier, 13 January 1595: Min. cent. XIX 331 f15. They agreed to the rate of 14 *ecus* per *toise* for the intramural section of the gallery and 21 *ecus* per *toise* for the extramural segment, which was more expensive because foundations had to be built for this part.

24. Masonry contract for the Grande Galerie, 12 March 1601: Min. cent. XIX 343 f80. After his death in 1599, Florent Fournier was replaced by his son Isaïe, who was named royal architect in 1602.

25. These events are reported in the new masonry contract dated 19 February 1603: Mallevoüe, 108–9. Requests for payment by the masons, 24 and 26 July 1600: Berty, 2:201–4.

26. Masonry contract for the Grande Galerie, 19 February 1603: Mallevoüe, 107–11.

27. ". . . une advance, saillant tant d'un costé que d'autre hors le corps des murs et au dessus une forme de balcon semblable et pour cymetrier celuy du bout de la petite gallerye": Mallevoüe, 110.

28. On Le Vau's reconstruction of the Petite Galerie and the Salle des Antiques: Christiane Aulanier, *Histoire du Palais et du Musée du Louvre,* vol. 5, *La Petite Galerie* (Paris: n.d.), 30–32; Louis Hautecoeur, *Le Louvre et les Tuileries de Louis XIV* (Paris: 1927), 105–19.

29. ". . . comme aussy de changer d'architecture en la façade depuis led. balcon et advance jusques et vers led. rampart": Mallevoüe, 110.

30. Sauval, 2:40. On the dolphin order at Fontainebleau: Nathan Whitman, "Fontainebleau, the Luxembourg, and the French

Domed Entry Pavilion," *JSAH* 46 (1987): 363.

31. Sauval, 2:40.

32. Marot's engraving shows one less bay between the moat and the passageway to the west than the 1603 plan.

33. One day after signing the first contract, Fournier subcontracted the extramural segment of the gallery to several other masons; among them were René Fleury and Remy Collin: Min. cent. XIX 331 f19, 15 Jan. 1595. There is no evidence that they executed the contract, either in 1595 or at a later date.

34. Berty 2:91. Thomas Coryate, *Coryat's Crudities* (1611; Glasgow: 1905), 175.

35. Carpentry contract for the Petite Galerie des Tuileries, 11 May 1609: Mallevoüe, 141–44.

36. Métezeau's appointment on 19 October 1594 and the crown's response to Ducerceau's complaint on 19 April 1599: Mallevoüe, 104–6.

37. Sauval, 2:53.

38. The documented work by Jacques II Androuet Ducerceau is limited to the Hôtel de Bellegarde (later renamed the Hôtel de Séguier; 1611–14) and the Hôtel de Mayenne (1613), but we do not know what his designs entailed: Babelon, *Demeures parisiennes,* 241.

39. Coope, *Salomon de Brosse and the Development of the Classical Style in French Architecture* (University Park, Pa.: 1972), 34. Ecole nationale supérieure des Beaux-Arts, *Arts français ancien XIIe–XVIIIe siècle . . . tirés en majeure partie de la donation Jean Masson* (Paris: 1936), no. 44. The drawing (29.9 cm × 54.1 cm; Ecole des Beaux-Arts, Dessin 093), rendered in pen and brown wash, does not have a watermark.

40. Canadian Centre for Architecture, *Architecture and Its Image* (Montreal: 1989), 308–9; Janet Byrne, "Some Sixteenth-Century Designs for Tombs and Fountains in the Metropolitan Museum," *Master Drawings* 21/3 (Autumn 1983): 263–70; idem, *Renaissance Ornament Prints and Drawings* (New York: 1981); idem, "Some Attributions Undone," *Master Drawings* 13/3 (Autumn 1975): 240–48; idem, "Du Cerceau Drawings," *Master Drawings* 15/2 (Summer 1977): 147–61.

41. Contracts for the king's apartment, 21 January 1606: Collard, 60–61. Contract for the queen's chapel, 13 June 1606: Collard, 62. Contract for reliefs in the Petite Galerie, 5 April 1606: Collard, 53. Contracts for the Salle des Antiques, see note 60. Contract for marble columns, 2 October 1602: Min. cent. XIX 347 f360. Métezeau also designed marble columns which may have been placed at the entrances to the Grande Galerie. In 1607 he was ap-

pointed concierge of the Tuileries and keeper of its furnishings, another indication of his importance in the decoration of the palace: Berty, 2:79. For the duties they performed as royal architect in 1608, Métezeau was paid 2,000 *livres,* Ducerceau 1,200 *livres;* evidently the former was more highly valued. Métezeau received an additional 400 *livres* for his role as concierge of the Tuileries and keeper of its furnishings: Berty, 2:205.

42. Germain Brice, *Description nouvelle de ce qu'il y a de plus remarquable dans la ville de Paris,* 2 vols. (Paris: 1684), 1:33. Brice incorrectly credited Louis Métezeau with the dam at La Rochelle; it was designed in 1627–28, long after his death, by his brother Clément. In the third edition of his guide, Brice attributed the western section of the Grande Galerie to Etienne Dupérac: Brice, *Description nouvelle,* 3rd ed., 2 vols. (Paris: 1698), 1:71. While this attribution is unlikely, it cannot be absolutely dismissed until we learn something about Dupérac's work as an architect. Dupérac made designs for gardens and for interior decoration; however, no evidence has yet been found of any building he designed.

43. David Thomson, *Renaissance Paris* (Berkeley/London: 1984), 152. Thomson did not cite his archival source.

44. Coope, *Salomon de Brosse,* 32–34.

45. The pavilion at the north end of the Tuileries is drawn on a patch; evidently the draftsman made a hole in the vellum in attempting to scrape away a mistake. No underdrawings are visible beneath the patch.

46. In 1612, a garden was planted in this area, and in 1617, Clément Métezeau designed an orangery on the site of the curtain wall: Collard, 68–73. Henri IV's plan projected both of these projects.

47. Jean de Saulx-Tavannes described a project of Henri IV for this area, but it does not conform to the 1603 plan: "une grande terrasse de laquelle on pourroit descendre par degrez, comme d'un theatre, les degrez deça au dela du portail qui seroit au mitan, qui contiendroit en longueur des deux tiers de la terrasse": *Mémoires de très-noble et très-illustre Gaspard de Saulx, seigneur de Tavannes,* 3 vols., Collection complète des mémoires relatifs à l'histoire de France, ed. Petitot, vols. 23–25 (Paris: 1822), vol. 25, 205–6.

48. "Si le roy Henri IV eust vescu, aymant les bastimens comme il faisoit, il pouvoit en faire un remarquable, achevant le corps de logis du Louvre, dont le grand escalier ne marque que

la moitié, et au bout d'iceluy faire une mesme gallerie que celle qui est à la sortie de sa chambre, en tirant vers St.-Honoré, et depuis là faire une pareille galerie que celle qui regarde sur la rivière, qui allast finir entre le pavillon des Tuilleries qui n'est pas faict, et l'escuyrie; et au lieu de gallerie, s'y pouvoit construire des logis pour loger des ambassadeurs; et ruinant toutes les maisons entre les deux galleries, le Louvre et les Tuilleries, se fust trouvée une grande cour admirable": Saulx-Tavannes, 205–6. According to Saulx-Tavannes, Henri IV also planned to demolish the buildings between the Louvre and the church of St. Germain l'Auxerrois in order to create a monumental forecourt to the palace; this report is unconfirmed by any other source.

49. Peter Heylyn, *A Survey of the Estate of France* (London: 1656), 117.

50. Cited in note 48.

51. The edict begins as follows: "Comme entre les infinis biens qui sont causez par la paix, celluy qui provient de la culture des arts n'est pas des moindres, se rendant grandement florissant par icelle, et dont le public a reçu une tres grande commodité, nous avons eu aussy cest esgard en la construction de nostre gallerie du Louvre d'en disposer le bastiment en telle forme que nous y puissions commodément loger quantité des meilleurs et plus suffizans maistres qui se pourroient recouvrer, tant de peinture, sculture, orfevrerie, orlogerie, insculture en pierreries, que aultres de plusieurs et d'excellentz artz, tant pour nous servir d'iceulx, comme pour estre par mesme moyen emploiez par noz subjectz en ce qu'ilz auroient besoing de leur industrye, et aussy pour faire comme une pepiniere d'ouvriers de laquelle, soubs l'aprentissaige de sy bons maistres, il en sortiroit plusieurs qui par après se repandroient par tout nostre royaulme et qui sçauroient très bien servir le publicq." The edict also named the artists who were given apartments: A.N. O1 1045, 22 Dec. 1608, published by J. J. Guiffrey, "Logements d'artistes au Louvre," *Nouvelles archives de l'art français,* 1873: 19–20.

52. In response to the first patent letters on 5 September 1607, the Parlement proposed two restrictions: each Grande Galerie resident could grant the *maîtrise* to no more than one apprentice every five years, and goldworkers would enjoy no exemptions from guild regulations: Félibien, 5:42–43. The crown rejected the proposed changes and on 7 January 1608 again instructed the Parlement to approve the edict: *Archives de l'art français, Documents,* III (Paris: 1853–55), 312–13.

53. Contracts for masonry, paving, and carpentry in the artists' apartments: Min. cent. XIX 355 f136, 11 April 1606 (this document was published by Collard, 57, but his transcription has many errors); Mallevoüe, 119–20, 29 March 1608; 124–25, 21 June 1608; 125–27, 24 July 1608.

54. Carpentry contract for the installation of the Mint, 11 July 1609: Mallevoüe, 128–30. The Mint occupied the fourth, fifth, and sixth bays west of the pavilion.

55. The tapestry weavers were Maurice Dubois, Girard Laurent, and Pierre Dupont. Apartments were also given to sculptor Jean Séjourné, who designed a grotto for Henri IV at St.-Germain-en-Laye; stone engraver Julien de Fontenay; and painter Pierre des Martins, whose work is now unknown. Métezeau probably was not named in the edict of 1608 because he was already living in the Louvre. Georges Huard, "Les logements des artisans dans la grande galerie du Louvre sous Henri IV et Louis XIII," *BSHAF,* 1939, 18–39.

56. Pierre Dupont, *Stromatourgie ou d'excellence de la manufacture des tapits dits de Turquie* (Paris: 1632; reprint: 1882), 38. The tapestryworks established by Dupont in 1627 later became the Savonnerie.

57. The history of the Grande Galerie is surveyed in Christiane Aulanier, *Histoire du Palais et du Musée du Louvre,* vol. 1, *La Grande Galerie* (Paris: n.d.).

58. Antoine Schnapper, "The King of France as Collector in the Seventeenth Century," *Journal of Interdisciplinary History* XVII/1 (Summer 1986): 189–90.

59. André Félibien, *Tableaux du Cabinet du Roi. Statues et bustes antiques des maisons royales* (Paris: 1677), Preface.

60. Contracts for the interior decoration of the Salle des Antiques: Collard, 56, 27 Jan 1606; 58, 26–27 June 1608. Mallevoüe, 111–13, 8 Feb. 1604; 115–18, 29 March 1608. Some of the marblework was executed by Robert Menart, whom we will meet at the Place Dauphine.

61. Sauval, 2:42.

62. Painting contract with Bunel, 9 December 1609: Mallevoüe, 134–35.

63. Antoine Schnapper, *Le Géant, la licorne, la tulipe* (Paris: 1988), 184–86. "Abbregé d'inventaire des pièces que le sieur de Bagarris a en main pour dresser un Cabinet à Sa Majesté de toutes sortes d'antiquitez, suyvant le commandement donné audit sieur de Bagarris par Sa Majesté tant de bouche que par lettre du

22me mars 1602": B.N. Ms. fr. 9540, f226–227. Philippe Tamizey de Larroque, *Les correspondants de Peiresc,* fasc. XII: *Pierre-Antoine de Rascas, sieur de Bagarris* (Aix: 1887).

64. Painting contract with Dubreuil, 28 November 1601: Collard, 54–55. The document does not specify the scenes to be painted. In conjunction with the decoration of the vault, two large coats of arms were commissioned from Barthélemy Tremblay for each end of the Petite Galerie, and plaster reliefs designed by Métezeau were commissioned from Jean Mansart: Collard, 50, 9 May 1601; 53, 5 April 1606.

65. Sauval, 2:38–39.

66. "Il est pardonnable aux hommes particuliers eslevez en hautes dignitez (qui n'osent pas ramener en mémoire le nom de leurs ancestres pour la honte de leur petitesse) de rechercher des fables et ornemens estrangers à l'embellissement de leurs maisons: et encor aux Princes nouvellement establis en leurs estats modernes. Mais à notre Roy, qui peut produire le plus venerable et authentique Arbre de Généalogie de Rois ses Ancestres, qui se puisse voir sur la face de la terre . . . , ce seroit un grand crime d'emprunter ailleurs ce qu'il a si abondamment chez soy": Antoine de Laval, "Des Peintures convenables aux basiliques et palais du Roy. Mesmes à sa gallerie du Louvre à Paris" (1600), *Desseins de professions nobles et publiques* (Paris: 1605), 9. Jacques Thuillier, "Peinture et politique: une théorie de la galerie royale sous Henri IV," A. Châtelet and N. Reynaud (eds.), *Etudes d'art français offertes à Charles Sterling* (Paris: 1975), 175–205.

67. Contract with Bunel, 22 May 1607, "de . . . peindre à huylle et sur toille tous les pourtraicts des Roys et Reynes, princes, princesses, seigneurs et dames que le Roy veult estre representez et apposez en 28 trumeaux ou espaces qui sont entre les croisées de sa petite gallerie du Louvre . . . ; le tout au naturel en habits et vestement du temps de chaque regne et suivant les originaux qui en seront fourny aud. Bunel et ceux qu'il pourra recouvrer par ses dilligences et industrie. A commancer par les tableaux de leurs majestez à present regnantes et finir au Roy St. Louis . . .": Collard, 53–54. Collard's transcription omits the price: 360 *livres tournois* for each large painting and accompanying smaller portraits; Min. cent. XIX 357 f168. For a list of all the portraits: Ludovic Lalanne, "Estat des tableaux qui sont en la galerie de Paris," *Archives de l'art français, Documents,* III,

54–58. The Petite Galerie is placed in the context of other decorative portrait cycles in French châteaux in Antoine Schnapper, *Le Géant,* 127–29; Margaret MacGowan, "Le phénomène de la galerie des portraits," Roland Mousnier and Jean Mesnard, eds., *L'Age d'or du mécénat (1598–1661)* (Paris: 1985), 411–22.

68. Schnapper, *Le géant,* 123–27, 132, 237–40.

69. Nicolas Claude Fabri de Peiresc, *Lettres de Peiresc,* ed. Ph. Tamizey de Larroque, 7 vols. (Paris: 1888–98), VII: 627–29.

70. Sauval, 2:38.

71. Peiresc, *Lettres de Peiresc,* VI: 695, VII: 755–56. Peiresc sustained his friendship with Bunel's widow.

72. Joinery contract for windows in the Grande Galerie, twenty on each side beginning at east end, 24 May 1608: Mallevoüe, 122–23. Paving contracts for the upper floor of the Grande Galerie, 5 April 1606 and 31 December 1618: Collard, 56, 58–59.

73. The contract for the triumphal arch at the east end has not been found. The arch was completed by 1606 when it is mentioned in the paving contract cited in the previous note. The four marble columns designed by Métezeau and delivered to the Louvre in 1602 may have been for this arch: Min. cent. XIX 347 f360, 2 Oct. 1602. Contract to move statues and polish marble columns with Robert Menart, 31 July 1609: Mallevoüe, 130–31.

74. Joinery contracts for Delorme's southern gallery, 15 March 1603: Mallevoüe, 136–38. Masonry and paving contracts for Bullant's pavilion and Delorme's adjoining gallery, 17 March 1603: Mallevoüe, 138–40.

75. Contract with Bunel for "les peintures et enrichissements de la vouste et pignons de la grande salle haute du vieil logis du pallais des Thuilleries," 27 March 1601: Min. cent. XIX 343 f57. Painting contract with Bunel for the vault, 17 February 1604: Edouard-Jacques Ciprut, "Nouveaux documents sur Etienne Dupérac," *BSHAF,* 1960: 171–72.

76. Contract for the tribune, 27 May 1603: Mallevoüe, 140–41.

77. Min. cent. XIX 329 f257, f259, 29 June 1594; summarized in Catherine Grodecki, *Histoire de l'art au XVIe siècle, 1540–1600, Documents du Minutier central* (Paris: 1985) t. 1, 342–44. The contract with Pierre Le Nostre in 1572 is also excerpted in Grodecki, *Histoire de l'art au XVIe siècle,* 340–41.

78. Contracts for the pond, 31 January 1607 and 24 March 1608: Mallevoüe, 240–42. Carpentry

contracts for the arbor (*berceau*) and seven pavilions, 1 April 1605: Mallevoüe, 236–39.

79. Masonry contract for the orangery, 9 September 1602: Ciprut, "Nouveaux documents," 170–71.

80. Masonry contract for the retaining wall, 91 *toises* long, 16 February 1601: Min. cent. XIX 343 f53.

81. Marble contract for the fountain, 9 March 1601: Ciprut, "Nouveaux documents," 170.

82. Gardening contracts with Mollet, 22 October 1599 and 7 March 1600, Grodecki, *Histoire de l'art au XVIe siècle,* 344; 5 February 1609: Mallevoüe, 245–48. Kenneth Woodbridge provides an excellent discussion of the plantings, but he mistakenly attributed the parterre designs to Sully and Henri IV: *Princely Gardens* (New York: 1986), 112–18.

83. No book surveys the nineteenth-century building history of the Louvre. Lefuel in particular awaits his biographer. See Babelon, "L.T.J. Visconti et le Louvre," in *'Il se rendit en Italie': Etudes offertes a André Chastel* (Rome/Paris: 1987), 617–32; idem, "Travaux de Henri IV au Louvre"; Jean-Claude Daufresne, *Louvre et Tuileries: architectures de papier* (Liège: [1987]); Emmanuel Jacquin, "La Seconde République et l'achèvement du Louvre," *BSHP,* 1986–87: 375–401.

84. Duban made minor changes to Métezeau's design; he raised the bull's-eye window on the river facade of the Petite Galerie and added sculptural decoration to the area left incomplete by Henri IV: J.-P. Babelon, "Les photographies des estampages pris sur les façades de la Grande Galerie du Louvre avant sa restauration," *Revue de l'Art* 58–59 (1983): 41–52. Jacques de Caso, "Duban et l'achèvement de la Galerie du bord de l'eau: la frise des frères L'Heureux," *BSHAF,* 1973: 333–43.

85. Cited in Daufresne, *Louvre et Tuileries,* 271.

Chapter 2: The Place Royale

1. Mallevoüe, 27–47. Louis Lambeau, *La Place Royale* (Paris: 1906); idem, "Communication relative à la place Royale et au lotissement du parc des Tournelles," *CVP,* 25 January 1908: 19–31; idem, "La Place Royale. Nouvelles contributions à son histoire," *CVP Annèxe,* 20 November 1915: 1–159. Lambeau's studies of individual hôtels are listed in the bibliography. Maurice Dumolin, "Les Propriétaires de la place Royale (1605–1789)," *La Cité* 95–96

(July–Oct. 1925): 273–319; 97–98 (April 1926): 1–30.

2. Jean-Pierre Babelon, "Le palais des Tournelles et les origines de la place des Vosges," EPHE, 1975–76: 695–714.

3. Laffemas described his many years of service to the king as tailor, *valet de chambre,* and merchant in his first pamphlet *Source de plusieurs abus* (Paris: 1596), 1. Laffemas's writings are listed in the Bibliography. Charles Cole wrote of Laffemas, "It is almost impossible to deny him the rank of the first great mercantilist minister of France, and not to see him [as] the Colbert of the reign of Henri IV": *French Mercantilist Doctrine Before Colbert* (New York: 1931), 112. On Laffemas's proposals: P. Boissonnade, *Le Socialisme d'Etat* (Paris: 1927), 164; Henri Hauser, "Le Système social de Barthélemy de Laffemas," *Revue Bourguignonne de l'enseignement supérieur* 12/1 (1902): 113–31; Gustave Fagniez, *L'Economie sociale de la France sous Henri IV 1589–1610* (Paris: 1897), 91; Paul Laffitte, "Notice sur Barthélemy Laffemas, contrôleur général du commerce sous Henri IV," *Journal des economistes,* ser. 3, 142/125 (May 1876): 181–218.

4. The Commission on Commerce was composed of two merchants and sixteen officers of the law courts and Parlement. The Commission evaluated inventions and commercial projects; those it recommended for royal support were submitted to the king's council, the Conseil d'Etat. The Commission reviewed proposals for water pumps, windmills, looms for the blind and crippled, a canal linking the Atlantic Ocean to the Mediterranean Sea, the cultivation of asparagus, and the breeding of stallions. It had the largest impact on textile production. After the first two hectic years, from July 1602 through October 1604, when the Commission met weekly, it played a more passive role, only arbitrating disputes and awaiting results from the numerous projects it had already launched. Its activities are chronicled in the minutes of its proceedings: *Recueil presenté au Roy de ce qui se passe en l'Assemblée du commerce* (Paris: 1604) in Archives curieuses de l'histoire de France, ed. Cimber and Danjou, ser. 1, vol. 14 (Paris: 1837), 219–45 (hereafter *Recueil de l'Assemblée du commerce*); *Registre des délibérations de la Commission consultative sur le faict du commerce (1601–1604)* in Documents historiques inédits, ed. Champollion Figeac, vol. 4 (Paris: 1848), 1–282 (hereafter *Délibérations de la Commission du commerce*).

5. A.N. E4B f161, 4 Oct. 1602.

6. Olivier de Serres, *La Cueillete de la soye par la nourriture des vers qui la font* (Paris: 1599); idem, *La seconde richesse du meurier blanc* (Paris: 1603).

7. The crown paid the merchants Jean-Baptiste Le Tellier and Nicolas Chevalier 120,000 *livres;* this sum was raised from a tax imposed on the participating regions: A.N. E4B f161, 4 Oct. 1602; Fagniez, *L'Economie sociale,* 109–10. Le Tellier wrote two pamphlets on sericulture: *Brief discours contenant la maniere de nourrir les vers à soye* (Paris: 1602); *Memoires et instructions pour l'establissement des meuriers et art de faire la soye en France* (Paris: 1603). *Brief discours,* dedicated to Sully's wife, was illustrated with six engravings by Philippe Galle after Jan van der Straet. It was far more elaborate than the other manuals and was probably intended for distribution to noble land owners.

8. The merchants described the difficulties they encountered to the Commission on Commerce on 11 April 1603: *Délibérations de la Commission du commerce,* 80; B.N. Ms. fr. 16740 f73–75v, f77. In 1605, the king compelled the clergy to cultivate mulberry trees and silkworms on their estates. The manual on sericulture cited in note 9 was dedicated to the clergy.

9. Benigne Le Roy, Jacques de Chabot, Jean Van der Vekene and Claude Moullet [sic], *Instruction du plantage et proprietez des meuriers et du gouvernement des vers à soye* (Paris: 1605). Laffemas called attention to Mollet's cultivation of mulberry groves in *Lettres et exemples de la feu royne mère* (Paris: 1602) in Archives curieuses, ed. Cimber and Danjou, ser. 1, vol. 9 (Paris: 1836), 130. Mollet wrote that he successfully cultivated mulberry trees and silkworms in 1606, producing silk "aussi belle comme celle qui vient d'Italie, laquelle j'ay vendue la mesme année 4 escus la livre à M. Sainctot, un des notables bourgeois de cette ville de Paris et Marchand de soye": Mollet, *Le Théâtre des plans et jardinages* (Paris: 1652), 340.

10. George Carew, "A Relation of the State of France" (1609), *An Historical View of the Negotiations between the Courts of England, France, and Brussels* (London: 1749), 431.

11. Pierre-Victor Palma-Cayet praised the groves at Madrid: *Chronologie Septenaire* (Paris: 1605) in Mémoires pour servir à l'histoire de France, ed. Michaud and Poujoulat, vol. 12 (Paris: 1838), 259.

12. "Mon amy, je vous prie de faire haster la charpente et couverture de mon orangerie des Tuilleries, affin que ceste année je m'en puisse servir a y faire elever la graine des vers a soie que j'ai faict venir de Valence en Espagne, laquelle il faudra faire eclore aussy tost que les meuriers auront jetté de quoy les pouvoir nourrir. Vous scavés comme j'affectionne cela: c'est pourquoy je vous prie encore un coup d'y pourveoir et les faire haster": *Lettres missives* 6:63. Master mason Jean Coin was hired to build the orangery on 9 September 1602: Min. cent. XIX 347 f308, published in Ciprut, "Nouveaux documents sur Etienne Dupérac," *BSHAF*, 1960: 170–71. The *allée* of mulberry trees still existed in 1652: Adolphe Berty et al., *Topographie historique du vieux Paris*, 6 vols. (Paris: 1866–97), 2:94.

13. B. Laffemas, *Le Tesmoinage certain du profict et revenu des soyes de France* (Paris: 1602), 4–5. Manfredo Balbani, a native of Lucca, came to Paris with a staff of Genoese workers to maintain the royal nurseries: de Serres, *Le Théatre d'agriculture*, bk. 2, chap. 3; Fagniez, *L'Economie sociale*, 108–9. Balbani later became active as a contractor in municipal and royal projects: A.N. E14B f71, f208, 6 and 15 Sept. 1607.

14. Noël and Estienne Parent, master workers in silk cloth, operated an atelier near the Temple by 1601; they were bankrupt two years later: Laffemas, *Neuf advertissements pour servir à l'utilité publique* (Paris: 1601), 5; *Délibérations de la Commission du commerce*, 68–69, 79. In 1604, they opened a new workshop in Mantes: Min. cent. CXII 251, 7 April 1605. Workshops specializing in the "art of drawing and threading gold in the custom of Milan" were opened in 1603 by Andrea Turrato, a Milanese merchant, and Alexandre de Vieux, perfumer and valet in the king's chamber; the latter hired two Italian master gold drawers to operate his shop: A.N. E5A f125, 15 Feb. 1603; f294, 16 March 1603. Other ateliers are mentioned in A.N. X1A/8645 f153, Aug. 1603 and in Palma-Cayet, *Chronologie Septenaire*, 259.

15. On Sainctot's trip to Fontainebleau: *Délibérations de la Commission du commerce*, 1. Royal edict: A.N. X1A/8645 f151–152, Aug. 1603.

16. The financial arrangements between the silk partners are explained in Min. cent. XC 170, 29 Dec. 1610. The crown had previously solicited Moisset's support for other workshops, but he failed to honor his pledges. In 1603, his default brought the silk workshop of the Parent brothers to bankruptcy, and his exploitation of the leather artisans led to the intervention of the Commission on Commerce: *Délibérations de la Commission du commerce*, 142. In 1605, Moisset spent 4,621,000 *livres* to purchase a tax farm (*ferme général des gabelles*); his investment of 45,000 *livres* in the silkworks was a meager sum by comparison. Moisset was remembered for swindling and dishonesty in the journal of Pierre de L'Estoile, *Journal pour le règne de Henri IV,* vol. 2, ed. André Martin (Paris: 1958), 51, 407. On Moisset: H. de Carsalade Du Pont, *La Municipalité parisienne à l'époque d'Henri IV* (Paris: 1971), 285–311; Léo Mouton, "Deux financiers au temps de Sully: Largentier et Moisset," *BSHP* 64 (1937): 65–104; *Registres* 13:214, 277.

17. On Sainctot: Françoise Bayard, *Le monde des financiers au XVIIe siècle* (Paris: 1988), 156–57, 350–57, 417–18; Jean-Louis Bourgeon, *Les Colbert avant Colbert* (Paris: 1973), 83; *Délibérations de la Commission du commerce*, 47; *Registres* 13:345–46.

18. On Claude Parfaict: *Lettres missives* 7:7–8; Inventory after death, Min. cent. CVIII 64/2 f237, 13 Dec. 1624.

19. On Camus: Bayard, *Le monde des financiers,* 156, 245, 388; Bourgeon, *Les Colbert,* 81–82, 251–54; Ernest O'Reilly, *Mémoires sur la vie de Claude Pellot,* vol. 1 (Paris: 1881), 137–38; Tellemant des Reaux, *Les Historiettes,* vol. 3 (Paris: 1834), 122.

20. Both Lumague and Mascranny were born in the Grisons in the Swiss Alps; although many documents bear the signatures Paolo Mascrani and Gio Andrea Lumaga, they were not Italian: Bourgeon, *Les Colbert,* 112–13. I have followed Bourgeon and Bayard in using the spelling Lumague rather than Lumagne as the name frequently appears. Lumague's investment in the silk venture was shared with three brothers and with Mascranny; however, they were not named in the act of August 1603: Min. cent. CXII 258, 10 Jan. 1609. On Lumague: Bayard, *Le monde des financiers,* 360–66, 373, 388, 417–18; Marie-Félicie Pérez, "Le Mécenat de la famille Lumague (branche française) au XVIIe siècle," *La France et l'Italie au temps de Mazarin*, ed. Jean Serroy (Grenoble: 1986), 153–65.

21. Bourgeon, *Les Colbert,* 85. Fernand Braudel, *The Perspective of the World* (New York: 1984), 326–37. Frank Spooner, *The International Economy and Monetary Movements in France*

1493–1725 (Cambridge, Ma.: 1972), 252–56.

22. Colbert's resignation from the business was authorized in patent letters dated 28 September 1604: B.N. Ms. fr. 18174 f165; Bourgeon, *Les Colbert*, 116; O'Reilly, *Mémoires de Claude Pellot*, 1:136.

23. On Guillaume Parfaict: *Lettres missives* 7: 7–8.

24. Royal edict: A.N. X1A/8645 f151. Confirmation of letters of nobility for silk partners: B.N. Ms. fr. 4139 f106v, f158, 19 Oct. 1604.

25. The king promised 90,000 *livres* for the linenworks and 100,000 *livres* for the Flemish tapestryworks: Mallevoüe, 13–16; *Registres* 14:170–74; *Lettres missives* 7:131. Further details on the financing of the silkworks are given in note 38.

26. A few days after the November meeting with Sainctot, Sully informed the Commission on Commerce that "pour le regard de l'entreprise de M. Sainctot, il l'approuvoit fort, mais qu'il trouvoit de la difficulté à luy fournir l'argent que Sa Majesté avoit promis leur advancer": *Délibérations de la Commission du commerce*, 133. The edict of January 1604, which does not survive, is mentioned in the following documents concerning the land donation: Letters of commission addressed to Sully, *Grand Voyer de France*, instructing him to refer the matter to the Treasurers of France (hereafter Sully's Commission), 4 March 1604; Measurement of the site by Jean Fontaine, 10 March 1604; Report of the Treasurers of France, 24 March 1604; Patent Letters by Henri IV confirming the donation, April 1604; Confirmation by the Parlement, 9 April 1604; Confirmation by the *Chambre des comptes*, 2 August 1604; Confirmation by the Treasurers general, 7 September 1604. This set of documents exists in three copies: A.N. Q1/1234; A.N. X1A/8645 f154–155v; A.P. H.D. 60.350.

27. "Ayant une particuliere affection d'establir en ceste nostre bonne ville de Paris les artz et manufactures specialement celles de soye, or, et argent fillé à la façon de Milan, nous y avons faict venir des pais estrangers des ouvriers tant pour dresser les moulins, mestiers, et autres choses necessaires pour lesd. manufactures, que pour commencer à y travailler et monstrer à ceulx de noz subjects qui aurons desir d'y apprendre. . . . Mais d'autant que nous n'avons peu trouver en ceste notred. ville aucun logis assez spacieux, propre, ny commode pour la grande quantité de mestiers et moulins qu'il conviendra

dresser ny pour loger et habiter les ouvriers qui y travailleront, nous avons jugé à propos d'en faire bastir ung expres en la place antiennement appellee le parc des Tournelles à nous appartenant et de faict, apres avoir esté nous mesurés sur les lieux, nous en avons promis et accordé en don aux sieurs de Moisset et Sainctot, Lumague, Camus et Parfaict entrepreneurs dudict establissement jusques à la quantité de 100 thoises de long sur 60 de large pour y faire bastir et construire les maisons propres et necessaires pour lesd. manufactures et ouvriers d'icelles suivant le desseing qui nous en a esté monstré . . ." Sully's Commission, 4 March 1604: A.N. Q1/1234; A.N. X1A/8645 f154–155v; A.P. H.D. 60.350.

28. On the Hôtel des Tournelles: Jean-Pierre Babelon, "Le palais des Tournelles et les origines de la place des Vosges," 696–703; Maurice Roy, "Les travaux de Philibert de Lorme à Paris: Hôtel des Tournelles," *Artistes et monuments de la Renaissance en France* (Paris: 1929), 351–54. The crown sold the lots on the site of the Hôtel des Tournelles "à la charge d'y faire bastir et edifier maisons et manoirs habitables, commodes et convenables pour la decoration de notred. ville selon les portraits et devis qui en feront pour ce faire": A.N. X1A/8625 f174, 28 Jan. 1564; Félibien, 4:817–18. I have found references to only two sales: lot 64, "entre la muraille dud. parcq et les egousts," sold to the convent of Ste. Catherine du Val des Ecoliers (A.N. S 1025, 7 Sept. 1576), and lot 65, which was included in the land given to the silk manufacturers, sold to Simon Mouquet in June 1564 (A.N. E19B f224, 18 Dec. 1608). A royal decree on 6 April 1585 ordered the transfer of the horse market from the Porte St. Honoré to the parc des Tournelles: *Registres* 8:438; Félibien, 2:1090; A.N. S 2857, 12 Oct. 1581.

29. Henri IV encouraged the settlement of the area by giving away land in the parc des Tournelles. In 1594, he gave Sully 1,800 square *toises* directly north of the tract later given to the silk entrepreneurs; Sully's property is now bounded by the rues des Minimes and de Turenne: Félibien, 5:26; B.N. Ms. fr. 18159 f431, 10 Nov. 1594; A.N. Z1F/559 f109, Jan. 1610. Sully sold the land for 7,500 *livres* in 1600 to Louis de l'Hospital, marquis de Vitry, who built an hôtel which is seen on Nicolay's map: Min. cent. III 462bis, 23 Jan. 1600. In 1603, the king gave Estienne Prevost, violinist in the king's chamber, 61 square *toises* on the east side of the rue des

Tournelles; Prevost subdivided the land and sold the parcels for approximately 7 *livres* per square *toise.* All but one of the fourteen buyers were craftsmen; they included three masons involved in construction of the silkworks — Guillaume Pingard, Balthazar Monnard, and Jean Poussard. The documents do not disclose why Prevost received this gift of land: Min. cent. CV 292, 24 March, 3, 10, 22, 23, 28 April, 14 May 1604; CV 293, 29, 30 July, 3, 4, 7 Aug. 1604. The royal donation to the silk partners in 1605 thus formed part of a broader effort to develop the parc des Tournelles.

30. The property given to the silk entrepreneurs was delimited by four streets projected in 1564: to the north, a street 6 *toises* wide bordering the Hôtel de Vitry (now the rue des Minimes); to the east, a street aligned with the rue des Tournelles "which is to be built to the ramparts"; to the south (today the north side of the Place des Vosges), "the site marked for the rue d'Anjou . . . running from the couture Sainte Catherine"; and to the west, a street along the open sewer, now the rue de Turenne. Measurement of the site, 10 March 1604: A.N. Q1/1234; A.N. X1A/8645 f154–155v; A.P. H.D. 60.350.

31. Report of the Treasurers of France, 24 March 1604: A.N. Q1/1234; A.N. X1A/8645 f154–155v; A.P. H.D. 60.350.

32. Min. cent. CVIII 34bis f316, 2 Sept. 1604.

33. The only information we have about the distribution of the silk buildings comes from a document postdating construction of the Place Royale. It refers to silk buildings "aux bouts de lad. place Royalle"; in other words, silk buildings remained standing beyond the 72 *toises* occupied by the Place Royale pavilions: Min. cent. XC 168, 2 Oct. 1608; A.P. H.D. 60.350. Do the silk buildings at the far corners of the site tell us anything about the plans of the silk partners in 1605? If twelve houses (each 3½ × 14–15 *toises*) and the pavilion (4 × 5 *toises*) were built side by side, with the short side of the houses facing the street, the buildings would have spanned only 46–47 *toises.* But if the full complement of twenty houses were built side by side, they would have formed a street wall 74–75 *toises* long. Perhaps the silk partners had a long-term plan to construct buildings across the full length of their property. No views of the silk buildings have been found. They were depicted on a woodcut map from 1604/5 (now lost), described by Bonnardot in 1851; he saw two long buildings running east-west at the

parc des Tournelles which were captioned "Batiments pour les soyes": Alfred Bonnardot, *Etudes archéologiques sur les anciens plans de Paris des XVIe, XVIIe, et XVIIIe siècles* (Paris: 1851), 73–75.

34. "[L]a grande maison des moulins à soye . . . contenant icelle 18 toises de face de longueur avec les bastimens en esquerre, court, puits, et issue sur la rue neufve du costé du rampart": Min. cent. XC 168, 2 Oct. 1608; A.P. H.D. 60.350.

35. Laffemas, *Recueil de l'Assemblée du commerce,* 222. Laffemas boasted that the king had commissioned "le dessein de la plus belle maison qui soit en l'Europe audit Paris pour les manufactures": *Le Naturel et profit admirable du meurier* (Paris: 1604), 17. According to Palma-Cayet, the king began in early 1605 "un superbe bastiment au parc des Tournelles près la porte St. Anthoine pour loger les ouvriers des manufactures des soyes": *Chronologie Septenaire,* 283. He can only be referring to the *maison des moulins* because the Place Royale pavilions had not yet been begun. Sully passed a carpentry contract with the carpenter Charles Marchant on 1 July 1606 for "ouvraiges de charpenterie d'eschaffaux, escalliers et porticques à faire en la court et place du logis des Manufactures . . . de la longueur de 90 toises de long et 45 de large, revenant le tout à 370 toises . . .": Mallevoüe, 263. These measurements confirm that the ceremony was not planned for the Place Royale, which was already laid out as a 72 *toises* square. Because of a plague epidemic, the king instructed Sully to transfer the baptismal celebrations from "la place des Manufactures" to Fontainebleau, in a letter dated 23 July 1606: Sully, *Oeconomies royales,* ed. Michaud and Poujoulat, 2:162.

36. The earliest apprenticeship contract thus far uncovered is dated 31 March 1605: Min. cent. CXII 251. Many more apprenticeship contracts were passed between 1606 and 1611: Min. cent. CV 295, 300; CXII 253, 258, 260–62; CXV 15–20. During July 1606, one notary witnessed no less than nine apprenticeship contracts (Min. cent. CXV 15). These documents identify a sizable community of silk artisans, spinners, and gold-beaters, mostly Milanese, who lived in the parc des Tournelles and worked at the silkworks.

37. Complaint against Turato, "soy disant maistre batteur d'or à la façon de Milan," for mismanagement: A.N. E12B f98, 15 March 1607; Min. cent. CXII 254, 23 April 1607.

Contract passed by Sainctot and his associates with Pestalossi: Min. cent. CXII 255, 24 July 1607.

38. The silk partners made an account of their debts on 29 December 1610 (Min. cent. XC 170), when they liquidated their partnership. This document provides considerable information about the financial organization of the enterprise. Financial transactions with the crown are summarized in A.N. S 6148, liasse 6, 31 Oct. 1671. The crown financed the royal subsidy with proceeds from the *Ferme des gabelles du Lyonnais, Forest, et Beaujolais,* a tax farm held by Guillaume de Balme; the silk partners acknowledged receipt of the subsidy on 10 December 1613. I found no receipts for repayment of the 150,000 *livres* loaned by the crown; the investors may eventually have been excused from repaying the debt.

39. "Mon amy, ceste-cy sera pour vous prier de vous souvenir de ce dont nous parlasmes dernierement ensemble, de cette place que je veux que l'on fasse devant le logis qui se fait au marché aux chevaux pour les manufactures, afin que si vous n'y avez esté vous alliez pour la faire marquer; car baillant le reste des autres places a cens et rente pour bastir, c'est sans doute qu'elles le seront incontinent, et je vous prie de m'en mander les nouvelles": Sully, *Oeconomies royales,* ed. Michaud and Poujoulat, 2:26.

40. *Lettres missives* 6:442, 29 May 1605.

41. "Ayant diliberé pour la commodité et l'ornement de nostre bonne ville de Paris, d'y faire une grande place bastye de quatre costés, laquelle puisse estre propre pour ayder à establir les manufactures des draps de soye, et loger les ouvriers que nous voulons attirer en ce royaume, le plus qu'il se pourra, et par mesme moyen puisse servir de proumenoir aux habitants de nostre ville, lesquelz sont fort pressez en leurs maisons à cause de la multitude du peuple qui y afflue de tous costés, comme aussi aux jours de resjouissance lorsqu'il se fait de grandes assemblees, et à plusieurs autres occasions qui se rencontrent auxquelles telles places sont du tout necessaires, Nous avons resolu en nostre conseil . . . de destiner à cest effet le lieu à present appelé le Marché-aux-Chevaulx, anciennement le parc des Tournelles, et que nous voullons estre doresnavant nommé la place Royalle . . ." A.N. X1A/8645 f284.

42. *Délibérations de la Commission du commerce,* 262–63, 5 Oct. 1604.

43. Carew, "State of France," 434. Contracts with four master gold-beaters—three Italians and one Frenchman—passed by Lumague in 1610 shed light on the wages paid to the silk artisans: Min. cent. CXII 260, 3, 4 March 1610. The highest wage, which went to the Frenchman, was 9 *livres* per week plus 90 *livres* per year, while the best-paid Italian received 8 *livres* per week (after a lower salary for the first eighteen months) plus 45 *livres* a year. They were all given free lodgings. In addition to free housing, the director of the silkworks, Pestalossi, was given a base annual salary of 1,000 *livres* plus compensation relating to the amount and type of cloth produced: Min. cent. CXII 255, 24 July 1607.

44. On the sixteenth-century *lotissements:* Françoise Boudon, "Paris: architecture mineure et lotissements au milieu du XVIe siècle," *La Maison de ville à la Renaissance,* ed. A. Chastel and J. Guillaume (Paris: 1983), 25–29; J.-P. Babelon, "Paris: un quartier residentiel, la couture Sainte-Catherine durant la seconde moitié du XVIe siècle," *La Maison de ville,* 31–35; idem, "De l'hôtel d'Albret à l'hôtel d'O. Etude topographique d'une partie de la Culture Sainte-Catherine," *BSHP* 97 (1970): 87–145; Maurice Dumolin, "Le lotissement de la Culture Sainte-Catherine et l'hôtel Carnavalet," *Etudes de topographie parisienne,* vol. 3 (Paris: 1931), 289–392; Léon Mirot, "La formation et le démembrement de l'hôtel Saint-Pol," *La Cité* 60 (Oct. 1916): 269–319.

45. The design of the bridge is attributed to Fra Giocondo. Miron Mislin, "Paris, Ile de la Cité: die Uberbauten Brucken," *Storia della città* 17 (Oct. 1980): 11–36.

46. "[Nous] avons fait marquer une grande place vis-à-vis du logis qui a esté basty depuis peu par les entrepreneurs des manufactures, contenant 72 thoises en carré . . . [et nous] avons baillé les places . . . au tour dud. carré . . . à ceux qui se sont presentez pour y bastir selon nostre desseing, et pour cest effect leur avons delaissé lesd. places . . . à la charge . . . de bastir sur la face desd. places chacun un pavillon ayant la muraille de devant de pierre de taille et de bricque, ouverte en arcades et des galleries au dessoubz avec des bouticques pour la commodité des marchandises selon le plan et les elevations qui en ont esté figurés, tellement que les trois costez qui sont à faire pour la tour de lad. place devant led. logis des manufactures soient tous bastiz d'une mesme cimettrie pour

la decoration de nostred. ville . . ." A.N. X₁A/8645 f284. Excerpts from the documents in A.N. X₁A/8645 f266v–285v were published by Lambeau, "Communication relative à la place Royale," *CVP*, 25 Jan. 1908: 19–31.

47. The stipulation reads as follows: "la charge de faire bastir par led. sieur achepteur, sur la face de lad. place, ung pavillon couvert d'ardoise ayant des arcades et une gallerie au dessoubs avec des bouticques ouvertes dans lad. gallerie, ayant led. pavillon la muraille estant sur lad. place Royale de pierre de taille et de bricque selon le desseing qui en a esté dressé par commandement de Sa Majesté." This language was included in all the land deeds: Min. cent. III 462ter; published by Mallevoüe, 27–47.

48. Josiane Sartre, *Châteaux "brique et pierre" en France* (Paris: 1981). Babelon, "Découverte de la 'maison Jacques Coeur' dans l'ancienne rue de l'Homme-Armé, 38 à 42, rue des Archives. Place de cet édifice dans l'architecture parisienne de brique et pierre," *CVP*, 1971: 10–26.

49. Catherine Grodecki, "La Construction du château de Wideville et sa place dans l'architecture française du dernier quart du XVIème siècle," *Bulletin Monumental* 136/2 (1978): 135–75. E.-J. Ciprut, "Documents inédits sur quelques châteaux d'Ile-de-France (XVIe–XVIIe s.)," *MSHP* 16–17 (1965–66): 137–43.

50. The development of the French hôtel in the sixteenth century is discussed by Babelon, "Du 'Grand Ferrare' à Carnavalet. Naissance de l'hôtel classique," *Revue de l'Art* 40–41 (1978): 83–108; idem, "Sur trois hôtels du Marais à Paris datant du règne d'Henri III," *Bulletin Monumental* 135/3 (1977): 223–30; idem, "Les hôtels de Sandreville, d'Alméras et de Poussepin," *BSHP* 99–100 (1972–73): 63–107; idem, "Hôtel de Savoury, rue Elzevir 4," *CVP*, March 1971: 35–51; Myra Nan Rosenfeld, "The Hôtel de Cluny and the Sources of the French Renaissance Urban Palace, 1350–1500," Ph.D. diss., Harvard University, 1971; Babelon, "L'Hôtel de Mayenne, 21 r. St-Antoine, 4e," *CVP*, December 1970: 16–35; François-Charles James, "L'Hôtel de Mayenne avant son acquisition par Charles de Lorraine," *BSHP* 97 (1970): 43–85.

51. Philibert Delorme, *Le Premier Tome de l'Architecture* (Paris: 1567) Livre VIII, Chap. XVII, f253r. Delorme's acquisition of the lot

is documented in Mirot, "Hôtel Saint-Pol," 313–16.

52. On French medieval squares: Alain Lauret et al., *Bastides. Villes nouvelles du Moyen-Age* (Toulouse: 1988); Françoise Divorne et al., *Les Bastides d'Aquitaine, du Bas-Languedoc et du Béarn* (Brussels: 1985); Jacques Le Goff, ed., *La Ville médiévale*, Histoire de la France urbaine, vol. 2 (Paris: 1980); Charles Higounet, *Paysages et villages neufs du Moyen Age* (Bordeaux: 1975); Pierre Lavedan and Jeanne Hugueney, *L'Urbanisme au Moyen Age* (Geneva: 1974).

53. Wolfgang Lotz, "Sixteenth-Century Italian Squares," "The Piazza Ducale in Vigevano," in *Studies in Italian Renaissance Architecture* (Cambridge, Ma.: 1977), 74–139. Alberti and Palladio made two further recommendations that the Place Royale failed to satisfy: a public square should be rectangular, following the Roman practice, and the height of the buildings should be between ⅓ and ⅔ the width of the square. The Place Royale buildings were 11 *toises* tall and the square 72 *toises* wide, yielding a ratio of 1:6.5.

54. There are two manuscript versions of Serlio's sixth book, one in Avery Library at Columbia University, the other in the Bayerische Staatsbibliothek in Munich. Serlio probably sold both manuscripts to Jacopo Strada, who in turn sold them by 1576. The Munich version does not concern us because it entered the collection of Duke Albert V of Bavaria and thereafter remained in Germany. The Avery version seems to have remained in France throughout the seventeenth century, although we do not know who bought it from Strada. In 1673, François Blondel referred to Serlio's manuscript: "Il y a un livre de luy qui traite des bastimens des particuliers, à commencer depuis la cabane de berger jusqu'aux palais du Roy, lequel n'a jamais été imprimé, quoyqu'il pû être de quelque utilité": Louis Savot, *L'Architecture françoise de bastiments particuliers*, ed. F. Blondel (Paris: 1673), 345; I would like to thank Claude Mignot for bringing this passage to my attention. Mignot has also informed me that, in the unpublished opinion of F. Ch. Jammes, the handwriting of Jacques Androuet Ducerceau appears on the Avery manuscript. Relying on this opinion, Mignot hypothesized that Serlio's manuscript passed from Ducerceau to his nephew Salomon de Brosse, but there is no hard evidence to support this speculation; see Pierre Le Muet, *Manière de Bien*

Bastir with an Introduction by Claude Mignot (Paris: 1981), xii. According to the inventory of de Brosse's belongings made after his death, the architect owned "trois *livres* d'architecture couverts de parchemyn . . . ," but the titles are not stated: Rosalys Coope, *Salomon de Brosse and the Development of the Classical Style in French Architecture from 1565 to 1630* (University Park, Pa.: 1972), 15. On the provenance of the Avery manuscript, also see: Rosenfeld, "Introduction," in Sebastiano Serlio, *On Domestic Architecture* (New York: 1978), 27–28; William Bell Dinsmoor, "The Literary Remains of Sebastiano Serlio," *Art Bulletin* 24 (1942): 55–91.

55. On Serlio and French bourgeois housing: Michele Humbert, "Serlio: il sesto libro e l'architettura borghese in Francia," *Storia dell'arte* 43 (1981): 199–240; Marco Rosci, *Il trattato di architettura di Sebastiano Serlio* (Milan: 1967), 80; Martin Huber, "Sebastiano Serlio: sur une architecture civile alla parisiana," *L'Information d'Histoire de l'Art,* 1965: 9–17; Pierre Du Colombier and Pierre D'Espezel, "L'Habitation au XVIe siècle d'après le sixième livre de Serlio," *Humanisme et Renaissance* 1 (1934): 31–49. Serlio's seventh book included a design for "una loggia da mercanti per negotiare" with a top floor of dormer windows, and he commented "sopra l'ultime cornice saranno habitationi al costume di Francia": *Il settimo libro d'architettura* (Frankfurt: 1575), chap. 73, 194.

56. The masonry and carpentry contracts for the King's Pavilion are published in Mallevoüe, 158–62. Sully itemized the building expenses as follows: masonry, 23,142 *livres;* carpentry, 6,237 *livres;* roofing, 2,300 *livres;* metalwork, joinery, and glazing, 1,000 *livres:* A.N. 120 AP 49, Liasse des ponts et chaussées pour l'année 1607, f29, "Conte arresté pour la despence du pavillon du roy à la place roialle. 1607." The charge of concierge was assigned to de Court by letters of commission published in A. de Montaiglon, "Jean et Charles de Court, peintres du roi," in *Archives de l'art français, Documents,* VI (Paris: 1858), 81–88, and in Lambeau, "Communication sur la place des Voges," *CVP,* 18 Dec. 1902: 289–90. The crown sold the pavilion in 1674 for 8,800 *livres:* A.N. Q1/1234, 10 May 1674.

57. The middle window of the first floor originally had a broken pediment. The bust of Henri IV was added at a later date.

58. Whitman, "Fontainebleau, the Luxembourg, and the French Domed Entry Pavilion," *JSAH* 46/4 (1987), 356–73.

59. According to a list of expenses incurred for the Place Royale in 1605, the crown spent 26,235 *livres* to demolish houses and compensate their owners: A.N. 120 AP 49 f254, Ponts et chaussées, 1607. Most, if not all, of these indemnities were for the rue Birague. An additional payment of 4,750 *livres* was allocated on 24 July 1607 to Jean de Trillart, who owned property on the rue Birague: A.N. E14A f109. The following year, he entered into construction contracts to rebuild his house on the street: Min. cent. CV 300, 26–27 March 1608.

60. For the reasons discussed in Chapter 1, it is not yet possible to evaluate the styles of Ducerceau and Métezeau. Nonetheless, Hautecoeur and Lavedan attributed the Place Royale to Métezeau based on its similarities to the Place Ducale in Charleville, which Métezeau's younger brother Clément designed in 1608. There were important political and symbolic reasons why Clément would have used the Parisian square as his model, whether or not it was designed by his brother. In any event, it does not follow from the formal similarities of the squares that they were designed by brothers. Lacking sufficient formal evidence to attribute the square to either man alone, Blunt and Babelon prudently suggested that the two royal architects collaborated on the project. Pierre Lavedan, *Histoire de l'urbanisme à Paris* (Paris: 1975), 232; Louis Hautecoeur, *Histoire de l'architecture classique en France,* 2nd ed., t. 1, pt. 3, *L'Architecture sous Henri IV et Louis XIII* (Paris: 1966), 300; Anthony Blunt, *Art and Architecture in France 1500 to 1700,* 4th rev. ed. (New York: 1986), 160; J.-P. Babelon, "L'urbanisme d'Henri IV et de Sully à Paris," *L'Urbanisme de Paris et l'Europe 1600–1680,* ed. Pierre Francastel (Paris: 1969), 57. The Place Royale is also attributed to Louis Métezeau by Emile Baudson, *Un urbaniste au XVIIe siècle, Clément Métezeau architecte du roi,* Cahiers d'Etudes ardennaises 1 (Mézières: 1956); idem, "La place Royale de Paris et la place ducale de Charleville," *BSHAF,* 1935: 204–21.

61. Ulf Johnsson, *Le Marais, Place Vendôme, les Invalides. Dessins d'architecture des XVIIe et XVIIIe siècles provenant des collections du Nationalmuseum de Stockholm,* Centre Culturel Suédois, Paris (Paris: 1972), 9.

62. Coope, *Salomon de Brosse,* 252.

63. Both Babelon and Ulf Johnsson state that the drawing dates from 1605, but they offer no supporting evidence: Babelon, "Le palais des Tournelles," 710; Johnsson, *Le Marais,* 9.

64. "Cesar et Henry ont esté grands architectes pour embellir de beaux edifices leurs villes. L'un fit bastir dans Rome un theatre somptueux pour le plaisir public: Et l'autre la Place Royalle dans Paris, pour y faire travailler toutes sortes d'artisans": Bandole, *Les Paralleles de Cesar et de Henry IIII* (Paris: [1609]), 115.

65. "Pour le regard de l'opposition que le sieur de Montmagny a faite lorsque vous aves esté apres a faire tirer les fondemens pour les maisons qu'il faut faire bastir au marché aux chevaulx, je suis d'advis que vous luy en partiés de ma part, et qu'estant une chose que j'affectionne pour l'ornement et embellissement de ma ville de Paris, il ne s'y devroit opposer; au pis aller, en luy payant la terre que l'on est constraint de prendre dans son jardin, et luy dire qu'estant une oeuvre publique on luy pourroit mesme contrainre a la vendre, non a son mot, mais comme il seroit jugé juste": *Lettres missives* 6:439, 27 May 1605.

66. By the terms of an agreement concluded on 23 January 1607, de Montmagny was paid 20,110 *livres* for 1,293½ square *toises* of land, a rate of 15½ *livres* per square *toise*: A.N. S 1025; E12A f18, 16 Jan. 1607. The price of land at the square is given below in the text. Two other parties were indemnified: the Remy Royer family and the priory of Ste. Catherine du Val des Ecoliers. The heirs of Remy Royer sold the crown 310 square *toises* of land with a house and its dependencies for 15,500 *livres* on 10 March 1607: A.N. X1A/8646 f28v – 32. In exchange for their land at the Place Royale, the priory accepted 8½ *arpents* between the rues Française, Pavée, Montorgueil, and Mauconseil: A.N. S 1025, 4 July 1615; A.N. E24A f25, f33, 6 Oct., 3 Dec. 1609. A drawing in A.N. S 1025 made between 1606 and 1615 depicts the territory on the west side of the square over which the priory claimed seignorial rights.

67. Pierre Fougeu, Noël Regnouart, Claude Chastillon, Hilaire Lhoste, and Daniel de Massy, all recipients of land at the Place Royale, were involved in the construction of Henrichemont: Rosalys Coope and Catherine Grodecki, "La création d'Henrichemont par Sully (1608 – 1612)," *Cahiers d'archéologie et d'histoire du Berry* 41 (June 1975): 21 – 48.

68. At the low end of the range, Daniel de Massy, Lieutenant at the Bastille, sold approximately 198 square *toises* for 850 *livres:* Min. cent. III 462ter, 3 Jan. 1606. At the high end was the sale by Jacques Bouhier, *maître d'hôtel du Roi*, of 176 square *toises* for 1,200 *livres:* Min. cent.

LXVIII 86, 8 and 23 July 1606. Etienne Prevost sold land on rue des Tournelles in 1604 for 7 *livres* per square *toise; see* note 29.

69. The dimensions of various lots in *toises* (t) and *pieds*(') compare as follows:

LOT	WIDTH	LENGTH
Place Dauphine	4t	4 – 8t
Serlio House K	6t 4'	14½t
Serlio House I	7t	17t
House of Philibert Delorme	6t 4'	27½t
Place Royale	8t	22 – 32t
Forecourt only		
Hôtel Carnavalet (16th century)	9t	10t
Hôtel du Grand Ferrare	17t	22t

70. The one-and-a-half-pavilion parcels were owned by Pierre Castille, *Maître des requêtes;* Antoine Ribauld, *Intendant des finances;* Philippe Collanges, *Secrétaire du Roi;* Nicolas Le Gras, *Trésorier général de Paris;* and Charles Marchant, who owned two such plots. The two-pavilion parcels were owned by Pierre Fougeu and Jean Péricard, *Conseiller du Roi.*

71. A.N. E14A f63r, 17 July 1607.

72. Min. cent. XIX 354, 12 Aug., 27 Dec. 1605.

73. The crown spent approximately 13,000 *livres* to compensate property owners for the extension of the port St. Paul: A.N. E7A f318, 21 Aug. 1604; A.N. E11B f187, 19 Aug. 1606; A.N. 120 AP 38 f4, 1605; A.N. 120 AP39 f8, 1606. Expulsion of the horse market: A.N. E11B 87, 8 Aug. 1606.

74. Public Record Office, London SP 78/52 f73, 16 March 1605. Mathew's description was first published by David Buisseret, *Henry IV* (London: 1984), 128 – 29.

75. "J'ay appris par le controlleur [général des bâtiments Jean de] Donon qu'il se trouvoit quelque difficulté avec les entrepreneurs des manufactures, pour ce qu'ils vouloient abattre tout le logis. Ce n'est pas mon advis et me semble que ce seroit assez qu'ils fissent une de galerie devant, qui auroit la face de mesme que le reste": *Lettres missives* 7:203, 27 April 1607.

76. Paul Deyon, "Manufacturing Industries in Seventeenth-Century France," *Louis XIV and Absolutism,* ed. Ragnhild Hatton (Columbus, Ohio: 1976), 241.

77. Babelon found only one example of an hôtel with shops built during the first half of the

seventeenth century, the hôtel of François de Chabannes on the rue St. Honoré in 1617: *Demeures parisiennes sous Henri IV et Louis XIII* (Paris: 1977), 90.

78. In December 1607, Pierre Fougeu d'Escures had his mason Jonas Robelin undertake "le bouchement faict après coup des quatre arcades du costé du passage de la gallerye": BHVP Ms. C.P. 3365, Toisé de maçonnerie, 10 Dec. 1607.

79. Dallington, *The View of Fraunce* (London: 1604; reprint, London: 1936), Q1v.

80. An agreement passed by the entrepreneurs on 2 October 1608 refers to the edict issued·by the Conseil d'Etat in April 1607 calling for the destruction of the silkworks. This edict has not been found, and in the index of acts passed by the Conseil d'Etat during Henri IV's reign, there is a gap between 31 March and 10 May 1607: Noël Valois, *Inventaire des arrêts du Conseil d'Estat de Règne de Henri IV*, vol. 2 (Paris: 1893).

81. "Devis des pavillons qu'il convient construire en la place Royalle en la partye de Septentrion au lieu ou maintenant est basty le corps de logis des Manufactures et sur le mesme allignement . . .": A.N. 120 AP 49 f31–33, Liasse des ponts et chaussées pour l'année 1607, Voirie 1607. This document is published in Appendix A2a.

82. "Tous lesquelz neuf pavillons sur leurs allignemens contiendront ensemble pareille longueur que les neuf aultres qui leur sont directement opposez en ladicte partye de Midy. Savoir en tout la quantité de soixante et douze toises, longueur et largeur, bornée pour la quadrature de ladicte place, et dont les deux extremitez desdictz neuf pavillons à bastir doibvent se rapporter justement et à l'eraze des pavillons à present ja bastiz de partye d'orient que d'occident pour fournir l'angle droict": A.N. 120 AP 49 f31. See Appendix A2a.

83. ". . . une gallerye d'arcades publique et commune pour aller à couvert soubz iceulx . . .": A.N. 120 AP 49 f31. See Appendix A2a.

84. Babelon incorrectly assumed that the corner entry pavilions were planned from the start: "Le palais des Tournelles," 707. The entry pavilion or *guichet* at the northwest corner was planned but not yet built by 1630; this is made clear when Lumague and his wife sold their pavilion at the west end of the north range and ceded "tout et tel droit qu'ils peuvent avoir aux voultes qui doibvent estre faictes aux despens de Sa Majesté à l'entree de lad. Place Royalle pour l'arcade qui joindra à lad. maison": Min. cent. CXII 299, 22 Aug. 1630. There are now three additional bays at the east end of the north range which must have been built following the destruction of the *guichet* in 1822. There is one additional bay at the west end of the north range which was built by 1702, when it appears on the *terrier* plan (Fig. 73).

85. Min. cent. XC 168, 2 Oct. 1608; Min. cent. LXXXVI 185, 8 Jan. 1609. Both contracts are copied in A.P. H.D. 60.350 (hereafter Partage). Moisset, the largest investor, was given the axial pavilion and the six adjoining bays to the east. Sainctot and the Parfaict brothers were each given a pavilion and a half, leaving Camus and Lumague with one pavilion each at either end of the range. To compensate for their smaller share, they were allocated the residue of land extending beyond the end pavilion. On the land between Lumague's pavilion at the west end of the north range and the rue de l'Egout (rue de Turenne) were two houses, which Lumague owned and which may have been built in 1604 as part of the silkworks: Min. cent. CXVII 258, 10 Jan. 1609. I did not find any documents concerning Camus's construction on his property at the east end of the north range.

86. Carpentry contract, Min. cent. CVIII 37 f79, 28 Feb. 1608. Masonry contract with Balthazar Monnard, Min. cent. CVIII 37, 8 March 1608. A few days later, Monnard hired a bargeman to deliver a minimum of 15 cubic *toises* of rubble to the building site every week for the price of 13 *livres* per cubic *toise*: Min. cent. CV 300, 19 March 1608. The rubble was probably used for the foundations and walls of the pavilions. Balthazar Monnard was the uncle of mason Claude Monnard, contractor of the Collège de France. Among the witnesses at Claude Monnard's wedding in 1609 was Claude Parfaict which suggests that there were close ties between the Monnard family and Parfaict: Min. cent. CVIII 39 f213, 13 May 1609.

87. Min. cent. XC 170, 29 Dec. 1610.

88. Contract with Pestalossi, Min. cent. XC 169, 26 March 1609. Pestalossi fulfilled the agreement, at least in part, by hiring four women living in Lyon, relatives of a silk artisan employed at the Place Royale. They agreed to work in the *maison des moulins* for five and a half years: Min. cent. CVX 20, 14 June 1609.

89. Sainctot, Camus, Lumague, and the Parfaict

brothers jointly hired Balthazar Monnard to build the seven houses on the rue du Foin. This contract, which I did not find, is mentioned in the land division of January 1609. Monnard subcontracted the work to masons Jean Langevin and Thomas Bourdon. In May 1608, Langevin and Bourdon in turn hired a mason to undertake minor construction "en la place Royale du costé de M. de Vitry [rue des Minimes] en trois logis des manufactures d'or, d'argent et soye" and agreed to pay him at the same rate they were being paid by Monnard: Min. cent. CXV 18, 16 May 1608. Two months later, Langevin and Bourdon hired a journeyman mason, Jean Corberon, to undertake "touttes et chacunes les ouvrages de massonnerye qu'il convient faire en une maison scize a la place Roialle appellee la maison des manufactures d'or, d'argent et soie": Min. cent. XXVI 28, 28 July 1608. On the block west of the rue de Béarn, three houses were built by October 1608, and on the block east of the rue de Béarn, four houses were under construction in January 1609. The documents do not indicate whether the crown or the land owners paid for laying in the new streets.

90. The land division of January 1609 named three silk craftsmen (two of whom were certainly Italian) who were living in three of the new houses. The owners equipped the houses with the tools needed for spinning silk cloth and even advanced the artisans money to start up their workshops. The owners, however, only turned part of the houses over to silk workers and rented the courtyards, rooms, or entire wings of the houses to paying tenants. Leases for the houses on the rue des Minimes entered into by the entrepreneurs with silk artisans and other tenants are listed in App. A5; one lease is published in App. A6.

91. In 1610–11, Lumague hired six master gold-beaters, five of whom were Italian; he gave them free lodgings and required them to engage French apprentices: Min. cent. CXII 260, 3, 4 March 1610; CXII 261, 12 July, 15 Nov. 1611; CXII 262, 7 April 1611. In 1611, Lumague declared that he had sold 100 *marcs* of threaded gold and 36 *marcs* of threaded silver to a merchant in Rouen, "lesquels or et argent estoit fabriqué à Paris en la fabrique dud. sieur Lumague": Min. cent. CXII 262, 16 May 1611. A dispute with a client over the terms of a sale also proves that Lumague continued to manufacture silk, gold, and silver cloth: Min. cent. CXII 260, 30 April 1610.

There was, however, some suspicion among rival merchants that Lumague and his associates were selling illicit, imported cloths and not goods of their own manufacture: *Registres* 15:161, 23 July 1612. This suspicion may have arisen because Lumague was commissioned by the king in 1610 to purchase 300,000 *livres* worth of precious cloths for the festivities in honor of the queen's coronation. In 1615, Lumague appealed to the crown for permission to continue selling these cloths in addition to the inventory of the *manufactures* without forfeiting his title of nobility: A.N. X1A/ 8648 f288, 6 Aug. 1615.

92. Montchrétien also wrote that Henri IV's program might have met with greater success "if those to whom His Majesty entrusted the conduct of his business had seconded him with a judgement equal to his affection": cited by Cole, *French Mercantilist Doctrine Before Colbert* (New York: 1931), 130–31. It is generally believed that Montchrétien was referring to Sully, who detailed his opposition to the silk venture in his memoirs: *Oeconomies royales,* ed. Michaud and Poujoulat, 1:514–16. But Sully's memoirs are unreliable, and there is contemporary evidence that Sully supported the silk program. In 1604, the sericulture campaign was centered in Poitiers because Sully, the governor of the region, lent his support to the enterprise.

93. A.N. E14A f63, 17 July 1607.

94. Another craftsman who had multiple jobs at the Place Royale was carpenter Jean Vivier. He was hired by the silk partners to dismantle the workshops and then hired by Lumague, Sainctot, and Claude Parfaict to build their houses: Min. cent. CVIII 37, 19 May, 8 Nov. 1608. These contracts instructed Vivier to use the wood from the construction site of the Hôpital St. Louis. The arrangement was probably made by Sainctot who in his capacity as governor of the Hôtel Dieu was overseeing construction of the new hospital. It indicates that the extensive construction in Henri IV's Paris provoked some large-scale organization of the supply of materials.

95. Projects to remodel several hôtels later in the seventeenth century are discussed in A. Braham and P. Smith, *François Mansart,* 2 vols. (London: 1973), 1:223, 269; Babelon, *Demeures parisiennes,* passim; idem, "L'hôtel de Chaulnes, 9, place des Vosges," *CVP,* 1968–69: 19–30; Maurice Dumolin, "Les Propriétaires de la place Royale (1605–1789)," *La Cité,* July–Oct. 1925: 273–316, April 1926:

1–30; and in the articles by Lambeau.

96. Fougeu held the following offices: *Lieutenant général sur le fait des rivières; Intendant des levées et turcies des rivières de Loire, Cher et Allier;* and *Maréchal des logis des armées du Roy.* He was also assigned by Sully to review a proposal to link the Seine and Loire rivers. Fougeu's career and architectural patronage are addressed by Catherine Grodecki, "L'architecture en Berry sous le règne de Henri IV," *Mémoires de l'Union des Sociétés savantes de Bourges* 3 (1951–52): 77–131; David Buisseret, "A Stage in the Development of the French Intendants: The Reign of Henry IV," *The Historical Journal,* 9/1 (1966): 33–34; G. Baguenault de Puchesse, "Pierre Fougeu d'Escures," *Mémoires de la société archéologique et historique de l'Orléanais* 34 (1913): 7–59.

97. Masonry contract with Jonas Robelin, Min. cent. XXXIX 38 f223, 17 March 1606. The rear block was built at a later date; the contract for it has not been found. The total cost of construction is disclosed in an inventory of documents concerning Fougeu's house that mentions a "mémoire de ce qui a esté payé par d'Escures aux ouvriers qui ont travaillé en lad. maison, montant 23,711 livres tournois": BHVP Ms. C.P. 3365 f6. On Fougeu's one-pavilion house: BHVP Ms. C.P. 3365 f17v–29; Min. cent. 358, 10 March 1608.

98. Land donation, Min. cent. CXVII 469 f182, 10 March 1607.

99. Contract with Robelin for "le bouchement faict après coup des quatre arcades du costé du passage de la gallerye": BHVP Ms. C.P. 3365, Toisé de maçonnerie, 10 Dec. 1607. Sale to Phelypeaux: Min. cent. XIX 358, 10 March 1608; BHVP Ms. C.P. 3365 f63–65. Shortly after purchasing Fougeu's house, Phelypeaux rented a house on the quai St. Paul for 450 *livres,* half the rent he charged for his house at the Place Royale: Min. cent. XIX 362, 5 Oct. 1609. In 1617, the king allowed Phelypeaux to annex part of the Pavillon du Roi, and a year later he moved into his enlarged Place Royale house.

100. Fougeu raised a minimum of 36,700 *livres:* 25,500 *livres* from the sale of his first house at the square, 1,200 *livres* from the two lots sold to Pericard (Min. cent. CXVII 469 f235, 3 April 1607), and 10,000 *livres* from the sale of a house to Jean Coin (Min. cent. CXVII 470 f220, 26 April 1608). The contracts of sale with François de Lomenie and Charles Marchant do not state the price of the lots that

they bought from Fougeu (Min. cent. CXVII 469 f215, 23 March; f236, 4 April 1607). The building history of Fougeu's two-pavilion house remains largely undocumented and therefore the total cost of construction is unknown; only the contract for the stables has been found: Min. cent. CVIII 43 f56, 25 Feb. 1611. A description of the house is given in the sale contract: Min. cent. CXV 87, 7 March 1644. Assuming that it cost 50,000 *livres* to build the two-pavilion house, slightly more than twice the cost of his one-pavilion house, then a substantial share of the expenses was covered by his recent sales at the square.

101. Fougeu's will: Min. cent. CXII 37, 18 March 1641. Sale to the duc de Chaulnes: Min. cent. CXV 87, 7 March 1644. This hôtel occupies an L-shaped parcel (Fig. 74). The short stem of the L, amounting to 54 square *toises,* was acquired by the duc de Chaulnes on 5 September 1644 and was used for the service court and a garden: Min. cent. CXV 88. See also Babelon, "L'hôtel de Chaulnes," *CVP,* 1968–69: 19–30; Lucien Lambeau, "La Place Royale. L'Hôtel de Chaulnes et de Nicolay," *BSHP,* 1911: 49–72; idem, "La Place Royale: L'Hôtel de Chaulnes et de Nicolay," *La Cité,* Jan. 1916: 26–58.

102. Du Ry was instructed to complete the masonry work "in compliance with the four designs which have been made and given to the said du Ry," a formulation that indicates that he did not invent the designs: Min. cent. XC 172, 2 March 1612. Du Ry often acted as the contractor for his brother-in-law, Salomon de Brosse, which introduces the possibility that de Brosse was the designer of Moisset's house. The only noteworthy feature of the hôtel was the main stair, placed at the corner of the Queen's Pavilion and the wing on the rue de Béarn. Barrel-vaulted flights (*voustes rampans*) rising to groin-vaulted landings wrapped around a rectangular stairwell; the entire stair chamber was covered by a vault. It was one of the earliest instances of this type of stair in France, giving further cause to consider a possible role played by de Brosse, who designed a similar vaulted stairwell at Coulommiers in 1613. The masonry contract for the stair required the masons to "faire les palliers qui seront posees sur lesd. vouste d'arrestes pour parachevement dudit escalier jusques à la haulteur dudit premier estage du grand pavillon lequel sera couvert d'une vouste": Min. cent. XC 173, 15 May 1613. Other documents concerning the stair are

in Min. cent. XC 173, 4 and 11 Sept., 22 Oct. 1613. On the relationship between du Ry and de Brosse: Coope, *Salomon de Brosse,* 9, passim.

103. Monnard was hired by Marchant as well as by royal mason Jean Fontaine, who owned the adjoining lot. Monnard subcontracted both jobs by verbal agreement to a mason who began construction then let it out to two other masons: Min. cent. CV 300, 9 June 1608. Marchant's contract with Monnard has not been found. Marchant passed a joinery contract on 21 April 1608 with Jan van Laubych, *compagnon menuisier,* who was instructed to build the *porte cochère* "suivant le desseing fait par led. sieur Marchant" and otherwise to build as he, Laubych, had already done in other houses at the Place Royale: Min. cent. XIX 359 f130. Lease: Min. cent. CXVII 471 f366, 16 June 1609. For Fontaine, Monnard built a pavillon 8 *toises* wide by 5 *toises* deep with a double file of rooms. Behind it, he built a small pavillon and a short side wing. Fontaine's masonry contract with Monnard: Min. cent. CXVII 469 f477, 24 Aug. 1607.

104. I have not found any documents concerning Le Redde's acquisition of the site from de Fourcy. Le Redde sold a house on the rue de la Cerisaie and used the proceeds "à parachever le bastimens qu'ils ont entrepris faire en ung grand pavillon qu'ils ont fait construire et bastir tout à neuf au parc Royal autrement le parc des Tournelles": Min. cent. XIX 358 f361, 9 Nov. 1607. A.N. Q1/1099/34A, Declaration au papier terrier du roi, 20 Dec. 1703.

105. Two houses were sold by 1608: one by Fougeu and one by Jean Coin. Master mason Coin paid Daniel de Massy 850 *livres* for a lot on the south range, adjoining Fougeu's house: Min. cent. III 462ter, 3 Jan. 1606. No building contracts for Coin's house have been found. Upon completion, he sold it to Pierre Chastellain, a royal treasurer, for an undisclosed amount: Min. cent. CV 300, 22 March 1608. It is most likely that Coin built the house on speculation. Following the Place Royale sale, Coin paid 10,000 *livres* for a house on the rue St. Antoine near the Place Royale, where he lived until his death shortly before April 1614: Min. cent. CXVII 470 f220, 26 April 1608. Presumably the Place Royale sale financed this purchase. Coin's most noteworthy building projects were the Petite and Grande Galeries of the Louvre and the château of Coulommiers, where he

worked with de Brosse in 1613.

106. The land deed names Hilaire Lhoste as the recipient of the lot, but Lhoste was fronting for Arnauld, his brother-in-law, and later disclaimed any rights to the property: Min. cent. III 462ter, 4 June 1605, 21 Jan. 1608. Sale of stone to Arnauld, Min. cent. CV 295, 18 Oct. 1605. Mason's receipt for payment: Min. cent. CXV 18, 5 Jan. 1608. Sale: A.S. 4 AZ 1153, 14 April 1612.

107. Masonry contract with Robelin: Min. cent. CVIII 36 f203, 12 May 1607.

108. Lease: Min. cent. CVIII 43 f283, 2 Sept. 1611.

109. Fougeu's sale of two lots to Péricard: Min. cent. CXVII 469 f235, 3 April 1607. Construction contracts for roofing: Min. cent. CV 170, 1 June 1607; for joinery: Min. cent. CV 170, 13 June 1607; for metalwork: Min. cent. CV 171, 8 Aug. 1607; for plasterwork: Min. cent. CV 174, 13 June 1608; and for paving: Min. cent. CV 175, 21 July 1608. Lease: Min. cent. LXII 46, 25 Aug. 1610.

110. "Si Sa Majesté commande de louer les boutiques de lad. place Royalle pour y habiter marchans ou autres artisans, ou que les autres proprietaires des autres maisons de lad. place Royale louent les bouticques desd. autres maisons, en ces cas ou l'un deux, led. sieur bailleur pourra louer comme les autres les quatre bouticques qui sont des deppendances de lad. maison baillee à son proffict et comme non comprises au present bail à la charge que dans l'un desd. bouticques il laissera ung passage pour aller à lad. place Royalle": Min. cent. XIX 359 f56, 15 April 1608.

111. Chastillon's leases: Min. cent. CXVII 470 f431, 25 Aug. 1608; Min. cent. CV 316, 3 May 1614. Upon Chastillon's death in 1616, his heirs, all residing in Chaalons, immediately sold the property: Min. cent. XLV 22 f79, 21 Feb. 1617. It is possible that Fougeu made Orléans his primary residence at various points.

112. Marchant acted as the contractor, supplying the building materials to the workers he hired to undertake construction. He bought 24,000 pieces of slate for delivery to the port St. Paul in May 1607, for the price of 14 *livres* per thousand: Min. cent. XIX 357, 12 April 1607. He bought 100 cubic *toises* of rubble from a quarrier for delivery to the Place Royale in weekly installments of 5 cubic *toises,* for the price of 12 *livres* 10 sols per cubic *toise.* The next day the quarrier hired a bargeman to transport the stone to the port St. Paul and then haul it to the square for 46

sols per cubic *toise:* Min. cent. CXV 18, 24–25 Feb. 1608. Marchant often hired craftsmen to work on several sites. For example, on 4 April 1606, he hired masons to build a house in the Marais as well as the houses at the Place Royale: Min. cent. XIX 355. This contract proves that Marchant expected the land donation before he was actually given title in March 1607. In the following months, he passed contracts for roofing, carpentry, and joinery: Min. cent. XIX 357 f159, 17 May 1607; Min. cent. XIX 358 f311, 14 Sept.; f368, 13 Nov. 1607. Marchant agreed to provide the joiner with a workshop where the artisan could work with two assistants.

113. The only lease thus far uncovered was passed by Marchant's son in 1617 for the house at the north end of the west range for 1,200 *livres:* Min. cent. CVIII 54 f20, 13 Jan. 1617; f183, 14 June 1617.

114. Sainctot's will: Min. cent. LXXXVI 261, 27 May 1639. Sainctot owned two other houses in Paris, a seignorial estate, and other rural property, with a total value of 353,800 *livres.* The Place Royale house accounted for 22 percent of his investment in real estate.

115. Sale of Sainctot's house by his heirs: Min. cent. CVIII 87 f83, 26 March 1641.

116. Claude Parfaict sold the two houses on his Place Royale property for a total of 55,000 *livres:* Min. cent. CVIII 61 f205, 20 June 1620; Min. cent. CVIII 64(2) f166, 13 Aug. 1624. At the time of his death on 1 August 1623, Parfaict owned nine houses, seven of which he acquired as a result of participating in the royal silkworks: Min. cent. CVIII 64(2) f237, 13 Dec. 1624. The heirs of his brother Guillaume sold a six-bay house at the square in 1630 for 20,000 *livres* plus 2,500 *livres* of *rente:* Min. cent. CVIII 68(5) f139, 5 June 1630. I do not know the prices for which Camus, Lumague, and Moisset sold their houses.

117. Guillaume Parfaict's leases: Min. cent. CVIII 45 f223, 27 June 1612; Min. cent. CVIII 47 f183, 3 June 1613; Min. cent. CVIII 48 f135, 6 June 1614; Min. cent. CVIII 52 f203, 5 Oct. 1616; Min. cent. CVIII 52 f230, 4 Nov. 1616; Min. cent. CVIII 59 f159, 10 May 1619. On a lot six bays wide, Parfaict built one and a half pavilions with two side wings bordering a front court. There were stables along a rear court and a *porte cochère* on the rue du Foin. The rent was lowered for the first time in 1622 from 2,000 to 1,500 *livres* because the tenant was required to make various repairs: Min. cent. CVIII 62(4) f127, 22 April 1622.

118. Leases passed by Sainctot: Min. cent. LXXXVI 187, 22 Aug. 1611, 6 Sept. 1611; Min. cent. LXXXVI 225, 10 and 12 Feb. 1618. Although I did not find the building contracts for Sainctot's Place Royale houses, they are described in the leases and the sale contract: Min. cent. CVIII 87 f83, 26 March 1641.

119. ". . . lequel ayant esté basty . . . au milieu de la France, par les glorieux travaux de l'Hercule François Henry le Grand, La Reine Mere et Regente desire de le rendre plus durable que celuy quui fut jadis basty à Athene pour adorer la mesme Divinite; elle y employa le ciment de cette double Alliance qui sembloit devoir donner à l'Europe une paix eternelle, et une felicite parfaite": Marc de Vulson, sieur de La Colombière, *Le Vray theatre d'honneur et de chevalerie ou le miroir heroique de la noblesse,* 2 vols. (Paris: 1648), 1: chap. 24, not paginated. The celebration is also described by Honoré Laugier, *Le Camp de la Place Royalle* (Paris: 1612); François de Rosset, *Le Romant des chevaliers de la gloire* (Paris: 1612); Anonymous, *Le Carousel des pompes* (Paris: 1612); Anonymous, *Le Triomphe royale* (Paris: 1612); André Stegmann, "La Fête parisienne à la Place Royale en avril 1612," in *Les Fêtes de la Renaissance,* ed. Jean Jacquot and Elie Konigson, vol. 3 (Paris: 1975), 373–92.

120. Engravings by Crispin de Passe of men in armor playing chivalric games in the Place Royale illustrate Pluvinel's treatises on equitation: *Maneige royal* (Paris: 1623); *L'Instruction du Roy en l'exercise de monter à cheval* (Paris: 1625). On Pluvinel: Frances Yates, *The French Academies of the Sixteenth Century* (London: 1947), 277.

121. On the Minim convent: Odile Krakovitch, "Le couvent des Minimes de la Place-Royale," *MSHP* 30 (1979): 87–258. The Minims acquired the land from Louis de l'Hospital, sieur de Vitry: Min. cent. CXV 21, 27 Oct. 1609; A.N. S* 4300. The masonry contract stipulated that the vaults around the cloister were to be built like those at the Place Royale: A.N. S* 4293A, 2 Sept. 1611. Simon Le Gras, Pierre Sainctot, and the Parfaict brothers, "qui ont desiré assister lesd. relligieux en son bon oeuvre," attended the closing of the land sale: Min. cent. CXV 21, 24 Oct. 1609. The heirs of Captain Charles Marchant, his son Charles and his son-in-law Nicolas Le Jay, bought a chapel in the Minim church; they financed this purchase with the rent collected from the houses on the Pont aux Marchands: A.N. S* 4300.

122. On Mansart's project: Braham and Smith, *Mansart,* 1:111–15, 247–49; idem, "Mansart Studies V: The Church of the Minimes," *Burlington* 57/744 (March 1965): 123–32; E.-J. Ciprut, "Documents inédits sur l'ancienne église des Minimes de la Place Royale," *BSHAF,* 1954: 151–74.

123. Anatole de Montaiglon, *Notice sur l'ancienne statue équestre ouvrage de Daniello Ricciarelli et le Biard le fils elevée à Louis XIII en 1639 au milieu de la place Royale à Paris* (Paris: 1874); Sieur de Grenaille, *La Place Royale ou la statue dressée à Louis le Juste* (Paris: 1639).

Chapter 3: The Place Dauphine, Pont Neuf, and Rue Dauphine

1. "[Henri IV] . . . avoit faict faire le Parc-Royal a dessein qu'il deust servir de place de Change ou de Bourse; mais estant en un des coins de la ville et trop loin du Palais, où tous les Banquiers ont tousjours affaire à la sortie de la Court, qui est à l'heure du Change, il commença ceste année à faire bastir la place Dauphine à la pointe de l'Isle du Palais, et d'un lieu qui estoit comme inutile, en faire la plus belle et la plus utile place de Paris . . .": *Mercure françois* (Paris: 1608), 312v.

2. Mallevoüe, 23–24; Jean-Pierre Babelon, "Le site parisien de la place Dauphine sous Henri IV," *MSHP* 25 (1974): 136–37; idem, "Nouveaux documents sur la place Dauphine et ses abords," *CVP,* 7 March 1966: 32–43. Jacques de Brunhoff's posthumously published monograph, *La Place Dauphine et l'Ile de la Cité* (Paris: 1987), surveys the square from its origins to the present day. The author made the original discovery of Harlay's sale contracts, which Babelon published in 1966, but the book provides no further information about the creation of the square.

3. There are two essential sources for the history of the Pont Neuf: building documents from November 1577 to October 1578 (Bibliothèque de l'Institut de France ms. 282) which were published by R. de Lasteyrie, "Documents inédits sur la construction du Pont-Neuf," *MSHP* 9 (1882): 1–94; and minutes of the building commission from October 1578 through 1605 which are recorded in a manuscript notebook entitled "Plumitif concernant le Pont Neuf, 1578–1605," A.N. Z1F/1065 (hereafter cited as Plumitif). The

manuscript has been numbered by two different systems. I have followed the sixteenth-century pagination, indicated by Roman numerals in the upper right corner of each recto. In several respects noted below, I have revised the standard history of the Pont Neuf based on evidence in the Plumitif, a manuscript that had not been previously tapped by scholars because of the enormous paleographic problems it presents. Future scholars will no longer face those problems since the manuscript has recently been published (unfortunately after my research was completed): Yves Metman, ed., *La construction du Pont-Neuf. Le Registre ou Plumitif de la construction du Pont-Neuf* (Paris: 1987). Debates over the designer of the Pont Neuf dominate the secondary literature, with Baptiste Androuet Ducerceau, Pierre des Isles, and Guillaume Marchant the leading candidates. It is misguided, I believe, to suppose that the bridge was designed by a single architect. As the documents make clear, each of the three successive projects resulted from the collaboration of several masons. On the Pont Neuf: Metman, 1987; Musée Carnavalet, *Pont Neuf 1578–1978* (Paris: 1978); François Boucher, *Le Pont Neuf,* 2 vols. (Paris: 1925–26); F. de Dartein, *Etudes sur les ponts en pierre,* vol. 1, *Ponts français antérieurs au XVIIIe siècle* (Paris: 1912), 77–140; Heinrich von Geymüller, *Les Du Cerceau* (Paris: 1887).

4. The history of the site is discussed by Babelon, "Nouveaux documents sur la place Dauphine," 34–35; Jean Guerout, "Le Palais de la Cité des origines à 1417, essai topographique et archéologique," *MSHP* 1 (1949): 57–212, 2 (1950): 21–204, 3 (1951): 7–101; Boucher, *Le Pont Neuf,* 1:70–71; Berty et al., *Topographie historique du vieux Paris,* vol. 5, *Région occidentale de l'Université* (Paris: 1887), 51–52; J.-B. Jaillot, *Recherches critiques, historiques et topographiques sur la ville de Paris,* 5 vols. (Paris: 1772–74), 1:185; Nicolas Delamare and Le Clerc du Brillet, *Traité de la Police,* 4 vols. (Paris: 1705–38), 1:98; Sauval, 1:99–100.

5. The commissioners overseeing construction of the Pont Neuf described both functions as follows: "par ce moyen en seroient receues deux commoditez, l'une de la traverse de la rue St. Honoré au coste de l'Université, l'autre commodité de venir au Louvre et de tout le quartier des Halles et St. Honoré pour aller au Palais par la porte qui est en ladite isle, et le charroy qui pourroit entrer en la cité de

ce costé la": Lasteyrie, 22, 10 Nov. 1577.

6. The report is published in Lasteyrie, 27–33, 3 March 1578.

7. The course of the street, 5 *toises* wide (9.9 meters), was described in the experts' report: "pour faire lad. rue outre led. quay pour aller à Nostre-Dame, convient et est necessaire entrer dedans l'enclos de la cour du Palais et passer à costé des deux petites tournelles estans au portail par lequel on entre de la cour du Palais en lad. Isle du Palais, et pourchasser lad. rue entre icelle deux tournelles et une masure estans à costé du pavillon neuf de la Chambre des comptes, et continuer lad. rue jusques au bout du pont St. Michel, à l'endroit de la rue du Marché-Neuf, et pour ce faire, couper et retrancher les jardins de derrière des maisons des chanoines de la Sainte Chapelle estans dud. costé . . .": Lasteyrie, 32–33, 3 March 1578.

8. The painting in the Musée Carnavalet (Inv. P.621) correctly illustrates two other features of the original project: the three-sided projections on the piles, "becs à trois pans," and the two filled-in arches between the raised street and the pavilion: Lasteyrie, 30–31. On the basis of these structural similarities, several writers concluded that the painting depicts the original design of the bridge, despite the fact that the decorative features are not mentioned in the *expertise* of 3 March 1578; Boucher, *Le Pont Neuf,* 1:83; Babelon, "Nouveaux documents sur la place Dauphine," 32; Musée Carnavalet, *Pont Neuf,* 15.

9. Lasteyrie, 66, 28 May 1578.

10. The second project can be partially reconstructed from the commission's deliberations (Plumitif, f5–20) and from the masonry contract for the southern vaults (Lasteyrie, 75–81, 25 Nov. 1579).

11. The date of the decision to build houses on the Pont Neuf has been disputed. Pierre Lavedan, *Histoire de Paris* (Paris: 1975), 154–55, and Lasteyrie, 14, argued that houses were planned from the start because the original specifications in 1578 pointed to the Pont Notre-Dame, a bridge with houses, as a model. The specifications do not, however, mention houses. Boucher (*Le Pont Neuf,* 1:106) and Babelon ("Nouveaux documents sur la place Dauphine," 32–33) concluded, as I do, that houses were not introduced until 1579. The vaults as planned in 1578 were insufficiently wide (7 *toises*) to accommodate houses, but they were enlarged the following year when houses are for the first time men-

tioned in the minutes: "[Il] faut faire et dresser les encorbellemens qui seront en saillie hors le corps desd. remplages desd. voultes, pour sur lesd. encorbellemens faire l'advencement des maisons dud. pont": Lasteyrie, 76, 25 Nov. 1579.

12. On 17 July 1579, mason Jacques Leroy was hired to build the abutments and flanking walls of the platform and to terrace the land between the bridge and the garden wall: Plumitif, f9–12; Lasteyrie, 82–87. Five months later, Leroy transferred the masonry contract to François Petit, Guillaume Marchant, and des Isles, the principal builders of the Pont Neuf: Plumitif, f20, 2 Dec. 1579. At a meeting of the supervisory commission on 30 June 1580, the new masons complained that the stone used by Leroy was too soft; Baptiste Ducerceau and other experts advised the commissioners that the platform required a harder stone: Plumitif, f24. Petit's team reinforced the abutments with "pierre dure de cliquart," and on 5 April 1581, the commissioners ordered an estimate of the supplementary work in order to pay the masons, which suggests that their work on the platform had been completed: Plumitif, f37v.

13. The Plumitif records discussions about the street on 15 April 1580 (f23v), 12 June 1581 (f28v), and 4 August 1581 (f42), before the adjudication of the masonry contract on 22 August 1581 (f42v). Leroy was paid 1,900 *ecus* (5,700 *livres*) between 1581 and 1584 for work on the raised street: Plumitif, f44v, 6 Nov. 1581; f47v, 20 Feb. 1582; f61v, 31 Aug. 1582; f75, 13 Sept. 1583; f80v, 27 Jan. 1584; f89, 8 Jan. 1585. The crown also indemnified private property owners whose shops, houses, and walls were destroyed to make way for the street.

14. "Il soit faict marque et devis de toutes et chacunes les rues qui seront necessaires pour aller dud. pont neuf dans nostre pallais et en autres lieulx et endroictz de nostred. ville, et pour faire lesd. rues et passages, abbatre si besoing est quelques maisons affectees aux prebends d'aucuns chanoines de nostre Saincte Chapelle de nostred. Palais, s'aider de leurs jardins, mesme de prendre telle quantité de terre et place dans nostre jardin du bailliage et maison des estuves que besoin sera pour icelles rues dresses, faire faire de toutes les places quilz verront et congnoistront estre propres à bastir maisons et demeurances; et apres les affiches et proclamation mises, estre icelles places par eulx adjugees à dernier d'entree et

delivrees au plus offrans . . . à la charge d'y faire bastir maisons par les acquereurs dedans le temps et selon les plans et desseings qui leur seront prescriptz par lesd. sieurs commissaires pour les rendre uniformes et semblables si possible est, de mesme face et front sur rue pour la decoration d'icelle . . .": Plumitif, f91v–92r, 11 June 1584. It is possible that construction of houses on the tip of the island was already considered in 1580, if not by the crown by the municipal building office, the *Bureau*. In trying to persuade the commissioners of the Pont Neuf not to build a fifth arch on the south arm of the Seine, the city argued that it "gasteroit les places à bastir en l'isle du pallais et es environs dudit pont": Plumitif, f23, 22 March 1580.

15. The Parlement stipulated "qu'en faisant lesdits quaiz il ne sera faict aucun edifice et bastiment le long de la salle S. Louis jusques au pont aux Musniers qui puisse apporter aucun incovenient aux edifices et aisances dudit palais; et que le quai qui sera faict dudit costé ne passera oultre ladite salle St. Louis . . .": Félibien, 5:17–18, 11 July 1584. The crown abandoned this policy in 1611, when it began to give away the land bordering the Palace along the quai de l'Horloge; between 1611 and 1614, a row of small shops and stalls was built up to the pont au Change: A.N. Z1F/561 f28v, 30 Nov. 1614; A.N. X1A/8649 f112, 1 Sept. 1618; f242v, 11 Jan. 1620; A.P. H.D. 25/171.991, 19 April 1617; A.S. DQ10 91/1115, 128/3286, 101/1713, 1812.

16. Boucher, *Le Pont Neuf,* 1:164.

17. Plumitif, f94v, 2 July 1586.

18. The Maison des Etuves was mentioned in an inventory in May 1607: Boucher, *Le Pont Neuf,* 1:70. The flowers grown in the Jardin du Bailliage were engraved by Pierre Vallet, *Le Jardin du roy tres chrestien Henry IV* (Paris: 1608).

19. In the contract dated 17 May 1599, the masons promised to complete the south arm of the bridge by the following October: Plumitif, f113v. In April 1601, the municipality requested the king "faire don à lad. Ville du fondz et proprieté dud. Pont pour y bastir et ediffier maisons et ediffices, ainsi que sur le Pont Nostre Dame," a request that was denied: *Registres* 12:413. Because of this appeal, Boucher (1:113) and Babelon ("Nouveaux documents sur la place Dauphine," 33) argued that the decision to banish buildings from the Pont Neuf was not made until 1601, but the city's request does not presuppose a

prior agreement to build houses; on the contrary, it may have been an attempt to have the crown reconsider its plan to exclude houses.

20. Du Breul, 246.

21. Germain Brice wrote of the Pont Neuf, "on peut encore conter entre ces avantages la belle veue que l'on y découvre, qui passe pour une des plus agréables et des plus riches qu'il y ait au monde." He rated it the third greatest vista in the world, after the view from the ports of Constantinople and Goa: *Description nouvelle . . . de Paris* (Paris: 1684), 283–84.

22. On 28 April 1601, Petit and Marchant promised to complete the north section of the bridge within three years: Plumitif, f120v–121. In June 1603, Henri IV crossed the bridge on planks laid across the piles, a challenge that had sent others tumbling into the Seine according to Pierre de L'Estoile, *Journal pour le règne de Henri IV (1589–1600),* vol. 2, ed. André Martin (Paris: 1958), 105. The Pont Neuf was paved in 1605 (A.N. Z1F/1065, 30 March 1605), and the Conseil d'Etat ordered the final inspection and *toisé* in July 1606 (A.N. E11A f30).

23. Construction contracts for the pumphouse, the reservoir in the cloister of St. Germain l'Auxerrois, and water conduits, as well as a maintenance contract with Lintlaer were published by Mallevoüe, 145–52. An undated manuscript signed by Lintlaer describes his duties in maintaining the pump: B.N. Ms. fr. 16652 f97. The pavilion was rebuilt in 1665, destroyed and rebuilt by Robert de Cotte in 1711–15, and finally dismantled in 1813. There are descriptions of the original building in Peter Mundy, *The Travels of Peter Mundy in Europe and Asia, 1608–1667,* ed. Richard Temple, The Hakluyt Society, 2nd ser., 17 (Cambridge: 1907), 125; Musée Carnavalet, *Pont Neuf,* 19–20.

24. "Sa Majesté a déclaré son intention estre de passer ses annees en ceste ville et y demeurer comme vrai patriote, rendre ceste ville belle, [splendide] . . . et pleine de toutes commoditez et ornemens qu'il sera possible. Voullant le parachevement du Pont Neuf et restablissement des fontaines, ayant Sa Majesté entendu que, par le deffault des eaus des fontaines, plusieurs personnes subjectz a des maladies de gravelle, desireux non seullement de nous preserver de noz ennemis, mais aussy soigneux de noz santez, nous ayant donné la paix, veult décorer ceste ville par le parachevement du Pont Neuf et restablissement des fontaines qui y souloient couler,

usant de ces motz qu'il veult faire un monde entier de ceste ville et un miracle du monde, en quoy certainement nous faict cognoistre un amour plus que paternel": *Registres* 12:386, 16 March 1601.

25. In a letter to Sully, the king instructed his minister to provide the city with funds to complete the fountains at the Palace and the Croix de Tirouer and the Portes St. Bernard and du Temple: "Et parce que je desire que lesd. portes et fontaines se parachevent au plus tost, je vous fais ce mot et vous depesche ce laquais, expres pour vous dire que je seray tres aise scavoir pourquoy les deniers destinez aux dicts ouvrages ont esté devertis et detournez et que tous teniés la main à ce que cela ne soit, me mandant les occasions pour lesquelles on l'a ainsy ordonné": *Lettres missives* 6:613, 18 May 1606.

26. A bronze statuette was sent from Florence to Paris in 1604, and a wax portrait bust of Henri IV was sent back to Giambologna's studio in 1606. The horse was cast by September 1607. Work on the figure was interrupted after Giambologna's death in 1608 and was resumed by Pietro Tacca following Henri IV's death in 1610. The monument arrived in Paris on 24 July 1614, and the dedication took place the following month, on 23 August. The statue of the king was destroyed in 1792 and replaced in 1818 by a statue of Henri IV by Lemot; only the slaves and a few fragments of the original equestrian monument survive. The statue is discussed by Katherine Watson, *Pietro Tacca Successor to Giovanni Bologna* (New York: 1983); Arts Council of Great Britain, *Giambologna 1529–1608 Sculptor to the Medici*, ed. Charles Avery and Anthony Radcliffe (London: 1978); Deborah Marrow, *The Art Patronage of Maria de' Medici* (Ann Arbor: 1982); Mila Mastrorocco "Pietro Francavilla alla corte di Francia," *Commentari* 26/3–4 (1975): 333–43; Robert de Francqueville, *Pierre de Francqueville* (Paris: 1968); idem, "Le sculpteur Francheville, sa vie, ses oeuvres d'après des documents d'archives," *BSHAF*, 1965: 33–54; John Pope-Hennessy, *Italian High Renaissance and Baroque Sculpture* (London: 1963), vol. 3, pt. 2:91–92; Eugène Muntz, *Les Archives des arts* (Paris: 1890), 79–84.

27. The four prisoners, today in the Louvre, were begun by Pietro Francavilla and completed by Francesco Bordoni in 1618. They were also responsible for the pedestal reliefs of the battles of Arques and Ivry, and the king's entry into Paris. The battles of Amiens and Montmélian were recorded in reliefs by Barthélemy du Tremblay and Thomas Boudin which were not placed on the pedestal until 1628.

28. The following pamphlets were published at the time of the statue's inauguration: N. Bergier Remois, *Le Cheval de Domitian* (Paris: 1614); Charles Jourdan, *Embarquement, conduite, peril et arrivée du cheval de bronze* (Paris: 1614); [D. Le Conte], *Météorologie ou l'excellence de la Statue de Henry le Grand eslevée sur le Pont-Neuf* (Paris: 1614); Louis Savot, *Discours sur le sujet du colosse du Grand Roy Henry posé sur le milieu du Pont-Neuf de Paris* (Paris: n.d.); Jean-Philippe Varin, *Discours de la statue et representation d'Henry le Grand* (Paris: 1614); Denis Rouillard, *Explication de tout ce qui est contenu aux plaques et inscriptions mises au piédestal de la statue de bronze de Henry le Grand* (Paris: 1636).

29. The crown must have decided to place the statue on the *terre-plein* by 1604. It is the *terminus post quem* that is at issue. According to Deborah Marrow, "One of the Queen's most important commissions during the early years, and one which was entirely her own idea, was the equestrian monument to Henri IV on the Pont Neuf": *Art Patronage of Maria de' Medici*, 9. A similar point is made by Katherine Watson, "Sugar Sculpture for Grand Ducal Weddings from the Giambologna Workshop," *Connoisseur* 199/799 (Sept. 1978): 22–25; Mastrorocco, "Pietro Francavilla," 343; Boucher, *Le Pont Neuf*, 2:67; Sauval, 1:235.

30. Arnold Van Buchel, "Description de Paris par Van Buchel d'Utrecht (1585–1586)," ed. L.-A. Van Langeraad and A. Vidier, *MSHP* 26 (1899): 121.

31. The bronze horse was cast by Daniele da Volterra before his death in 1566. It remained in Rome until 1622 when it was brought to Paris by Richelieu who installed it in the Place Royale in 1639. The history of Catherine de' Medici's commission is examined by Malcolm Campbell and Gino Corti, "A Comment on Prince Francesco de Medici's Refusal to Loan Giovanni Bologna to the Queen of France," *Burlington* 115/845 (Aug. 1973): 507–12; Anatole de Montaiglon, *Notice sur l'ancienne statue équestre ouvrage de Daniello Ricciarelli et le Biard le fils elevée à Louis XIII en 1639 au milieu de la place Royale à Paris* (Paris: 1874).

32. At least two of the rejected schemes for the Pont Neuf included statuary, although not equestrian figures, on the platform of the bridge. Guillaume Marchant submitted a design with a triumphal arch on the *terre-plein* (Sauval, 1:233), and Jacques Androuet Ducerceau's design of a bridge, presumed to be for the Pont Neuf, had a circular *place* at the midpoint of the bridge with a colonnaded tempietto in the center (B.N. Est. Ed 2p res. f17).

33. Boucher typifies this attitude in writing, "Si le terre-plein lui même fut amenagé en vue de reçevoir la statue royale, il n'est pas exageré de supposer que l'entreprise de la place Dauphine doit aussi quelque chose au project de la reine": Boucher, *Le Pont Neuf*, 1:167.

34. On Livorno: Cornelia Danielson, "Livorno: A Study in 16th Century Town Planning in Italy," Ph.D. diss., Columbia University, 1985; Dario Matteoni, "La construzione della città nuovo," in *Livorno: progetto e storia di una città tra il 1500 e il 1600* (Pisa: 1980).

35. The land donation to Harlay was published by Mallevoüe, 23–24.

36. "Mon amy, je vous fais ce mot pour vous dire qu'incontinent que vous l'aurés receue vous voyiés M. le premier president, pour resouldre la place Dauphine selon le dessein que vous m'en avés monstré, affin qu'elle soit faicte en trois ans. Que s'il ne le veut faire, trouvés quelque autre qui l'entreprenne, et luy dites qu'il aura le profit du fonds": *Lettres missives* 7:238–39, 13 May 1607.

37. The engraving does not clearly represent the elevation. Do the arched shopfronts alternate with doorways or with pilasters? A pilaster certainly rises at the left corner, but other bays are more ambiguous, and if they were pilasters, then where are the entrances to the houses? Chastillon's engraving is inaccurate in the following respects: it depicts 24 arches along the north range whereas the de Cotte plan delineates 30 arches and 15 doors (Fig. 89); the file of quoins demarcating every three-bay unit is not shown; the stone tablets between the windows are too wide; the dormers are crowned by triangular rather than segmental pediments; the number of houses on the quai east of the rue de Harlay is grossly exaggerated; and a grill was not erected around the statue of Henri IV until 1662. The date of the engraving is uncertain. It is signed "J. Poinssart ex A PARIS avec previlege du Roy 1640." Without presenting any supporting evidence, Dumolin suggested that an unidentified artist had made the engraving before Chastillon's death in 1616, and that Poinssart later added the inscription: Maurice Dumolin, "Essai sur Claude Chastillon et son oeuvre," B.N. Est. typewritten manuscript (c. 1930), 19, 45, 141–42.

38. According to the de Cotte plan, the interior angle at the southeast corner was approximately 64°, about 12° more acute than the interior angle at the northeast corner (see Fig. 89). An inscription on the plan indicates that the exterior side of the south range was 68 *toises* long while the north range was 64.3 *toises* long, a difference of 4.3 *toises*. The north range tapered by approximately 2 *toises*.

39. Jaillot wrote, "Il eut été à souhaiter que ceux qui ont eu l'inspection de cet ouvrage eussent placé cette statue en face de l'ouverture de la Place Dauphine et de la porte du Palais": *Recherches critiques, historiques et topographiques sur la ville de Paris*, 5 vols. (Paris: 1772–74), 1:182.

40. "Sans doute le Sculpteur et le Maçon eurent tous deux bien peu d'industrie, d'avoir tourné si mal le pied d'estal et la figure, qu'on ne les voit presque point du dedans de la place Dauphine, et que le Roi en regarde l'entrée de travers et de mauvais oeil. On me dira qu'ils l'ont dressé à la pointe de l'Isle, dans le centre de la place qui separe les deux ponts [terreplein], et qu'ainsi à l'égard de cette difformité on s'en doit prendre à François Petit, conducteur de la place Dauphine, pour avoir donné à un des quais beaucoup plus de largeur qu'à l'autre, ce qui est cause que la pointe de cette place n'est pas planté dans le milieu de l'Isle du Palais. J'avoue que cette raison peut servir à les defendre [i.e., sculptor and mason], et qui pourtant est la seule, cependant elle ne satisfait pas trop, car ils devoient prévoir qu'à faute d'assujettir cette figure à l'entrée de la place c'etoit ôter au pont un enrichissement qui leur étoit très necessaire; si bien qu'en l'état où étoit pour lors la pointe de l'Isle du Palais, il leur étoit aisé d'établir son centre où ils eussent voulu; et peut-être est-ce pour celà que Petit ne s'est pas soucié de placer précisement dans le milieu de l'Isle la pointe de la place Dauphine": Sauval, 1:235.

41. G. Dechuyes, *La Guide de Paris* (Paris: [1647]), 153, 160; Sauval, 1:627.

42. Sauval, 1:629.

43. Harlay was imprisoned by the League in January 1589 for supporting Henri III. After eight months of captivity in the Bastille, Harlay fled the insurrectionary capital and

rejoined the Parlement, exiled in Tours. When Henri IV ascended the throne later that year, Harlay immediately threw his support to the new king. On Harlay: E. Pilastre, *Achille III de Harlay. Premier Président du Parlement de Paris sous le règne de Louis XIV* (Paris: 1904); P. Lafleur de Kermaingant, *L'Ambassade de France en Angleterre sous Henri IV. Mission de Christophe de Harlay, Comte de Beaumont (1602–1605)* (Paris: 1895); Père Anselme, *Histoire généalogique*, vol. 8 (Paris: 1733), 799–800; Jacques de la Valée, *Discours sur la vie, actions et mort de très-illustre Seigneur Messire Achilles de Harlay* (Paris: 1616) in Archives curieuses de l'histoire de France, ed. Cimber and Danjou, ser. 1, vol. 15 (Paris: 1837), 423–57.

44. Part of the wall was demolished at the king's expense in 1610: A.N. Z1F/559 f2v, 9 Sept. 1610. The crown sold the salvaged building materials and gave the proceeds of the sale to a canon of the Ste. Chapelle, Jacques Gillot, in partial payment for the loss of the chapel's land: A.N. E27B f143, 19 Aug. 1610. The Ste. Chapelle also profited by selling its part of the Palace wall destined for demolition to a mason who reused the dressed stone: Min. cent. XIX 363 f96, 20 April 1610; A.N. Z1F/559 f2v, 19 Aug., 9 Sept. 1610.

45. Petit and Marchant resumed work on the south quai in compliance with an order in June 1603: Plumitif, f127. In 1608, Petit was paid "sur les ouvrages de maçonnerie qu'il faict pour la confection des murs des quais et abbreuvoirs du costé du petit cours de la riviere . . .": A.N. Z1F/1065, Estat par Henry Estienne, 20 Jan. 1610.

46. Masonry contract with Petit for north quai: A.N. Z1F/150 f101v, f108, 14 Aug. 1608. After the first building season, he was paid 24,000 *livres*: A.N. Z1F/1065, Estat du Pont Neuf, 1608. In July 1612, the quai was approaching the bridgehead of the Pont au Musnier; the sale contract of a lot backing onto the Conciergerie required the owner to begin construction as soon as the quai was completed: Min. cent. LXXVIII 187, 17 July 1612.

47. A.N. E21 f102, 11 April 1609.

48. The proceeds from Harlay's *lotissement* of the Ile du Palais break down as follows: 86,556 *livres* from eleven lots at the square; 14,661 *livres* from five lots abutting the Palace on the quai de l'Horloge; and 2,400 *livres* from one lot abutting the Palace on the quai des Orfèvres. Harlay also sold a small lot lodged

between two towers of the Conciergerie on the quai de l'Horloge for 75 *livres* per *toise*, higher than the standard rate of 72 *livres* for quai property, but the owner was not required to comply with the royal facade design: Min. cent. LXXVIII 187, 17 July 1612. Harlay gave away two lots to compensate the recipients for property which was appropriated for the square. The lot at the southeast corner of the Place Dauphine was given to Etienne Gillot, royal counselor and canon of the Ste. Chapelle, in exchange for a section of the chapel's garden on which the rue de Harlay houses were built: Min. cent. XXIX 163, 30 May 1611. Gillot was an early supporter of Henri IV and co-author of the anti-League satire *La Satyre ménippée* published in Tours in 1593. Germaine Durand, widow of Germain Pilon, was given one lot on the quai de l'Horloge plus a payment of 1,800 *livres*, to compensate for the destruction of her house adjoining the Maison des Etuves: Min. cent. LXXVIII 184, 11 July 1609: Edouard-Jacques Ciprut, "Chronologie nouvelle de la vie et des oeuvres de Germain Pilon," *GBA* 74 (1969): 343.

49. The son of a master mason from Beauvais, Petit was *juré du Roi en l'office de maçonnerie* by 1588. There are references to Petit throughout the minutes of the *Bureau* in connection with the Pont Neuf (1578–1604), the Valois chapel (1582), the Porte St. Germain (1599), the Grande Galerie of the Louvre (1602), a reservoir at the Halles (1600), and the chapel of St. Esprit (1608). On Petit: Rosalys Coope, "John Thorpe and the Hotel Zamet in Paris," *Burlington* 124/956 (Nov. 1982): 671–81; idem *Jacques Gentilhâtre*, Catalogue of the Drawings Collection of the Royal Institute of British Architects, vol. 6 (London: 1982), f35v, fig. 27; J.-P. Babelon, *Demeures parisiennes sous Henri IV et Louis XIII* (Paris: 1977), 258; Jules Guiffrey, *Artistes parisiens* (Paris: 1915), 223–24; Ch. Bauchal, *Nouveau dictionnaire biographique et critique des architectes français* (Paris: 1887), 469; Adolphe Lance, *Dictionnaire des architectes français*, 2 vols. (Paris: 1872), 2:200–201; B.N. Ms. fr. nouv. acq. 12167 (Fichier Laborde). On Petit's work for the Augustins, see the section on the rue Dauphine below.

50. Min. cent. LXXVIII 183, 28 Aug. 1608.

51. Receipt by Petit for payment "sur et tant moings des ouvrages de maçonnerie et tailles faites et à faire pour led. seigneur en la place Dauphine": Min. cent. LXXVIII 184, 14

Aug. 1609.

52. Min. cent. LIX 42 f269, 12 March 1610; f280, 18 March 1610.

53. Min. cent. LXXVIII 186, 20 June 1611.

54. The rue de Harlay houses were rented in 1611–12 for 600 *livres* annually. In 1613, the rent was lowered to 500 *livres* except for the house on the north corner with three shops which remained at 600 *livres* and the smaller house on the south corner which cost 450 *livres*. See Appendix B2.

55. Contract for maintenance of roofs and of lead in the rue de Harlay houses: Min. cent. LXXVIII 205, 16, 20, and 21 Jan. 1617.

56. Harlay survived his only child Christophe (+1615) and gave his grandson Achille II "les deux premieres maisons basties et deux autres à son choix et option en la rue traversante," according to a will appended on 10 March 1614: Min. cent. LXXVIII 188, 23 Dec. 1613. In a later will dated 9 October 1616, he assigned all his goods to his nephews and nieces: Min. cent. LXXCIII 204. Achille III de Harlay's sale of the rue de Harlay houses is documented in A.N. Q1/1099/25B.

57. The turnover of empty lots was largely eliminated at the Place Dauphine. Of the twenty-six men who bought land from Harlay, only two men did not build at all, each exceptional cases. The first, Gillot, was in the same position as Harlay, having been given his lot in order to profit from its sale (see note 48), and he subdivided and sold the land accordingly, making a profit of 9,198 *livres:* Min. cent. LXVI 30, 12 Sept., 27 and 28 Nov. 1614. Gillot sold one lot to a distant relative by marriage, Hierosme Ferrier (c. 1576–1626), the Protestant theologian from Nîmes infamous for attacking the pope as the antichrist. Chased from Nîmes in 1613, he came to Paris and ended his life there as a Catholic, writing pamphlets in support of Richelieu. The second person who failed to build at the square was Abel Langelier, one of the most important publishers and booksellers in Henri IV's Paris and a faithful supporter of the king during the Wars of Religion: Henri-Jean Martin, *Livres, pouvoirs et société à Paris au XVIIe siècle (1598–1701),* 2 vols. (Geneva: 1969), 1:348. His shop was located in the Palace, and presumably he planned to relocate or open a second shop at the new square, but he died in 1610 before breaking ground on his property. His widow continued the publishing firm in the Palace, abandoning the land at the Place Dauphine. The crown regained possession of

the parcel and gave it to an officer of the Parlement, Jacques Chevalier: A.N. Z1F/563 f62v, 5 May 1618; Min. cent. LXVI 89, 9 March 1641. The difficulty of tracing small property owners who did not have an established relationship with a notary proved insurmountable in four cases. I was unable to find any documentation concerning the houses of Baudoin Bacher, jeweler; André Belot, prosecutor (*procureur*) in the Grand Conseil; François Pepin, registrar at the Châtelet (*greffier*); and Nicolas Poullet, prosecutor in the *Chambre des comptes.*

58. Sancy's purchase of the north house: Min. cent. LXXVIII 183, 12 Sept. 1608.

59. Min. cent. LIV 479, 19 Aug. 1612.

60. Min. cent. LIV 249, 22 and 24 Oct. 1612. These transactions are listed in de Ligny's inventory after death: Min. cent. LIV 494 n°503, 5 Dec. 1619–3 June 1620.

61. Masonry: Min. cent. LIV 480, 30 April 1613 (see Appendix B5). Metalwork: LIV 480, 14 May 1613. Carpentry: LIV 480, 18 May 1613. Roofing: LIV 481, 26 Nov. 1613.

62. Min. cent. LXXVIII 184, 24 Jan. 1609.

63. Contract for dressed stone: Min. cent. LIX 42 f412, 16 April 1610. Metalwork contract: Min. cent. LIX 43 f103–4, 20 Jan. 1611. The inventory of Petit's notary Jean Le Camus (Min. cent. LIX) lists declarations made by Marrier and Chaillou to Petit on 24 January 1609, the same date that Marrier and Chaillou bought the lots from Harlay. The documents do not survive, and therefore it is not possible to confirm my hypothesis that Chaillou and Marrier renounced their rights to the lots at this time and acknowledged Petit as the rightful owner. Petit may have considered it necessary to conceal his ownership because of the large role he already had at the square. The arrangement between the men was certainly amicable because the three families were friendly; children of Marrier, Chaillou, and Petit were all godparents for the same infant: B.N. Ms. fr. nouv. acq. 12167 n°53.337.

64. Min. cent. LIX 45, 16 Aug. 1613.

65. ". . . ce qu'il conviendra pour parachever de bastir les maisons qui luy appartiennent en l'Isle du Pallais de ceste ville de Paris par luy encommancer à ediffier et dont les bastiments sont ja fort advancez et eslevez jusques aux combles; sans que pour raison de ce, lad. future epouse puisse pretendre ni demander aucun remplacement ni recompense": Min. cent. LIX 46 f902, 21 July 1614.

66. Purchase by Laborie and Deligny: Min. cent. LXXVIII 183, 23 Sept. 1608. Declaration to the Papier Terrier: A.N. Q1/1099/20, 1 Dec. 1667 (Deligny's house); A.N. Q1/1099/25B, 19 Oct. 1671 (Laborie's house). Michel Deligny is discussed in Jean Delay, *Avant Mémoire. D'une minute à l'autre, Paris 1555–1736* (Paris: 1979), 169, 173–74, 194.

67. Another arrangement was made by jeweler Baudouin Bacher, prosecutor André Belot (*procureur au Grand Conseil*), and barrister Olivier Montel (*avocat au conseil privé du Roi*) who divided their lot on the south side of the square into shares of 2/5, 1/5, and 2/5 respectively (see Fig. 112, Parcel 10). They satisfied the royal design on the quai side where each house had a facade 4 *toises* wide, confining irregularities to the facade on the square. Belot's parcel did not border the square, while Bacher and Montel each had L-shaped parcels: Min. cent. LXXVIII 184, 7 Jan. 1609.

68. Mutation fees were waived for the following lot owners: Robert Menart, A.N. Z 5965 f157v, 30 May 1609, published by J.-J. Guiffrey, *Nouvelles archives de l'art français*, 1873: 230; François Pepin, A.N. Z1F/563 f89v, 25 May 1609; Olivier Montel, A.N. Z1F f164, 6 June 1609; Michel Deligny, A.N. Z1F/560 f148v, 31 March 1610; and the heirs of Abel Langelier, A.N. Z1F/563 f62v, 5 May 1618.

69. Gillot sold the land at the southeast corner in 1614; see note 57.

70. Min. cent. LIV 253, 13 Oct. 1610. After Le Redde's death, this contract was taken over by master mason Claude Pouillet: Min. cent. LIV 254, 20 April 1611. The abutting parcel of the same size facing the square was owned by Charles Beranger, tailor to Queen Marguerite (see Fig. 112, Parcel 11B). He hired Pouillet to build a comparable house for only 4,650 *livres*: Min. cent. LIV 250, 17 March 1609. This contract excluded the cost of glass, doors, mantels, locks, and mullions, but it included the wall dividing the property of Béthune and Beranger. Pouillet also worked

for Menart (see note 73) and built the party wall shared by Béthune, Beranger, and their neighbor, merchant Antoine Mignollet: Min. cent. XXIX 161, 7 Sept. 1609; Min. cent. LXVI 22, 29 May 1609; Min. cent. LXVI 23, 16 Sept. 1609. Pouillet executed Salomon de Brosse's design for the Hôtel de Fresne in 1608.

71. Min. cent. LIV 480, 30 April 1613 (see Appendix B5).

72. Min. cent. VI 282, 14 June 1611.

73. Claude Pouillet was hired to build the foundations and party walls: Min. cent. XLII 48, 27 Dec. 1608. Jean Gobelin was hired for the facade: Min. cent. LXVI 24, 28 June 1610.

74. Mignollet and his wife sold a house on the rue St. Honoré for 6,800 *livres* "par eulx commetre et employer au paiement des bastimens et ediffices qu'ils pretendent faire . . . sur une place qu'ilz ont acquise depuis peu un l'isle du pallais . . .": Min. cent. XCIX 90, 6 Oct. 1608. Bunel borrowed 3,200 *livres* (Min. cent. XCVI 4 f70, 26 March 1611), Menart 1,600 *livres* (Min. cent. LXVI 24, 28 June 1610), and Montel 2,000 *livres* (Min. cent. XC 169, 7 Jan. 1609). All of these contracts specify that the money was borrowed to finance construction at the Place Dauphine.

75. Min. cent. LIV 253, 20 Sept. 1610. Min. cent. LXXVIII 187, 3 July 1612.

76. After paying Menart's creditors, who are listed in the contract of sale to Collier, Menart's heirs were left with only 7,500 *livres*: Min. cent. XLI 56, 5 and 7 Feb. 1613, 4 March, 18 May 1613.

77. Seventeen leases passed by François Petit between 1612 and 1618 have been found, including two renewals. Of the fifteen tenants named in the leases, ten were merchants and artisans, four minor officers, and one a widow. The lot numbers refer to Figures 111 and 112. Prices are given in *livres* and Roman numerals refer to documents in the Minutier central.

LOCATION	NAME	OCCUPATION	PRICE	DOC.	DATE
LOT 4					
quai de l'Horloge	Winter, Sébastien	gem cutter	450	LIX 47	17 Feb. 1615
	Maret, Denis	merchant	500	LIX 47	10 Mar. 1615
square	Jolly, Simon	joiner	450	LIX 47	7 Apr. 1615
	Renewal		450	LIX 53	4 Feb. 1619
	Prudent, Marin	founder	450	LIX 47	7 Apr. 1615

LOCATION	NAME	OCCUPATION	PRICE	DOC.	DATE
LOT 6					
rue de Harlay	Fauvel, François	*sec. du Roi*	350	LIX 45	29 Jan. 1613
	Guytard, Jacques	*sec. du Roi*	350	LIX 47	13 Jan. 1615
	Belleval, François	wine merchant	400	LIX 52	7 Feb. 1618
square	Bailly, Guillaume	*sec.* Queen Marguerite	350	LIX 42	4 Apr. 1612
	Riviere, Sébastien	*sec. des finances*(?)	350	LIX 44	29 May 1612
	Danzet, Jean	goldsmith	350	LIX 46	12 June 1614
	Renewal		400	LIX 52	5 May 1618
	Legendre, Aymond	leather gilder	400	LIX 47	10 Mar. 1615
LOT 7					
rue de Harlay	Jolly, Leger	pin maker	350	LIX 45	4 Mar. 1613
square	Croust, David	goldsmith	400	LIX 44	23 Mar. 1612
	Barjot, Marguerite	widow	350	LIX 49	26 May 1616
	Vaux, Nicolas	wood turner	350	LIX 52	7 Feb. 1618

78. Min. cent. LIV 484, 23 March 1615. De Ligny also rented a house with one shop to an innkeeper for 550 *livres* (Min. cent. LIV 484, 12 May 1615) and another house on the quai de l'Horloge to a master jeweler for 450 *livres* (Min. cent. LIV 490, 5 April 1618). Several other leases are mentioned in de Ligny's inventory after death: LIV 494, n°1600, 5 Dec. 1619–3 June 1620.

79. Bunel's purchase: Min. cent. LXXVIII 183, 24 Oct. 1608. Documents concerning Bunel's residence in the Louvre were published by Guiffrey, *Artistes parisiens*, 81–86. I was unable to find any of the construction contracts for his Place Dauphine buildings.

80. Some time before March 1611, Bunel negotiated a five-year lease with Jean Carrel, treasurer for Queen Marguerite. Carrel sublet the ground-floor shops, charging 200 *livres* to a belt-maker for a shop with two arches on the quai and 150 *livres* to a bookseller for a similar shop facing the passageway into the square: Min. cent. VI 282, 17 March, 13 June 1611. Sebastien Winter moved from a house that he rented from Bunel for 800 *livres* (Min. cent. XLII 53, 7 Dec. 1613) to a smaller house that he rented from Petit for 450 *livres* (see note 77 above).

81. Perrot's statement on 26 January 1623 is published in *Registres* 18:348.

82. Sauval, 1:246.

83. *Registres* 15:95–96, 126–29.

84. *Registres* 18:348. Jeannin never built the houses. Babelon thought that the houses abutting the north side of the Palace were built by Jeannin, but a series of documents establish that these stalls were built by numerous other people: see note 15 above.

85. Mallevoüe, lvi.

86. "Monsieur Achille de Harlay . . . estant en son lict mallade . . . [a] juré et affermé . . . que Monsieur le duc de Sully en sa grande faveur auroit violament extorqué de luy ung escript signé de la main dud. sieur de Harlay au prejudice du don qui avoit esté faict aud. seigneur de Harlay par le feu roy des places dans l'isle du pallais aud. seigneur; que Madame de Sully . . . le prioit de signer led. escript pour le contentement dud. sieur de Sully . . . lequel escript Monsieur Le Gras tresorier de France a du depuis dict en plain bureau . . . et portait proteste que led. escript ne luy puisse ny à ses heritiers [faire] prejudice . . ." Min. cent. LXXVIII 204, 10 Oct. 1616.

87. *Registres* 18:140–49, 213–16, 348.

88. "Les quais et lieux adjacentz doibvent estre conservez pour la decoration de la Ville, santé et salubrité des habitans d'icelle, et que l'ung des plus beaulx ornemens d'icelle Ville c'est l'isle du Pallais basty comme il est à present, revestu de quais spacieulx des deux costez de la riviere, sur lesquelz l'on ne peut faire aulcune constructions de bastimens sans ap-

porter incommodité à la structure et cimetrie desd. bastimens qui servent, en l'estat qu'ilz sont, d'un aspect agreable aux veues du chasteau du Louvre": *Registres* 18:348, 26 Jan. 1623.

89. Le Jay's parcel on the south side of the rue St. Louis measured 60 *toises* long by 3 *toises* wide. Babelon, "Nouveaux documents sur la place Dauphine," 41–42; Jaillot, 1:189; Sauval, 1:245; A.N. Q1/1099/1.

90. The requirements were set forth in a royal edict on 23 February 1671: Félibien, 5:220–25. At the same time, an entrance to the Palace was opened on the quai de l'Horloge, next to Parcel 18 on Figure 109.

91. On the projects to modify or destroy the Place Dauphine: Joerg Garms, "Projects for the Pont Neuf and Place Dauphine in the First Half of the Eighteenth Century," *JSAH* 26/2 (May 1967): 102–13; Ragnar Josephson, "Un projet de la Place Royale à la pointe de la Cité," *BSHAF*, 1928: 52–58; Pierre Patte, *Monuments érigés en France à la gloire de Louis XV* (Paris: 1765).

92. A.N. F14 906, Inspection of the *terre-plein*, 8 July 1810.

93. Boucher, *Le Pont Neuf*, 2:87, 105–6.

94. Plans for the expansion of the law courts and the elimination of the rue de Harlay houses are discussed in the minutes of the *Conseil municipal;* see for example A.N. F21 2370. On the reconstruction of the Palais de Justice during the nineteenth century: Katherine Fischer Taylor, "The Palais de Justice of Paris: Modernization, historical self-consciousness, and their prehistory in French institutional architecture (1835–1869)," Ph.D. diss., Harvard University, 1989.

95. The church of the Grands Augustins was the principal stop on the annual processions of the Order of the Holy Spirit, a chivalric confraternity founded by Henri III in 1578. Frances Yates suggested that the Pont Neuf was built to facilitate access between the Louvre and the church of the Grands Augustins: *Astraea* (London: 1975), 176. Such a link was certainly important for the processions of the order, and while the Pont Neuf was under construction, a temporary wooden bridge was erected across the tip of the island for these occasions. Henri III's designs for the Pont Neuf called for "a lane in the form of a passage [*allée*] to enter the large garden of the hôtel de Saint Denis from the quai": Lasteyrie, 29. The bridge would not have disturbed the medieval fabric of the Left Bank.

96. The Hôtel de Nevers was built at great expense during the 1580s by Louis de Gonzague on the site of the Hôtel de Nesle. After the Tuileries, it was the grandest building project in Henri III's Paris, and yet its history has not yet been written. On the patronage of the Gonzague family: Denis Crouzet, "Recherches sur la crise de l'aristocratie en France au XVI siècle; les dettes de la Maison de Nevers," *Histoire, économie, et société*, 1982: 7–50; Emile Baudson, *Charles de Gonzague duc de Nevers, de Rethel, et de Mantoue 1580–1637* (Paris: 1947).

97. Min. cent. VIII 568 f268, 29 March 1606.

98. This sum included 66,000 *livres* for the land and 6,000 *livres* for construction of a new monastic building: Min. cent. VIII 568 f268, 29 March 1606. The sale contract did not specify the amount of land purchased by the developers. Since Carrel, Corbonnois, and du Nesme equally divided the mutation tax, they probably were equal partners in the rue Dauphine development: Min. cent. XXIII 261, 3 Feb. 1623.

99. Roland Mousnier, *La Vénalité des offices* (Paris: 1971), 242–43.

100. Min. cent. CV 181, 26 Feb., 19 May 1610. In order to conceal his extensive purchases at the Place de France, Carrel had other men sign these contracts, which eliminates the possibility that he was only acting as the front man for other people in his various real estate transactions.

101. B.N. Ms. fr. 16744 f266–268.

102. Le Barbier was also responsible for developing the site of Marguerite de Valois's unfinished hôtel. His schemes were studied by Maurice Dumolin, *Etudes de topographie parisienne*, 3 vols. (Paris: 1929–31).

103. Du Nesme's imprisonment: B.N. Ms. fr. 18174 f97, 22 Nov. 1608; f187, 18 Dec. 1608. A financial transaction by Corbonnois in 1621 is mentioned in F. Bayard, *Le monde des financiers au XVIIe siècle* (Paris: 1988), 100.

104. Miron de l'Espinay published a letter purportedly written by *Prévôt des marchands* François Miron to Sully in October 1604 concerning a proposal by Carrel to build the rue Dauphine, but the authenticity of the letter is questionable: *François Miron et l'administration municipale de Paris sous Henri IV* (Paris: 1885), 269–71.

105. Min. cent. CXVII 469 f243, 6 Feb. 1607.

106. "Ventre Saint Gris! mes Peres, l'argent que vous retirerez du revenu des maisons vaut bien des choux." This statement is reported

by L'Estoile, *Journal pour le règne de Henri IV*, 2:225.

107. Min. cent. CXVII 469 f184, 12 March 1607. Berty and Tisserand mistakenly wrote that the developers bought a second tract of land from the Augustins for 30,000 *livres*, but this purchase was made by the crown: *Topographie historique du Vieux Paris*, vol. 5, *Région occidental de l'Université* (Paris: 1887), 368.

108. Min. cent. CXVIII 469 f243, 4 April 1607. The terms of this contract were met by late 1608 when François Petit was paid 2,000 *livres* for construction of the walls and underground passage: A.N. Z1F/1065, Estat du Pont Neuf, 1608. The passage was closed by 1640 and rediscovered during an excavation in 1839: Claude Malingre, *Les Antiquitez de la Ville de Paris* (Paris: 1640), 368; *L'Echo du Monde savant*, 12 Oct. 1839, 481:645.

109. A.N. E19B f116, 13 Dec. 1608.

110. A.N. E20B f324, 31 March 1609. The crown paid 220 *livres* for clearing land for the rue Dauphine and only 83 *livres* for paving, insignificant sums: A.N. 120 AP 41 f16v, Estat pour la grande voirie de France 1609; A.N. 120 AP 42 f62, Estat pour la grande voirie 1610. Carrel and his associates submitted a request to the King's Council in 1611 "à estre remboursé pour le terre employé par commandement du roy Henri IV pour les rues Dauphine, Cristine, et d'Anjou, et du pavé qui a esté appliqué pour la commodité publique": A.N. E30 f354, 28 May 1611. There is no evidence that the crown granted this request.

111. Du Breul, 769.

112. A clause in the sale contracts suggests that the buyers may have made earlier commitments: "lors que led. Carrel fust l'acquisition des maisons, masures, jardins, cours, et autres appartenances de l'hostel Saint Denis et maison des chappes scizes pres les Augustins, ils fur-

ent promesse de place à . . . [name of buyer] de luy bailler et delaisser une place prise dans le jardin dudit hostel St. Denis sur la grande rue qui seroit faicte au travers d'icelluy hostel pour y bastir et ediffier une maison." These contracts are listed in note 115 below.

113. "Sur ce que j'ay advertiy que l'on commence de travailler aux bastimens qui sont en la rue neufve qui va du bout du Pont-Neuf à la porte de Bussy, je vous ay bien voulu faire ce mot pour vous dire je serais tres bien aisé que vous fissiez en sorte envers ceulx qui commencent à bastir en ladicte rue qu'ils fissent le devant de leurs maisons toutes d'un mesme ordre, car celà seroit d'un bel ornement de voir au bout du dict pont ceste rue tout d'une mesme façade": *Lettres missives* 7:219, 2 May 1607.

114. Min. cent. XXIII 234 f356, 25 June 1607.

115. Listed below are eight documented sales made by Carrel, Corbonnois, and du Nesme of land on the site of the Hôtel Saint Denis. The following men acquired lots on the rue Dauphine, but the sale contracts have not yet been located: Jean Antoine, master tapestry-worker; Jean Autissier, master mason; Gilbert Chappelle, magistrate in the *Chambre des comptes;* Philibert Gillot, barrister; Jacques Le Breton, wine merchant; Hierosme Luillier, *maître des requêtes;* Samuel Menjot, solicitor; François Petit, master mason; and Guillaume Rousseau, master joiner. For this group of seventeen land owners, I have found only three construction contracts: carpentry contract passed by Guillaume Rousseau with Pierre Bourdellet, master carpenter, Min. cent. XXIII 234 f778, 6 Dec. 1607; masonry contract passed by Claude de Paris with Jean Poussart, master mason, Min. cent. XC 168, 24 March 1608; masonry contract passed by Jean Anthoine with Simon Puthois, master mason, Min. cent. XXIII 237 f12, 3 July 1608.

DATE	DOC. (Min. cent.)	NAME	PROFESSION	AREA (sq. *toises*)	PRICE (*livres*)
18 Oct. 1607	LI 18	Boucher, Jean	merchant	(c. 40)	2,000
22 Nov. 1607	LI 18	Maillet, Pierre	solicitor	24	1,200
25 Apr. 1608	LI 20	Baudu, Jean	*sec. du Roi*	96	4,800
25 Apr. 1608	LI 20	LeTenneur, Abraham	*sec. du Roi*	42.5	2,125
25 Apr. 1608	LI 20	LeTenneur, Benjamin	*sec. des finances*	143	7,150
8 May 1608	LI 20	Mylon, Benoist	*con. du Roi*	57	2,850
22 May 1608	LI 20	Paris, Nicolas de	auditor	120	6,000
14 June 1608	LI 20	Paris, Nicolas de		(c. 12)	60
27 Feb. 1612	*	Sevin, Marie	widow	248	7,600
TOTAL				c. 782.5	33,785

* Mentioned in XXIII 261, 10 Feb. 1623.

116. Several men still lived on the rue Dauphine in 1623: Min. cent. XXIII 261, 3 Feb. 1623. Leases have been found for only two of Carrel's clients, Jacques Le Breton and Marie Sevin: Min. cent. CXXII 1570 f 72, 16 May 1609; Min. cent. XXXV 188 f353, 6 Dec. 1611.

117. Corbonnois and du Nesme passed a carpentry contract for the "maisons qu'ils entendent faire construire . . . durant la presente annee et la suivante dans le jardin de l'hostel Saint Denis sciz allentour des Augustins sur 12 thoises de longueur et de 23 pieds de largeur dans oeuvre pour chacun des grands corps du logis. Et pour 4 petites maisons sur pareille longueur et 3 thoises ou environ dans oeuvre . . .": Min. cent. LI 15, 16 March 1607. Contracts for the purchase of wood and for paving are located, respectively, in Min. cent. LI 15, 9 March 1607, and Min. cent. LI 21, 23 Sept. 1608. As for the houses owned by Carrel and Coursin, building contracts have not been found; the only relevant document thus far uncovered is a receipt from two carpenters acknowledging payment for work in three houses built by Coursin: Min. cent. CXXII 1575 f84, 30 June 1611. The two men used their seven rue Dauphine houses as security against a loan: Min. cent. XXIII 261, 3 Feb. 1623.

118. Dumolin, "L'hôtel de la reine Marguerite," *Etudes de topographie parisienne*, 1:101–220.

119. The masonry contract passed by Menjot and Autissier required the mason to provide a facade design: Min. cent. XXIII 234 f356, 25 June 1607. Three other building contracts for Menjot's house have been found: carpentry, Min. cent. XXIII 234 f572, 18 Sept. 1607; roofing, Min. cent. XXIII 236 f477, 17 June 1608; chimney mantels, Min. cent. XXIII 237 f246, 17 Oct. 1608. Autissier bought stone and rubble for delivery "tant en l'hostel de lad. Reine [Marguerite] et rues Christine et Dauphine": Min. cent. XXIII 234 f463, 29 July 1607. Other purchases of stone and tiles by Autissier are recorded in Min. cent. XXIII 234 f455, 27 July 1607; f471, 2 Aug. 1607. The only contract thus far located for the construction of Autissier's house on the rue Dauphine concerns carpentry work: Min. cent. XXIII 234 f776, 6 Dec. 1607.

120. Masonry contract with Petit: Min. cent. LXVI 19, 19 Oct. 1607. Other contracts for the houses owned by the Augustins on the rue Dauphine follow: carpentry, Min. cent. LXVI 20 and 29 Feb. 1608; roofing, Min.

cent. LXVI 21, 2 Oct. 1608; receipts from artisans, Min. cent. LXVI 23, 4 and 7 Dec. 1609.

121. Leases passed by the Augustins for the ten houses are located in Min. cent. LXVI 23, 31 Oct., 6 and 11 Nov. 1609. The houses generated 2,640 *livres* in rental revenue; the corner house with entrances on the quai and rue Dauphine cost 400 *livres,* but the nine others ranged in price from 240 to 260 *livres.*

122. The Grands Augustins owed Petit 25,973 *livres* for his masonry work. This sum was reduced by 3,473 *livres* which Petit agreed to pay the convent to settle a law suit. The Grands Augustins had initiated suits against four rue Dauphine residents — Philibert Gillot, Samuel Menjot, François Petit, and Marie Sevin — for damaging the convent by building houses against its walls; records of these suits are located in A.N. S 3632–3633. Petit was left with net earnings of 23,500 *livres:* A.N. S 3632–3633, dossier 3, n°4, 19 July 1610. Each of his houses had two shops and three floors above. Leases passed by Petit for his rue Dauphine houses are located in: Min. cent. LIX 41 f53, 11 July 1608; f287, 4 Sept. 1608; f294, 9 Sept. 1608; f383, 30 Sept. 1608. Min. cent. LIX 42 f255, 9 March 1610. Min. cent. LIX 44 f700, 14 June 1612. Min. cent. LIX 46 f55, 13 Jan. 1614.

123. *Registres* 14:220, 6 Nov. 1607.

Chapter 4: The Hôpital Saint Louis

1. There are no reliable mortality figures for these epidemics. One contemporary source put the death toll during the plague of 1560–62 at 68,000 people: *Registres* 14:178. L'Estoile estimated that 30,000 Parisians died in 1580: *Journal pour le règne de Henri III (1574–1589),* ed. Louis-Raymond Lefèvre (Paris: 1943), 250.

2. Pierre de L'Estoile, *Journal pour le règne de Henri IV,* vol. 2, ed. André Martin (Paris: 1958), 212.

3. These studies include Pierre-Nicolas Sainte Fare Garnot, *L'Hôpital Saint-Louis* ([Paris]: 1986); Dieter Jetter, "Betrachtung-mogligkeiten historischer am Hôpital St. Louis in Paris," *Das Krankenhaus,* March 1967: 108–9; Benassis, "Promenades medicales: l'Hôpital Saint-Louis et les sanitats," *Revue thérapeutiques des alcaloides,* ser. 4, 1937: 7–17, 39–48, 71–82; R. Sabouraud, *L'Hôpital Saint Louis* (Lyon: 1937); Maurice Dogny, *Histoire de l'Hôpital Saint-Louis* (Paris: 1911).

4. Ambroise Paré, "Traicté de la peste" (1568), *Oeuvres,* 6th ed. (Paris: 1607), 825.

5. L'Estoile, *Journal pour le règne de Henri III*, 250.
6. The Parlement of Paris described the outcast status of the city during the plague of 1596: "Sous pretexte de la Contagion . . . les gouverneurs, capitaines, maires, et eschevins, et autres qui commandent aux villes circonvoisines, mesmement aux bourgs et villages qui sont sur les avenues et grands chemins de lad. ville de Paris, refusent de recevoir, et laisser passer, et loger ceulx qui viennent de cetted. ville, et les empescher par violence, et voye de fait mesmement les vivandiers et autres qui se retirent en leurs maisons qui est entreprise prejudiciable au public dont peut advenir grand scandale et inconvenient . . .": A.N. U* 415 f103, 19 Aug. 1596.
7. "C'est pourquoy recognoissans asses que le chef se trouvant malade, tous les membres en auront ressentiment, nous avons jugé que cestuy cy qui est des plus éloignés y debvoit accourir de bonne heure, pour l'importance du negoce et du passage ausdictes nations": *Registres* 13:303, 3 June 1604.
8. Collège des maistres chirurgiens jurez de Paris, *Traicté de la peste avec les remedes certains et approuvez pour s'en preserver et garantir* (Paris: 1606), 13; Noé Legrand, "La peste à Paris en 1606. Mesures de defense prises par le Collège de Chirurgie de Paris," *Bulletin de la société française de l'histoire de la medecine* 10/4 (April 1911): 236–38.
9. See, for example, Estienne Gourmelon, *Advertissement tant pour se preserver de la peste comme aussi pour nettoyer la ville et les maisons qui y ont esté infectées* (Paris: 1581).
10. Measures to satisfy the demand for paving stones: A.N. E3B f264, 8 Nov. 1601. Sully's order to inspect the streets of Paris: A.N. E4B f224, 19 Oct. 1602; *Registres* 13:45. Paving was financed by the crown and a municipal tax: A.N. E11A f10, 4 July 1606; A.N. E11B f510, 30 Dec. 1606; A.N. E23B f123, 12 Sept. 1609. In 1605, the crown spent only 5,000 *livres* on paving; the amount more than tripled in 1606 (17,000 *livres*) and thereafter stayed at high levels—in 1608, 13,500 *livres*, in 1609 and 1610, 23,000 *livres*: A.N. 120 AP 38–42. Long-term paving contract with master pavers: A.N. E19B f179, 18 Dec. 1608. Regulations were also imposed on the residents of Paris concerning garbage dumping and street sweeping: A.N. 120 AP 1, Reiglement sur le faict des boues, Sept. 1608.
11. Henri IV's endowment of a military hospital was much celebrated by contemporary authors such as André Du Chesne, *Les Antiquitez et recherches des villes* (Paris: 1609), 120–21. It is, however, unclear if the Maison de la Charité continued to operate in later years. The foundation edicts were published by Félibien, 4:28–34.
12. The site of the Maison Royale de la Charité Chrétienne along the Bièvre stream had been devoted to therapeutic tasks since the thirteenth century, when the widow of St. Louis founded the Hôpital de Lourcine there. Houël's orphanage was organized as a learned academy with instruction in Greek, Hebrew, arithmetic, and music. He envisioned several schools, an apothecary, botanical garden, hospital, chapel, and an academy for artisans, all housed in arcaded Renaissance buildings. In May 1585, Houël claimed that he had already begun several "beaux edifices," but there is no indication that any buildings were realized: Félibien, 3:726–27. Houël's death in 1587 led to the abandonment of the project. On Houël: Frances Yates, *Astraea. The Imperial Theme in the Sixteenth Century* (London: 1975), 187–91, 204–7; Jules Guiffrey, "Nicolas Houël," *MSHP* 25 (1898): 179–270; Nicolas Houël, *Advertissement et declaration de l'institution de la maison de la charité chrestienne establie es fauxbourgs St. Marcel* (Paris: 1580); idem, *Ample discours de ce qui est nouvellement survenu es faulxbourgs S. Marcel* (Paris: 1579).
13. Pierre de L'Estoile, *Journal pour le règne de Henri IV*, vol. 1, 1589–1600, ed. Louis-Raymond Lefèvre (Paris: 1948), 459.
14. *Registres* 11:138.
15. On poor-relief measures in fifteenth- and sixteenth-century Europe: H. L. Beier, *Masterless Men: The vagrancy problem in England 1560–1640* (London: 1985); Bronislaw Geremek, *The Margins of Society in Late Medieval Paris* (1976; Cambridge: 1987), chap. 6, "Charity and Beggars"; Natalie Zemon Davis, "Poor Relief, Humanism, and Heresy," *Society and Culture in Early Modern France* (Stanford, Calif.: 1975), 17–64; Geremek, "La lutte contre le vagabondage à Paris au XIVe et XVe siècles," *Richerche storiche ed economiche memoria di Corrado Barbagallo*, 3 vols. (Naples: 1970), 2:211–36; Jacques LeGoff, "Ordres mendiants et urbanisation dans la France médiévale: état de l'enquête," *Annales ESC* 25 (1970): 924–46.
16. The city also had vagrants work on the trenches around Paris, *Registres* 9:23, 5 Jan. 1589; 9:371, 9:381, 5 and 15 June 1589; the Portes St. Victor and Buci, *Registres* 11:229, March 1596; and the Porte du Temple, *Registres* 12:559, 561–62, 576, March–May 1602.

17. Nicolas Ellain, *Advis sur la peste* (Paris: 1604).

18. *Registres* 14:40–41, 18 Jan. 1606. In 1611, the first Parisian hospitals to enclose beggars were opened: La Pitié in the faubourg St. Victor, maison de Scipion in the faubourg St. Marcel, and the Hôpital de St. Germain in the faubourg St. Germain. On 27 August 1612, the queen regent issued a decree requiring the enclosure of all beggars. This movement is discussed in Jacques Depauw, "Pauvres, pauvres mendiants, mendiants valides ou vagabonds? Les hésitations de la legislation royale," *Revue d'histoire moderne et contemporaine* 21 (July–Sept. 1974): 401–18; Christian Paultre, *De la repression de la mendicité* (Paris: 1906), 95–98; *Memoires concernans les pauvres que l'on appelle enfermez* (1617) in Archives curieuses de l'histoire de France, ed. Cimber and Danjou, ser. 1, vol. 15 (Paris: 1837), 241–70.

19. On the response to the plague in sixteenth-century Paris: Jean-Noël Biraben, *Les hommes et la peste en France*, vol. 1, *La peste dans l'histoire* (Paris: 1975); Claude Hohl, "Les pestes et les hôpitaux parisiens au XVIe siècle," thesis Ecole des Chartres, 1960, deposited at the Archives de l'Assistance Publique, Paris; Marcel Fossoyeux, "Les Epidémies de peste à Paris," *Bulletin de la société française de l'histoire de la médecine* 12/2 (Feb. 1913): 115–41; Léon Lallemand, *Histoire de la Charité*, vol. 4, *Les Temps modernes*, pt. 1 (Paris: 1910); C. Tollet, *De l'Assistance publique et des hôpitaux jusqu'au XIXe siècle* (Paris: 1889); Guillaume Potel, *Discours des maladies épidémiques ou contagieuses advenues en ceste ville de Paris es années 1596 et 1597 et es années 1606 et 1607 comme aussi en l'année 1619* (Paris: 1623).

20. In addition to the Salle du Légat, the Hôtel Dieu consisted of the Salle St. Thomas, which bordered the Seine; the Salle de l'Infirmerie, built during the second quarter of the thirteenth century; the Salle Neuve and Chapelle du Petit Pont, built from 1250–60. The history of the Hôtel Dieu is discussed in Jean Imbert, ed., *Histoire des hôpitaux en France* (Paris: 1982); Musée de l'Assistance Publique, *Dix siècles d'histoire hospitalière parisienne. L'Hôtel Dieu de Paris, 651–1650* (Paris: 1961), 93–94; Marcel Fossoyeux, *L'Hôtel-Dieu de Paris au XVIIe et XVIIIe siècles* (Paris: 1912).

21. Assistance Publique, Fonds Hôtel Dieu (hereafter A.P. H.D.) 69.607M f4.

22. *Registres* 1:226, 233–35. The project was realized more than a century later, when the Hôtel Dieu built the Pont-au-Double (1626–32) across the Seine.

23. A.P. H.D. 11.74/630, 13 Aug. 1519.

24. "[Nous] avons eté advertis que au moien de la contagion qui pourroit estre aud. hostel de la Charité durant les temps de peste, en pourrait advenir inconvenient en nostre hostel et chastel du Louvre qui nous tourneroit à grand prejudice": A.P. H.D. 11.74/635, 13 Sept. 1527.

25. "L'Hostel Dieu est scitué au meilleu de la ville, comme le coeur au meilleur [sic] de l'homme, qu'au moyen du mauvais air ordinaire estant en icelluy, peult infecter tout le reste du corp et tous les membres et endroitz d'icelle ville; aussi, s'il estoit permis faire led. accroissement, ce seroit muys du boys au feu, du venyn avec du venyn": *Registres* 3:131, 6 July 1548.

26. Claude Haton described the "tentes et pavillons à la mode d'ung camp hors la ville . . . pour y faire mener les malades par faultes de maison commune à cest effect": *Mémoires contenant le récit des événements accomplis de 1553 à 1582*, vol. 2 (Paris: 1857), 1013–14. In Bordeaux, the third city of France, the municipality bought a plot of land outside the city in 1586 and built small, uniform huts, a well, chapel, and cemetery: J. Barraud, "Les hôpitaux de peste à Bordeaux," *Archives historiques du dépt. de la Gironde* 42 (1907): 498–500. The use of huts and tents is discussed by Biraben, *Les Hommes et la peste en France*, vol. 2, *Les hommes face à la peste* (Paris: 1976), 171. On Constant's ex-voto: Jacques Choux, "Deux toiles de Rémond Constant au Musée Lorrain," *Musée Lorrain. Quelques enrichissements récents* (Nancy: 1958).

27. On the difficulties in financing the Hôpital de Grenelle: *Registres* 8:228; Félibien, 5:11. According to Félibien (2:1162), two thousand victims of the famine of 1587 were lodged in the Grenelle hospital. Mayenne's demolition order: *Registres* 9:548, 7 Dec. 1589.

28. Pierre Fayet's description is cited by Hohl, "Les pestes et les hôpitaux parisiens au XVIe siècle," 269.

29. On the Lazaretto of San Gregorio: John Thompson and Grace Goldin, *The Hospital. A Social and Architectural History* (New Haven: 1976), 51–53; Luigi Gallingani, "Il Lazzaretto fuori Porta orientale à Milano," *Atti Primo Congresso Italiano di Storia ospitaliera*, Reggio Emilia, 14–17 June 1956 (Reggio Emilia: 1957); Gian Piero Bognetti, "Il Lazzaretto di Milano e la peste del 1630," *Archivio Storico Lombardo* 50 (1923): 388–442; Luca Beltrami, *Il Lazzaretto di Milano* (Milan: 1882).

30. Alessandro Tadino, *Raguaglio dell'origine et giornale successi della gran peste* (Milan: 1648), 132.

31. Félibien, 5:31–32.

32. On 17 July 1606, the city bought two adjoining houses from Daniel Voisin and Antoine Lemaire for 15,000 *livres* and 5,000 *livres,* respectively: A.P. H.D. 10.69A–B. This money was raised by levying a municipal tax on the citizens of Paris: *Registres* 16:332–33.

33. "Les malades de la contagion transportés au logis de Voisin, au faubourg St. Marceau sont contraints d'en sortir, pour le mauvais traictment qu'on leur fait, jusques à les laisser mourir de faim et leur avancer les jours. A raison de quoi, ils se dressent des cabannes aux champs . . . , s'epandant partout où ils peuvent, au grand détriment du public et infection du pauvre, lequel par faute de police est contraint de souffrir toutes les extrémités du monde": L'Estoile, *Journal pour le règne de Henri IV,* 2:201.

34. *Registres* 14:177–180, May 1607.

35. On each *minot* of salt sold in the *généralité* of Paris, the king granted the Hôtel Dieu 10 *sols:* 5 *sols* for fifteen years, and 5 in perpetuity. The king had granted the same benefice to the Hôtel Dieu in 1597, but only for a short term. The 1607 measure had been preceded by a fiscal reform in 1600, when the crown verified the privileges claimed by all hospitals, lazarettos, and hospices in France. This measure was intended to locate misused funds that could be reassigned to feed the poor and support the soldiers' hospice: A.N. X1A/8644 f133, 20 March 1600.

36. The arches supporting the Salle St. Thomas were rebuilt in 1602, after experts advised the governors of Hôtel Dieu that they were about to collapse. This work and other repairs were undertaken between 1602–6 by Claude Vellefaux: M. Möring and L. Brièle, *Inventaire-Sommaire des Archives hospitalières antérieurs à 1790. Hôtel Dieu,* vol. 2 (Paris: 1884), 212–13; Léon Brièle, *Délibérations de l'ancien Bureau de l'Hôtel-Dieu,* Collection de documents pour servir à l'histoire des hôpitaux de Paris, vol. 1 (Paris: 1881), 33–35.

37. According to the royal decree, the Hôtel Dieu had to provide up to 120,000 *livres* "or a larger sum, if necessary": *Registres* 14:179.

38. In 1608, Pierre Parfaict, the brother of silk merchants Claude and Guillaume Parfaict, joined the governing board.

39. The operation of Italian health boards is surveyed by Carlo Cipolla in *Faith, Reason, and the Plague: A Tuscan Story of the Seventeenth Century* (Brighton: 1979); idem, *Public Health and the Medical Profession in the Renaissance* (Cambridge, 1976); idem, *Cristofano and the Plague. A Study in the History of Public Health in the Age of Galileo* (Berkeley: 1973). On the response to the plague elsewhere in Europe: Giulia Calvi, *Histories of a Plague Year: The social and the imaginary in baroque Florence* (Berkeley: 1989); Paul Slack, *The Impact of Plague in Tudor and Stuart England* (London: 1985).

40. On the Petites Maisons: Paultre, *Repression,* 73–74; Sauval, 3:28.

41. A.P. H.D. 1440¹.6545 f67. There is an unregistered masonry contract for the Hôpital St. Germain dated 5 June 1606 in *Registres* 14:93–94, but the documents thus far uncovered give no indication of what was actually built.

42. The repairs included reroofing, building new stairs, and glazing the windows. The construction work, operating procedures of the hospital, and its periods of use are detailed in A.P. H.D. 1440¹.6545 f30v–33, 42, 44, 54, 79, 94, 97v, 99v, 103, 119v, 141v, 161v, 196. In 1623, there were 912 patients in the Hôpital St. Marcel. During the following decades, the facility became overcrowded as the surrounding area was more densely settled. In 1646, the pesthouse was relocated to a more remote area, the faubourg St. Jacques, because Queen Anne of Austria had decided to build the Val-de-Grâce on the site of the Hôpital St. Marcel.

43. The plan, A.P. Plan 210 (492mm × 758mm), probably dates from 1618, when the property was surveyed: A.P. H.D. 69K, Arpentage, 6 Sept. 1618. Marcel Candille, *Catalogue des plans et dessins d'architecture du fonds de l'ancien Hôtel-Dieu de Paris* (Arpajon: 1973), 210.

44. The land on which the hospital was built belonged to the convent of St. Lazare and to various private individuals. Construction began before the property had been legally acquired by the Hôtel Dieu; either the governors had made verbal agreements with the property owners at an earlier date, or else the Hôtel Dieu acted on the assumption that it had the right of eminent domain. Between 1607 and 1617, the Hôtel Dieu accumulated 27 *arpents* at a total cost of approximately 6,000 *livres;* rates ranged from 160 to 300 *livres* per *arpent.* The land did not become increasingly expensive over this ten-year period. Furthermore, the Hôtel Dieu paid a lower purchase price for some parcels of land than the prior owners had paid a decade earlier. The sale contracts are collected in A.P. H.D. 8.62B–M.

45. On 26 July 1605, the city hired Pierre Noblet to rebuild the Porte du Temple: *Registres* 13:387–88. An inspection of the completed gate was ordered on 20 June 1607: *Registres* 14:185.

46. A.P. H.D. 1440¹.6545 f41v.

47. Ellain, *Advis sur la peste*, 37.

48. A.P. H.D. 1440¹.6545 f58.

49. Brièle, *Délibérations*, 48, 54.

50. Henri IV's attempt to associate himself with St. Louis may have inspired the publication of two books: a new edition of Jean de Joinville, *Histoire et chronique de tres-chrestien roy Sainct Loys* (1547; Paris: 1609); and an anonymous text dedicated to Henri IV, *La Vie, Legende et Miracles du Roy Sainct Louys* (Paris: 1610). A common theme in the funeral orations for Henri IV was his similarities to St. Louis: Jacques Hennequin, *Henri IV dans ses oraisons funèbres* (Paris: 1977), 201–4.

51. Möring and Brièle, *Inventaire-Sommaire des Archives hospitalières*, 214.

52. On 1 July 1607, payment of 36 *livres* was made to a messenger "pour son sallaire d'avoir porté en dilligence a Monsieur Sainctot estant a Fontainebleau deux plans du bastiment de la Santé pour les faire veoir au Roy": ibid., 214; A.P. H.D. 1440¹.6545 f42.

53. "Le roy aiant veu les trois plants qui luy ont esté representés pour la maison de la Santé a ordonné que le present sera suivy. Faict a Fontainebleau par nous Grand Voier de France Maximilien de Bethune." Candille dated this plan between 1607 and 1609, but in view of the design changes during construction, the plan could not possibly have been made any later than 1607: Candille, *Catalogue des plans*, 29.

54. A.P. H.D. 8.63Aa, 1 June–11 Aug. 1607.

55. The plan, A.P. Plan 191, is drawn on vellum in colored ink and measures 606mm × 621mm: Candille, *Catalogue des plans*, 115. The Assistance Publique also has a site plan of the hospital made in 1675, A.P. Plan 192.

56. On 23 April 1608, the governors ordered that "les pavillons des entree et sortie de la maison de la Santé seront faits de pareille structure l'un que l'autre, et se seront les portes en forme de portes cochere": A.P. H.D. 1440¹.6545 f62.

57. A.P. H.D. 8.63Aa f5, 1 June–11 Aug. 1607.

58. A.P. H.D. 8.64T, 16 Sept. 1611.

59. A.P. H.D. 1440¹.6545 f76, 17 Dec. 1608. According to the 1607 plan, seven chimneys had originally been planned in each of these buildings; only five were built: A.P. H.D. 1440¹.6545 f61v, 18 April 1608.

60. According to the 1607 plan, the two galleries had originally been designed with solid walls on the ground floor. The ground-floor arcade was introduced in 1608: A.P. H.D. 1440¹.6545 f71, 12 Sept. 1608.

61. *Lettres missives* 7:535, 28 April 1608.

62. A.P. H.D. 1440¹.6545 f63, 9 May 1608.

63. A.P. H.D. 8.64Q, 1 June 1611.

64. Attempting to cut corners, some masons plastered the chimney tops, but the governors had the masons redo the work in brick, as the contract required. A.P. H.D. 1440¹.6545 f60v, 11 April 1608.

65. On the church: Amédée Boinet, *Les églises parisiennes*, 3 vols. (Paris: 1958–62), 2:26–31. The black marble tablets on the facade were made by Robert Menart, the marble cutter who built a house at the Place Dauphine: A.P. H.D. 1440¹.6545 f75v, 5 Dec. 1608. Nicolas de Cambrai sculpted stone figures of the Virgin, St. John, and St. Louis which were placed inside the church: A.P. H.D. 1440¹.6545 f85v–86, 3 July 1609. Jacques and Abraham Sallé, master sculptor and painter, respectively, delivered stone for the statues of the king and queen and presumably made the figures as well: A.P. H.D. 1440¹.6545 f50, 5 March 1614.

66. According to Rosalys Coope, Vellefaux worked on the Hôtel de Gondi shortly before 1584: *Jacques Gentilhâtre*, Catalogue of the Drawings Collection of the Royal Institute of British Architects: vol. 6 (London: 1972), f37v. The earliest reference to Vellefaux in Paris that I was able to locate dates from January 1585: B.N. Ms. fr. Fichier Laborde 64787. Letters of naturalization: A.N. P 2666 f489v, 27 Oct. 1600.

67. B.N. Ms. fr. Fichier Laborde 64791, 64794. Vellefaux lived on the rue de Seine in 1610 (Min. cent. LXXIII 275, 13 Aug. 1610) and in the cloître St. Benoist in 1627 (Min. cent. LXXIII 96 f215v, 27 April). He regularly used the notary Nicolas Bontemps, whose notarial registers, however, shed little light on Vellefaux's architectural activity.

68. Vellefaux was first mentioned as *entrepreneur des bastiments* of the Hôtel Dieu in 1602. In 1603, he produced a plan "touchant les chambres qu'il fault faire sur les pilliers neufs," and in 1605 completed repairs in the Salle St. Thomas. The Salle St. Denis was rebuilt in 1617 "suivant le dessein qu'en a faict Claude Vellefaux": Brièle, *Délibérations*, 32–52. Vellefaux's will is dated 27 April 1627: Min. cent. LXXIII 196 f215v. By May 1629, he had died: A.P. H.D. 7b. 433/50.

69. A.P. H.D. 1440¹.6545 f45v, 24 Aug. 1607. Vellefaux also took charge of building the fountain in the center of the quadrangle and laying the water pipes.

70. "La Compagnie a delivré mandement à Claude Vellefaux juré du roi es oeuvres de massonerie de la somme de 257 livres 3 sols tournois pour son remboursement de ce qu'il a paié a eulx qui lui ont aidé a faire le dessein et modele en elevation de la maison de la Santé . . . et pour les fraiz et depense de bouche faite a diverses fois lors que les jurez massons ont esté visité les ouvrages de massonerie qui se faisoient en lad. maison et autres fraiz . . .": A.P. H.D. 1440¹.6545 f52v, 27 Nov. 1607.

71. Although seventeenth-century writers identified Vellefaux as the architect of the Hôpital St. Louis, later authors rejected this attribution: Du Breul, 1003; Sauval, 1:561. According to Bauchal and Lance, the hospital was designed by Chastillon and Quesnel: Bauchal, *Nouveau dictionnaire biographique* (Paris: 1887), 562; Lance, *Dictionnaire des architectes français* (Paris: 1872), 2:316–17. The case for Chastillon has recently been made by Pierre-Nicolas Sainte Fare Garnot, *L'Hôpital Saint-Louis* ([Paris]: 1986), 66–68. He does not question Vellefaux' responsibility for the modifications made during construction; only the authorship of the 1607 plan is at issue. Sainte Fare Garnot believes that Henri IV would not have entrusted the staff architect of the Hôtel Dieu with the design of a royal building. Among the architects in the king's circle, the most likely author of the 1607 plan, according to Sainte Fare Garnot, was the military engineer Chastillon because the hospital resembles a citadel (*château fort*). I believe that there are more significant affiliations between the Hôpital St. Louis and château planning, and thus disagree with the formal analysis on which Sainte Fare Garnot's attribution is based.

72. A.P. H.D. 1440¹.6545 f50, 28 Sept. 1607; f110v, 6 Oct. 1610; f121, 13 July 1611; f134v, 4 Aug. 1612.

73. On Ducerceau's designs: Ilaria Toesca, "Drawings by Jacques Androuet Du Cerceau the Elder in the Vatican Library," *Burlington,* May 1956, 153–57. The 1626 edition of Philibert Delorme's treatises included a hospital design based on Filarete's model. This project had not appeared in the first edition of 1567, published during his lifetime, and Delorme's authorship of the scheme remains uncertain. Dieter Jetter described the Hôpital St. Louis as

follows: "The principles of its form deviate to such an extent from anything up to then that it is not possible to point to any predecessors"; see "Erwägungen beim Bau französischer Pesthäuser," *Archives internationales d'histoire des sciences* 76 (Sept. 1966): 251–52.

74. Peter Heylyn, *A Survey of the Estate of France* (London: 1656), 74.

75. The masons were Antoine Lemercier and Pierre and Jacques Saffres: A.P. H.D. 8.63A, 10 Sept. 1607.

76. A.P. H.D. 8.63C, 19 Oct. 1607.

77. A.P. H.D. 8.63G, 3 July 1609.

78. A.P. H.D. 1440¹.6545 f55v, 13 Feb. 1608. The construction process can be followed in several *toisés:* A.P. H.D. 8.63L, March 1610; A.P. H.D. 8.64S, July 1611; A.P. H.D. 8.64U, June 1612.

79. Du Breul, 1003. Payments to day workers: A.P. H.D. 1440¹.6545 f87v, f95; A.P. H.D. 67.577, 17 April 1613.

80. A.N. Z1F/567 f93. At the start of construction, the governors of the Hôtel Dieu had recognized that the building costs would exceed royal revenues from the salt tax, and that the long-term operation of the hospital would require further subsidies. Consequently, they sought additional benefactors for the new foundation. Ten paintings of the hospital were commissioned from master painters and given to prospective patrons, among them Queen Marguerite and the *Prévôt des marchands:* A.P. H.D. 1440¹.6545 f44–46, 54–55, 62. A budget, probably dating from 1616, mentioned "quelques modelles tant de carte qu'en painture du bastiment dud. hospital dont deux ont esté donnez au roy et un autre à la royne Marguerite" (see Appendix C). The *modelles* were probably not three-dimensional models, but rather paintings. The word *modèle* was often used interchangeably with *portrait;* for example, the minutes refer to "le dessein et modele en élévation de la maison de la Santé": A.P. H.D. 1440¹.6545 f52v.

81. A.P. H.D. 1440¹.6545 f186, 31 Oct. 1618.

82. A.P. H.D. 66.557.

83. Tenon, *Mémoires sur les hôpitaux de Paris* (Paris: 1788), 71.

84. John Howard, *Prisons and Lazaretos,* vol. 1, *The State of the Prisons in England and Wales* (4th ed., London: 1792; reprint, Montclair: 1973), 1:176–77.

85. Fossoyeux, *L'Hôtel Dieu de Paris au XVIIe et XVIIIe siècles,* 270.

86. The following buildings survive from the seventeenth century: the central quadrangle, with remodeled axial pavilions; the L-shaped

buildings, except for the one at the southwest corner; the arcaded gallery at the southwest corner and the one leading to the service courtyard; the church; the governor's pavilion; and the two northern guard houses. The entrance pavilion for the sick and the pavilion opposite the apse of the church have both been substantially remodeled.

Chapter 5: Unfinished Projects: The Place de France and Collège de France

1. A.N. X1A/8646, f254. The only study of the project is a thesis by Lydia Mérigot. I was unable to obtain the author's permission to read the thesis and relied on a brief published summary: Mérigot, "La Place de France et le lotissement de la couture du Temple à Paris, 1608–1630," *Ecole nationale des Chartes, Positions des thèses*, 1966, 87–92. My interpretation differs from Mérigot's in two major respects. First, she believes that plans to develop the couture du Temple proceeded from a prior decision to build the Place de France, not vice versa as I argue. Second, Mérigot characterizes the Place de France design as more advanced than that of Henri IV's two earlier squares. I suggest that different sets of design considerations shaped the squares and that the greater interest in circulation demonstrated at the Place de France does not necessarily constitute an advance.

2. Appraisal of the gardeners' plantings, 5 Aug. 1608, and survey of the couture du Temple, 18 Dec. 1608: A.N. S 5063A. Minutes of the auction, 20–29 Dec. 1608: A.N. X1A/8646, f251v–269.

3. Further details on the amount of land controlled by each of the associates is given in Mérigot, 89. Declarations by Pigou of his purchase on behalf of du Nesme and Rousselet: Min cent. CV 181, 19 May 1610.

4. A.N. X 1A 8646, f269–273v. Between January and October 1609, only one action was taken. On 16 July 1609, the crown issued an order to survey the privately owned land that was needed to execute the 1608 street plan: A.N. E23A f29.

5. "Le Roy en son Conseil, voulant reunir à son domaine vingt cinq arpents de terre ou environ acquis du commandeur du Temple par Pigou destinez par Sa Majesté pour y bastir des rues et maisons et autres edifices pour la décoration de sa bonne ville de Paris dont la plus-

part se doibt construire des deniers que Sa Majesté sera délivre pour cest effect, a ordonné et ordonne que ledict commandeur du Temple sera assigné à jour certain en son conseil pour y veoir licquider la recompense qu'il pourroit demander et pretendre à l'occasion de lad. reunion": A.N. E24A f24, 6 Oct. 1609.

6. The first reference to the Porte and Place de France is dated 19 November 1609: A.N. E24B f111.

7. B.N. Est. rés. Ve 9, Coll. Hennin XVIII, 1636.

8. ". . . selon la cimeterye qui sera ordonné par M. le Grand Voyer pour lad. place et bastiment qui y sera fait": Min. cent. CV 181, 14 Oct. 1609.

9. Masonry contract with René Besnard, 19 March 1603: Mallevoüe, 267–69. Payments to Besnard from 1605 through 1609 are detailed in the budgets of the *Grand Voyer*: A.N. 120 AP 38 f12 (1605); A.N. 120 AP 39 f12 (1606); A.N. 120 AP 40 f10v (1608); A.N. 120 AP 50 f59v (1608); A.N. 120 AP 41 f13v (1609).

10. Carrel's proposal, detailed in B.N. Ms. fr. 16744 f266–268, was identical to a separate proposal made by the hydraulic engineer Hugues Cosnier, reproduced by Félibien, 5:804–6. Both Carrel and Cosnier refer to unnamed associates, and I assume they were partners. Their project entailed construction of a new wall from the Porte St. Denis to the Tuileries, a project originally planned by Charles IX when the Tuileries was under construction, and shown on the Nicolay and Quesnel maps of Paris. Secondly, the proposal contemplated a navigable canal 10 *toises* wide in the *fossé* of this enlarged circuit. The canal was to be inside the wall, not outside it as in the 1609 maps. Third, the project included six ports and three gates. Finally, the developers offered to demolish Charles V's wall. In exchange, Carrel and Cosnier asked for three things: payment of 300,000 *livres*, ownership of the land underlying the demolished wall, and the right to develop the territory lying between the old and new walls. Royal engineer Jean de Beins also submitted a proposal for the canal: B.N. Ms. fr. 16740 f285–286. The city government discussed the proposed canal in 1612: *Registres* 15:210–13. Le Barbier's development of the *fossés jaunes* in the 1630s was in many respects anticipated by the project of Carrel and Cosnier. On the *fossés jaunes*: Dumolin, "L'enceinte des Fossés-Jaunes et la formation du quartier Richelieu," *Etudes de*

topographie parisienne, vol. 2 (Paris: 1930), 111–340.

11. Several royal decrees referred to "les sept pavillons et logis du Grand Conseil," for instance A.N. E24B f111, 19 Nov. 1609.

12. David Buisseret, "Les Ingénieurs du roi au temps de Henri IV," *Bulletin de la section de géographie,* 1964, 77. In the preface to Alleaume's mathematical treatise, the publisher recounted the history of the manuscript after the author's death as well as that of an unpublished work, "L'Usage du Compas optique et perspectif": Aleaume [sic], *La Perspective speculative et pratique* (Paris: 1643).

13. A.N. E24B f111, 19 Nov. 1609. After the gardeners appealed for compensation, the crown agreed to assess their plants and trees: A.N. E24C f393, 29 Dec. 1609.

14. The sale contracts are gathered in two duplicate sets: Min. cent. CV 181, 1609–12; A.N. S 5064A–C, 1610–32.

15. Mérigot, "La place de France," 90.

16. On the market: A.N. Z1F/561 f54–55, March 1615; f103v–104v, Aug. 1615. On later subdivisions in the couture: Mérigot, "La place de France," 90–92.

17. Jean de Serres, *Inventaire général de l'histoire de France* (Paris: 1627), 1118–19.

18. Félibien, 2:985–87, 3:577–78. Du Breul, 762. On the history of the royal college: Abel Lefranc, *Histoire du Collège de France* (Paris: 1893); Abbé Claude-Pierre Goujet, *Mémoire historique et littéraire sur le Collège Royal de France* (Paris: 1758).

19. The following account is drawn from L.W.B. Brockliss, *French Higher Education in the Seventeenth and Eighteenth Centuries* (Oxford: 1987).

20. B.N. Ms. fr. 7801 f212–243.

21. *Mercure françois* (Paris: 1611), f407.

22. Du Breul, 763. By Henri IV's reign, there were thirteen royal professors holding chairs in Hebrew, Greek, Arab, Mathematics, Philosophy, Eloquence, Medicine, and Theology.

23. Jacques Verger, ed., *Histoire des universités en France* (Toulouse: 1986), 155–58.

24. Masonry contract with Claude Monnart, 5 April 1610: Mallevoüe, 170–73. Carpentry contract with Alexandre Gaultier, 10 February 1610: Mallevoüe, 174–76. Roofing contract with Léon Thomas, 10 February 1610: Mallevoüe, 177–78.

25. Coope, *Salomon de Brosse and the Development of the Classical Style in French Architecture from 1565 to 1630* (University Park, Pa.: 1972), 284–85.

26. The birthdate of Paul de Brosse is unknown, but two confirmed dates suggest he was an adolescent in 1610: his father was married in 1592, and he died in 1666.

27. B.N. Ms. fr. 7801 f212–243.

28. Min. cent. LIV 480, 13 March 1613.

Chapter 6: The Image of Paris: Maps, City Views, and the New Historical Focus

1. Pioneering work on the ideological content of maps has been done by J. B. Harley; see his "Maps, knowledge and power," *The Iconography of Landscape,* ed. D. Cosgrove and S. J. Daniels (Cambridge: 1988), 277–312; idem, "Silences and Secrecy: the Hidden Agenda of Cartography in Early Modern Europe," *Imago Mundi* 40 (1988), 57–76; idem, "Meaning and Ambiguity in Tudor Cartography," *English Map-Making 1500–1650,* ed. Sarah Tyacke (London: 1983), 22–45. Other important articles include: Richard Helgerson, "The Land Speaks: Cartography, Chorography and Subversion in Renaissance England," *Representations* 16 (Fall 1986): 50–85; Victor Morgan, "The Cartographic Image of 'the Country' in Early Modern Europe," *Transactions of the Royal Historical Society* ser. 5, 29 (1979): 129–54; John Pinto, "Origins and Development of the Ichnographic City Plan," *JSAH* 35 (March 1976): 35–50; Juergen Schulz, "Jacopo de Barbari's Views of Venice: Map Making, City Views, and Moralized Geography before the Year 1500," *Art Bulletin* 60 (September 1978): 425–74. Seventeenth-century French maps have not been given a symbolic reading with one exception: Louis Marin's comments on the Merian map of Paris (1615) in *Utopics: Spatial Play* (Atlantic Highlands, N.J.: 1984), 209–26.

2. On Deventer: B. Van'T Hoff, *Jacob van Deventer* (The Hague: 1953); Johannes Keuning, "XVIth Century Cartography in the Netherlands," *Imago Mundi* 9 (1952): 35–63; Jacques Deventer, *Atlas des villes de la Belgique aux XVIe siècle,* 2 vols. (Brussels: 1884–1929); H. E. Wauwermans, *Histoire de l'école cartographique Belge et Anversoise du XVIe siècle,* 2 vols. (Brussels: 1895). On Wyngaerde: Richard Kagan, ed., *Spanish Cities of the Golden Age: The Views of Anton van den Wyngaerde* (Berkeley: 1989); idem, "Philip II and the Art of the Cityscape," *Journal of Interdisciplinary History* 17/1 (Summer 1986): 115–35; Egbert Haverkamp-Bege-

mann, "The Spanish Views of Anton van den Wyngaerde," *Master Drawings* 7 (1969): 375–99.

3. On Saxton: Sarah Tyacke and E. John Huddy, *Christopher Saxton and Tudor Map-Making* (London: 1980); R. A. Skelton, *Saxton's Survey of England and Wales and the Maps from it: with a Facsimile of Saxton's Wall-Map of 1583,* ed. J. B. Harley (Amsterdam: 1974); Helgerson, "The Land Speaks"; Edward Lynam, *The Mapmaker's Art. Essays on the History of Maps* (London: 1953).

4. R. Hervé, "L'Oeuvre cartographique de Nicolas de Nicolay et d'Antoine Laval (1544–1619)," *Bulletin de la section de géographie,* 1955: 223–63; Leo Bagrow, *A. Ortelii catalogus cartographorum,* 2 vols. (Gotha: 1928–30).

5. The first French edition of Ortelius's *Theatrum* was published in 1572, trailing the original edition by two years. It was followed by five other sixteenth-century French editions in addition to a popularized version, *Le Miroir du Monde,* which went through eight printings between 1577 and 1607.

6. Gilles Guéroult, *Premier livre des figures et pourtraitz des villes plus illustres et renommées d'Europe* (Lyon: 1552), retitled and enlarged as *Epitome de la corographie d'Europe* (Lyon: 1553). Antoine du Pinet, *Plantz, pourtraitz et descriptions de plusieurs villes et forteressses* (Lyon: 1564).

7. On Belleforest's atlas: Mireille Pastoureau, *Les Atlas français XVIe–XVIIe siècles* (Paris: 1984), 55–56.

8. On Bouguereau's atlas: Pastoureau, *Atlas français,* 81–83; François de Dainville, "Le Théâtre français de M. Bouguereau, 1594. Premier atlas national de France," in *Actes du 85e Congrès national des sociétés savantes, Section de géographie,* Chambéry-Annecy, 1960 (Paris: 1961): 3–50; Ludovic Drapeyron, "Le premier atlas national de la France (1589–1594)," *Bulletin de géographie historique et descriptive* 1 (1890).

9. On Tavernier: Mary Pedley, "The map trade in Paris 1650–1825," *Imago Mundi* 33 (1981): 33–45; R.-A. Weigert, "Le commerce de la gravure en France au XVIIe siècle: les Tavernier," *Overdruk uit de gulden passer* (Antwerp: 1975), 409–40; idem, "Graveurs et marchands d'estampes flamands à Paris sous le règne de Louis XIII," *Miscellanea Jozef Duverger,* 2 vols. (Ghent: 1968), 2:531.

10. ". . . je diray en verité que ce qui m'a principalement induit à cest oeuvre a esté affin que sur le subject de chacune Province je peusse noter à propos au Greffe de l'immortalité les actes valeureux (joincts de la pieté et miseri-

corde) de nostre grand Hercule, Henry de Bourbon quatriesme": Bouguereau, *Le Théâtre françois* (Tours: 1594; facsimile reprint, Amsterdam: 1966), "Preface aux echevins de Tours," not paginated.

11. ". . . la Paix nous soit envoyée du Ciel sous sa domination, pour tous ensemble n'avoir qu'un Dieu, un Roy, une Foy, et une Loy": ibid.

12. Filippo Pigafetta, *Relatione dell'assedio di Parigi* (Rome: 1591), 21. Pigafetta included an engraving of Henri IV's siege of Paris in 1590. Ignoring the conventions of Parisian maps, Pigafetta placed the Right Bank (north) on the right side of his plan; it was always shown on the left side. Jules Cousin, "Les deux éditions du plan de Pigafetta (Siège de Paris en 1590)," *BSHP* 9 (1882): 28–29; Alfred Franklin, "Notice sur le plan de Paris de Pigafetta," *MSHP* 2 (1875): 398–401.

13. In a letter to Peiresc in January 1608, Malherbe reported rumors that the king was planning to demolish the wall between the Louvre and Tuileries and build a new wall enclosing the faubourg St. Honoré and Tuileries gardens. Although the projected wall, originally planned by Henri II, appears on the Nicolay and Quesnel maps, it was never begun by Henri IV.

14. Robert Dallington, *The View of Fraunce* (1604; reprint, London: 1936), D4.

15. Ibid., D3v. J. R. Hale, "To fortify or not to fortify? Machiavelli's contribution to a Renaissance debate," *Renaissance War Studies* (London: 1983), 189–209.

16. On Sully's work on the fortifications: Bernard Barbiche, *Sully* (Paris: 1978), 132–41; David Buisseret, *Sully and the Growth of Centralized Government in France 1598–1610* (London: 1968), 120–39; idem, "Les ingénieurs du roi au temps de Henri IV," *Bulletin de la section de géographie* 77 (1964): 13–84; idem, "Organisation défensive des frontières au temps de Henri IV," *Revue historique de l'Armée* 20/4 (1964): 25–31; Gaston Zeller, *L'Organisation défensive des frontières du Nord et de l'Est au XVIIe siècle* (Paris: 1928).

17. The seminal study of the royal engineers is Buisseret, "Les ingénieurs du roi au temps de Henri IV."

18. On Errard: Jean Errard, *Le Premier livre des instruments mathématiques méchaniques* (Nancy: 1583); idem, *Le Géométrie et practique d'icelle* (Paris: 1594); idem, *La fortification reduicte en art et demonstrée* (Paris: 1600); Euclid, *Les neuf premiers livres des elemens d'Euclide,* trans. Errard (Paris: 1604); Marcel Lallemend and Alfred

Boinette, *Jean Errard de Bar-le-Duc* (Paris: 1884). Henri IV referred to Errard as his principal engineer: *Lettres missives* 6:119, 3 July 1603.

19. In a stereographic view or profile, the observer stands on the ground or close to it. In a perspective or bird's-eye view, there is an oblique, elevated viewpoint. Types of city views in the sixteenth century are discussed in R. A. Skelton's Introduction to Georg Braun and Frans Hogenberg, *Civitates Orbis Terrarum 1572–1618* (Amsterdam: 1965), x–xi; R. A. Skelton, "Tudor Town Plans in John Speed's *Theatre*," *The Archaeological Journal* 108 (1951): 109–20.

20. De Beins's maps are reproduced in facsimile in François de Dainville, *Le Dauphiné et ses confins vus par l'ingénieur d'Henri IV Jean de Beins*, 2 vols. (Geneva: 1986). The letters of nobility are cited by Dainville, 1:65.

21. David Buisseret, "The Cartographic Definition of France's Eastern Boundary in the Early Seventeenth Century," *Imago Mundi* 36 (1984): 72–80. Buisseret points out that boundary lines had appeared earlier on maps published by Ortelius.

22. The only evidence of Sully's proposed map gallery is given by Antoine de Laval, "Des Peintures convenables aux basiliques et palais du Roy, mesmes à sa gallerie du Louvre à Paris (1600)," *Desseins de professions nobles et publiques* (Paris: 1605). In *La France metallique* (Paris: 1636), Jacques de Bié reproduced a medal of 1604 (now lost) which represented Henri IV as Atlas supporting a globe and standing in front of the Grande Galerie. Babelon cleverly suggested that the medal alluded to the proposed map gallery, but Sully's idea concerned the decoration of the Petite Galerie, not the Grande Galerie: Babelon, "Les Médailles de Henri IV," 34. A variant of Sully's idea was revived in 1626, when Louis XIII endorsed a project to decorate the Grande Galerie with views of French towns, but only two bays were ever completed.

23. Roberto Almagià, *Le Pitture murali della Galleria delle carte geografiche*. Vol. 3 Monumenta Cartographica Vaticana (Vatican City: 1952).

24. Juergen Schulz, "Maps as Metaphors: Mural Map Cycles of the Italian Renaissance," *Art and Cartography*, ed. David Woodward (Chicago: 1987), 97–122.

25. A native of Lyon, Nicolay's birth and death dates are unknown. The only documented phase of his life corresponds with Henri IV's reign: Buisseret, "Les Ingénieurs de Henri

IV," 74–76; Gabriel Marcel, "Quelques mots sur Vassallieu," *BSHP*, 1893: 189–90; idem, "Nouvelles notes sur B. de Vassalieu, auteur du plan de Paris de 1609," *BSHP*, 1907: 179–82.

26. The six watercolor plans of Crèvecoeur, Breedevort, Lochem, Groenloo, Lingen, and Oldenzaal are identical in style and format, although only the plan of Groenloo bears Nicolay's signature: B.N. Est., Coll. Lallemant de Betz Vx 27 pp. 365, 387, 397, 401, 495, and 525. The only other known drawing by Nicolay is a signed manuscript plan of St. Jean de Luz dated 1614 (B.N. Cartes et Plans Ge C1758). On the maneuvers of the French army in the United Provinces: Geoffrey Parker, *The Army of Flanders and the Spanish Road, 1567–1659. The Logistics of Spanish Victory and Defeat in the Low Countries' Wars* (Cambridge: 1972).

27. On the 1604 commission: A.N. 120 AP 5 f102.

28. *Recueil du Reiglement General de l'ordre et conduitte de l'Artillerye tant pour marcher en Campagne que pour la placer et dresser Batteryes aux sieges et auttres affaires*, 1613 (B.N. Ms. fr. 592). There is a second, undated copy of this manuscript in a larger format with additional drawings dedicated to Gaston d'Orléans: *Discours et Desseins par lesquels s'acquiert la congnoissance de ce qui s'observe en France en la conduite et employ de l'artillerie* (B.N. Ms. fr. 388).

29. On Nicolay's map: L.-M. Tisserand, ed., *Atlas des anciens plans de Paris* (Paris: 1880); A. Franklin, *Les Anciens plans de Paris*, 2 vols. (Paris: 1878–80), 1:90–100 (a transcription of the map's nomenclature); A. Bonnardot, *Etudes archéologiques sur les anciens plans de Paris de XVIe, XVIIe, et XVIIIe siècles* (Paris: 1851), 85–87.

30. There are seven sixteenth-century views of Paris: the Gouache plan (c. 1535), a painted work destroyed in 1871 but recorded in photographs; the Münster plan, from his atlas *Cosmographia* (Basel: 1550); the Basel (or Truschet and Hoyau) plan (c. 1550), a woodcut wall map; the Saint Victor plan (c. 1551), an engraved wall map attributed to Jacques Androuet Ducerceau; the Braun plan, from the *Civitates Orbis Terrarum* (Cologne: 1572); the Belleforest plan, from his *Cosmographie universelle* (Paris: 1575); and a tapestry (between 1569 and 1590), which is discussed in detail below. These maps are reproduced in Tisserand, ed., *Atlas des anciens plans de Paris*. Bonnardot and Longnon also described a seven-

teenth-century woodcut which can be dated to 1604/5 because the silkworks at the parc des Tournelles are depicted. All eight views were closely related, either copied from one another or copied from a lost prototype made in the 1530s, as some scholars have proposed. While the invention of a lost prototype appears to solve various interpretive problems, there is no documentary evidence that such a map ever existed. On the sixteenth-century views of Paris: Jean Dérens, "Le Plan de Paris par Truschet et Hoyau (1550) dit plan de Bâle," *Cahiers de la Rotonde* 9 (1986); idem, "Notes sur les plans de Paris au XVIe siècle," *BSHP* 107 (1980): 71–86; Michel Le Moël, "Les Plans de Paris," *Guide historique des rues de Paris,* ed. Charles Braibant et al. (Paris: 1965); Maurice Dumolin, "La famille du plan de la Tapisserie," *Etudes de topographie parisienne,* vol. 1 (Paris: 1929), 1–100; A. Franklin, *Les Anciens plans de Paris,* vol. 1; Jules Cousin, "Note sur l'attribution à Du Cerceau du plan de Paris sous Henri II, dit plan de St.-Victor," *BSHP* 3 (1876): 26–30; A. Longnon, "Catalogue des cartes et plans de Paris et de l'Ile-de-France exposés au Palais des Tuileries en 1875," *BSHP* 2 (1875): 141–60; A. Bonnardot, *Etudes archéologiques.*

31. The attribution to Gaultier was proposed more than a century ago by Bonnardot, *Etudes archéologiques,* 85. On Gaultier: André Linzeler, *Inventaire du fonds français. Graveurs du seizième siècle,* vol. 1 (Paris: 1932), 371–428; Roger-Armand Weigert, *Inventaire du fonds français. Graveurs du XVIIe siècle,* vol. 4 (Paris: 1961), 415–17; F. Baré, "Léonard Gaultier," *Bulletin des Beaux-Arts* 1 (1883–84): 1–2, 38–41, 54–60, 72–75, 81–86, 107–11, 142–44.

32. On Jean IV Le Clerc: R.-A. Weigert and Maxime Préaud, *Inventaire du fonds français. Graveurs du XVIIe siècle,* vol. 7 (Paris: 1976), 428–68.

33. On Le Clerc's atlas: Pastoureau, *Atlas français;* François de Dainville, "L'évolution de l'atlas de France sous Louis XIII. Théâtre géographique du Royaume de France des Le Clerc, 1619–1632," *Actes du 87e Congrès national des sociétés savantes, Section de géographie,* Poitiers, 1962 (Paris: 1963), 3–51; Raleigh Skelton, "Jean Le Clerc's Atlas of France, 1619," *British Museum Quarterly* 16 (1951): 60–61.

34. "Or afin que l'excellence de ceste grande ville soit notoire un à chacun, que les estrangers l'admirent, et que le tout redonde à la louage et à la gloire immortelle de vostre nom tres-Auguste, j'ay faict par vostre permission pour-

traire et buriner en cuivre le plan de vostre Ville, Cité et Université de Paris . . .": B.N. Est., Coll. Hennin XV 1352, Le Clerc's dedication to the king.

35. "Remarques singulieres de la ville, cité et université de Paris, sommairement recueillies des bon autheurs tant anciens que modernes par E.C. I.C. Lyonnais" comprised five sheets of text. The author was named in the second edition. The enlarged text from 1614 was reprinted by Abbé Valentin Dufour, *Anciennes descriptions de Paris,* vol. 6 (Paris: 1881).

36. Only one copy of the 1609 edition of Nicolay's map survives in Parisian libaries: B.N. Est., Coll. Hennin XV 1352.

37. Philippe Danfrie, *Declaration de l'usage du graphometre* (Paris: 1597). Danfrie's book reflects the growing interest in surveying techniques during the last third of the sixteenth century, when surveying manuals and new measuring devices proliferated. Among the French manuals on surveying were Didier Henrion, *L'Usage du compass de proportion* (Rouen: 1564); Jean de Merliers, *L'Usage du quarré geometrique* (Paris: 1573); Elie Vinet, *L'Arpanterie* (Bordeaux: 1583); J. Chauvet, *Instruction et usage de cosmometre* (Paris: 1585); J. Tarde, *Usage du Quadrant à l'Esquille aymantée* (Paris: 1594); Claude Flamand, *La Practique et usage d'arpenter* (Montbéliard: [1611]). Surveying techniques are discussed in G. Turner, "Mathematical instrument-making in London in the sixteenth century," *English Map-Making 1500–1650,* ed. Sarah Tyacke, 93–105; E. R. Kiely, *Surveying Instruments. Their History and Classroom Use* (New York: 1947); A. Laussedat, *Recherches sur les instruments, les méthodes et le dessin topographiques. Aperçu historique sur les instruments et les méthodes,* vol. 1 (Paris: 1898).

38. Classical scholars believe that the iconography of the Boscoreale cup (10cm high, 20cm diameter) copied the decorative program of a monument dedicated to Augustus: Fondation Eugène Piot, *Monuments et mémoires,* vol. 5 (Paris: 1899), 134–40; François Baratte, *Le Trésor d'orfèvrerie romaine de Boscoreale* (Paris: 1986), 69–76. On the iconography of the emperor's *submissio* and *clementia*: Richard Brilliant, *Gesture and Rank in Roman Art* (New Haven: 1963), 74–76.

39. Cesare Ripa, *Iconologia* (Rome: 1603; reprint, 1970), 149–50.

40. "Soubs le regne de ce grand roy/ Tres clement, tres vaillant, tres juste,/ Paris est

comme soubs Auguste/ Fut Rome du monde l'effroy."

41. P. A. Brunt and J. M. More, *Res Gestae Divi Augusti. The Achievements of the Divine Augustus* (Oxford: 1967), par. 34.

42. ". . . vous l'avez tellement embellie et enrichie de sompteux bastimens et de superbes edifices, qu'elle est maintenant beaucoup plus grande, plus belle, plus opulente, et plus magnifique qu'elle ne fut jamais, et pouvez dire avec verité, que l'ayant trouvée bastie de plastre, vous la laisserez toute de pierre et de marbre à la posterité": B.N. Est., Coll. Hennin XV 1352, Le Clerc's dedication.

43. Suetonius, *The Twelve Caesars,* trans. Robert Graves (New York: 1979), 69, sec. 28. A French translation of Suetonius by Guillaume Michel, *Les faicts et geste des douze Césars,* was first published in 1520. The latest edition that may have been consulted for Nicolay's map was printed in 1569.

44. Augustus commissioned Agrippa to produce a world map showing the full extent of the Roman empire; Dilke believes that the emperor also commissioned a map of Rome, although it is not mentioned by ancient sources: O.A.W. Dilke, *Greek and Roman Maps* (London: 1985), 41–53, 105; idem, "Maps in the Service of the State: Roman Cartography to the End of the Augustan Era," *The History of Cartography,* ed. J. B. Harley and David Woodward, vol. 1 (Chicago: 1987).

45. Given the motto, it is surprising that the Pont Neuf was not represented on the medal. The arms of Paris appear on the obverse: B.N. Médailles armoire 8, tiroir 265, no. 32; diameter 29mm. Babelon, "Médailles de Henri IV," 35; F. Feudardent, *Jetons et méreaux depuis Louis IX jusqu'à la fin du Consulat de Bonaparte,* 3 vols. (Paris: 1904–15), 1: no. 3487; A. d'Affry de la Monnoye, *Les Jetons de l'échevinage parisien* (Paris: 1878), no. 104; Jacques de Bié, *La France metallique,* 217.

46. ". . . pouvoit bien dire de sa Cité notre Auguste comme l'autre fit de la sienne, que de plâtre qu'il la trouva, il la randit toute de marbre": Laval, "Oraison funebre de Henry le Grand IIII," *Desseins de professions nobles,* 2nd ed. (Paris: 1612), f185. André Du Chesne extended the trope to the entire realm: "Je dis des Provinces de ceste France, que non content d'avoir mises en Paix, il rend encore d'avoir mises en Paix, il rend encore comme un autre Auguste sur la fin de son regne, toutes de marbre, bien qu'il ne les ayt trouvées que de brique au commencement": *Les Antiquitez et recherches des villes, chasteaux, et*

places plus remarquables de toute la France (Paris: 1609), "Epitre," not paginated. Imperial imagery was also invoked in pamphlets on the equestrian statue on the Pont Neuf (see Chapter 4) and in numerous other books and images: Antoine de Bandole, *Paralleles de Cesar et de Henri III* (Paris: 1609); Maximilien de Béthune, duc de Sully, *Paralleles de Cesar et de Henry le Grand* (Paris: 1615). On the iconography of Henri IV: Jacques Hennequin, *Henri IV dans ses oraisons funèbres* (Paris: 1977); Françoise Bardon, *Le portrait mythologique à la cour de France sous Henri IV et Louis XIII* (Paris: 1974).

47. "Les autres villes de ce Royaume ont l'oeil jetté sur Paris, comme sur leur aisnée, se conforment à ses actions, servent à ses intentions, et la reverent comme la Dame et Maistresse des Villes de France. [Comme] Pline disoit de Rome . . . il en est autant de Paris qui est nostre Françoise Rome, et qui ne cede en rien à ceste vieille Rome, autrefois pleine de si grand credit et authorité": Du Chesne, *Antiquitez et recherches des villes,* 57.

48. On Quesnel: Jean Adhémar, *Les Clouet et la cour des rois de France* (Paris: 1970), 52–55; Louis Dimier, *Histoire de la peinture de portrait en France au XVIe siècle,* 3 vols. (Paris: 1925), 1:157–61, 2:218–59; Frédéric Reiset, *Notice des dessins . . . au Musée Impérial du Louvre,* pt. 2, *Ecole française* (Paris: 1869), 413–15; Auguste Jal, *Dictionnaire critique de biographie et d'histoire* (Paris: 1867), 1025–56.

49. Michel Marolles, *Le Livre des peintres et graveurs,* ed. Georges Duplessis (Paris: 1877), 42–43.

50. On Quesnel's map, entitled "Carte ou description nouvelle de la ville, cité, université et fausbourg de Paris 1609": Tisserand, ed., *Atlas des anciens plans de Paris;* Franklin, *Les Anciens plans de Paris,* 1:80–89; Bonnardot, *Etudes archéologiques sur les anciens plans de Paris,* 75–84 (transcription of nomenclature). Quesnel is known to have made only one other map, a small manuscript plan made with Claude Vellefaux in 1615 to resolve a property dispute involving the abbey of St. Germain (A.N. S 869): Franklin Hazlehurst, *Jacques Boyceau and the French Formal Garden* (Athens, Ga.: 1966), 54; A. Berty et al., *Topographie historique du Vieux Paris,* 6 vols. (Paris: 1866–97) vol. 3, *Région du faubourg Saint-Germain,* 292; L.-M. Tisserand, "Note sur les travaux du service historique de la Ville de Paris," *BSHP* 3 (1876): 89–90; R. de Lasteyrie, "Un dessin de François Quesnel," *BSHP* 1 (1874): 71.

51. On Dupérac: Naomi Miller, "Etienne Dupérac," *Macmillan Encyclopedia of Architects* (New York: 1982), 1:613; Henri Zerner, "Observations on Dupérac and the *Disegni de le ruine di Roma e come anticamente erono*," *Art Bulletin* 47 (1965): 507–12; Edouard-Jacques Ciprut, "Nouveaux documents sur Etienne Dupérac," *BSHAF*, 1960, 161–73; Francesco Ehrle, *Roma prima di Sisto V. La Pianta di Roma du Pérac-Lafréry del 1577* (Rome: 1908).

52. Jacques Androuet Ducerceau, *Livre des edifices antiques romains* (n.p.: 1584), "Notice au Lecteur," not paginated.

53. These facts are disclosed in the printing privilege. "François Quesnel maistre paintre à Paris nous a faict dire et remonstrer que des sa premiere jeunesse s'estant addonné à la painture tant pour l'excellence de l'art qui est mise entre les sciences liberalles que pour avoir esté aymé des Roys noz predecesseurs et nous, il y auroit continué jusques à present et desirant profficter au public et en laisser quelque marque se seroit advisé de paindre et representer en platte paincture notre bonne ville et citté de Paris et la faire veoir tout aultrement et avec plus de grace et de verité que l'on ne la veue par cy devant principallement en ce temps ou soubz l'heureux succes de notre regne, elle a esté comme rebastye tout du nouveau et rendu en l'estat des plus superbes villes qu'on vit jamais auquel labeur led. Quesnel a apporté tant de continuation et tant d'industrie qu'il n'y a lieu signalle en lad. ville qui n'y soit despaint avec ses mesures et dimentions geometricques et non content de l'avoir paincte avec tant de travail l'auroit encore faict tailler en bois et en cuivre chacune description contenant douze grandes planches ce qui luy revient à de grandz fraiz et pour ce qu'il crainct que d'aultres imitans ses ouvraiges luy ravissent l'honneur de son long travail et le fruict de sa depense s'il ne luy est pourveu de noz lettres à ce necessaire": A.N. X1A/8646 f300–301, 4 Jan. 1608. For unknown reasons, the Parlement delayed registration of these patent letters. The king sent a second request for verification on 8 April 1608 (A.N. X1A/8646 f201), and the Parlement complied on 14 April. An excerpt of the registration is published by Félibien, 5:46.

54. Pierre Vallet, *Le Jardin du roy tres chrestien Henry IV* (Paris: 1608). A second edition was published in 1623 with a new dedication to the queen mother. Vallet collaborated with botanist and royal gardener Jean Robin on this book. As one of the earliest florilegia it was of great interest to botanists and flower collectors. On Vallet: G. K. Nagler, *Die Monogrammisten*, vol. 5 (Munich: 1879), 249; F. Robert-Dumesnil, *Le Peintre-Graveur français*, vol. 6 (Paris: 1842), 123.

55. Of the seven plans, the only other large-scale work besides the tapestry was the Gouache plan, which measured 5.14m × 4.42m. The Münster, Braun, and Belleforest plans were single-sheet printed maps; the Basel and Saint Victor plans were small wall maps. The analysis of the tapestry by Dérens ("Le Plan de Paris," 36–42) supersedes A. Franklin, *Etude historique et topographique sur le plan de Paris de 1540 dit plan de Tapisserie* (Paris: 1869), which contains two significant errors: the tapestry is incorrectly dated c. 1540, and the Gouache plan is incorrectly described as a seventeenth-century copy of the tapestry. The depiction of the Collège des Grassins, founded in 1569, establishes a *terminus post quem* for the tapestry. The arrest of Cardinal de Bourbon in 1588 provides the *terminus ante quem*.

56. The de Gaignières copy measures 56cm × 46cm, one ninth the size of the tapestry. In the secondary literature, the de Gaignières copy is misleadingly called the tapestry plan.

57. Named cardinal in 1548 and archbishop of Rouen in 1550, he presided over several important abbeys. With the fortune derived from these benefices, he remodeled the château of Gaillon (1566–76). On Cardinal Charles de Bourbon: Frederic Baumgartner, *Radical Reactionaries: the political thought of the French catholic League* (Geneva: 1975), 161–72; R. Limouzin-Lamothe, "Charles de Bourbon," *Dictionnaire de Biographie française*, vol. 6 (Paris: 1951), 1394; Eugène Saulnier, *Le Rôle politique du Cardinal de Bourbon (Charles X) 1523–1590* (Paris: 1912).

58. It is a peculiar oversight that Quesnel used the cipher of Henri II and Catherine de' Medici in the collar of the Order of the Holy Spirit. Evidently, he failed to modernize the prototype that he copied. The arms of the crown and the city are placed in the same location on the Gouache, Basel, and Belleforest plans. Only the municipal arms appeared on the St. Victor and Braun plans.

59. The arrangement of three cartouches with texts in praise of Paris at the bottom of the tapestry also appears on the Gouache, Basel, and St. Victor plans. The text on the Basel plan was taken from Gilles Corrozet, *La Fleur des antiquitez de la noble et triomphante ville et cité de Paris* (Paris: 1550).

60. The full text reads as follows: "L'Antiquité de la ville de Paris. La ville de Paris fut fondée selon aucuns par un Roy des Celtes, nommé Luce, duquel elle tire son nom de Lutece l'an du monde 2550. Autres assurent qu'elle fut bastie par un Gaulois nommé Paris qui estoit de la race de . . .(?) Samothe, lequel du temps de Noel institua les Gaulois en tous honnestes exercice. Clovis 5e roy de France y establyt son siege et la feit la ville capitale du royaume, Pepin le Bref y establit le parlement l'an 755. Charlemaigne y institua l'université qu'il retira de Rome l'an 807. Philippe Auguste enrichit beaucoup cette ville: en l'an 1190, il crea le Prevost des Marchans et Eschevins d'icelle et luy donna pour ces armoiries une naivre d'argent sur gueulle, le chef d'azur semé de fleurs de lys d'or; il feit paver. Mais Henry 4e la plus illustre qu'aucun des ces predecesseurs tant par infinis beaux edifices que cette carte represente, que par ses bonne loix qui y sont sainctement gardées et observées à l'honneur et gloire de sa Majesté."

61. The most famous exposition of the Trojan origins of Paris was Pierre Ronsard's epic poem *Franciade* (1572), which was modeled after the Aeneid. On sixteenth-century ideas about the origins of France: Claude Dubois, *Celtes et Gaulois au XVIe siècle: le développement d'un mythe nationaliste* (Paris: 1972); George Huppert, *The Idea of Perfect History* (Urbana: 1970); idem, "The Trojan Franks and their Critics," *Studies in the Renaissance* 12 (1964): 27–241.

62. The full text of the dedication follows: "Au Roy, Sire, C'est à vous seul à qui la raison et le debvoir veulent que je dedie cette carte, ou plustost ce tableau qui represente en petit volume vostre belle grande ville de Paris qui n'est pas tant obligée à ces premiers fondateurs (qui ne l'avoient qu'esbauchée) qu'à vous qui l'avez regenerée, redifiée, et parfaicte apres l'avoir retirée par votre valeur invincible des extremitez ou elle estoit reduicte. Aussi estiez vous dès longtemps destiné pour estre le Persée de la France, et le sien, le soing que vous avez eu d'elle, la colleguée en la preminence de toutes les villes de l'univers, sans qu'aucunes marques de ses malheurs passez ne la difforment. Vous l'avez si magnifiquement decorée et rembellie qu'elle n'est maintenant comparable qu'à elle mesme pour le nombre des edificies, maisons, pallais, eglises, hospitaux, colleges, rues, ponts, fontaines et portes dont elle est composée de sorte qu'elle est à present plustost une grande province qu'une ville. Or affin que les

Estrangers qui ne l'ont veue voient les merveilles que vous avez faictes en elle, je l'ay designée et pourtraité avec une exacte observation de toutes les dimensions et mesures, avec art et simetrie et non à bouleveue, prenant un aspect differant des aultres. Puis je l'ay faict graver en planche de cuivre pour satisfaire au desir des curieux. Le tout a vostre gloire, veuillez (Sire) avoir pour agreable l'offerte que j'en fais à vostre Majesté, laquelle je supplie de m'aprouver pour, Vostre tres humble serviteur et subject Francoys Quesnel. De Paris ce 2me may 1609."

63. On Gallicanism: J.H.M. Salmon, "Gallicanism and Anglicanism in the age of the Counter-Reformation," *Renaissance and Revolt* (Cambridge: 1987), 155–88; Jonathon Powis, "Gallican Liberties and the Politics of Later Sixteenth-Century France," *The Historical Journal* 26/3 (Sept. 1983): 515–30; Nannerl Keohane, *Philosophy and the State in France* (Princeton: 1980); Donald Kelley, *Foundations of Modern Historical Scholarship* (New York: 1970); Pierre Pithou, *Le Traité des libertez de l'Eglise gallicane* (n.p.: 1594).

64. The Belle Cheminée was dismantled in 1725 and remounted in a different form in 1825. The white marble equestrian relief was originally set against a black marble ground and framed by personifications of Peace and Clemency. Michèle Beaulieu, *Description raisonnée des sculptures du Musée du Louvre*, t. 2, *Renaissance française* (Paris: 1978), 107–9; Jean Ehrmann, "La Belle Cheminée du château de Fontainebleau," *Actes du colloque international sur l'art de Fontainebleau*, ed. André Chastel (Paris: 1975), 117–25; A. Chastel, ed., *L'Ecole de Fontainebleau* (Paris: 1972), 411–13; E.-J. Ciprut, *Mathieu Jacquet, sculpteur d'Henri IV* (Paris: 1967); idem, "Le Chef-d'oeuvre de Mathieu Jacquet de Grenoble. La 'Belle Cheminée' du château de Fontainebleau," *GBA* 53 (May–June 1959): 271–82; Père Pierre Dan, *Le Trésor des merveilles de la maison royale de Fontainebleau* (Paris: 1642), 139–41.

65. The motto, a traditional oath of royal unity, had been directed against the Huguenots. During the ceremonies for Henri II's entry to Paris in 1549, the *Prévôt* invoked the motto in a speech attacking heretics: *Registres* 3:185, 4 July 1549. L'Hospital changed the political meaning of these words when he appealed for tolerance and unity in a speech before the Estates-General in 1560: "La division des langues ne faict la séparation des royaumes, mais celle de la religion et des loyx, qui d'ung

royaume en faict deux. De là sort le vieil pro-
verbe, Une foy, une loy, un roy"; *Oeuvres com-
plètes de Michel l'Hospital,* vol. 1 (Paris: 1824),
398. On the Gallican motto: Kelley, *Foundations of Modern Historical Scholarship,* 254.

66. "Nous reunissans tous ensemble, recognois-
sans que nous somme subjects d'un même
Roy, . . . Et reprenans pour nostre devise
celle de nos peres et ancestres, vivons en fin
tous sous UN DIEU, UN ROY, UNE FOY,
UNE LOY": Antoine Loisel, "Remonstrance
III" (1582), *La Guyenne qui sont huit remon-
strances faictes en la Chambre de Justice de
Guyenne sur le subject des edicts de pacification*
(Paris: 1605), 99.

67. "Sur la devise de Paris. Un Dieu, un Roy./
Paris pour sa devise a un Dieu, et un Roy,/
Ayant l'appuy des deux son regne est de
dureé./ Rien ne le scauroit vaincre et il sera
l'effroy/ De toute nation et de toute contrée./
Sa grandeur ne sera jamais en desaroy/ Toujours dans son palais sera la Saincte Astrée./
Son estat sera ferme, assisté de sa loy/ Et d'une
bele paix durable et assurrée."

68. Frances Yates, *Astrea. The Imperial Theme in
the Sixteenth Century* (London: 1975).

69. "Sur la devise de Paris. Une Foy, une Loy./
Une Loy, une Foy entretient en concorde/ Et
en vraye amitie les peuples empeschant/ Que
parmy leur repos neglisse la discorde/ Qui
faict contre le bon animer le mechant/ Garde
ces quatre point, Paris, et te recorde/ Toujours
d'un Dieu, d'un Roy, d'une Foy et tachan,/
Qu'avecques une Loy ta volonté s'acorde/
Nul trouble par ainsi nira ton hur Faschant."

70. On Chastillon: Pastoureau, *Atlas français,* 97–
98; Buisseret, "Ingénieurs du roi," 40–51;
Maurice Dumolin, "Essai sur Claude Chastillon et son oeuvre," typewritten manuscript
(c. 1930) deposited at B.N. Est.; Colonel Au-
goyat, "Notice sur les Chastillon, ingénieurs
des armées, sur Claude Chastillon, Topo-
graphe du Roi et sur l'oeuvre de cet artiste,"
Spectateur Militaire, 15 Aug. 1856.

71. *Lettres missives* 5:46, 9 Oct. 1598.

72. E. Pognon has argued that the earliest engraved views and plans of towns appeared in
connection with military encounters: "Les
plus anciens plans de villes gravés et les événements militaires," *Imago Mundi* 22 (1968): 13–
19.

73. Boisseau had Chastillon's drawings engraved,
altered many of the plates that were made
during the engineer's lifetime, and added the
work of other artists to *Topographie Françoise.*
Later editions appeared in 1648 and 1655. On

Topographie Françoise: Pastoureau, *Atlas français,* 98–124; R.-A. Weigert, *Inventaire du
fonds français* 2:307–81; Françoise Boudon,
"La *Topographie française* de Claude Chastillon. Proposition pour une grille d'analyse des
gravures," *Les Cahiers de la recherche architecturale* 18 (1985): 54–73; Jeannine Gaugué-
Bourdu, "Montlhéry sous Henri IV, d'après
Claude Chastillon," *Bulletin Monumental*
139/3 (1981): 165–79; Marie Herme-Renault,
"Claude Chastillon et sa *Topographie française,*" *Bulletin Monumental* 139/3 (1981): 141–
63.

74. It is unclear when the drawings were engraved. Mathieu Merian probably engraved
the Hôtel de Ville and Place Royale during
Chastillon's lifetime. Jacques Poinssart engraved the Place Dauphine and Hôpital St.
Louis after the engineer's death. Neither the
engraver nor date of the Place de France and
Collège de France plates are known.

75. Claude Gilbert Dubois, *La Conception de l'his-
toire en France au XVIe siècle (1560–1610)*
(Paris: 1977); George Huppert, *The Idea of Per-
fect History;* Donald Kelley, *Foundations of
Modern Historical Scholarship;* J.G.A. Pocock,
"Introductory: the French Prelude to Modern
Historiography," *The Ancient Constitution and
the Feudal Law* (Cambridge: 1957); Roger
Chartier, "Comment on écrivait histoire au
temps des guerres de religion," *Annales ESC*
29/4 (July–Aug. 1974): 883–87 (a review of
Huppert's book); Corrado Vivanti, "Paulus
Aemilius Gallis condidit historias?" *Annales
ESC* 19 (Nov.–Dec. 1964): 1117–24. On his-
tory writing in seventeenth-century France:
Orest Ranum, *Artisans of Glory. Writers and
Historical Thought in Seventeenth-Century
France* (Chapel Hill: 1980).

76. Claude Fauchet's *Recueil des antiquitez gauloises
et françoises* (Paris: 1579), the best-known of
the group, was joined by an array of local
works: Elie Vinet, *L'Antiquité de Bordeaux*
(Poitiers: 1564); idem, *L'Antiquité de Saintes*
(Bordeaux: 1571); Léon Trippault, *Antiquité de
la ville d'Orléans* (Orléans: 1572); Noël Taille-
pied, *Recueil des Antiquitez et singularitez de la
ville de Pontoise* (Rouen: 1587); François Des
Rues, *Les Antiquitez, fondations, et singularitez
des plus celebres villes, chasteaux, et places remarquables du Royaume de France* (Paris: 1605,
1608, 1614). For a complete list of the antiquity books, see Jacques Lelong, *Bibliothèque
historique de la France* (Paris: 1768).

77. Du Chesne also compiled a bibliography on
the subject: *Bibliothèque des autheurs qui ont*

escript *l'histoire et topographie de la France* (Paris: 1618).

78. Gilles Corrozet, *La Fleur des antiquitez,* Prologue. On Corrozet: S. M. Bouchereaux, "Recherches bibliographiques sur Gilles Corrozet," *Bulletin du bibliophile et du bibliothecaire,* 1948 and 1949; A. Bonnardot, *Gilles Corrozet et Germain Brice. Etudes bibliographiques sur ces deux historiens de Paris* (Paris: 1880). Corrozet published a new edition in 1550 with a modified title and expanded material on churches, courts, hospitals, and the bishops of Paris: *Les Antiquitez, histoires et singularitez de Paris, ville capitale du Royaume de France* (Paris: 1550).

79. On sixteenth-century books about Paris: Maurice Dumolin, "Notes sur les vieux guides de Paris," *MSHP* 47 (1924): 209–85. Bonfons brought out an enlarged edition in 1561, which went through several reprintings: *Les Antiquitez, chroniques et singularitez de Paris par Gilles Corrozet et depuis augmentées par N.B.* (Paris: 1561). It was enlarged in 1576 and reprinted in 1577, 1581, and 1586–88. Bonfons added woodcut illustrations of the royal tombs at St. Denis, transcribed the epitaphs, and added lists of bishops and magistrates in various jurisdictions. The street list was expanded and regrouped in sections on the Cité, Université, and Ville, without however following a consistent geographical order.

80. Pierre Bonfons, *Les Fastes, antiquitez et choses plus remarquables de Paris* (Paris: 1605).

81. *Les Antiquitez et choses plus remarquables de Paris.* Recueillies par M. Pierre Bonfons, augmentées par Frère Jacques Du Breul (Paris: 1608). Du Breul's Christian faith inspired him to add extensive material on the religious orders in France. He cast Clovis, the first Christian king, rather than the pagan Merovich, as the king who "established the foundation of the entire grandeur of the kingdom," and he concluded the tome with the absolution of Henri IV by Pope Clement VIII.

82. A second edition of *Le Théâtre des antiquitez* was brought out by royal historiographer Claude Malingre in 1639, followed by a folio edition in 1640 from which he eliminated Du Breul's name: Claude Malingre, *Les Antiquitez de la ville de Paris* (Paris: 1640). On Malingre, who was appointed royal historiographer in 1614: François Fossier, "A propos du titre d'historiographe sous l'Ancien Régime," *Revue d'histoire moderne et contemporaine* 32 (July–Sept. 1985): 404.

83. On Du Breul: Le Roux de Lincy and A. Bruel, "Notice historique et critique sur Dom Jacques Du Breul, prieur de St. Germain des Prés," *Bibliothèque de l'Ecole des Chartes,* ser. 6, 4 (1868): 56–72, 479–512. *Le Théâtre* was followed by a supplementary volume in Latin on abbeys and monasteries: Jacobo Du Breul, *Supplementum Antiquitatem urbis Parisiacae* (Paris: 1614).

Conclusion

1. Michel de Montaigne, *The Complete Essays of Montaigne,* trans. Donald Frame (Stanford, Calif.: 1965), "Of Vanity" (III: 9), 743.

2. Henri IV "avoit fait commencer la structure d'un College Royal à Paris pour y appeler par des gages plus grands qu'en aucune université du monde les plus grands hommes du monde. Pour la facilité et richesse du comerce [sic], il a attiré en son Royaume les plus rares artisans des pays estrangers, pour y establir les manufactures des soyes, et autres façons estrangeres, à cause desquelles plus de six millions de livres se transportoient tous les ans hors de France: pour ce mesme subject il fit rebastir les ponts, que la fureur des guerres avoit démolis, en bastir de nouveaux, applanir les chemins, refaire les anciens pavez, et en faire d'autres. Recognoissant que les bastiments estoient des monuments eternels de la grandeur d'un Prince, et la puissance de ses richesses, un employ de toutes sortes d'artisans, et un gaignepain d'une infinité de pauvres manoeuvres et hommes de bras, qui faute d'estre occupez deviennent fayneans, vagabonds, et voleurs, il employa pour ceste consideration en edifices plus de huict millions de livres: il fit faire particulierement le pont-neuf de Paris, le canal de Briare, la tour de Courdouan, Montceaux, la grande galerie du Louvre, l'Hopital de S. Louis, la place Royale, la place Daulphine, la rue Daulphine, autant de rues dans les marests du Temple qu'il y a de Provinces en France, le grand College de la Fleche, une partie de l'Arsenal, du Louvre, et la meilleure partie des Tuilleries, de Saint Germain en Laye, de Verneuil, et de Fontainebleau . . .": Louis Savot, *Discours sur le sujet du colosse du Grand Roy Henry posé sur le milieu du Pont-Neuf de Paris* (Paris: [c. 1614]), 21–22.

3. On the urban planning of Sixtus V: Helge Gamrath, *Roma sancta renovata: studi sull' urbanistica di Roma nella seconda meta del sec. XVI* (Rome: 1987); René Schiffmann, *Roma felix: Aspekte der städtebaulichen Gestaltung Roms unter Papst Sixtus V* (Bern: 1985); Jean Delumeau, *Vie économique et sociale de Rome dans la seconde moitié du XVIe siècle,* vol. 1 (Paris: 1957); Ludwig

von Pastor, *The History of the Popes,* vol. 22
(London: 1932); idem, *Sixto V: il creatore della
nouva Roma* (Rome: 1922).

4. J.-B. Colbert, *Lettres, Instructions et Mémoires,*
ed. P. Clément (Paris: 1861–73), 7:288.

Appendix D: Charles Marchant

1. Félibien, 5:44–45. Carpentry contracts: Min.
cent. XIX 357, 10 June 1607; XIX 360 f330,
5 Nov. 1608. Joinery contract: XIX 358 f366,
24 Oct. 1607. Roofing contract: XIX 357
f159, 17 May 1607.

2. Leases for houses on the Pont aux Marchands:
Min. cent. CVIII 39 f1–25, 10 Jan.–19 Aug.
1609; CVIII 41, 20 Jan., 6 May 1610; CVIII 43
f11, 11 Jan. 1611, f62, 28 Feb. 1611.

3. Pierre de L'Estoile, *Journal pour le règne de Henri
IV,* vol. 2, ed. A. Martin (Paris: 1958), 412.

4. Min. cent. CVIII 35 f336, 24 Oct. 1606.

5. *Registres* 11:317.

6. Min. cent. XIX 358, 14 Aug. 1607.

7. Masonry contracts for the house on the rue des
Minimes: Min. cent. XIX 355, 4 April 1606;
XIX 358 f300, 14 Sept. 1607. The other houses
included three on the rue de la Mortellerie,
three on the rue Roi de Sicile, one on the rue
Ste. Catherine, where Marchant lived, and one
on the rue de la Verrerie, where his daughter
Magdeleine and her husband, Nicolas Le Jay,
President of the Parlement, lived: Min. cent.
LIV 250, 29 Jan. 1609; CVIII 57 f206, 7 May
1618.

8. A.N. S 1958.

9. Sauval, 1:71. The property was confiscated
from his heirs in 1620.

10. Min. cent. LIV 250, 29 Jan. 1609.

11. Min. cent. CVIII 57 f206, 7 May 1618.

SELECTED BIBLIOGRAPHY

I. PRIMARY SOURCES

Alleaume, Jacques. *La Perspective speculative et practique.* Paris: 1643.

Alphand, Michaux, and L.-M. Tisserand, eds. *Atlas des anciens plans de Paris,* 4 vols. Paris: 1880.

Bandole, Antoine de. *Les Paralleles de Cesar et de Henry IIII.* Paris: [1609].

Barbiche, Bernard, ed. *Lettres de Henri IV.* Vatican City: 1968.

Bautier, Robert-Henri, and Aline Vallée-Karcher. *Les Papiers de Sully aux Archives Nationales.* Paris: 1959.

Berger de Xivrey, Jules, and Jules Guadet. *Recueil des lettres missives de Henri IV,* 9 vols. Collection de documents inédits sur l'histoire de France. Paris: 1843–76.

Béthune, Maximilien de [Sully]. *Paralleles de Cesar et de Henry le Grand.* Paris: 1615.

———. *Sages et royales Oeconomies d'Estat.* 1st ed. vol. 1: 1638, vol. 2: 1662. Nouvelle collection des mémoires pour servir à l'histoire de France, ed. Michaud and Poujoulat, ser. 2, vols. 2–3. Paris: 1837.

[Béthune, Philippe de.] *Le Conseiller d'Estat.* Paris: 1641.

Bié, Jacques de. *La France metallique.* Paris: 1636.

Bonfons, Nicholas, ed. *Les Antiquitez, histoires et singularitez de Paris de Gilles Corrozet.* Paris: 1561.

Bordier, Henri, and Léon Brièle. *Les Archives hospitalières de Paris.* Paris: 1877.

Brice, Germain. *Description nouvelle de ce qu'il y a de plus remarquable dans la ville de Paris,* 2 vols. Paris: 1684.

Brièle, Leon. *Collection de documents pour servir à l'histoire des hôpitaux de Paris.* Vol. 1 Délibérations de l'ancien Bureau de l'Hôtel-Dieu (1531–1767). Paris: 1881.

Buchel, Arnold Van. "Description de Paris par Van Buchel d'Utrecht (1585–1586)," eds. L.-A. Van Langeraad and A. Vivier, *MSHP* 26 (1899), 59–195.

Bugato, P. *I Fatti di Milano al contrasto della peste.* Milan: 1578.

Candille, Marcel. *Catalogue des plans et dessins d'architecture du fonds de l'ancien Hôtel-Dieu de Paris.* Arpajon: 1973.

Carew, George. "A Relation of the State of France with the Characters of Henry IV and the Principal Persons of that Court," *An Historical View of the Negotiations between the Courts of England, France, and Brussels from the year 1592 to 1617,* ed. Thomas Birch. London: 1749.

Le Carousel des pompes et magnificences faictes en faveur du mariage du tres-chrestien Roy Louis XIII. Paris: 1612.

Chastillon, Claude. *Topographie françoise ou représentations de plusieurs villes.* Paris: 1648.

Chereau, Achille. *Les Ordonnances faictes pour eviter dangier de peste, 1531.* Paris: 1873.

Cholet, Estienne. *Remarques singuliers de la ville, cité, et université de Paris.* Paris: 1614.

Citoys, François. *Advis sur la nature de la peste et sur les moyens de s'en preserver et guerir.* Paris: 1623.

Clavareau, N. M. *Mémoire sur les hôpitaux civils de Paris*. Paris: 1805.

Clement, Gabriel. *Le Trespas de la peste*. Paris: 1626.

College des maistres chirurgiens jurez de Paris. *Traicté de la peste et les remedes certains*. Paris: 1606.

Copie d'une missive envoyée de Paris à Lyon contenant nouvelle de la santé. Lyon: 1580. Rpt. Archives curieuses de l'histoire de France, ed. M. L. Cimber and F. Danjou, ser. 1, vol. 9. Paris: 1835, 321–26.

Corrozet, Gilles. *Les Antiquitez, histoires et singularitez de Paris*. Paris: 1550.

_____. *La Fleur des antiquitez de la noble et triomphante ville et cité de Paris*. Paris: 1532.

Coryate, Thomas. *Coryat's Crudities*, 2 vols. (London: 1611). Glasgow: 1905.

_____. "Voyage à Paris (1608)," ed. R. de Lasteyrie, *MSHP* 6 (1879), 24–53.

Coulon, Louis. *L'Ulysse françois ou le voyage de France, de Flandre et de Savoye*. Paris: 1643.

Dallington, Robert. *The View of Fraunce* (London: 1604), Shakespeare Facsimiles 13. London: 1936.

Dechuyes, G. *La Guide de Paris*. Paris: [1647].

Defoe, Daniel. *A Journal of the Plague Year*. London: 1722. Rpt. New York: 1969.

Delamare, Nicolas, and Le Clerc du Brillet. *Traité de la police*, 4 vols. Paris: 1705–38.

Delorme, Philibert. *Traités d'architecture: Nouvelles Inventions pour bien bastir et à petits fraiz* (1561); *Premier Tome de l'Architecture* (1567). Paris: 1988.

Des Rues, François. *Les Antiquitez, fondations, et singularitez des plus celebres villes, chasteaux, et places remarquables du royaume de France*, 2nd ed. Paris: 1608.

Discours sur la vie, actions et mort de tres-illustre Seigneur Messire Achille de Harlay. Paris: 1616. Rpt. Archives curieuses de l'histoire de France, ed. M. L. Cimber and F. Danjou, ser. 1, vol. 15. Paris: 1837, 423–57.

Du Breul, Jacques. *Supplementum antiquitatem urbis Parisiacae*. Paris: 1614.

_____. *Le Théâtre des antiquitez de Paris*. Paris: 1612; 2nd ed. 1639.

_____, ed. *Les Antiquitez et choses plus remarquables de Paris de Pierre Bonfons*. Paris: 1608.

Ducerceau, Jacques Androuet. *Livre des edifices antiques romains*. N.p.: 1584.

_____. *Les plus excellents bastiments de France*, 2 vols. Paris: 1576–79.

Du Chesne, André. *Les Antiquitez et recherches des villes, chasteaux, et places plus remarquables de toute la France*. Paris: 1609.

Dupont, Pierre. *Stromatourgie ou d'excellence de la manufacture des tapis dits de Turquie*. Paris: 1632. Repub. by Alfred Darcel and Jules Guiffrey, *La Stromaturgie de Pierre Dupont*. Documents relatifs à la fabrication des tapis de Turquie, Paris: 1882.

Du Port, François. *Pestilentis luis domandae ratio. Moien de cognoistre et guarir la peste*. Paris: 1606.

[Ellain, Nicolas.] *Advis sur la peste*. Paris: 1604.

Errard, Jean. *La Fortification reduicte en art*. Paris: 1600.

Estienne, Charles. *L'Agriculture et maison rustique*. Paris: 1564.

Eve, Clovis. *La Vie, legende et miracles du Roy Saint Louys*. Paris: 1610.

Fabri, Claude. *Paradoxes de la cure de peste*. Paris: 1568.

Fardoil, N. *Remerciment à Monsieur Myron*. Paris: 1606.

Fauchet, Claude. *Les Oeuvres*. Paris: 1610.

Félibien, André. *Description de l'arc de la place Dauphine*. Paris: 1660.

Félibien, Michel, and Guy-Alexis Lobineau. *Histoire de la ville de Paris,* 5 vols. Paris: 1725.

Filarete. *Treatise on Architecture,* trans. and intro. John Spencer, 2 vols. New Haven: 1965.

Fioravanti, Leonardo. *Del regimento della peste.* Venezia: 1565.

Flamand, Claude. *La Guide des fortifications et conduitte militaire.* Montbéliard: [1611].

_____. *La Practique et usage d'arpenter et mesurer toutes superficies de terre.* Montbéliard: [1611].

[Fonteny, J. de.] *Antiquitez, fondations, et singularitez des plus celebres villes, chasteaux, places remarquables, eglises, forts, forteresses du royaume de France.* Paris: 1614.

Frutaz, Amato Pietro. *Le Piante di Roma,* 3 vols. Rome: 1962.

Giraldi, Giuliano. *Esequie d'Arrigo quarto.* Firenze: 1610.

Gourmelon, Estienne. *Advertissement tant pour se preserver de la peste comme aussi pour nettoyer la ville et les maisons qui y ont esté infectées.* Paris: 1581.

Grenaille, sieur de. *La Place Royale ou la statue dressée à Louis le Juste.* Paris: 1639.

Grillot, J. *Lyon affligé de contagion.* Lyon: 1629.

Grodecki, Catherine. *Histoire de l'art au XVIe siècle, 1540–1600, Documents du Minutier Central.* Paris: 1985.

Habicot, N. *La Recette chasse-peste.* Paris: 1619.

Haton, Claude. *Mémoires contenant le récit des événements accomplis de 1553 à 1582,* 2 vols. Paris: 1857.

Heroard, Jean. *Journal de Jean Heroard sur l'enfance et la jeunesse de Louis XIII (1601–1628),* ed. Eud. Soulié and Ed. de Barthélemy, 2 vols. Paris: 1868.

Heylyn, Peter. *A Survey of the Estate of France and of some of the adjoyning lands.* London: 1656.

Houël, Nicolas. *Advertissement et declaration de l'institution de la maison de la charité chrestienne.* Paris: 1580.

_____. *Ample discours de ce qui est nouvellement survenu es faulxbourgs S. Marcel les Paris ensemble les miracle advenus en la maison de la charité chrestienne.* Paris: 1579.

_____. *Traité de la peste.* Paris: 1573.

Howard, John. *The Principal Lazarettos in Europe.* London: 1789.

_____. *Prisons and Lazarettos (1777).* Vol. 1 The State of the Prisons in England and Wales. 4th ed., London: 1792. Rpt. Montclair: 1973.

Husson, Armand. *Etude sur les hôpitaux considérés sous le rapport de leur construction.* Paris: 1862.

Huval, Baltazar. *Discours et sommaire recueil de plusieurs personnes guaries de la maladie contagieuse.* Paris: 1583.

Jaillot, Jean-Baptiste. *Recherches critiques, historiques et topographiques sur la ville de Paris,* 5 vols. Paris: 1772–74.

Joinville, Jean de. *Histoire et chronique du tres-chrestien roy Sainct Loys.* Paris: 1547. Rpt. 1609.

Laffemas, Barthélemy de. *La Commission edit et partie des memories de l'ordre et establissement du Commerce general des manufactures.* Paris: 1601.

_____. *Les Discours d'une liberté generale et vie heureuse pour le bien du peuple.* Paris: 1601.

_____. *Discours sur la figure du Roy eslevée à la porte de la Maison de Ville.* Paris: 1607.

_____. *La Façon de faire et semer la graine de meuriers.* Paris: 1604.

_____. *L'Incredulité ou l'ignorance de ceux qui ne veulent cognoistre le bien et repos de l'Estat.* Paris: 1600.

_____. *Lettres et exemples de la feu royne mère. Avec la preuve certaine de faire les soyes en ce royaume.* Paris: 1602. Rpt. Archives curieuses de l'histoire de France, ed. M. L. Cimber and F. Danjou, ser. 1, vol. 9. Paris: 1836, 121–36.

_____. *Le Naturel et profit admirable du meurier.* Paris: 1604.

_____. *Neuf advertissements pour servir à l'utilité publicque.* Paris: 1601.

_____. *Le Plaisir de la noblesse et autres qui ont des eritages aux champs sur la preuve certaine et profict des estauffes et soyes qui se font à Paris.* Paris: 1603.

_____. *Recueil presenté au Roy de ce qui se passe en l'assemblée du commerce au Palais à Paris.* Paris: 1604. Rpt. Documents historiques inédits, ed. Champollion Figeac, vol. 4. Paris: 1848, 282–301.

_____. *Reglement general pour dresser les manufactures et ouvrages en ce royaume.* Rouen: 1597.

_____. *Remonstrances au peuple suivant les edicts et ordonnances des roys à cause du luxe et superfluité des soyes.* Paris: 1601.

_____. *La Ruine et disette d'argent qu'ont apporté les draps de soyes en France.* Paris: 1608.

_____. *Source de plusieurs abus et monoples.* Paris: 1596.

_____. *Le Tesmoinage certain du profict et revenu des soyes de France.* Paris: 1602.

Laffemas, Isaac de. *L'Histoire du commerce de France.* Paris: 1606. Rpt. Archives curieuses de l'histoire de France, ed. M. L. Cimber and F. Danjou, ser. 1, vol. 14. Paris: 1837.

_____. *Le Tesmoinage certain du profict et revenu des soyes de France.* Paris: 1602.

La Framboisiere, Nicolas Abraham de. "Le Gouvernment requis en temps de peste pour se garder de sa tyrannie," *Les Oeuvres,* vol. 1. Paris: 1613, 271–83.

Lamperiere, Jean de. *Traité de la peste.* Rouen: 1620.

Largentier, Nicolas. *Recueil des principaux poincts, raisons, et remonstrances.* Paris: 1610.

Lasteyrie, R. de. "Documents inédits sur la construction du Pont-Neuf," *MSHP* 9 (1882), 1–94.

Laugier, Honoré de. *Le Camp de la Place Royalle.* Paris: 1612.

Laval, Antoine de. *Desseins de professions nobles et publiques.* Paris: 1605.

Le Clerc, Antoine. *Stations faictes pour l'entrée de la Royne à Paris apres son coronnement.* Paris: 1611.

Le Conte, D. *Météorologie ou l'excellence de la statue de Henry le Grand eslevée sur le Pont-Neuf.* Paris: 1614.

Legrain, Baptiste. *Decade contenant la vie et gestes de Henry le Grand.* Paris: 1614.

Le Maire, C. *Paris ancien et nouveau,* 3 vols. Paris: 1685.

Le Muet, Pierre. *Manière de bastir pour touttes sortes de personnes.* Paris: 1623; 2nd ed. 1648.

Le Roy, Benigne, Jacques de Chabot, Jean Van der Vekene, and Claude Moullet [sic]. *Instruction du plantage et proprietez des meuriers et du gouvernement des vers à soye.* Paris: 1605.

L'Estoile, Pierre de. *Journal pour le règne de Henri III (1574–1589),* ed. Louis-Raymond Lefèvre. Paris: 1958.

_____. *Journal pour le règne de Henri IV.* Vol. 1 (1589–1600), ed. L.-R. Lefèvre. Paris: 1948. Vol. 2 (1601–9), ed. André Martin. Paris: 1958.

Le Tellier, Jean-Baptiste. *Memoires et instruction pour l'establissement des meuriers et art de faire la soye en France.* Paris: 1603.

———. *Brief discours contenant la maniere de nourrir les vers à soye.* Paris: 1602.

Lister, Martin. *A Journey to Paris in the Year 1698,* ed. Raymond Stearns. Urbana: 1967.

Locatelli, Sebastien. *Voyage de France (1664–1665),* ed. Adolphe Vautier. Paris: 1905.

Loisel, Antoine. *La Guyenne qui sont huit remonstrances faictes en la chambre de Justice de Guyenne sur le subject des edicts de pacification.* Paris: 1605.

Malingre, Claude. *Les Antiquitez de la ville de Paris.* Paris: 1640.

Mallevoüe, F. de. *Les Actes de Sully passés au nom du Roi de 1600 à 1610 par-devant Maître Simon Fournyer notaire du Châtelet.* Collection de documents inédits sur l'histoire de France. Paris: 1911.

Matthieu, Pierre. *L'Entrée de Henry IIII en sa bonne ville de Lyon.* Paris: 1595.

———. *Histoire de France et des choses memorables advenues aux provinces estrangeres durant sept années de paix du regne de Henry IIII.* Paris: 1605.

Memoires concernans les pauvres que l'on appelle enfermez. Paris: 1617. Rpt. Archives curieuses de l'histoire de France, ed. M. L. Cimber and F. Danjou, ser. 1, vol. 15. Paris: 1837, 241–70.

Menestrier, Claude François. *Traité des tournois, joustes, carrousels, et autres spectacles publics.* Lyon: 1669.

Le Mercure françois, 2 vols. Paris: 1611.

Metman, Yves, ed. *La construction du Pont-Neuf. Le Registre ou Plumitif de la construction du Pont-Neuf.* Paris: 1987.

Mizauld, Antoine. *Singuliers secrets et secours contre la peste.* Paris: 1562.

Mollet, Claude. *Théatre des plans et jardinages.* Paris: 1652.

Möring, Michel, and Léon Brièle. *Inventaire-Sommaire des archives hospitalières antérieures à 1790. Hôtel-Dieu,* 4 vols. Paris: 1882–89.

Mundy, Peter. *The Travels of Peter Mundy in Europe and Asia 1608–1627.* Vol. 1 *Travels in Europe,* ed. Richard Temple, The Hakluyt Society, 2nd ser., 17. Cambridge: 1907.

Nancel, Nicolas de. *Discours tres ample de la peste.* Paris: 1581.

Odier, Jeanne. *Voyage en France d'un jeune gentilhomme morave en 1599 et 1600.* Paris: 1926.

Ordonnances, statuts, reglemens et arrests concernant le mestier des maistres maçons. Paris: 1721.

O'Reilly, Ernest. *Mémoires sur la vie publique et privée de Claude Pellot (1619–1683),* 2 vols. Paris: 1881–82.

Palma-Cayet, Pierre-Victor. *Chronologie Septenaire.* Vol. 12 Nouvelle collection des mémoires pour servir à l'histoire de France, ed. Michaud and Poujoulat. Paris: 1838.

Paré, Ambroise. *Les Oeuvres.* Paris: 1568; 6th ed. 1607.

Pasquier, Etienne. *Les Recherches de la France,* rev. ed. Paris: 1607.

Perefixe, Hardouin de. *Histoire du Roy Henry le Grand.* Paris: 1661.

Perret, Jacques. *Des Fortifications et artifices d'architecture et perspective.* Paris: 1597.

Pigafetta, Filippo. *Relatione dell'assedio di Parigi.* Rome: 1591.

Platter, Thomas. "Description de Paris (1599)," *MSHP* 23 (1896): 167–224.

Pluvinel, Antoine de. *L'Instruction du Roy en l'exercise de monter à cheval.* Paris: 1625.

———. *Maneige royal ou l'on peut remarquer le defaut et la perfection du Chevalier.* Paris: 1623.

Potel, Guillaume. *Discours des maladies epidimiques.* Paris: 1623.

_____. *Traicté de la peste.* Paris: 1624.

La Prevosté des Marchans. Paris: 1605.

Raynaud, Gaston, ed. "Paris en 1596. Récit de F.-G. d'Ierni," *BSHP*, 1885, 164–70.

Registre des délibérations de la Commission consultative sur le faict du commerce général et de l'establissement des manufactures (1601–1604). Rpt. Documents historiques inédits, ed. Champollion Figeac, vol. 4. Paris: 1848, 1–282.

Registres des délibérations du Bureau de la Ville de Paris (1499–1628), eds. Paul Guerin, et al. 19 vols. Paris: 1883–1958.

Remois, N. Bergier. *Le Cheval de Domitian.* Extrait du premier livre des Bocages de P. Statius Papinius: et mis en françois pour servir de parallele au cheval de Henry le Grand posé sur le Pont Neuf à Paris. Paris: 1614.

Rosset, François de. *Le Romant des chevaliers de la gloire.* Paris: 1612.

Rubys, Claude. *Discours sur la contagion de peste.* Lyon: 1577.

Salazar, Ambrosio de. *Tratado de las cosas mas notables que se veen en la grand ciudad de Paris.* Paris: 1616.

[Saulx-Tavannes, Jean de.] *Mémoires de très-noble et très-illustre Gaspard de Saulx, seigneur de Tavannes,* 3 vols. Collection complète des mémoires relatifs à l'histoire de France, ed. Petitot, vols. 23–25. Paris: 1822.

Sauval, Henri. *Histoire et recherches des antiquités de la ville de Paris,* 3 vols. Paris: 1724.

Savot, Louis. *L'Architecture françoise des bastimens particuliers* (Paris: 1624), ed. F. Blondel. Paris: 1673.

_____. *Discours sur le suject du colosse du Grand Roy Henry posé sur le milieu du Pont-Neuf de Paris.* Paris: n.d.

Serlio, Sebastiano. *On Domestic Architecture.* Intro. Myra Nan Rosenfeld. New York: 1978.

_____. *Il sesto libro delle habitationi di tutti i gradi degli huomini,* ed. Marco Rosci. Milan: 1967.

_____. *Il settimo libro d'architettura.* Frankfurt: 1575.

Serres, Jean de. *Inventaire général de l'histoire de France.* Paris: 1627.

Serres, Olivier de. *La Cueillete de la soye.* Paris: 1599.

_____. *La Seconde richesse du meurier blanc.* Paris: 1603.

_____. *Le Théâtre d'agriculture et mesnage des champs.* Paris: 1600.

Sully, duc de. *See* Béthune, Maximilien de

Tadino, Alessandro. *Raguaglio dell'origine et giornali successi della gran peste.* Milan: 1648.

Tenon, [Jacques René.] *Mémoires sur les hôpitaux de Paris.* Paris: 1788.

Textor, Benoit. *De la maniere de preserver de la pestilence.* Lyon: 1551.

Le Triomphe royale: Contenant un brief discours de ce qui s'est passé au Parc Royal à Paris au mois d'avril 1612. Paris: 1612.

Valladier, André. *Harangue funebre de Henry le Grand.* Paris: 1610.

_____. *Labyrinthe royal de l'Hercule Gaulois triomphant.* Avignon: [1601].

Vallet, Pierre. *Le Jardin du roy tres chrestien Henry IV.* Paris: 1608.

Valois, Noel. *Inventaire des arrets du Conseil d'Estat de Henri IV,* 2 vols. Paris: 1886, 1893.

Vinet, Elie. *La Maison champestre et agriculture.* Paris: 1607.

Vulson, Marc de, sieur de La Colombière. *Le Vray theatre d'honneur et de chevalerie ou le miroir heroique de la noblesse,* 2 vols. Paris: 1648.

II. SECONDARY SOURCES

d'Affry de la Monnoye, Alfred. *Les jetons de l'échevinage parisien.* Paris: 1878.

Almagià, Roberto. *Le Pitture murali della Galleria delle carte geografiche.* Vol. 3 Monumenta Cartographica Vaticana. Vatican City: 1952.

Arts Council of Great Britain. *Giambologna 1529–1608, Sculptor to the Medici,* ed. Charles Avery and Anthony Radcliffe. London: 1978.

Aulanier, Christiane. *Histoire du palais et du musée du Louvre,* 10 vols. Paris: 1948–1971.

Babelon, Jean-Pierre. "Architecture et emblématique dans les médailles d'Henri IV," *Revue de l'Art* 58–59 (1983), 21–40.

──────. "Les chiffres de Henri IV et de Gabrielle d'Estrées sur les façades du Louvre," *CVP,* 2 April 1979, 5–13.

──────. "Découverte de la 'maison Jacques Coeur' dans l'ancienne rue de l'Homme-Armé, 38 à 42, rue des Archives. Place de cet édifice dans l'architecture parisienne de bricque et pierre," *CVP* 7–9 (1971), 10–26.

──────. "De l'hôtel d'Albret à l'hôtel d'O. Etude topographique d'une partie de la Culture Sainte-Catherine," *BSHP,* 1970, 87–145.

──────. *Demeures parisiennes sous Henri IV et Louis XIII.* Paris: 1965; 2nd ed. 1977.

──────. "Documents inédits concernant Salomon de Brosse," *BSHP,* 1962, 141–56.

──────. "Du 'Grand Ferrare' à Carnavalet. Naissance de l'hôtel classique," *Revue de l'Art* 40–41 (1978), 83–108.

──────. *Henri IV.* Paris: 1982.

──────. "Henri IV, urbaniste au Marais," *Festival du Marais,* ed. Association pour la sauvegarde et la mise en valeur de Paris historique. Paris: 1966, 99–109.

──────. "L'hôtel de Chaulnes, 9, place des Vosges," *CVP,* 1968–69, 19–30.

──────. "L.T.J. Visconti et le Louvre," *'Il se rendit en Italie': Etudes offertes à André Chastel.* Rome/Paris: 1987, 617–32.

──────. "Nouveaux documents sur la place Dauphine et ses abords," *CVP,* 7 March 1966, 32–43.

──────. "Le Palais de l'Arsenal à Paris. Etude architecturale et essai de répertoire iconographique critique," *Bulletin Monumental* 128/4 (1970), 267–310.

──────. "Le palais des Tournelles et les origines de la place des Vosges," *EPHE,* 1975–76, 695–714.

──────. *Paris au XVIe siècle.* (Nouvelle Histoire de Paris). Paris: 1986.

──────. "Les photographies des estampages pris sur les façades de la Grande Galerie du Louvre avant sa restauration," *Revue de l'Art* 58–59 (1983), 41–52.

──────. "Les relations entre urbanisme et architecture: les châteaux d'Henri IV," *Cahiers du Centre de recherches et d'études sur Paris et l'Ile-de-France* 1 (April 1983): 188–91.

──────. "Le site parisien de la place Dauphine sous Henri IV," *MSHP* 26 (1974), 136–37.

_____. "Sur trois hôtels du Marais à Paris datant du règne d'Henri III," *Bulletin Monumental* 135/3 (1977), 223–30.

_____. "Les Travaux de Henri IV au Louvre et aux Tuileries," *MSHP* 29 (1978), 55–130.

_____. "L'Urbanisme d'Henri IV et de Sully à Paris," *L'Urbanisme de Paris et l'Europe 1600–1680*, ed. Pierre Francastel. Paris: 1969, 47–60.

Baguenault de Puchesse, G. "Pierre Fougeu d'Escures (1554–1621)," *Mémoires de la société archéologique et historique de l'Orléanais* 34 (1913), 7–59.

Ballon, Hilary. "The Rive Droite Remodelled," *Oxford Art Journal* 5/2 (1983), 50–52.

Barbiche, Bernard. "Henri IV et la surintendance des bâtiments," *Bulletin Monumental* 142/1 (1984), 19–39.

_____. "L'influence française à la cour pontificale sous le règne de Henri IV," *Mélanges d'archéologie et d'histoire* 77 (1965), 277–99.

_____. *Sully.* Paris: 1978.

_____. "Sully et ses mémoires," *Bulletin de la société des sciences, lettres et arts de Pau*, ser. 4, 7 (1972), 115–27.

Bardet, Jean-Pierre, et al. "Une nouvelle histoire des villes," *Annales ESC* 32/6 (1977), 1237–54.

Bardon, Françoise. *Le portrait mythologique à la cour de France sous Henri IV et Louis XIII.* Paris: 1974.

Barroux, Maurice. *Le département de la Seine et la ville de Paris. Notions générales et bibliographiques pour en étudier l'histoire.* Paris: 1910.

Batiffol, Louis. "Les Travaux du Louvre sous Henri IV d'après de nouveaux documents," *GBA*, 1912/1, 173–90, 417–35.

Baudson, Emile. *Charles de Gonzague duc de Nevers, de Rethel et de Mantoue 1580–1637.* Paris: 1947.

_____. "La place Royale de Paris et la place ducale de Charleville," *BSHAF*, 1935, 204–16.

_____. *Un urbaniste au XVIIe siècle, Clément Métezeau.* Vol. 1 Les Cahiers d'études ardennaises. Mézières: 1956.

Bayard, Françoise. *Le monde des financiers au XVIIe siècle.* Paris: 1988.

Bédarida, François. "The growth of urban history in France: some methodological trends," *The Study of Urban History*, ed. H. J. Dyos. London: 1968, 47–60.

Béguin, Sylvie. "Toussaint Dubreuil, premier peintre de Henri IV," *Art de France* 4 (1964), 86–107.

Beltrami, Luca. *Il Lazzaretto di Milano.* Milan: 1882.

Benassis. "Promenades medicales: l'Hôpital Saint-Louis et les sanitats," *Revue thérapeutique des alcaloides*, 1937, 7–17, 39–48, 71–82.

Berty, Adolphe, H. Legrand, and L. M. Tisserand. *Topographie historique du vieux Paris*, 6 vols. Paris: 1866–97.

Biraben, Jean-Noël. *Les Hommes et la peste en France*, 2 vols. Paris: 1975–76.

Blunt, Anthony. *Art and Architecture in France 1500–1700*, 4th rev. ed. The Pelican History of Art. Harmondsworth: 1982.

_____. *Philibert de l'Orme.* London: 1958.

Bognetti, Gian Piero. "Il Lazzaretto di Milano e la peste del 1630," *Archivio Storico Lombardo* 50 (1923), 388–442.

Boinet, Amedée. *Les églises parisiennes,* 3 vols. Paris: 1958–62.

Boislisle, Arthur de. "Nicolas Delamare et le Traité de la Police," *BSHP* 3 (1876), 79–85.

————. "Notices historiques sur la place des Victoires et la place de Vendôme," *MSHP* 15 (1888), 1–272.

Boissonnade, Prosper. *Le Socialisme d'Etat. L'Industrie et les classes industrielle en France pendant les deux premiers siècles de l'ère moderne (1453–1661).* Paris: 1927.

Bonnardot, Alfred. *Dissertations archéologiques sur les anciennes enceintes de Paris.* Paris: 1852–53.

————. *Etudes archéologiques sur les anciens plans de Paris des XVIe, XVIIe, et XVIIIe siècles.* Paris: 1851.

————. *Gilles Corrozet et Germain Brice. Etude bibliographique sur ces deux historiens de Paris.* Paris: 1880.

Borsook, Eve. "Art and Politics at the Medici Court IV: Funeral Decor for Henry IV of France," *Mitteilungen des Kunsthistorischen Institutes in Florenz* 14 (1969), 201–34.

Boucher, François. *Le Pont Neuf,* 2 vols. Paris: 1925–26.

Bouchereaux, Suzanne-Marie. "Recherches bibliographiques sur Gilles Corrozet," *Bulletin du bibliophile,* 1948.

Boudon, Françoise. "Tissu urbain et architecture: l'analyse parcellaire comme base de l'histoire architecturale," *Annales ESC,* July–Aug. 1975, 773–818.

————. "La *Topographie française* de Claude Chastillon. Proposition pour une grille d'analyse des gravures," *Les Cahiers de la recherche architecturale* 18 (1985): 54–73.

————, and Jean Blécon. *Philibert Delorme et le château royal de Saint-Léger-en-Yvelines.* Paris: 1985.

————, et al. *Système de l'architecture urbaine. Le quartier des Halles à Paris,* 2 vols. Paris: 1977.

Boulay de la Meuthe, Henry. *Notice sur la place des Vosges.* Mirecourt: 1848.

Bourgeon, Jean-Louis. *Les Colbert avant Colbert. Destin d'une famille marchande.* Paris: 1973.

Boyer, H. *Histoire de la principauté souveraine de Boisbelle-Henrichemont.* Paris: 1904.

Braham, Allan, and Peter Smith. *François Mansart,* 2 vols. London: 1973.

————. "Mansart Studies V: The Church of the Minimes," *Burlington* 57/744 (1965), 123–32.

Braibant, Charles, et al. *Guide historique des rues de Paris.* Paris: 1965.

Brinckmann, A. E. *Platz und Monument.* Berlin: 1908.

————. *Stadtbaukunst.* Berlin: 1920.

Brunhoff, Jacques de. *La Place Dauphine et l'Ile de la Cité.* Paris: 1987.

Buisseret, David. "The Cartographic Definition of France's Eastern Boundary in the Early Seventeenth Century," *Imago Mundi* 36 (1984): 72–80.

————. "The Communications of France during the reconstruction of Henri IV," *Economic History Review* 18/2 (1965), 267–77.

————. *Henry IV.* London: 1984.

———. "Les ingénieurs du roi au temps de Henri IV," *Bulletin de la section de géographie* 77 (1964), 13–84.

———. "The Legend of Sully," *The Historical Journal* 5/2 (1962), 181–88.

———. "Organization défensive des frontières au temps de Henri IV," *Revue historique de l'Armée* 20/4 (1964): 25–31.

———. "A Stage in the Development of French Intendants: The Reign of Henry IV," *The Historical Journal* 9/1 (1966), 27–38.

———. *Sully and the Growth of Centralized Government in France, 1598–1610.* London: 1968.

Burlen, Katherine, et al. *Versailles. Lecture d'une ville.* Paris: 1979.

Cadet de Gassincourt, F. *Les Origines de l'Hôpital Saint-Louis.* n.p.: n.d.

Campbell, Malcolm, and Gino Corti. "A Comment on Prince Francesco de' Medici's Refusal to Loan Giovanni Bologna to the Queen of France," *Burlington* 115/845 (1973), 507–12.

Candille, Marcel. "Contribution à l'histoire de l'urbanisation de la capitale: la collection des plans et dessins d'architecture du fonds de l'ancien Hôtel-Dieu de Paris," *Société française d'histoire des hôpitaux* 33 (1976), 73–88.

Carsalade Du Pont, Henri de. *La Municipalité parisienne à l'époque d'Henri IV.* Paris: 1971.

Caso, Jacques de. "Duban et l'achèvement de la Galerie du bord de l'eau: la frise des frères L'Heureux," *BSHAF*, 1973, 333–43.

Castelnau, Jacques Thomas de. *Le Paris de Louis XIII (1610–1643).* Paris: 1928.

Castex, Jean, et al. *Formes urbaines: de l'îlot à la barre.* Paris: 1977.

Chassagne, Serge. "L'Histoire des villes: une opération de renovation historiographique?" *Villes et campagnes XVe–XXe siècles,* Université de Lyon II, Centre d'histoire économique et sociale de la région lyonnaise. Lyon: 1977, 217–300.

Choay, Françoise. "L'histoire et la méthode en urbanisme," *Annales ESC* 25/4 (1970), 1143–54.

Cipolla, Carlo. *Cristofano and the Plague. A Study in the History of Public Health in the Age of Galileo.* Berkeley: 1973.

———. *Faith, Reason and the Plague: A Tuscan Story of the Seventeenth Century.* Brighton: 1979.

———. *Public Health and the Medical Profession in the Renaissance.* Cambridge: 1976.

Ciprut, Edouard-Jacques. "L'architecte du palais abbatial de Saint-Germain-des-Prés," *BSHAF*, 1956, 218–21.

———. "Documents inédits sur l'ancienne église des Minimes de la Place Royale," *BSHAF*, 1954, 151–74.

———. "Documents inédits sur quelques châteaux de l'Ile-de-France," *MSHP* 16–17 (1965–66), 131–88.

———. *Mathieu Jacquet, sculpteur d'Henri IV.* Paris: 1967.

———. "Nouveaux documents sur Etienne Dupérac," *BSHAF*, 1960, 161–73.

———. "Oeuvres inconnues de Clément Métezeau," *BSHAF*, 1954, 143–48.

Cole, Charles. *French Mercantilist Doctrine Before Colbert.* New York: 1931.

Coope, Rosalys. *Jacques Gentilhâtre.* Vol. 6 Catalogue of the Drawings Collection of the Royal Institute of British Architects. London: 1972.

———. "John Thorpe and the Hôtel Zamet in Paris," *Burlington* 124/956 (1982), 671–81.

———. *Salomon de Brosse and the Development of the Classical Style in French Architecture from 1565 to 1630.* University Park, Pa.: 1972.

———, and Catherine Grodecki. "La création d'Henrichemont par Sully (1608–1612)," *Cahiers d'archéologie et d'histoire du Berry* 41 (1975), 21–48.

Coüard, E. "Thomas Francini Intendant général des eaux et fontaines de France 1572–1651," *Réunion des sociétés des beaux-arts des départements,* 1894, 1459–92.

Cousin, Jules. "Note sur l'attribution à Du Cerceau du plan de Paris sous Henri II, dit plan de St.-Victor," *BSHP,* 1876, 26–30.

———. "Notice sur un plan de Paris du XVIe siècle nouvellement découvert à Bâle," *MSHP* 1 (1875), 44–57.

Curzon, Henri de. *La Maison du Temple de Paris, histoire et description.* Paris: 1888.

Dainville, François de. *Le Dauphiné et ses confins vus par l'ingénieur d'Henri IV Jean de Beins,* 2 vols. Paris: 1968.

———. "*Le Théâtre françois* de M. Bouguereau, 1594. Premier atlas national de France," *Actes du 85e Congrès national des sociétés savantes, Section de géographie,* Chambéry-Annency, 1960. Paris: 1961, 3–50.

Dartein, F. de. *Etudes sur les ponts en pierre.* Vol. 1 *Ponts français antérieurs au XVIIIe siècle.* Paris: 1912.

Davis, Natalie Zemon. "The Sacred and the Body Social in Sixteenth Century Lyon," *Past and Present* 90 (1981), 40–70.

———. *Society and Culture in Early Modern France.* Stanford: 1965.

Dérens, Jean. "Notes sur les plans de Paris au XVIe siècle," *BSHP* 107 (1980): 71–86.

———. "Le Plan de Paris par Truschet et Hoyau (1550) dit plan de Bâle," *Cahiers de la Rotonde* 9 (1986).

Descimon, Robert. "L'échevinage parisien sous Henri IV (1594–1609)," *La ville, la bourgeoisie et la génèse de l'état moderne (XII-XVIIIe siècles),* ed. Neithard Bulst and J.-Ph. Genet. Paris: 1988, 113–50.

———, and Jean Nagle. "Les quartiers de Paris du Moyen Age au XVIIIe siècle. Evolution d'un espace plurifonctionnel," *Annales ESC,* Sept. 1979, 956–83.

Deyon, Paul. *Amiens capital provinciale. Etude sur la société urbaine au 17e siècle.* Paris: 1967.

———. "Manufacturing Industries in Seventeenth-Century France," *Louis XIV and Absolutism,* ed. Ragnhild Hatton. Columbus: 1976.

Dickerman, Edmund. *Bellièvre and Villeroy. Power in France under Henry III and Henry IV.* Providence: 1971.

Diefendorf, Barbara. *Paris City Councillors in the Sixteenth Century. The Politics of Patrimony.* Princeton: 1983.

Dogny, Maurice. *Histoire de l'Hôpital Saint-Louis depuis sa fondation jusqu'au XIXe siècle.* Paris: 1911.

Dubois, Claude. *Celtes et Gaulois au XVIe siècle: le développement d'un mythe nationaliste.* Paris: 1972.

———. *La Conception de l'histoire en France au XVIe siècle (1520–1610).* Paris: 1977.

Du Colombier, Pierre. "Autour des Métezeau," *Bibliothèque de l'Humanisme et Renaissance* 3 (1943), 168–89.

———, and Pierre d'Espezel. "L'Habitation au XVI siècle d'après le sixième livre de Serlio," *Humanisme et Renaissance* 1 (1934), 31–49.

Dufour, A. "Histoire du siège de Paris sous Henri IV en 1590," *MSHP* 7 (1880), 175–270.

Dumolin, Maurice. *Etudes de topographie parisienne*, 3 vols. Paris: 1929–31.

———. "Notes de topographie parisienne. Hôtel de Saint-Géran," *La Cité* 93–94 (1925), 220–31.

———. "Notes sur les vieux guides de Paris," *MSHP* 47 (1924), 209–85.

———. "La place Vendôme," *CVP*, 1927, 1–52.

———. "Les Propriétaires de la place Royale (1605–1789)," *La Cité* 95–96 (1925), 273–316; 97–98 (1926), 1–30.

Ehrle, Francesco. *Roma prima di Sisto V. La Pianta di Roma du Pérac-Lafréry del 1577.* Rome: 1908.

Ehrmann, Jean. "La Belle Cheminée du château de Fontainebleau," *Actes du colloque international sur l'art de Fontainebleau*, ed. André Chastel. Paris: 1975, 117–25.

Fagniez, Gustave. *L'Economie sociale de la France sous Henri IV 1589–1610.* Paris: 1897.

Ferro, Filippo. "La peste nella cultura lombarda," *Il Seicento lombardo.* Milan: 1973, 83–124.

Fleury, Michel. "Le plan archéologique de Paris du XIIIe au XVIIe siècles et la *Topographie du Vieux Paris*," *Bulletin municipal officiel de la ville de Paris*, 8–9 Feb. 1959, 292–94.

———. "Recherches sur l'oeuvre de Sauval," *EPHE*, 1975–76, 629–37.

Fossoyeux, Marcel. "Les Epidémies de peste à Paris," *Bulletin de la société française de l'histoire de la médecine* 12/2 (1913), 115–41.

———. *L'Hôtel-Dieu de Paris au XVIIe et XVIIIe siècles.* Paris: 1912.

Foucault, Michel. *The Birth of the Clinic.* New York: 1973.

———, et al. *Les Machines à guérir aux origines de l'hôpital moderne.* Paris: 1976.

Fournier, Edouard. *Histoire du Pont-Neuf*, 2 vols. Paris: 1862.

Francqueville, Robert de. *Pierre de Francqueville, sculpteur des Médicis et du roi Henri IV (1548–1615).* Paris: 1968.

Franklin, Alfred. *Les Anciens plans de Paris. Notices historiques et topographiques*, 2 vols. Paris: 1878–80.

———. "Notice sur le plan de Paris de Pigafetta," *MSHP* 2 (1875), 398–401.

Gallingani, Luigi. "Il Lazzaretto fuori Porta orientale à Milano," *Atti Primo Congresso Italiano di Storia ospitaliera*, Reggio Emilia, 1956. Reggio Emilia: 1957.

Garms, Joerg. "Projects for the Pont Neuf and Place Dauphine in the First Half of the Eighteenth Century," *JSAH* 26/2 (1967), 102–13.

Garnier, Noel. "Le President Jeannin," *Mémoires de la société bourguignonne de géographie et d'histoire* 28 (1913), 287–589.

Gerard, Albert. "La révolte et le siège de Paris en 1589," *MSHP* 33 (1906), 65–150.

Geymüller, Heinrich von. *Les Du Cerceau, leur vie et leur oeuvre.* Paris: 1887.

Goldthwaite, Richard. *The Building of Renaissance Florence.* Baltimore: 1980.

Goubert, Pierre. "Economie et urbanisme en France dans la première moitié du XVIIe siècle," *L'Urbanisme de Paris et l'Europe 1600–1680,* ed. Pierre Francastel. Paris: 1969, 37–45.

Greengrass, Mark. *France in the Age of Henri IV: The Struggle for Stability.* London: 1984.

Grimault, Aimé. *Anciennes enceintes et limites de Paris.* Paris: 1966.

Grivel, Marianne. *Le Commerce de l'estampe à Paris au XVIIe siècle.* Geneva: 1986.

Grodecki, Catherine. "L'Architecture en Berry sous le règne de Henri IV," *Mémoires de l'Union des sociétés savantes de Bourges* 3 (1951–52), 77–131.

———. "La Construction du château de Wideville et sa place dans l'architecture française au dernier quart du XVIe siècle," *Bulletin Monumental* 136/2 (1978), 135–75.

———. "Un marché de Gilles Le Breton pour le château de Fleury-en-Bière," *L'Information d'histoire de l'art* 19/1 (1974), 37–41.

———. "Au Minutier central des notaires de Paris. XVIe et XVIIe siècles," *Revue de l'Art* 54 (1981), 35–42.

Guerout, Jean. "Le Palais de la Cité des origines à 1417, essai topographique et archéologique," *MSHP* 1 (1949), 57–212; 2 (1950), 21–204; 3 (1951), 7–101.

Guiffrey, Jules. "Logements d'artistes au Louvre. Liste général des brevets de logement sous la grande galerie du Louvre," *Nouvelles archives de l'art français,* 1873, 1–221.

———. "Nicolas Houël, apothicaire parisien," *MSHP* 25 (1898), 179–270.

———, ed. *Artistes parisiens de XVIe et XVIIe siècles.* Paris: 1915.

Guillaume, Jean. "Le phare de Cordouan, merveille du monde et monument monarchique," *Revue de l'Art* 8 (1970), 33–52.

Harley, J. B. "Maps, knowledge and power," *The Iconography of Landscape,* ed. D. Cosgrove and S. J. Daniels. Cambridge: 1988, 277–312.

———. "Meaning and Ambiguity in Tudor Cartography," *English Map-Making 1500–1650,* ed. Sarah Tyacke. London: 1983, 22–45.

Hauser, Henri. "La Liberté du commerce et la liberté du travail sous Henri IV," *Revue historique* 80/2 (1902), 257–300.

———. *Les Sources de l'histoire de France, XVIe siècle.* Vol. 4, *Henri IV (1589–1610).* Paris: 1915.

———. "Le Système social de Barthélemy de Laffemas," *Revue Bourguignonne de l'enseignement supérieur* 12/1 (1902), 113–31.

Hautecoeur, Louis. "Un album de dessins de Salomon de Brosse au Musée du Louvre," *Beaux-Arts* 11 (15 June 1923), 167–68.

———. *Histoire de l'architecture classique en France. La formation de l'idéal classique,* 4 vols., 2nd ed. Paris: 1963–67.

———. "Les places en France au 18e siècle," *GBA* per. 6, 85 (1975), 89–116.

Hayden, J. Michael. *France and the Estates General of 1614.* Cambridge: 1974.

Hennequin, Jacques. *Henri IV dans ses oraisons funèbres.* Paris: 1977.

Herme-Renault, Marie. "Claude Chastillon et sa *Topographie française,*" *Bulletin Monumental* 139/3 (1981): 141–63.

Hilaire, Françoise. "Architecture hospitalière du Moyen Age au XVIIIe siècle," *Monuments historiques* 114 (1981), 8–15.

Hillairet, Jacques. *Dictionnaire historique des rues de Paris,* 2 vols., 5th ed. Paris: 1963.

Hohl, Claude. "Les Pestes et les hôpitaux parisiens au XVIe siècle." Thesis Ecole des Chartes, Paris, 1960. (Typescript deposited at Archives de l'Assistance Publique.)

Huard, Georges. "Les logements des artisans dans la Grande Galerie du Louvre sous Henri IV et Louis XIII," *BSHAF*, 1939, 18–36.

Huber, Martin. "Paris sous la Ligue," *Art de France*, 1964, 104–15.

Hubert, Jean. *Histoire de Charleville depuis son origine jusqu'en 1854*. Charleville: 1854.

Humbert, Michele. "Serlio: il sesto libro et l'architettura borghese in Francia," *Storia dell'arte* 43 (1981), 199–240.

Huppert, George. *The Idea of Perfect History. Historical erudition and historical philosophy in Renaissance France*. Urbana: 1970.

Husson, François. *Artisans français*. Vol. 3 *Maçons et tailleurs de pierre. Etude historique*. Paris: 1903.

Imbert, Jean. *Histoire des hôpitaux en France*. Paris: 1982.

———. "Les Prescriptions hospitalières du Concile de Trente et leur diffusion en France," *Atti del Primo Congresso Italiano di Storia Ospitaliera*, Reggio Emilia, 1956. Reggio Emilia: 1957, 349–75.

Jadart, Henri. "Sully et les plantations des arbres," *Revue Henri IV* 1/20 (1906), 59–65.

Jetter, Dieter. "Betrachtung-moglichkeiten historischer am Hôpital St. Louis in Paris," *Das Krankenhaus*, March 1967, 108–9.

———. "Erwägungen beim Bau französischer Pesthäuser," *Archives internationales d'histoire des sciences* 76 (1966), 227–62.

———. *Geschichte des Hospitals*. Wiesbaden: 1966.

Josephson, Ragnar. "Les projets pour la place Vendôme," *Architecture*, 1928, 83–95.

Jurgens, Madeleine, and Pierre Couperie. "Le logement à Paris aux XVIe et XVIIe siècles: une source, les inventaires après décès," *Annales ESC* 17/2 (1962), 488–500.

Kelley, Donald. *Foundations of Modern Historical Scholarship. Language, law, and history in the French Renaissance*. New York: 1970.

Keohane, Nannerl. *Philosophy and the State in France*. Princeton: 1980.

Kierstead, Raymond. *Pomponne de Bellièvre. A Study of the King's Men in the Age of Henry IV*. Evanston: 1968.

Konvitz, Josef. *Cities and the Sea. Port City Planning in Early Modern Europe*. Baltimore: 1978.

Kordi, Mohamed El. *Bayeux aux XVIIe et XVIIIe siècles. Contribution à l'histoire urbaine de la France*. Mouton: 1970.

Krakovitch, Odile. "Le couvent des Minimes de la Place-Royale," *MSHP* 30 (1979), 87–258.

Labasse, Jean. *L'Hôpital et la ville, géographie hospitalière*. Paris: 1980.

La Croix, Horst de. "Military Architecture and the Radial City Plan in Sixteenth Century Italy," *Art Bulletin* 42/4 (1960), 263–90.

Lacroix, Paul. "La porte et place de France sous le règne de Henri IV," *GBA*, June 1870, 561–66.

Laffitte, Paul. "Notice sur Barthélemy Laffemas, contrôleur général du commerce sous Henri IV," *Journal des economistes* 142/125 (1876), 181–218.

Lafolie, Ch. J. *Mémoires historiques relatifs à la fonte et l'élévation de la statue équestre de Henri IV sur le terre-plein du Pont-Neuf à Paris*. Paris: 1819.

Lafond, Paul. "François et Jacob Bunel, peintres de Henri IV," *Réunion des sociétés des beaux-arts des départements*, 1898, 557–606.

Lallemand, Léon. *Histoire de la charité*, Vol. 4 *Les Temps modernes*, 2 vols. Paris: 1910–12.

Lallemand, Marcel, and Alfred Boinette. *Jean Errard de Bar-le-Duc*. Paris: 1884.

Lambeau, Lucien. "Communication relative à la place Royale," *CVP*, 25 Jan. 1908, 19–31.

——. "Communication sur la place des Vosges," *CVP*, 23 Oct. 1902, 175–216; 18 Dec. 1902, 262–94.

——. "Compte-rendu d'une visite," *CVP*, 29 Nov. 1924, 130–40, 142–49.

——. "L'Hôtel de Rotrou. Le Pavillon du Roi," *CVP*, 28 Oct. 1922, 96–109.

——. *La Place Royale*. Paris: 1906.

——. "La Place Royale," *CVP Annexe* 31 Jan. 1925, 1–41.

——. "La Place Royale. L'Hôtel d'Aumont," *BSHP* 39, (1912), 174–208.

——. "La Place Royale: l'Hôtel d'Aumont," *La Cité* 138 (1936), 81–114.

——. "La Place Royale. L'Hôtel de Chaulnes," *BSHP* 38 (1911), 49–72.

——. "La Place Royale. L'Hôtel de Chaulnes et de Nicolay," *La Cité* 57 (1916), 26–58.

——. "La Place Royale. Nouvelles contributions à son histoire," *CVP Annèxe*, 20 Nov. 1915, 1–159.

——. "La Place Royale: ses habitants en 1697," *La Cité* 59 (1916), 180–89.

——. "Quatre hôtels de la place des Vosges," *CVP*, 16 Dec. 1922, 136–61.

——. "Rapport sur le classement comme monuments historiques des pavillons de la place des Vosges, dits pavillon du Roi et de la Reine," *CVP*, 4 April 1914, 50–52.

Laprade, Jacques de. "Note sur quelques portraits d'Henri IV gravés d'après François Bunel," *Revue des Arts* 2 (1953), 89–92.

Lavedan, Pierre. *Histoire de l'urbanisme à Paris*. Paris: 1975.

——, et al. *L'Urbanisme à l'époque moderne (XVIe-XVIIIe siècles)*, rev. ed. Geneva: 1982.

Lecestre, Paul. "Notice sur l'Arsenal royal de Paris jusqu'à la mort de Henri IV," *MSHP* 42 (1915), 185–281.

Legrand, Noé. "La Peste à Paris en 1606," *Bulletin de la société française de l'histoire de la médecine* 10/4 (1911), 236–38.

Le Moël, Michel. "Archives architecturales parisiennes en Suède," *L'Urbanisme de Paris et l'Europe 1600–1680*, ed. Pierre Francastel. Paris: 1969, 105–92.

——. "Aux origines de la Place Royale," *Festival du Marais*, ed. Association pour la sauvegarde et la mise en valeur de Paris historique. Paris: 1966, 111–15.

Lequenne, Fernard. *Olivier de Serres*. Paris: 1983.

Le Roux de Lincy. "Recherches historiques sur la chute et la reconstruction du Pont Nôtre-Dame à Paris (1499–1510)," *Bibliothèque de l'Ecole des chartes* ser. 2, 2 (1845–46), 32–51.

——, and A. Bruel. "Notice historique et critique sur Dom Jacques Du Breul, prieur de St.-Germain-des-Prés," *Bibliothèque de l'Ecole des chartes* ser. 6, 4 (1868), 56–72, 479–512.

Le Roy Ladurie, Emmanuel, ed. *La Ville classique de la Renaissance aux Revolutions.* Vol. 3 Histoire de la France urbaine. Paris: 1981.

————, and Pierre Couperie. "Le mouvement des loyers parisiens de la fin du Moyen Age au XVIIIe siècle," *Annales ESC* 25/4 (1970), 1002–23.

Letrait, Jean-Jacques. "La Communauté des maîtres maçons de Paris au XVIIe et au XVIIIe siècles," *Revue historique de droit français et étranger* per. 4, 24 (1945), 215–66; 26 (1948), 96–136.

Lowry, Bates. "Palais du Louvre 1528–1624. Development of a Sixteenth-Century Architectural Complex." Ph.D. diss. University of Chicago, 1956.

La Maison de la ville à la Renaissance. Recherches sur l'habitat urbain en Europe aux XVe et XVIe siècles. Centre d'études supérieures de la Renaissance. Actes du colloque, Tours, May 1977. Paris: 1983.

Marcel, Gabriel. "Nouvelles notes sur B. de Vassalieu, auteur du plan de Paris de 1609," *BSHP*, 1907, 179–82.

Mareuse, E. "Sur quelques anciens plans de Paris," *BSHP*, 1877, 167–71.

Marrow, Deborah. *The Art Patronage of Maria de' Medici.* Ann Arbor: 1982.

Martin, Henri-Jean. *Livres, pouvoirs et société à Paris au XVIIe siècle (1598–1701),* 2 vols. Geneva: 1969.

————, and Roger Chartier, eds. *Histoire de l'édition française.* Vol. I *Le livre conquérant du Moyen Age au milieu du XVIIe siècle.* Paris: 1983.

Maser, Edward. "A Statue of Henry IV in Saint John Lateran," *GBA* per. 6, 56 (1960), 147–56.

Mastrorocco, Mila. "Pietro Francavilla alla corte di Francia," *Commentari* 26/3–4 (1975), 333–43.

————. "Lo scultore Pietro Francavilla: la sua attività alla corte dei Granduchi di Toscana Francesco I et Ferdinando I (1572–1606)," *Commentari* 26/1–2 (1975), 98–120.

Maugis, Edouard. *Histoire du Parlement de Paris,* 2 vols. 1913–16. Rpt. Geneva: 1977.

Mazerolle, Fernand. *Les Médailleurs français du XVe siècle au milieu du XVIIe,* 3 vols. Paris: 1902–4.

Mérigot, Lydia. "La place de France et le lotissement de la couture du Temple à Paris (1608–1630)," *Ecole nationale des chartes. Positions des thèses,* 1966, 87–92.

Mettam, Roger. *Power and Faction in Louis XIV's France.* Oxford: 1988.

Mignot, Claude. "Henri Sauval entre l'érudition et la critique d'art," *XVIIe Siècle* 138 (1983), 51–66.

————. "Travaux récents sur l'architecture française: du Maniérisme au Classicisme," *Revue de l'Art* 32 (1976), 78–85.

Miller, Naomi. "A Volume of Architectural Drawings ascribed to Jacques Androuet Ducerceau the Elder in the Morgan Library, New York," *Marsyas* 11 (1962–64), 33–41.

Miron de l'Espinay, Albert. *François Miron et l'administration municipale de Paris sous Henri IV de 1604 à 1606.* Paris: 1885.

Mirot, Léon. "La formation et le démembrement de l'hôtel Saint-Pol," *La Cité* 60 (1916), 269–319.

_____. "Les origines de l'Hôtel et la censive du prieuré de la couture Ste. Catherine dans la rue St. Antoine," *BSHP* 38 (1911), 77–95.

Mislin, Miron. "Paris, Ile de la Cité: die Uberbauten Brucken," *Storia della città* 17 (1980), 11–36.

Montaiglon, Anatole de. *Notice sur l'ancienne statue éqeustre ouvrage de Daniello Ricciarelli et le Biard le fils elevée à Louis XIII en 1639 au milieu de la place Royale à Paris.* Paris: 1874.

Mousnier, Roland. *The Assassination of Henry IV. The Tyrannicide Problem and the Consolidation of the French Monarchy in the Early 17th Century,* trans. Joan Spenser. London: 1973.

_____. *The Institutions of France under the Absolute Monarchy 1598–1789,* 2 vols., trans. Brian Pearce and Arthur Goldhammer. Chicago: 1979–84.

_____. *Paris capitale au temps de Richelieu et de Mazarin.* Paris: 1978.

_____. *La Venalité des offices sous Henri IV et Louis XIII,* 2nd ed. Paris: 1971.

Mouton, Léo. "Deux financiers au temps de Sully: Largentier et Moisset," *BSHP*, 1937, 65–104.

Musée de l'Assistance Publique à Paris. *Dix siècles d'histoire hospitalière parisienne. L'Hôtel Dieu de Paris (651–1650),* ed. Marcel Candille and Claude Hohl. Paris: 1961.

Musée Carnavalet. *Pont Neuf 1578–1978.* Paris: 1978.

Musée National de Pau; Archives Nationales. *Henri IV et la reconstruction du royaume.* Paris: 1989.

Nudi, Giacinto. *Storia urbanistica di Livorno dalle origini al secolo XVI.* Venice: 1959.

Pagès, Georges. *La Monarchie d'Ancien Régime en France de Henri IV à Louis XIV.* Paris: 1928.

Pannier, Jacques. *L'Eglise réformée de Paris sous Henri IV.* Paris: 1911.

Pastoureau, Mireille. *Les Atlas français XVIe–XVIIe siècles. Répertoire bibliographique et étude.* Paris: 1984.

_____. "Les atlas imprimés en France avant 1700," *Imago Mundi* 32 (1980), 45–72.

Paultre, Christian. *De la repression de la mendicité et du vagabondage en France sous l'Ancien Régime.* Paris: 1906.

Pérouse de Montclos, Jean-Marie. *L'Architecture à la française. XVIe, XVIIe, XVIIIe siècles.* Paris: 1982.

Pinsseau, Pierre. *Le canal Henri IV ou canal de Briare (1604–1943).* Orléans: 1943.

Pinto, John. "Origins and Development of the Ichnographic City Plan," *JSAH* 35/1 (1976), 35–50.

Poëte, Marcel. *Une vie de cité. Paris de sa naissance à nos jours,* 3 vols. Paris: 1924–31.

Poirson, Auguste. *Histoire du règne de Henri IV,* 4 vols. Paris: 1862–67.

Pope-Hennessy, John. *Italian High Renaissance and Baroque Sculpture,* 2nd. ed. London: 1970.

Powis, Jonathon. "Gallican Liberties and the Politics of Later Sixteenth-Century France," *The Historical Journal* 26/3 (1983): 515–30.

Pronteau, Jeanne. "Etude des historiens de Paris au XVIe et XVIIe siècles," *EPHE,* 1964–65, 296–301; 1965–66, 336–43.

_____. "Recherches sur les travaux d'urbanisme à Paris du XVIIe au XIXe siècle," *EPHE*, 1972–73, 477–89.

Quenedey, Raymond. "L'Habitation urbaine et son evolution," *Annales d'histoire économique et sociale* 6 (1934), 62–68, 138–47.

Ranum, Orest. *Artisans of Glory. Writers and Historical Thought in Seventeenth-Century France*. Chapel Hill: 1980.

_____. *Paris in the Age of Absolutism. An Essay*. New York: 1968.

Rosci, Marco. *Il trattato di architettura di Sebastiano Serlio*. Milan: 1967.

Rosenfeld, Myra Nan. "The Hôtel de Cluny and the Sources of the French Renaissance Urban Palace, 1350–1500." Ph.D. diss. Harvard University, 1971.

_____. "Serlio's Late Style in the Avery Version of the Sixth Book on Domestic Architecture," *JSAH* 28 (1969), 155–72.

Rousset-Charny, Gérard. "Le relevé d'architecture chez Jacques Ier Androuet du Cerceau: *Les plus excellents bâtiments de France* (1576–1579)," *L'Information d'histoire de l'art* 19/3 (1974), 114–24.

Roux, Simone. "L'habitat urbain au Moyen Age: le quartier de l'Université à Paris," *Annales ESC* 24/5 (1969), 1196–1219.

Sabouraud, R. *L'Hôpital Saint-Louis*. Lyon: 1937.

Sainte Fare Garnot, Pierre-Nicolas. *L'Hôpital Saint-Louis*. [Paris]: 1986.

Salmon, J.M.H. *Renaissance and Revolt*. Cambridge: 1986.

_____. *Society in Crisis. France in the Sixteenth Century*. London: 1975.

Sartre, Josiane. *Châteaux 'brique et pierre' en France*. Paris: 1981.

Schnapper, Antoine. *Le Géant, la licorne, la tulipe. Collections françaises au XVIIe siècle*. Vol. I Histoire et histoire naturelle. Paris: 1988.

Stegmann, André. "La fête parisienne à la Place Royale en avril 1612," *Les Fêtes de la Renaissance*, vol. 3, ed. Jean Jacquet and Elie Konigson. Paris: 1975, 373–92.

Stein, Henri. "Mesures prises contre le choléra à Paris (1596)," *BSHP*, 1884, 86–91.

Tamizey de Larroque, Philippe. *Les Correspondants de Peiresc*, fasc. XII: *Pierre-Antoine de Rascas, sieur de Bagarris*. Aix-en-Provence: 1887.

Taxil, M. L. "Communication sur le bail d'une maison de la place Dauphine," *CVP*, 25 Oct. 1919, 135–37.

Teisseyre-Sallman, Line. "Urbanisme et société: l'exemple de Nîmes aux XVIIe et XVIIIe siècles," *Annales ESC*, Sept. 1980, 965–86.

Tesson. "Visite à l'Hôpital Saint-Louis," *CVP*, 6 July 1899, 211–16.

Thompson, John, and Grace Goldin. *The Hospital: A Social and Architectural History*. New Haven: 1975.

Thomson, David. *Renaissance Paris. Architecture and Growth 1475–1600*. Berkeley: 1984.

Thuillier, Guy. "Politique et économie au XVIIe siècle: le 'Conseiller d'Estat' de Philippe de Béthune," *Revue Economique*, Jan. 1958, 144–50.

Thuillier, Jacques. "Economie et urbanisme au XVIIe siècle: Philippe de Béthune," *Art de France* 1 (1961), 311–12.

_____. "Peinture et politique: une théorie de la galerie royale sous Henri IV," Albert Châtelet and Nicole Reynaud, eds. *Etudes d'art français offertes à Charles Sterling*. Paris: 1975, 175–205.

Toesca, Ilaria. "Drawings by Jacques Androuet Du Cerceau the Elder in the Vatican Library," *Burlington* 48/638 (1956), 153–57.

Tollet, C. *De l'Assistance publique et des hôpitaux jusqu'au XIXe siècle.* Paris: 1889.

Vallery-Radot, Pierre. *Deux siècles d'histoire hospitalière de Henri IV à Louis-Philippe (1602–1836).* Paris: 1947.

Vignon, E.-J. *Etudes historiques sur l'administration des voies publiques en France au XVIIe et XVIIIe siècles,* 3 vols. Paris: 1862.

Viguerie, Jean de, and Evelyne Saive-Lever. "Essai pour une géographie socio-professionelle de Paris dans la première moitié du XVIIe siècle," *Revue d'histoire moderne et contemporaine* 20/3 (1973), 424–29.

Vitry, Paul. "Quelques bustes et statues du roi Henri IV," *GBA,* Dec. 1898, 452–66.

Vivanti, Corrado. "Henri IV, the Gallic Hercules," *Journal of the Warburg and Courtauld Institutes* 30 (1967), 176–97.

Ward, W. H. *French Châteaux and Gardens in the XVIth Century.* London: 1909.

Watson, Katherine. *Pietro Tacca Successor to Giovanni Bologna.* New York: 1983.

———. "Sugar Sculpture for Grand Ducal Weddings from the Giambologna Workshop," *The Connoisseur* 199/799 (Sept. 1978), 20–26.

Whitman, Nathan. "Fontainebleau, the Luxembourg, and the French Domed Entry Pavilion," *JSAH* 46/4 (1987), 356–73.

Yardeni, Myriam. *La Conscience nationale en France pendant les guerres de religion (1559–1598).* Louvain: 1971.

———. "Le mythe de Paris comme élément de propagande à l'époque de la Ligue," *MSHP* 20 (1969): 49–63.

Yates, Frances. *Astraea. The Imperial Theme in the Sixteenth Century.* London: 1975.

INDEX

Figure numbers appear in italics following page numbers.